D0458861

17990

Killing Dragons

Also by Fergus Fleming

Barrow's Boys

Killing Dragons

The Conquest of the Alps

FERGUS FLEMING

The Henry S. Hall Jr.
American Alpine Club Library
710 10th St., Suite 15
Golden, CO 80401 U.S.A.
303-384-0112

Atlantic Monthly Press
New York

DQ
823
.F613
2000
c.2

Copyright © 2000 by Fergus Fleming

All rights reserved. No part of this book may be reproduced in any form or by
any electronic or mechanical means, including information storage and
retrieval systems, without permission in writing from the publisher, except by
a reviewer, who may quote brief passages in a review. Any members of
educational institutions wishing to photocopy part or all of the work for
classroom use, or publishers who would like to obtain permission to include
the work in an anthology, should send their inquiries to Grove/Atlantic, Inc.,
841 Broadway, New York, NY 10003.

First published in Great Britain in 2000 by Granta Books, London, England

Published simultaneously in Canada
Printed in the United States of America

FIRST AMERICAN EDITION

Library of Congress Cataloging-in-Publication Data

Fleming, Fergus, 1959–
    Killing dragons : the conquest of the Alps / Fergus Fleming.
        p.   cm.
    Includes bibliographical references.
    ISBN 0-87113-778-X
    1. Mountaineering—Alps—History—19th century. 2. Mountaineers—
Biography. 3. Alps—Description and travel. I. Title.

DQ823 .F613 2000
914.94'7—dc21   00-04335

Atlantic Monthly Press
841 Broadway
New York, NY 10003

01 02 03 04   10 9 8 7 6 5 4 3 2 1

PREFACE AND ACKNOWLEDGEMENTS

Any account of the Alps must lead sooner or later to the events of July 1865. In that month an obscure printer named Edward Whymper became Europe's most talked-about man. The reason? He had climbed the Matterhorn, one of the world's legendary mountains and one of the last to be conquered in the Alps. But he had earned his glory at a horrible cost. A rope snapped during the descent and four of his seven-strong team fell to their deaths. Portions sufficient to fill three coffins were later retrieved. Of the fourth man – a Lord, no less – nothing was found save a shoe, a pair of gloves and a coat sleeve. A Reuters report gave the full, stomach-turning details but was swiftly suppressed. (And has been ever since: it now exists only as a yellowing document in the archives of the Alpine Club.) Rumours of its content, however, were enough to make people gawp. Here, for the first time, and in truly dramatic fashion, were revealed the perils and triumphs of mountaineering.

The Matterhorn disaster was one of those tragic events of which the Victorians were so fond and to which they were so prone. It ranked in popular imagination alongside Franklin's disappearance in the Arctic, Livingstone's death in Africa and, later, Scott's fate at the South Pole. It shaped the childhood perceptions of millions – amongst them Winston Churchill – and it had, uniquely, a survivor who could describe it at first hand. Edward Whymper, who was only in his mid-twenties at the time of the disaster, was bedevilled by it for the rest of his life. He loomed in popular imagination as a Titan and as he aged he came to look the part. Pipe in hand, his mouth set in a perpetual scowl, he delivered the same harsh lecture to audiences of thousands almost until the year he died. As an extraordinary man – and an extra-ordinarily odd one, too – Whymper could fill a book on his own. (He has done so: three of them.) So long is his shadow that even today he is the first person one associates with the Alps. His notoriety, however, is obstructive. Set in context Whymper becomes a memorable, but by no means the most important, character in a long history of Alpine exploration.

When one thinks of exploration one thinks primarily in terms of the poles and Africa, of ice caps and deserts, of furs and snake boots. Distance is paramount, foreignness all. Yet here, in the middle of the world's smallest, most densely populated continent, was a wilderness which was not properly mapped until the late nineteenth century and whose more inaccessible slopes are still being fought over today. The Alps lacked the sullen gravitas of the Arctic or the dry weirdness of the Sahara but they had the same aura of inaccessibility. Their higher zones were unknown and around them had been woven a web of myth and superstition. In the eighteenth century a respected sci-entist quite seriously enumerated the different species of dragon to be found there. For a long while people believed that the peaks were home to an alien race – and why not? They did not even know if humans could survive at such altitudes. It was a closed world. Whymper, and people like him, felt compelled to open it.

Exploration conjures up images of obsessive men – typically British – doing mad things in strange surroundings. The Alpine explorers were no different. Always fixated and sometimes peculiar, they shared a background of illness and phobia: sickly childhoods were ubiquitous; insomnia and indigestion were common; one man was afraid of heights, another of garlic. They had spiritual problems, being uncertain whether the Alps would lead them to God or confirm his non-existence. And yes, a lot of them were British. Then again, a lot of them were not. The Swiss, French, Germans and Italians were equally prone to arguments and insanity; they quibbled as pointlessly and displayed the same eccentricities. And while it is true that Britons made their mark – in particular members of the Alpine Club – their continental rivals were no less active. Were it not for one Genevan's politeness to a M. Dolomieu, for example, the Dolomites would now be known as the Saussures.

The Alps caused controversy when they were being explored and they continue to do so today. Everybody has a favourite region, a favourite mountain, a specialised area of interest, a unique appreciation of the peaks' beauties, an interpretation of their past and a vision of their future. Anything written on the subject raises bubbles of partisan outrage. It is with some trepidation, therefore, that I add this book to the cauldron. Those who know the Alps like the back of their hands, or who have a particular speciality, will doubtless smite me for a thousand heresies of omission or misdescription. To all these people I apologise. What I have tried to do is tell a tale of exploration in the simplest meaning of the word – of going where no man has gone before.

The subtitle, 'The Conquest of the Alps', is selective. I have narrowed the term 'Alps' to describe the central, western section running from the Massif des Écrins (or the Dauphiné, as it was previously called) through the Mont Blanc range to the Bernese Oberland and then south to the Valais. I have done so because these are among the highest and most impressive mountains and they were the ones people most wanted to explore. Their 'Conquest' has been similarly reduced. Diehard mountaineers claim that the conquest is ongoing and that there are many new routes and faces yet to be conquered. Here, however, the conquest is interpreted as the first ascent of major peaks, the ground-breaking investigation of glaciers and, because it represents the new wave of exploration (also because it is too good a story to miss out), the battle for the Eigerwand. As for those who did the conquering, self-censorship again prevails. Many fine explorers have been omitted, such as Father Placidus a Spescha, who roamed bravely through the eastern Alps; the Abbé Imseng, renowned for his ability to go up mountains and for the greasy cassock in which he did so; and Charles Barrington, the prize-winning Irish jockey, who climbed the Eiger on his winnings and a whim during his one and only visit to the Alps. The disastrous career of Francis Fox Tuckett, who was twice arrested as a spy and who survived so many avalanches, rockfalls and lightning strikes that it beggars belief, has barely been touched upon. One has to draw the line somewhere.

During the twelve months it has taken to research and write this book I have visited many (not all) of the places mentioned and have tried to get a feel for the area. My main sources of information, however, have been books, letters and documents. Most of the Alpine explorers published journals of their adventures, and their diaries and correspondence have been stored in archives across Europe. In making sense of this primary material I am indebted to several authors. First, Ronald Clark, whose numerous books on the Alps and those who climbed them are both fascinating and heartfelt. Second, Claire Engel, who has written fluently and wittily in two languages on the history of Alpine exploration. Both Clark and Engel speak from a lifetime's experience of the Alps. Without the benefit of their wisdom I would have floundered. G. De Beer's excellent anthologies of Alpine literature have been invaluable, as have Douglas Freshfield's life of Saussure, C. A. Mathews's history of Mont Blanc, and Frank Smythe's biography of Whymper.

I would like to thank the following for access to their archives and libraries and, where appropriate, for permission to quote from material in their possession: the Alpine Club, London; the Bibliothèque Publique et Universitaire, Geneva; the British Library; the Imperial College of Science, Technology, and Medicine London; Kensington and Chelsea Library, London; the London Library; Magdalen College, Oxford; the National Record of Archives, London; the Royal Geographical Society, London; the Royal Institution, London; the Scott Polar Research Institute, Cambridge; the Zentralbibliothek, Zurich.

I would also like to thank Gillon Aitken, my agent; Ben Ball; Anne

Barrett; Neil Belton, my editor; Robin Darwall-Smith; Alain Doubre; Margaret Ecclestone; Lyvia Gollancz; Robert Headland; Patrick Herring; Frank James; Bob Lawford; Isobel Pritchard; Angela Rose; Rachel Rowe; Janet Turner; and Rachel Unsworth. A special thanks to David Rose for correcting the manuscript's many errors – and an apology for sometimes ignoring his corrections.

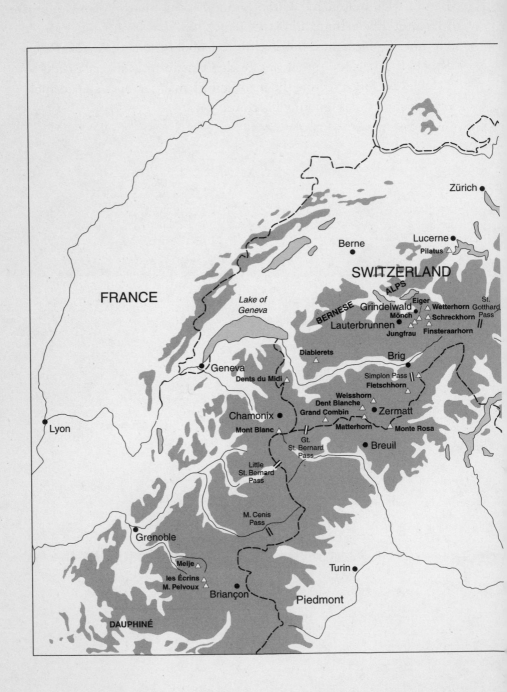

Zürich

Lucerne

Berne   Pilatus △

SWITZERLAND

BERNESE ALPS   St.
                                Eiger △ Wetterhorn   Gotthard
Grindelwald   Mönch △   △ Schreckhorn   Pass
Lauterbrunnen   △ Finsteraarhorn
               Jungfrau

FRANCE

Lake of
Geneva

Diablerets   Brig
△

                    Simplon Pass ‖ △
Dents du Midi △   Fletschhorn
Geneva   △

                    Weisshorn
                    Dent Blanche △
                    Grand Combin △   Zermatt
Chamonix   Matterhorn   Monte Rosa
Mont Blanc △   ‖   △
                  Gt.   Breuil
                  St. Bernard
Lyon   Pass

Little
St. Bernard
Pass ‖

M. Cenis
Pass ‖

Grenoble

Meije △   Turin
les Écrins △
M. Pelvoux △
Briançon   Piedmont

DAUPHINÉ

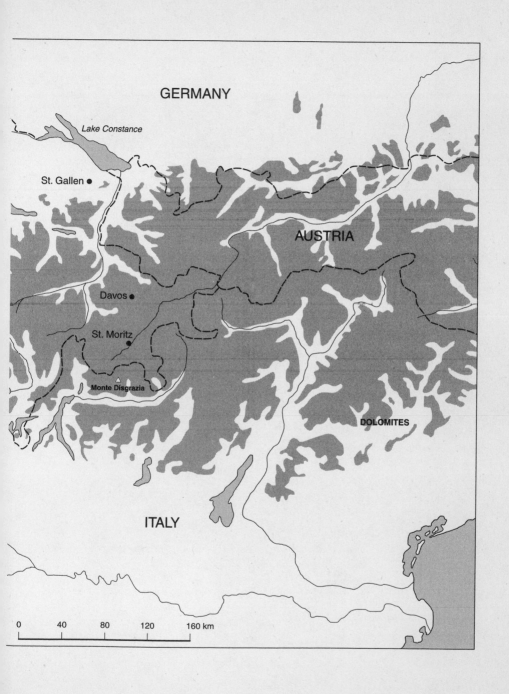

GERMANY

Lake Constance

St. Gallen ●

AUSTRIA

Davos ●

St. Moritz ●

△
Monte Disgrazia

DOLOMITES

ITALY

0   40   80   120   160 km

CHAPTER ONE

In 1541 the naturalist Conrad Gesner made an extraordinary decision. 'I am resolved,' he wrote to a friend, 'that as long as God grants me life, I will each year climb some mountains, or at least one, at the season when the flowers are in bloom, in order that I may examine these, and provide noble exercise for my body at the same time as enjoyment for my soul.'[1]

Gesner's decision was unusual for several reasons. In the short, uncertain and uncomfortable lifespans of the time, most people did not seek extra toil; climbing a mountain even once, let alone every year, was an unnecessary and profitless burden. Then there was the very fact of mountains; they were steep, nasty, cold, frightening and potentially hazardous. They were also high, and height was anathema. What could one do with height? Nothing. One could not till its thin soil. One could trade only with difficulty over its rocky passes. One could hardly even invade one's own neighbour if height intervened. It was a worthless and obstructive thing. All these factors made Gesner's decision unusual. But what made it extraordinary was his decision to climb not just mountains but Alps.

The Alps were – and are – Europe's most majestic mountain range. Springing in the west from the Tenda Pass above Nice, the main chain of summits ran in a 700-mile arc to the south-west of Vienna.

Lesser offshoots poked southwards to the Adriatic and the Balkans, but it was the main chain, and especially the western part of the main chain, in the regions of Piedmont, Savoy and Switzerland, that first sprang to mind when anybody mentioned the Alps.

Lying at the cultural crossroads of Europe, where French, German and Italian influences met, the western Alps should theoretically have been a vibrant, cosmopolitan area. And to an extent they were: in the sixth century BC they had witnessed the brilliant Celtic culture of La Tène; the Romans had marched over them, as had Hannibal and his Carthaginians; since the second century AD Christian missionaries had proselytised in the valleys; pilgrims from as far afield as Iceland had crossed the Great St Bernard Pass and other of the twenty-three major passes which led to Rome. For a brief period they were controlled by Saracen bandits. Every conceivable nationality had either passed over the Alps or settled below them. One region was proud of its Scandinavian heritage, another of its Prussian; one area venerated an Irish monk; in others the place names were clearly Arabic in origin; neighbouring valleys spoke different languages, held different political allegiances and embraced different religious beliefs.

Yet for all this diversity, for all this coming and going, the Alps were a blank on the map. Apart from a few pockets of civilisation such as Geneva, Berne and other cities which prospered in the mountains' shadow, and apart from the well-trodden passes (which had once been well maintained but since the fall of Rome had become increasingly ruinous), nobody cared about the rest. Scattered agricultural communities, inbred and disease-ridden, grazed livestock on the upper pastures. And that was all people knew or wanted to know about the place. The culprit, as usual, was height.

The Alps were, indeed, tremendously high. Within the central range, which was in places 120 miles wide, there were hundreds of peaks higher than 10,000 feet, dozens higher than 13,000 feet and one, Mont Blanc, which at 15,771 feet was the highest in western Europe. So high were the mountains that they formed one of the continent's great climatic barriers, wringing the moisture from prevailing winds to divide Europe into cold, wet north and warm, dry south. They were rough as well as high. Thrust up by the tectonic collision which welded Italy onto mainland Europe, they displayed the earth's crust in all its rawness. There were crags of black granite and sharp needles of pink; there were piles of disintegrating shale whose shards left silvery dust on the hands; there were vast, orange columns of limestone. On Alpine cliffs one could trace the swirls of petrified mud and hack from them the skeletons of tiny, fossilised fish. Veins of gold, silver, iron, lead, zinc and copper came to the surface; marble, slate and salt could be hewn from the hills; grottos yielded valuable crystals.*

Above all, however, the Alps were cold. Beyond the treeline lay a world of frigidity into which humans rarely ventured. In summer it was possible to put cattle and sheep up there, and farmers decamped to temporary stone shelters called chalets from which they kept an eye on their herds. But for most of the year the high peaks were clamped in snow, and between them lay field after field of year-round ice whose offshoots dribbled menacingly into the valleys below. In the first century AD a Roman chronicler wrote that 'everything in the Alps is frozen fast'[2] – and this was a relatively warm period. Three centuries later St Ambrose, Bishop of Milan, feared that the ice would suffocate all civilisation. By the Middle Ages monastic orders had erected hospices at the top of every pass to succour pilgrims and, in the case of the Great St Bernard hospice, to rescue them with snow-trained hounds. In 1690 the villagers of Chamonix, beneath Mont Blanc, imported the Bishop of Annecy to exorcise the glaciers which threatened to obliterate them. (It worked: allegedly the ice retreated one-eighth of a mile, thereby showing God's greatness and also justifying the large sum the Bishop charged for his services.)

The Alps were a world to themselves: they produced flowers found

---

*In the second century BC an Alpine gold strike was so large that it reduced the value of Roman bullion by two-thirds. Three hundred years later Pliny recorded the sale of a crystal vase which fetched the fantastic sum of 150,000 sesterces. Impressive as were these finds they were also rare; the physical cost of exploiting Alpine minerals deterred most prospectors.

nowhere else on the continent, tiny plants that had shrunk to cope with near-Arctic conditions, yet which retained in miniature all the beauty of their lowland equivalents; hidden by snow for much of the year they emerged in spring and summer to carpet the mountainside. There was an equally rare set of fauna: the chamois was unique, so were the Bouquetin ibex, the lammergeier, or bearded vulture, and the marmot, a burrow-dwelling member of the squirrel family which looked like a rabbit–beaver cross and emerged from its annual hibernation with a chorus of whistles – to be quickly knocked on the head and eaten.

Such was the ignorance surrounding the mountains that most of them had no names – if they did, they were called things like Accursed or Unapproachable – and the very term 'alp' was itself a misnomer: when early geographers had pointed at the peaks and asked what they were called, locals had replied *alpes*. But this referred only to the high-level pastures on which they grazed their stock; they had no word for the mountains themselves. Thus the name which appeared on world atlases became an unwitting reminder of just how little Europeans knew of the wilderness in their midst – and of how radical Gesner's decision was.

By Gesner's time the Alps were a source of terror and superstition. Plains-dwellers still shuddered at the thought of Hannibal's march in 218 BC. Philemon Holland, a sixteenth-century translator of Livy, painted a terrifying picture of the campaign, in which Hannibal's men smashed their way through the Alpine passes, shattering boulders with fire and vinegar before dragging their protesting elephants, 'ever readie and anone to run upon their noses', towards Italy. He described the invaders' fear at 'the height of those hills . . . the horses singed with cold . . . the people with long shagd hair' and the horrors of the journey where 'the snow being once with the gate of so many people and beasts upon it fretted and thawed, they were fain to go upon the bare yce underneath and in the slabberie snow-broth as it relented and melted about their heeles'.[3] And if Holland was not enough there were the words of Master John de Bremble, a Canterbury monk who had braved the Alps in 1188. 'I put my hand in my scrip that I might scratch out a syllable or two,' he wrote to his subprior, 'lo, I found my ink-bottle filled with a dry mass of ice; my fingers too refused to write; my beard was stiff with frost, and my breath congealed into a long icicle. I could not write the news I wished . . . Lord, restore me to my brethren that I may tell them that they come not to this place of torment.'[4] True, like many other pilgrims, Master John had chosen to cross the Alpine passes in early spring, the most changeable season as far as the weather was concerned. But this in no way diminished his message of woe.

One or two souls had braved the forbidding peaks. In 1358 a knight named Rotario of Asti climbed Roche Melon near Susa and deposited a bronze triptych on its 11,600-foot summit. In 1492, the year Columbus discovered America, Charles VII of France passed by Mont Aiguille near Grenoble – Mont Inaccessible as it was then called – and ordered his chamberlain to climb it. The chamberlain did so, surmounting its rocky, 7,000-foot mass by 'subtle means and engines' – which seems to have involved a rickety chain of ladders – to erect three crosses on the top. The feat was considered so astounding that it produced a flurry of official correspondence.

At one undetermined time in the fifteenth century, Leonardo da Vinci climbed what may have been Monte Rosa, near Zermatt, and recorded his impressions:

No mountain has its base at so great a height as this, which lifts itself above almost all the clouds; and snow seldom falls there, but only hail in the summer when the clouds are highest. And this hail lies there, so that if it were not for the absorption of the rising and falling clouds, which does not happen more than twice in an age, an enormous mass of ice would be piled up there by the layers of hail; and in the middle of July I found it very considerable, and I saw the sky above me was quite dark; and the sun as it fell on the mountain was far brighter here than in the plains below, because a smaller extent of atmosphere lay between the summit of the mountain and the sun.[5]

If Leonardo had reached the summit – which he almost certainly hadn't – he would have stood 15,203 feet above sea level.

Generally, however, the Alps were as distant from the normal world as was the moon. Anything could happen in this icy semi-circle of teeth that bit off Italy from the rest of Europe. To many they represented hell, combing the freezing conditions of a Nordic Niflheim with, in summer, the roasting inferno of Christianity. When people approached them, it was only to scuttle over their passes as speedily as they could, alert for impending danger. Many travellers were carried blindfold lest they be overwhelmed by the awfulness of the scenery. Here was a realm whose upper reaches were, by all accounts, home to a race of malformed and malevolent sub-humans. The peaks above were inhabited by demons of every kind. Witches were well attested, their presence being routinely exorcised by one form or other of social purging. It was an undisputed fact that dragons lived in Alpine caves, ready to incinerate any who set foot above the snowline. Now and then, an intrepid traveller might acquire a 'dragon stone', which could cure haemorrhage, dysentery, diarrhoea, poisoning, plague and nosebleeds. This miraculous stone could only be obtained by cutting open the forehead of a dragon as it slept in its lair – care had to be taken, however, for should the dragon awake the stone would lose its power. Naturally hard to come by, one specimen was preserved at Lucerne, having been dropped luckily, if illogically, by a passing serpent.

Representative of the rumours was Pilatus, a mountain near Geneva, that held a pond full of biblical terror. According to legend, Pontius Pilate had committed suicide rather than face the prospect of death at the hands of Emperor Tiberius. His body was weighed down with stones and hurled into the Tiber. The result was a bout of the most atrocious weather the Romans had ever seen. He was hastily recovered and taken to Vienne – in a show of contempt for its inhabitants – where he was thrown into the Rhône. Further storms and tempests ensued, so he was fished out once again and thrown into the waters at Lausanne. Here, too, Pilate worked his malevolence so he was salvaged for a third time and dumped in a lake on a mountain above Geneva. For good measure his wife Procla was tossed into a nearby pond. The storms were phenomenal.

When the local bishop strode forth to exorcise the lake he met with qualified success. The weather returned to normal but Pilate demanded a quid pro quo. Every Good Friday he would rise from the lake on his judge's throne, dressed in scarlet robes. Anyone who saw him would die before the year was out. The bargain was struck.

Pilate remained quiet, save that a number of locals died every year from unexplained causes – obviously they had seen the scarlet apparition – and now and then Pilatus would be subject to horrendous blizzards, clearly brought about by folk who taunted Pilate by throwing stones into the lake or by mobbing him in some other disrespectful fashion. To avert calamity the authorities expressly forbade anyone to approach the mountain without an approved guide. When six clerics tried to climb the hill unaided in 1387 they were imprisoned. For centuries Mount Pilatus, as it became known, was forbidden territory.

In the sixteenth century, a number of brave men put Pilatus to the test. In August 1518 Joachim von Watt, Burgomaster of St Gall, obtained permission from the authorities to go up the mountain. Following the advice of his guide he did nothing untoward near the lake and managed to climb one of Pilatus's peaks. He was followed in 1555 by Conrad Gesner who set out on 20 August with a small body of men – among them the court usher of Lucerne who carried on his back a sustaining quantity of wine – and reached the actual peak without disaster. He marked his conquest with a blast on an alpenhorn. Then, in 1585, Pastor Johann Müller of Lucerne did the unheard of: he climbed the mountain and deliberately threw stones into the lake. Nothing happened.

Of these three conquests, Müller's would appear initially to be the most important. He had set out to quash a superstition and he had been successful. It is Gesner's climb, however, that deserves most attention. For Gesner was not out to slay dragons. What he wanted to do was see the Alps in a new light, as spiritual totems whose summits would lead him to greater awareness of the world about him. In 1541, far ahead of his time, he declared that 'The consciousness is in some vague way impressed by the stupendous heights and is drawn to the contemplation of the Great Architect. Men of dull mind admire nothing, sleep at home, never go out into the Theatre of the World, hide in corners like dormice, through the winter, never recognise that the human race was sent out into the world in order that through its marvels it should learn to recognise some higher Power, the Supreme Being himself.'[6] Two years after climbing Pilatus he was able to express himself in greater detail. Writing in Latin, he told his limited readership that the Alps 'are the Theatre of the Lord, displaying monuments of past ages, such as precipices, rocks, peaks, chasms, and never-melting glaciers'. And, he added quaintly, even if the walking was tiresome, the accommodation bad and the perils numerous, 'it will be pleasant thereafter to recall the toils and dangers; it will gratify you to turn over these things in your mind and to tell them to friends'.[7]

Gesner was widely ignored and died in 1565. He did, however, set rolling a ball that would be caught almost two centuries later when Johann Scheuchzer, the Professor of Physics at Zürich University, wrote a definitive study of the Alps. From August 1702 he undertook nine journeys through the mountains and published his findings in 1723 under the title *Itinera per Helvetiae Alpinas Regiones*. Scheuchzer had a solid reputation in his field – the philosopher and mathematician Gottfried Leibniz was one of his supporters – and he was a notoriously modern thinker: he propagated Sir Isaac Newton's notions of gravity, for example, and opposed capital punishment for witchcraft. When his two-volume work came out, therefore, people were expecting something special. Scheuchzer did not disappoint. His enquiring mind made a number of botanical and mineralogical discoveries that were of benefit to science as well as a number of personal observations that were not. At Fürstenau he encountered a cheese that had been treated with wine and oil of cloves for so many years that it had become a porridge – 'which for connoisseurs of such food has a particularly delicious flavour'.[8] From the quarries of Oehningen he received a fossil that he believed was the missing link and which he triumphantly named *Homo diluvii testis*. (It was later found to be a species of giant newt.) He wondered at glaciers, and came to the conclusion that their movement was caused by the expansion of water trapped in their crevasses. Near Brig he discovered a super-intelligent community, most of whose members shared the surname Supersaxo, who were fluent in German, French, Italian and Latin and descended from a sixteenth-century Italian count who had sired twelve sons and eleven daughters.

Scheuchzer shunned the peaks. He was not, by inclination, a climber. At the Sègnes Pass he warned that people prone to giddiness should try another route. At the Gemmi Pass he decided that its name came from the sighs (Latin *gemitus*) of those who tried to cross it. And at Leukerbad he became exasperated: 'we have already climbed sufficient mountains, but we must get over one today which will give us enough to do'.[9] His visit to the St Gotthard Pass was endurable only because it gave him an opportunity to talk about the formation of crystals. He had a stab at Pilatus but 'partly because of bodily fatigue and partly because of the distance remaining to be traversed'[10] he did not reach the summit. 'Very few care for this laborious kind of pursuit, which is by no means lucrative,' he commented. 'It is not everyone who can take pleasure in climbing hills which reach the clouds.'[11] Nevertheless, he did cover a lot of ground and if some of his observations seemed absurd – such as his belief that certain chamois possessed a stone in their bellies which rendered them immune to bullets – others did not. His theory of glacial movement would not be bettered for almost 150 years. Above all, he set at rest a question that had haunted people for a long time. Yes, the Alps did contain dragons.

From a number of reliable witnesses, Scheuchzer compiled a list of these creatures. There was one that had the body of a snake and the head of a cat. Another had four short legs and a coxcomb. A third was a snake equipped with bat's wings. Some had crests. (Were crested dragons the cock of the species? he wondered.) The best specimen of all had the head of a ginger tom, a snake's tongue, scaly legs and a hairy, two-pronged tail. Its eyes sparkled horribly. All it lacked was physical stature, being a mere two feet long.

Scheuchzer dismissed most of the dragon tales. But those in which he believed – including all the above – were accorded full respect. The ginger tom, for example, came from the Grisons, an area, according to Scheuchzer, that was 'so mountainous and so well provided with caves, that it would be odd not to find dragons there'.[12] One could tell the real article from the false by the number of birds they inhaled during their flight. Without wishing to seem alarmist, he concluded that 'from the accounts of Swiss dragons and their comparison with those of other lands . . . it is clear that such animals really do exist'.[13]

Not everybody believed him. But for several years thereafter a respectful silence fell over the Alps.

The hush was broken in 1741 by two Britons, Messrs Pococke and Windham. In that year they led a small party of fellow countrymen to Chamonix, a valley in Savoy overlooked by Mont Blanc. It was an uneventful excursion by modern standards. The travellers entertained themselves by cracking whips and firing pistols to hear the echoes rattle off the mountains. They went up the Montenvers, marvelled at the 'terrible havock' made by avalanches, and gaped at the views, which were now '*delicious*' and now 'terrible enough to make most people's heads turn'.[14] Windham, the party's main chronicler, was amazed by his first glaciers, and was quite taken aback by the Mer de Glace, a tremendous snake of ice that curled away below the Montenvers into a distance of needle-like peaks. 'I own to you that I am extremely at a loss how to give a right idea of it,' he wrote to a friend in Geneva, 'as I know no one thing which I have ever seen that has the least resemblance to it. The description which travellers give of the seas of Greenland seems to come nearest to it. You must imagine your lake put in agitation by a strong wind, and frozen all at once, perhaps even that would not produce the same appearance.'[15] Witches, he was told, came to 'play their pranks on the glacieres [sic] and dance to the sound of their instruments'.[16]

They saw no witches; they saw no dragons; nor did they see any of the bandits they had been assured roamed the region, although

Windham advised future visitors to go armed – "'tis an easy precaution . . . and oftentimes it helps a man out of a scrape'.[17] In fact, the
worst shock they received was of a dietary nature – 'there are some
places where one can get no provisions, and the little there is to be
had in other places, is very bad'.[18] Pococke, who had recently visited
the Middle East and was a bit of a show-off, filled empty moments by
dressing as an Oriental potentate, thereby causing the guides some
anxiety. But otherwise a cheery time was had by all. They were
unabashed tourists, and Windham did not try to hide it: 'a man of
genius might do many things we have not done. All the merit we can
pretend to is having opened the way to others who may have curiosity of the same kind.'[19]

Others would indeed come to Chamonix, drawn as much by
Pococke and Windham as by a new flourish of Alpine literature. In
1732, the Swiss naturalist and philosopher Albrecht von Haller had
published the poem *Die Alpen*. Haller was widely respected throughout Europe and beyond. Such was his renown that, according to one
story, when pirates once captured a ship carrying a case of books
addressed to him they deposited the parcel at the next port with
instructions that it be forwarded. His poem, which addressed the
moral aspects of mountains rather than mountains themselves, was
treated with similar reverence. It was reprinted thirty times during his
lifetime and was recited by heart in the salons of France and
Germany. Then there was the French writer Jean-Jacques Rousseau,
the apostle of noble savagery, who was one of the first to suggest that
powdered wigs and court glitter might not be the only measure of
human worth. Rousseau favoured natural beauty over the artificial
and slightly squalid fashions of the time, and in doing so started a
craze for rugged scenery and rustic simplicity that has yet to abate.
The Alps were the closest example of ruggedness to hand and,
although Rousseau never did more than dally beneath them, his 1761
novel *La Nouvelle Héloïse* contained a long section describing their
emotional impact. 'There is something magical and supernatural in
hill landscape which entrances the mind and the senses,' ran one typical passage. 'One forgets everything, one forgets one's own being; one

ceases to know where one stands.'[20] Like Haller before him, he became one of the century's bestselling authors.

Rousseau and Haller drew people to the Alps for their spiritual qualities. Pococke and Windham did the same in respect of their physical beauties. The mountains became a place of pilgrimage for literary-minded Europeans and for wealthy young Britons doing the Grand Tour. The Alps were painted and written about and marvelled at, and their glacial waters were quaffed by the gallon by those who had heard of their supposedly health-giving properties. People became aware that mountains need not be feared but could actually be enjoyed. The medieval attitude, which had hailed towns as oases of comfort in a harsh world, was replaced by an anti-urban trend. Parisians, for example, became conscious that in certain conditions travellers could smell their city before they even saw it. Other centres were the same. Pure air, clear skies and green trees suddenly became valuable and nowhere were these qualities more plentifully available than in the Alps. But although people came to the Alps they did not climb them. The new wave of tourism lapped no higher than the snowline. Pococke and Windham, for example, had trampled through Chamonix without once mentioning their constant companion, Mont Blanc, the highest mountain in the Alps. Height, it seemed, was just as intimidating as ever.

Artists, writers and philosophers had popularised the Alps – or at least certain, easily accessible segments of them – but they had done little to explore them. Dragons, for all anyone knew, and hosts of demons and whole species of unknown humanity might yet inhabit the upper slopes. Nobody had a clue about glaciers, those monstrous seas of ice, constantly and inexplicably sliding downhill, whose snouts poked into most valleys; it was very seriously believed that they were the agents of the devil, and priests were routinely summoned to keep them at bay. The area remained a mystery, comprising 'great excrescences of earth, which to outward appearance indeed have neither use nor comeliness'.[21] It needed a scientific mind to probe its secrets, a mind such as belonged to a Genevan aristocrat named Horace Bénédict de Saussure.

CHAPTER TWO

A feature of eighteenth-century Geneva was its extraordinary number of suicides. Citizens hung themselves, shot themselves, poisoned themselves and flung themselves into either the lake or its inflowing rivers with weary regularity. One inhabitant hesitantly put this down to the influence of the English, who flocked to Geneva as an orderly, non-Catholic centre of the Enlightenment; an Englishman declared that this view could be 'summarily dismissed',[1] but did not offer an alternative diagnosis; and a Frenchman wondered whether it might not be caused by the oppressive landscape – a comment that the same Englishman thought preposterous.

Horace Bénédict de Saussure did not himself commit suicide – although several of his friends and relatives did – but he was undoubtedly influenced by the two supposedly disposing causes. Born in 1740, one year before Pococke and Windham entered Chamonix, he grew up in an English-style Genevan mansion built by his father in imitation of those he had seen on a visit to Yorkshire; he started his career in the then typically English fashion as a lawyer, hoping not to have anything to do with law but 'to gain knowledge of affairs'; and when he abandoned law in favour of a career as a geologist, he met and corresponded with his English counterparts, many of whom were among Geneva's regular visitors. A small, feisty state whose 1781 census counted some 25,000 inhabitants (of whom a staggering 6,000 were watchmakers), Geneva was one of the more prosperous members of the Swiss Confederation and prided itself on being the equal of any nation in every respect save pomp, cuisine and authoritarianism – the very virtues that eighteenth-century Englishmen considered to be the distinguishing features between themselves and their vainglorious French neighbours.

More than Englishness, however, Saussure was swayed by the other demon of self-destruction – the oppressive landscape. In general, Genevans had two things to look at: the lake and the mountains. For some this might have been depressing but Saussure found the sight invigorating. 'From childhood, I have had an absolute passion for the mountains,' he later wrote. 'I still remember the sensation I experienced when, for the first time, my hands touched the rocks of the Salève [in nearby Savoy] and my eyes enjoyed its vistas.'[2] His love of the mountains was more than a passion: it was an obsession. In 1760, while still a student at the Geneva Academy – in two years' time he would be appointed its Professor of Natural History – he became frustrated with the smaller hills available to him. He wanted to expand his scope to include the giant peaks visible in the distance. As he described it, 'I was desperately anxious to see at close quarters the great Alpine summits which look so majestic from the top of our mountains.'[3] So, at the age of 20, he walked the 50 miles to Chamonix on the trail of Pococke and Windham.

Saussure had not only read Albrecht von Haller's poem on the Alps but knew the old man personally. The ostensible purpose of his journey was to collect plants for Haller's collection. He was not particularly successful in this regard, for which he blamed the lack of specimens to be found. In all likelihood he was not looking very hard. 'I fear, eager as you are, that on your excursions you walk a little too quickly,' Haller chided him. 'One ought to go as slowly as possible, and above all on the alps to sit down from time to time, even to lie down, so as to get a close view of the growing plants.'[4] Lie down? No thought could have been further from Saussure's mind.

As a youth he had heard stories about the mountains surrounding

Chamonix, the largest of which was Mont Blanc. Its icy slopes and those of its adjoining chain of peaks were said to have been placed there to punish the sinful folk who lived below. The moment he entered the valley of Chamonix, however, Saussure was entranced. 'The fresh air one breathes . . . the good cultivation of the soil, the pretty hamlets met with at every step . . . give the impression of a new world, a sort of earthly paradise, enclosed by a kindly Deity in the circle of the mountains.'[5] As for the ice, it was to him not a punishment but a gift. 'These majestic glaciers, separated by great forests, and crowned by granite crags of astounding height cut in the form of great obelisks and mixed with snow and ice, present one of the noblest and most singular spectacles it is possible to imagine.'[6]

From the house of the local curé – the only decent lodging available – Saussure roamed his new-found paradise with enthusiasm. Where no plants were to be found he carried a gun and excused his expeditions on the ground of collecting Alpine birds. He climbed the Brévent, an 8,287-foot mountain opposite Mont Blanc. He crossed the Mer de Glace to visit a shepherd on one of the more distant and threadbare pastures and marvelled at the needles of rock which rose around him dizzyingly into the sky. When not exploring, he studied the locals. The women, he noted, did most of the agricultural work while the men busied themselves in the dangerous trades of chamois-hunting and crystal-gathering. (Rock crystal was a major component of eighteenth-century costume jewellery.) The Chamoniards were also renowned cheese-makers and in summer hired themselves out to other valleys, thereby diminishing the population considerably*. From those that remained, Saussure picked one, Pierre Simon, to help him through the wondrous but unknown landscape. 'He is short of stature,' wrote a contemporary, 'his head buried in a large hat; small bright eyes, a short coat, heavy nailed shoes, and a spiked stick, a peculiar language as difficult to understand as to

---

*The practice of seasonal work migration, common throughout the Alps, no doubt added weight to the rumours of strange, subhuman races. One summer traveller was disconcerted to find a village whose inhabitants were, to a man, either deformed or deranged.

speak for everyone . . . he was experienced, prudent, courageous and faithful.'[7] Little else is known about Pierre Simon, but he stands on record as one of the first Alpine guides, a breed whose knowledge and ice craft would later steer their employers through the glacial approaches to the summits themselves.

Saussure visited Chamonix again and again. By 1778 he had been there eight times – twice in 1776 – and still he wondered at everything he met. Even the approach thrilled him. At Balmes, for example, a local guide took him aside and in hushed tones informed him that fairies and other supernatural beings had once ruled the land. Moreover, he could show him the proof. There were places, he said, where they had turned snakes, snails and a variety of indescribable creatures into stone. Hastening to the spot, Saussure found nothing but ammonites and other fossils. Interestingly, however, he did not discount his guide's 'fairies' until he had seen the evidence for himself. Even to someone like Saussure, it seems, the existence of dragons and the like was not an impossibility. There was more to come. When the supernatural transmogrifications failed to convince his employer, the guide told Saussure of a palace the fairies had carved into the mountainside. It contained chambers lined with glittering columns and in the vastness of its main reception room lay a fathomless pit containing untold wealth. Saussure sallied forth to investigate. The Caverne de Balmes, as expected, was a lengthy grotto of stalactites and stalagmites. The only excitement for Saussure was walking on a layer of crystals that had formed on the surface of long since evaporated water to produce a shelf that was equidistant from floor and ceiling. Apart from this the cavern was unexceptional and Saussure recorded, disappointedly, that it did not even measure up to Pool's Hole in Derbyshire.

But the pit, down which he could not go because exploration of its 600-foot depth required ropes made to special order, remained a tantalising mystery. People had thrown stones into it and had heard them bounce off metal. On descending to find the fairy gold they had been driven back by a black goat that rose up from the abyss to bite their legs. Saussure dismissed the tales when he interviewed a man who had actually gone to the bottom of the pit. He was the surviving member of a twelve-strong team that had descended, clothed in crucifixes and other charms, to bring up the fairy treasure. What they had found was two copper bracelets, a number of chamois skeletons and some broken skulls of unidentifiable origin.

Saussure very much wanted to investigate the pit, especially when his informant told him that a man-made tunnel, on the wall of which was carved the image of a violin, led off to yet another cave. But the ropes were not available and he had to content himself with throwing rocks to judge its depth. It was small consolation. In his precise fashion he wrote that he could not be certain how far the rocks had dropped because they bounced off the sides on their way down. Once again, however, he did not dismiss superstition out of hand: when he wrote of the black goat in his journal he did so in respectful capitals.

Chamonix and its approaches were fine. But what captured Saussure's imagination more than anything else was Mont Blanc. Its presence had eluded Pococke and Windham – perhaps because from Chamonix it appears foreshortened and little more impressive than any of the adjacent peaks – but Saussure had seen it from Geneva and had recognised its importance. In his opinion it was the highest mountain in Europe, Africa or Asia and one that he must conquer. He was so besotted with Mont Blanc that he chose his *auberges* on the way to Chamonix not for their comfort but for the view they afforded of the peak. When he left Chamonix at the end of the summer of 1760 he had a notice posted in every parish of the valley. In it he offered a reward – the precise sum is not known – for the first person to climb Mont Blanc. In addition, he promised to recompense anybody for the time they spent on a failed attempt. On a second visit to Chamonix, in 1761, he repeated the offer. It was maybe a whim, a gesture by a well-meaning youngster with money to hand. But it was enough to set the Chamoniards thinking.

While Saussure was tinkling his purse at the locals, another man, Marc-Théodore Bourrit, was igniting the world with his visions of Mont Blanc. Bourrit, the Precentor of Geneva Cathedral, was an extraordinary man. Artist, singer, womaniser, snob and interminable raconteur, he was an endearing coward with a genius for self-promotion. One traveller portrayed him as 'long and thin, his complexion as dark as a negro's, his eyes burning and full of genius and life; his mouth marked by a touch of mobility and good nature which inspires confidence'.[8] Physically, this description fitted the bill. It omitted, however, Bourrit's various other attributes – such as his vocal chords, of which he was immodestly proud. 'I have been told in Paris that my voice can compete with the finest in Europe,' he said. 'I daresay that when my passion for music gets the better of me, I may feel tempted to make myself known to the world.'[9] He could paint, too – although not particularly well – and made a small name for himself as an Alpine artist, selling his watercolours to a gratifyingly important clientele that included the royalty of France, Russia, Sardinia and Prussia. And he could talk, squeezing from the smallest opportunity a lengthy torrent of words accompanied by gesticulations and, frequently, tears. But here his genius ended and a tetchy insecurity took over. He was touchy, and when crossed did not hesitate to use libel, slander and poison-pen letters against his perceived enemies.

Bourrit's one redeeming trait was his fascination with the Alps. He painted them, wrote about them and spoke about them. He travelled through them extensively. He dubbed himself the 'Historian of the Alps' and the 'Indefatigable Bourrit', and did all he could to make people – preferably wealthy, well-connected people – acquainted with their beauty. The one thing he could not do with the Alps was to climb them. He tried again and again – between 1869 and 1819 he made several attempts each year – but was thwarted by three debilitations: he dreaded cold, he disliked rain and he suffered from vertigo. He was the despair of his companions. He would wear impractical fur-lined shoes that had no grip; he would walk through pastures of cattle wearing a red cloak and carrying a large red umbrella; on slopes beyond a certain gradient he would lean so heavily on his guides that they almost collapsed. He would arrange a climb, delay it and then cancel it if the weather was not right. Even when painting he displayed a regrettable lack of surety. Approaching a glacier, he dithered at its edge, then decided the cold was too extreme for inspiration. On one rare occasion when he did climb a hill he planted his easel on the summit and took out his watercolours; after a while he noticed that he had sunk waist-deep in snow, and had to be dug out. He had no scientific accomplishments whatsoever: 'It may be wished he had explained himself with more precision,' complained a translator, having struggled to make sense of Bourrit's borrowed theories concerning glaciers. '[It is] a point in which he leaves the mind not fully satisfied.'[10] Instead, he was happier pottering over the foothills, exploring undiscovered valleys – which he did with some success – and telling female tourists how things should be done.

Bourrit did, however, have an undeniable feel for the Alps. Whereas Rousseau and the like were content to describe the hills from below, Bourrit did his best to tell people how they looked from above. On encountering his first glacier he was smitten.

A new universe came into view; what words can I use to describe a spectacle which struck us dumb? . . . The richness and variety of colours added to the beauty of the shapes. Gold, silver, crimson, and azure were shining everywhere, and what impressed me with a sense of even greater strangeness were the arches supporting snow-bridges over the crevasses, the apparent strength of which encouraged us to walk cross. We were even courageous enough to stop in the middle and gaze down into the abyss.[11]

Of the surrounding peaks that he could not reach he remarked only that they 'were serrated in innumerable ways'. When in 1775 he eventually managed to climb one of the smaller hills, Le Buet (it took him two years simply to locate it), he burst into such an extravagance of speech and song that a large boulder was named 'La Table au Chantre' in his honour.

His fellow countrymen mocked him, his fellow climbers abhorred him and the authorities noted crossly his continued absence from the cathedral. Yet his presence was inescapable, his knowledge seemingly endless and his enthusiasm so patent that people were drawn to the Alps if only to meet their most fanatical publicist. One such pilgrim was Prince Henry of Prussia, who paid a visit to Bourrit's studio, an episode that Bourrit never tired of relating. 'M. Bourrit pointed out to us his little staircase, which, in fact, is very narrow,' wrote an English visitor. 'He said that while going down it Prince Henry had said to his suite, "How many great staircases there are for little men! I am delighted to have found at last a great man with a little staircase." I hope for M. Bourrit's sake that there is a real disproportion between his staircase and himself, and that the prince's antithesis is sound . . . On looking at him I saw that his sleeve had a hole in it.'[12] Come nightfall, Bourrit camped in his courtyard on a little iron bedstead to prepare himself for conditions higher up. For all his faults it was hard to despise him.

Saussure was the very opposite of Bourrit. At the age of 24 he was, according to one acquaintance, 'already – without knowing it – a great savant, witty with a particular touch of naivete which could not fail to please, and though he was not easily embarassed, he almost invariably blushed when spoken to by a girl or young woman'.[13] Unlike Bourrit, who cut a dashing figure, Saussure had a pinched, prim look that reflected his methodical, scientific approach to the mountains. He wrote of his excursions that he 'made all these journeys with a miner's hammer in hand, merely for the purpose of studying natural history, climbing all accessible summits which seemed to promise interesting observations, and always carrying off specimens from the mines and mountains, especially those which threw any light on physical theories'.[14] He made it a rule to take notes on the spot and then transcribe them that evening in a journal that he would later rewrite for publication. He was painstakingly exact, at times overly so. '[He] instructs you frigidly, and sometimes sends you to sleep,'[15] complained one German writer.

Bourrit, in contrast, liked to pounce on unsuspecting victims and bore them to death. On one occasion he encountered an unsuspecting group of English tourists at Chamonix and waxed lyrical to their guides. 'Put yourself in the place of the strangers,' he began, 'who come from the most distant lands to admire the marvels of Nature in these wild and savage aspects, and justify the confidence they place in you . . .'[16] He carried on in similar vein, flanked by a visiting princess and the local chief of police, shedding the occasional tear as his fervour mounted. His audience goggled in bewilderment. In 1787 Baron de Frenilly happened to meet Bourrit – 'a man of volcanic imagination' – in an Alpine hospice. Bourrit began to describe a mountain sunrise. 'I believe that I listened to Bourrit for half an hour without falling asleep,' wrote the Baron. 'But at last, fatigue got the better of me, and I know not if he succeeded in getting the sun to rise.'[17]

Bourrit and Saussure, albeit at opposite ends of the spectrum, were in the vanguard of Alpine exploration. Initially, however, their efforts were fruitless. Saussure's bounty on Mont Blanc resulted in two desultory failures by Pierre Simon and for a while thereafter not much else. And for all Bourrit's raving and painting – he travelled throughout Europe trying to sell his pictures – he could not tempt tourists from the safety of their literary excursions. It was left to two Genevan brothers, Jean-André and Guillaume-Antoine De Luc, to make the first serious investigation of a mountain.

Born in 1717 and 1729 respectively, Jean-André and Guillaume-Antoine were amateur scientists of some renown. They were also admirers of Rousseau and in 1754 had rowed him and his mistress around Lake Geneva. Rousseau did not think much of the brothers, finding them rather boring, but this did not stop him pumping them for Alpine information that later found its way, unacknowledged, into *La Nouvelle Héloïse*. Whether or not this upset the brothers is unknown. At any rate, they joined their love of science with their love of the hills and decided to make some experiments at high altitudes. They had two aims: to determine by means of a barometer the differences in air pressure at the top of a mountain and at its base – thereby, they hoped, being able to calculate its height; and to measure how long it took a kettle of water to boil at various heights above sea level. The importance they attached to these simple goals speaks volumes of their lack of information regarding the Alps. They chose

Le Buet, an impressive but untaxing mountain of 10,167 feet, as a suitable site for their experiments.

The De Lucs' first expedition, in 1765, was a failure. Acting on the advice of peasants who were acquainted only with Le Buet's grazing, they climbed a long slope of grass and found themselves thwarted by precipices. It was useless to continue and anyway their thermometer had broken. In August 1770 they had another go, taking with them a local guide who was both cheese-maker and 'apprentice to a hunter'[18] – he liked to load his gun twice down the same barrel, he explained, so that he could get in a second shot if necessary. After a number of wrong turns they found themselves once again at a dead end. To salvage something from the day Jean-André set up his kettle and began to boil water. Their guide burst into laughter and took the opportunity to have a rest. He sat down heavily on Jean-André's foot, spraining his employer's ankle. Then, suddenly remembering that his cows had not been milked, he left the De Lucs to their own devices and went down the mountain. Guillaume-Antoine helped his crippled brother as best he could – which was not much according to Jean-André; he described with feeling the sensation of sliding on his back 'down 1,500 perpendicular feet'[19] – but they were unable to reach shelter and had to spend a night in the open. Their only blanket was the cloth in which they had bundled their provisions and which, when spread out, barely covered their legs. They slept badly and were so stiff and cramped on waking that it was some time before they could hobble to safety. Jean-André later explained, with forbearance, that the guide 'was not the expert we required'.[20]

Undeterred, they made a third attempt in September 1770, and this time they secured a man who knew the way if not to the peak then at least to the point from which it could be attained. They climbed ever higher, 'enjoying a multitude of agreeable sensations', until they reached the snowline. Here they felt slightly nervous. 'We were not shod for such an enterprise,' Jean-André explained. 'But our guide, with his thick, hobnailed boots, kicked the snow sideways as he ascended. In this way, he made little steps in the crust of snow which supported him, and by means of these we climbed up after him, supporting ourselves with our poles [until] we discovered the immense chain of the Alps, stretching for a distance of more than fifty leagues.'[21]

At once, Jean-André lit a fire and put the kettle on. While waiting, thermometer in hand, for the water to boil, he had time to admire the stupendous view. And as he did so he became aware of an uncomfortable fact: he was conducting his experiment on a cornice, a perilous, wind-blown coif of snow that projected from the summit without any support save that of its binding molecules. Five hundred feet of vertical space separated him from the rocks below. Nowadays, cornices are known to be inherently unstable, likely to break at any given moment. In his innocence, Jean-André took a different view. The weight of ice and snow was already so great, he reasoned, that a mere human and his kettle could not possibly affect matters. Teetering on the brink of disaster he boiled away, alternately consulting his watch and dipping his thermometer into the water. At his leisure he also took barometric readings. Then he packed his equipment and ambled back to the security of the summit.

The De Lucs' climb was an achievement. This was not because Le Buet was a particularly high or challenging hill to climb. According to one authority, 'the mountain is nothing but a long grind up meadows, steep scree slopes and a small, almost level glacier. The going is never difficult but extremely tedious.'[22] Even Bourrit later managed to climb it. Their ascent, however, was important in that it was the first time Le Buet had been climbed, and the first time that the vogue for scientific inquiry had penetrated above the lower slopes.

The De Lucs would make other water-boiling expeditions from which they returned – if their thermometers and barometers did not break, as often happened – with data that were original if not particularly useful. But they never climbed a really high peak. That privilege was left to the Abbé Murith, a priest of the Great St Bernard hospice. Murith was an amateur botanist and natural scientist who determined in 1779 to climb the Vélan, at 12,353 feet the highest mountain in his locality. Setting out on 31 August with two Chamois hunters, he successfully reached his goal. The hunters proved spineless guides, complaining of heat, tiredness and homesickness. That the party reached the summit intact was due only to Murith's browbeating; once, the Abbé had to personally hack steps in a steep ice slope and drag his companions after him. Along the way he dutifully took measurements with his barometer and his thermometer. He also listed the number and species of plants to be found at various altitudes. But what truly amazed him was the view from the top.

Had he been with him, he wrote to Saussure, 'You would have enjoyed the most splendid spectacle of mountains and glaciers you can imagine; you would have been able to gaze on a wide circle of peaks of different heights, from Turin to the Little St Bernard, from the St Bernard to the Lake of Geneva, from Vevey to the St Gotthard, from the St Gotthard to Turin.'[23] He expounded further in a letter to Bourrit. While admitting for the touchy Precentor's sake that the view from Le Buet was extremely fine, he avowed there was nothing to match that from the Vélan: 'you would have seen the universe under your feet, the points and needles of the highest hills looking like a tumultuous sea'.[24] By his calculations the summit was 'hardly less than 100 toises [650 feet] lower than the highest point of Mont Blanc . . . I believe I ascended one of the first great peaks ever climbed in Europe.'[25]

Officially, of course, the view Murith enjoyed and the height he attained were less important than his contributions to science. Nevertheless, he took a wry pleasure in underlining his achievement to Saussure. 'I cannot promise I will help you enjoy so ravishing a view,' he wrote. 'In spite of my own intrepidity, I had too much trouble in gaining the summit of this wintry giant.'[26] It was, he said, without going into details, 'a terrible climb'.

Steadily, the men of science were inching their way towards something important. They paid lip service to tales of dragons and demons and stories of witches who danced on glaciers, but what concerned them most were hard facts: the measurements of thermometers and barometers; the extent of electrical activity; the speed at which sound travelled; the quality and composition of rocks; the diversity of flora and fauna; the formation of glaciers; and the effects altitude had on the human frame. Yet even the sternest hearts experienced a near superstitious awe when considering the world they had set out to conquer.

'The high summits,' wrote Guillaume-Antoine De Luc after one expedition, 'could be descried, all white with fresh snow, through the gaps between the clouds; they appeared as many giants of an enormous size, as old as the world, who were at their windows looking down upon us poor little creeping creatures.'[27]

Chapter Three

Unlike Murith and the De Lucs, Saussure was not a trailblazer. Since 1760 he had combined a university career with vacation travels over well-trodden routes, sometimes alone, sometimes accompanied by friends and occasionally with his faithful guide, Pierre Simon. He was not, by nature, a hardy individual and rarely went anywhere without a manservant whose blue livery was so splendid that he was often taken for an army officer. During this period Saussure never climbed anything important but made his usual steady notes – a first draft, written as often as not sitting astride a mule, a second draft whenever he reached an inn and then, at home, a fair copy for the printers. He would have liked to do more but was constrained by his job at the Academy and by his wife, an heiress called Albertine Amélie Boissier who had no taste for cross-country tramps. She described herself in a teenage diary with remarkable candour: 'I am fifteen and a half: I am plain but not painfully so. Some people find an attraction in my air of gentleness and kindness. Am I clever? No: still I am not actually stupid . . . I am rather disposed to langour rather than to too much vivacity. I do not care for fashionable society, and, to put it shortly, idleness is my favourite passion.'[1] She would have preferred her husband to be idle too, and frequently berated him for his prolonged absences. At one point he was driven to retort that, 'you would like better to see me as fat as a canon and asleep all day in the chimney corner after a big dinner, than to see me achieve immortal fame by the most sublime discoveries at the cost of a few ounces of weight and several weeks' absence'.[2]

Despite his wife's opposition Saussure persevered in his travels. Between 1774 and 1784 he made a protracted exploration of the Alps. He went southwards from Geneva to the Duchy of Savoy and thence southwards again to Piedmont, the north Italian province which formed part of the Kingdom of Sardinia. He went eastwards to Switzerland, and roamed through the Bernese Oberland before dipping south to the canton of Valais. His objective, which was shared by most geologists of the time, was to discover at a fundamental level how the landscape had been formed. Theories of upheaval and erosion, basic as they may seem nowadays, were still under discussion in the eighteenth century. The principles were well understood but their application was hampered by the Bible, whose statement that the globe had at one time been submerged by water was accepted without question. The irrefutability of this doctrine rested entirely on the clergy whose power, when not overtly temporal, influenced the nobility whose decisions and patronage most certainly were. Every wealthy man hoped to buy his way to heaven – as attested by the richness of myriad chapels and churches – and those who had money were unwilling to risk damnation by sponsoring heretics who had none. So tight was the biblical straitjacket that even scientists of independent means, such as Saussure, refused to countenance a theory that excluded the Deluge.

Hampered from the start, Saussure tried his hardest to explain the Alps in religious terms. In 1778 he wrote:

Retracing in my brain the succession of the great revolutions which our globe has undergone, I saw the sea, covering the whole surface of the globe, form by successive deposits and crystallisations first the primitive mountains, then the secondary. I saw these deposits arrange themselves symmetrically in concentric beds, and subsequently the fire or

other elastic fluids contained in the interior of the globe lift
and break up this crust and thus press out the interior and
primitive part of this crust, leaving the exterior or secondary
portions piled up against the interior beds. I saw next the
waters precipitate themselves into the gulfs split open and
emptied by the explosion of the elastic fluids [and thus erode
the rocks]. I saw finally, after the retreat of the waters, the
germs of plants and animals, fertilised by the atmosphere
newly created, begin to develop on the ground abandoned by
the waters and in the waters themselves where they were
retained in the hollows of the surface.[3]

A few years later, having studied the rock strata more closely, he concluded from their contortions that the mountains had been raised by
compression rather than subterranean explosion. It was a step in the
right direction, but he still clung to the overall Flood theory.
Interestingly, he found himself unable to depict what he saw – perhaps because in his heart he could not reconcile his scientific and
religious beliefs. 'It is a terrible task,' he told his wife, 'to draw a
mountain in its detail, to make it come out clearly, so that the beds
and the joints do not look flat – that it does not resemble a split board.
Oh, this is really difficult! Still, I struggle on.'[4]

As to glaciers, Saussure was stumped. Once again he was trying to
make sense of phenomena which seem unremarkable today. Glaciers
accumulate in annual layers of snow which are marked by striations in
the ice. They move downhill thanks predominantly to their plasticity
and also to a process known as basal sliding, in which ice melted by
friction acts as a lubricant. Saussure and his contemporaries had
arrived at the latter theory – save that they believed the ice was
melted by the heat of the earth's crust. But the notion that ice could
flow, as if a congealed fluid, was hard to believe. Looking at the
vicious chunks which cracked off the Mont Blanc and Bernese
glaciers, it seemed implausible that their movement could be related
in any way to that of water. Saussure agreed with Scheuchzer that
glaciers were forced downhill by the expansion of water freezing in

their crevasses. As for glacial moraines, the lines of rock which retreating glaciers deposit on hillsides, Saussure noted them constantly in his journal but refused to associate them with their true cause. Instead, he explained them as debris left by the Deluge and proudly wove them into his biblical world view.

Finally, and on a very basic level, Saussure wanted to know where the various Alpine ranges were and how they were linked. Such maps as existed were so meagre as to be useless: no two were the same, or agreed on the whereabouts of a particular mountain; all gave different heights; and many included non-existent peaks. Mountains real and imaginary leaped across the atlas in a cartographical hopscotch that baffled the most astute. They were of no help to a traveller who strayed off the main highways – just to look at them induced a sense of despair, the peaks being portrayed in little blodges as if a pack of cats had run across the page – and they were certainly no help to a scientist like Saussure.

While battling with the terrain, the maps and his geological drawings – which he would eventually cast aside – Saussure recorded everything of interest that he stumbled upon. On one occasion, having climbed a ridge near Geneva he was astonished to find at its summit a level plateau of grass which was, on the first two Sundays of August, a trysting ground for the youths from the villages below. A couple had gone so far as to hold their wedding there, he was told, but the bride had slipped over the edge while admiring the view. The groom, in trying to catch her had also fallen to his death. 'A ruddy rock is pointed out which is reputed to be stained by their blood,'[5] Saussure commented. Less dramatically, he met a young couple walking along one of the valleys. They were engaged. She came from near Geneva; he came from the mountainous cantons. They were making a two-day hike so that the woman could assure herself that her husband-to-be had as good a home as he had promised. Elsewhere he described the gnome-like activities of those who burrowed into the Alps in search of gold, lead and other minerals. So long did they spend underground, and so hazardous was their task, that disused galleries were converted into chapels complete with altars, flickering candles and memorial tablets.

Some scenes were memorably unpleasant, such as a village near Aosta in Piedmont where every inhabitant seemed to be either cretinous or afflicted with a goitre. Both ailments were commonplace throughout Europe – the Isle of Wight was mildly notorious for its goitres – but nowhere were they more prevalent than in remote Alpine valleys. It would be a hundred years before medical science discovered that cretinism and goitres were caused by iodine deficiency. Until then doctors could only speculate – poor religious habits and bad hygiene were seen as disposing influences – and travellers could only shudder at the elephantine throats of the goitred and the stunted bodies, misshapen heads and dulled intellects of cretins. Saussure had never seen so many sufferers in one spot and he was appalled by the spectacle. As far as he could tell there was not an able-bodied man in the place.

I asked the first person I met what the name of the village was, and when he did not reply I asked a second, and then a third; but a dismal silence, or a few inarticulate noises were the only response I received. The stupid amazement with which they looked at me, their enormous goitres, their fat, parted lips, their heavy, drooping eyelids, their hanging jaws, their doltish expressions, were quite terrifying. It was as if an evil spirit had transformed every inhabitant into a dumb animal, leaving only the human form to show that they had once been men. I left with an impression of fear and sadness which will never be erased from my memory.[6]

These and other observations were woven into a hugely influential tome titled *Voyages dans les Alpes*, which came out in four volumes, two in 1786, and another two in 1796, and which secured Saussure's reputation as an Alpine expert. All the time, however, Mont Blanc loomed above him. Almost everywhere he went he could see it. Even as far afield as Lyons its pale, forbidding outline was visible. Saussure longed for it to be conquered. 'It had,' he later wrote, 'become with me a species of disease; my eyes never rested upon Mont Blanc . . .

without my undergoing a fresh attack of melancholy.'[7] Nothing could have tantalised him more than Murith's letter, written only a few years before the first two volumes of *Voyages* went to press. Surely, if Murith could climb the Vélan someone could get to the top of Mont Blanc? He was not alone: Bourrit was equally exasperated. In fact, as Saussure wrote with a tinge of anxiety, 'M. Bourrit is even keener than I to conquer Mont Blanc.'[8]

Ever since Saussure had put a price on Mont Blanc, Bourrit had positively frothed over the mountain. He had written several books on Chamonix and had analysed the different routes by which Mont Blanc might be climbed. He had gone up the Brévent, on the opposite side of the valley, and had given a torrid description of what was to most people an easy enough jaunt: 'It was infinite labour; the sweat ran down our faces; the instant we sometimes thought ourselves perfectly safe, in having grasped the solid rock, the edge would deceive us, and break off in our hands; or the stone upon which we set our foot would escape, and we were carried down with the rubbish.'[9] On reaching the top, he and his fellows 'looked at one another in expressive silence', and then began the journey down. It was even worse than the journey up: 'Perplexed, shaking and trembling at every step, our danger painted itself in all its terrors.'[10] Later, Bourrit navigated the Mer de Glace. The huge glacier had been crossed by Saussure without any difficulty but it gave Bourrit nightmares. 'Redoubling then my ardour I climbed afresh with inexpressible fatigue from rock to rock, and with the caution of a reptile making its way upon some bristly plant, I insinuated along the traces of these ornamental winding crypts . . . till astonished with the prodigious height at which I saw myself and still more with what remained to do, I at last discerned the full extent of my ability.'[11]

Bourrit was a dedicated and at times grovelling admirer of Saussure. He supplied the illustrations for *Voyages* – all from a distance, none from a height – and charted the approaches to Chamonix in exactly the same manner as had Saussure. He wrote, obsequiously, that Chamoniards raised their hats whenever Saussure's name was uttered. His attitude to Alpine exploration was, however, slightly different from Saussure's and veered towards the dramatic rather than the scientific. At Balmes, for example, he explored the same mysterious cavern with its tantalising pit. Whereas Saussure had wanted to get to the bottom of the hole, Bourrit simply threw down a grenade to see what would happen. (All his torches blew out.) Nevertheless, he reached a wide audience and was as much an agent of Mont Blanc's popularity as was Saussure.

Bourrit's outpourings and Saussure's bounty had resulted in a number of attempts on Mont Blanc. They had all been fruitless and in 1783, after three guides had failed yet again, Bourrit announced that he himself would climb the mountain. He felt confident that he could overcome at least some of his phobias, having embarked on an eccentric regime of acclimatisation – 'he sleeps during eight months in the year under a walnut-tree in his garden,' wrote an acquaintance, 'with a fur coat in July, and no greatcoat in January'.[12] The only drawback was that Bourrit needed to climb Mont Blanc for a reason. Wanting to reach the summit was not good enough in public opinion. The climb had to have scientific value. Bourrit begged Saussure for the loan of a barometer, that emblem of respectability. He begged in vain. He invited a Genevese naturalist, H. A. Gosse, to accompany him. Gosse refused. Finally, Bourrit secured the companionship of Michel-Gabriel Paccard, a 26-year-old Chamonix doctor whom Saussure described as 'a handsome youth, full, as it seemed, of intelligence, fond of botany . . . wanting to climb Mont Blanc or at least to attempt it'.[13]

Paccard, like so many of his educated Alpine brethren, was an amateur scientist. He corresponded with the Academy of Turin, was creating a garden of Alpine plants and had assisted several foreign visitors in their search for botanical specimens. These were not oustanding qualifications but they added the requisite gloss to Bourrit's attempt. Equally important, as far as Bourrit was concerned, was Paccard's mountaineering pedigree. Two of his cousins had been among those who had already made unsuccessful attempts on Mont Blanc. Paccard himself had scouted a possible route to the summit while on a plant-gathering expedition in 1775. He had also made a habit of recording every climb ever made on the mountain. And he owned a barometer.

Bourrit, Paccard and three guides set out on 15 September 1783, ascending via the central Glacier des Bossons. It was a failure, but a glorious one according to Bourrit. He told searingly of his tussles with snow and ice, of his sensation at being 'surrounded by horrible crevasses and great frozen cliffs'. He described how he and his team threw themselves into thick veils of rain to forge a passage. They came nowhere near the top but were rewarded, when the weather cleared, by 'a ravishing view' of the mountain and its surrounding needles of rock. 'Such were the magnificent scenes which compensated us for not having attained the summit of Mont Blanc,'[14] he wrote, wringing the greatest possible triumph from the occasion. Paccard also wrote an account of the trip. It was somewhat terser and did not quite coincide with that of his companion: 'I started with M. Bourrit, the miller Marie, and Jean-Claude Couttet . . . we arrived only at the glacier . . . Mont Blanc was covered with clouds, and M. Bourrit did not dare go on the ice.'[15] The following year both Paccard and Bourrit renewed their efforts. Significantly, they did not climb together.

On 9 September 1784, Paccard tried a new approach from the west, up the Glacier de Bionnassay. As was by now de rigueur, he did not succeed. 'My guide, Henri Pornet, fell ill, owing probably to the fatigue and the brandy he had taken,' Paccard wrote resignedly. 'On crossing the Bionnassay stream, I broke my barometer, and Joseph Jacques de Villette gave me his . . . The rock is rotten, and more dif-ficult to climb than it appears.'[16] Bad weather drove him back and, on the descent to Chamonix, 'I again broke the barometer.'

Seven days later, on 16 September, Bourrit followed exactly in Paccard's footsteps, taking with him a dog, four guides and a sketch-book. Events followed their habitual pattern. At a certain height Bourrit felt cold and sick. He sat down to sketch the scenery, and then, while two of the guides went ahead, he returned with the other two to safety. Bourrit wrote an overblown description of the climb, concluding with the information that at 11.00 p.m., while he was asleep in a chalet, the two missing men arrived and announced that,

'Thanks to God, they had returned from Mont Blanc without accident.'[17]

Paccard scratched drily in his ledger that on meeting the glacier Bourrit 'had a headache, felt extremely cold . . . was very pale'[18] and could go no farther. The two guides who had been last to return had arrived at 7.30, not 11.00, and had endured none of the difficulties at which Bourrit had hinted. In fact, they 'did not suffer . . . at all, and came down the hill like birds'.[19]

Paccard's history of Mont Blanc, which eventually ran as far as 1827, was not published in his lifetime. Even without his insights, however, cognoscenti detected a certain liberality in Bourrit's descriptions. 'Bourrit has just given a manuscript reduction of his new attempt on Mont Blanc,' Guillaume-Antoine De Luc wrote to his brother, who was currently in England. 'The title is very funny and so are several paragraphs of the text. It is easy to see it has not been corrected by his friend Bérenger.'[20] Bérenger, who acted as Bourrit's editor, generally toned down the Precentor's more inflammatory assertions. On this occasion he seems not to have been available, thus allowing Bourrit to escape with the inference that it was he, rather than Paccard, who first tried Paccard's route.

Bourrit was still expostulating in Chamonix when Saussure, teased beyond endurance by a letter from Paccard describing his climb of 9 September, decided to make his own attempt on Mont Blanc. He arrived in the summer of 1785 with the intention of following Paccard's route. He most certainly did not want to take Bourrit. Unfortunately, there was no way he could avoid doing so. Had not Bourrit published the route as his own discovery? To leave him out would have been an unforgivable insult. 'Though, as a rule, I infinitely prefer to make excursions of the sort alone with my guides, I could not refuse to associate M. Bourrit,'[21] he wrote. Bourrit took advantage of the situation to bring along his 21-year-old son who had no mountain experience but whose scientific achievements were said to be 'of no ordinary character'.

When the expedition departed on 14 September 1785, it comprised Saussure, Bourrit *père et fils*, and 17 porters whose luggage included

barometers, thermometers, hygrometers and electrometers, a seemingly random assortment of six sheets, five blankets and three pillows,
plus a huge amount of food and wine. Whether they needed the provisions was debatable. Previous climbers had found that the higher
they climbed the less they wanted to eat. Alcohol, which was an inte-
gral part of any endeavour, even in the lowlands, often became
abhorrent at altitude (though it was still drunk in large quantities,
perhaps in the hope that application would solve the problem). What
climbers wanted most was water to satisfy their unaccountable thirst.
And sometimes they did not even want that. A member of the 1783
three-man attempt had said that to climb Mont Blanc one should cast
everything aside; all one needed was an umbrella and a bottle of
smelling salts.

The party spent its first night at a small cabin of rock slabs which
Bourrit had had erected at the base of the Aiguille du Goûter. The
Bourrits felt ill and went early to bed while Saussure, who was already
experiencing 'a slight annoyance', stayed outside to admire the view
by starlight. Having spent so many years staring at Mont Blanc from
below, he experienced a near religious sense of awe now that he was
actually on the mountain. Exhilaration was mixed with dread. 'The
repose and deep silence cast over this huge expanse, and increased by
my imagination, inspired me with a sort of terror,' he wrote. 'I felt as
if I were the sole survivor in the universe, the dead body of which I
saw lying at my feet.'[22]

The morning of 15 September was cold, and the Bourrits refused to
leave the cabin before 6.20 a.m., far too late for Saussure's liking. The
slow-moving party climbed for five hours before being thwarted by
thick, soft snow. Two guides were sent ahead to scout the way and,
after a while, shouted down that it was impossible to go farther.
Reluctantly, Saussure agreed to retreat. He stayed awhile, however, to
take observations before rejoining the group at the cabin. There he
found to his dismay that the Bourrits had made arrangements for an
immediate retreat to the valley. Swearing that he would never again
climb accompanied by any other than guides, he settled down for a
second night in the cabin while his companions went downhill. On

looking over his measurements he calculated that they had climbed to 11,400 feet – 'a higher level than any observer before me had in the Alps'[23] – and had therefore come within 1,500 feet of the summit. He was wrong in his latter calculation by more than 2,000 feet.

When he eventually reached Chamonix, Saussure learned that the Bourrits had already started on their narratives. Keen to reassure his wife, Saussure made it a rule never to advertise the hazards he encountered on the hill. Bourrit, however, was circulating preposterous tales about the dangers that he and Saussure had faced. More, he was castigating Saussure's climbing skills. 'I could not but notice that the way in which you came down was not the happiest,' Bourrit told him. 'You might have fallen backwards, you might have been hit by the rocks dislodged by the guides, whom you made keep behind you, and we noticed the trouble they had to take to avoid this. As to my mode of coming down, I followed the advice of [my guide] who saw how impossible it was for me, with ruined boots which had lost their heels [Bourrit was wearing his usual, impractical fur slippers], to keep myself from falling. I was forced to put my feet in his footsteps; and if I rested on him, I took care to do so as lightly as possible.'[24] Saussure's reply was a model of restraint: 'No one perhaps believes more than I do in the kindness and modesty of your heart, but I know very well also that your flighty imagination often makes you see things in a false light. If you could put aside this tendency, there is no reason why you should not keep an agreeable recollection of our excursion.'[25]

Bourrit Jr. also had something to say. 'Sir,' he wrote to Saussure, 'do you not envy me my twenty-one years? Who will wonder if a youth of this age, who has nothing to lose, is bolder than a father of a family, a man of forty-six?'[26] Wearily, Saussure picked up his pen.

Monsieur, a moderate amount of boastfulness is no great crime, especially at your age . . . You say you descended agilely. It is true, you descended agilely enough in the easy places, but in the difficult places you were, like your father, resting on the shoulder of one guide in front and held up behind by another. I do not blame you for these precautions; they were wise, prudent, even indispensable; but in no language in the world is that the manner of progress styled agile climbing. But enough . . . After what I have written to you, sir, I am under no anxiety as to anything you may say or write, and am very far from asking you to show me your narrative. On the contrary, I desire there may be an end to this discussion.[27]

Silently, in his ledger, Paccard gave a dispassionate account of the whole business. He noted that Saussure had 'always shown a dislike for snowy tracks – though he was a good walker on rocky ground', and that he was roped 'like a prisoner'[28] to his guides. As for the Bourrits, father leaned on the shoulder of one guide and was gripped by his collar by another; son, meanwhile, suffered from mountain sickness and made the ascent hanging onto the tails of the guides' coats. They were all equally incompetent as climbers, he reckoned. And he didn't think much of Saussure's altitude measurements, either.

Saussure was discouraged by the failure. From Geneva he wrote to a friend that 'To reach this summit, then, it is essential to find some shelter for the night at a higher point than ours, and to select a year when the mountain is entirely stripped of [new] snow by the month of July, or at latest by the beginning of August, and even then the enterprise will be pretty dangerous and always infinitely laborious.'[29] Thinking of the distance he had left unclimbed, he wondered whether Mont Blanc might not be better conquered by balloon. 'But I believe it would be very dangerous,' he added mournfully, detailing with typical precision all the perils that would attend such an effort.

It had been a quarter of a century since Saussure had first offered his reward. He was now wondering if he would ever have to pay it. Mont Blanc was clearly impossible to climb.

CHAPTER FOUR

The year after Saussure and Bourrit had failed to capture Mont
Blanc, Paccard's diary, even drier than usual, contained the following entry: 'Our journey of the 8th of August, 1786; arrived six
hours twenty-three minutes; set out six hours fifty-seven minutes;
rested thirty-four minutes.'[1] Fleshed out, this skeletal account could
be interpreted thus: at 4.00 a.m. on 7 August, Paccard and a local
guide named Jacques Balmat had set out from Chamonix; after a
climb of more than fourteen hours during which they fought gales,
altitude sickness and snow blindness they reached, at 6.23 p.m. the
following day, the summit of Mont Blanc which they then left at 6.57
p.m. The impossible had been accomplished.

At the heart of the climb was Balmat, a short, boastful farmer-
cum-crystal-gatherer. He was not particularly pleasant and had a
twisty cast to his face, but he was supremely fit and was as determined as any of his more illustrious employers to reach the summit –
and, importantly, to earn Saussure's reward. 'In those days I really
was something worth looking at,' he recalled. 'I had a famous calf and
a stomach like cast-iron, and I could walk three days consecutively
without eating, a fact I found useful to me when lost on the Buet. I
munched a little snow – nothing more. Every now and then I cast a
sidelong look at Mont Blanc and said to myself, "My fine fellow,

whatever you may say or whatever you may do, I shall get to the top of you one day.'"[2]

Climbing the Brévent repeatedly to get a good view of Mont Blanc's slopes, he saw a possible way to the top. It led via the village of La Côte, through the Glacier de Taconnaz to the rocky outcrops known as the Grands Mulets and thence to the snowy mound of the Dôme du Goûter. From here, he hoped, a sudden lunge might capture the summit itself.

Balmat trained for every possible difficulty to such a degree that he dreamed of nothing else. 'I would plant my feet on pieces of rock and feel them shake like loose teeth,' he wrote, 'and the sweat would fall from me in great drops . . . Never mind, keep going! I was like a lizard on a wall. I saw the earth sinking away beneath me. It was all the same, I only looked at the sky. All I cared for was to reach the top . . . At that moment I was awakened by a vigorous box to the ear by my wife, and, would you believe it, I had caught hold of her ear and was tugging it as if it were indiarubber.'

Finally, on 5 June 1786, he put his dreams and his plans to the test. Telling his wife that he was going after crystals and would be back within two days – secrecy was essential, he decided, lest competitors steal the fruits of his reconnaissance – he reached the Grands Mulets without mishap. Here he was prevented from spying the ground ahead thanks to a cloud that enveloped both the peak and himself. Undeterred, Balmat then did the unheard of: he decided to spend the night where he was. Lacking as he did a tent, and provisioned with only a loaf of bread and a bottle of brandy, his decision would be considered foolhardy by any standards. By those of the time, it was unimaginable folly. Nobody had ever spent a night in the open at such high altitude. It was widely believed that any who did so would die.

Balmat's chosen resting place was a little perch of hard snow, about six feet long, surrounded by rocks. A few feet away yawned an 800-foot drop. For fear of rolling down the cliff in his sleep, Balmat remained awake, seated on his knapsack, beating his hands and feet together to combat the cold. Shortly before midnight, the mist turned to snow. 'My breath was frozen,' he recalled, 'and my clothes were soaked . . . soon I felt as if I was stark naked. I moved my hands and feet faster, and began to sing to drive away the thoughts that were seething in my brain.' His voice died away in the whiteness. There was no echo. 'Everything was dead in this ice-bound world and the sound of my voice almost terrified me. I became silent and afraid.'

At 2.00 a.m. the sky grew lighter and by 4.00 Balmat was confident that he had survived. (Though it would be more than twenty-four hours before his clothes thawed.) He spent another day and yet another numbing night on the mountain before deciding to go back. On the way down, however, he was horrified to meet a party of three guides coming up. Ostensibly they were looking for lost goats; but Balmat knew better. 'I felt that the men were trying to deceive, and at once surmised that they were about to attempt the journey which I had just failed to achieve.' And, if they were successful they would gain the reward. When they asked him what conditions were like higher up, his suspicions were confirmed. By now, Balmat had been climbing more or less continually for two days, but the prospect of being outstripped by the fresher men was more than he could bear. When they asked him to join them he accepted immediately. There was one problem: Balmat had promised his wife he would be back within two days. In an extraordinary display of vigour he therefore ran down to Chamonix, told his wife that he was back and then, having grabbed some food and a change of socks, told her he was off again.

He left his home at 11.00 p.m. and two hours later had caught up with the others. By 3.00 a.m. the whole party was standing on the Dôme du Goûter from where, in the early dawn, they could see the summit of Mont Blanc to the east. Here, the throng was swelled by yet another group of two guides. Their excuse that they had decided to climb to the Dôme for a wager was more than Balmat could stomach. Aghast at the prospect of having to share the reward with so many, he set out on his own and within a few hours was sitting astride a narrow ridge or arête leading to the summit. It 'seemed a path fit only for a rope dancer' and was interrupted by an ugly clump of rocks but, looking down, Balmat thought he could discern a route over the glacier below – the so-called Grand Plateau. Unfortunately, he was in no position to make the journey. He was starved of sleep, he had run out of provisions, and the weather was deteriorating. He had no choice but to retreat.

On reaching the Dôme he discovered that the others, too, had given up. They had gone home, expecting Balmat to follow. Rather than do so, however, he spent the rest of the day criss-crossing the Grand Plateau. That night he again slept uneasily on the mountainside. Thousands of feet below him, he could see the lights of Chamonix being extinguished one by one. It did little to raise his spirits. 'No man is made of iron,' he admitted, 'and I felt far from cheerful. During the short intervals between the crash of avalanches I heard distinctly the barking of a dog at Courmayeur [on the Italian side of Mont Blanc] though it was more than a league and a half to that village from the spot where I was lying. The noise served to distract my thoughts, for it was the only earthly sound that reached me. At about midnight the barking ceased, and nothing remained but the deathly silence of the grave.' Glaciers continued to crack explosively and avalanches to rumble, but they 'could reassure no human being, they could only frighten him'.

At 2.00 a.m. he awoke and began his descent. He reached home six hours later, badly sunburned and utterly exhausted. Rejecting his bedroom – 'I was afraid of being tormented by the flies' – he went into the barn and stretched out on a pile of hay where he slept for twenty-four hours. In all, his odyssey had taken the better part of five days during which he had slept, minimally, for only two nights. He had covered incredible vertical distances at an astonishing rate – his second ascent must have been at a run, even allowing for an exaggeration of his times. He had proved that it was possible to survive a night in the open at very high altitude and, above all, he had found a route to the summit. It really was an amazing achievement and if it yielded no immediate profit Balmat did not care. 'I was despondent, but not disheartened by these two vain attempts,' he recorded. 'I felt quite certain I should be more fortunate a third time.'

For three weeks Mont Blanc was shrouded in cloud. This was no use to Balmat. The clouds which looked so innocuous from below contained driving snow and sleet which even his constitution could not endure for long. Equally important, they meant that observers would be unable to see people on the summit. It was all very well to reach the top but it would be pointless to do so unless the conquest could be verified by telescope from below. And there was another thing: Balmat had to find a respectable person to climb with. Even if he reached the summit and turned somersaults in the full view of 1,000 spectators, it would be considered valueless without a man of science to hand with his barometer. Where could one find such a man in Chamonix? At the door of that silent, critical chronicler Dr Michel-Gabriel Paccard.

Paccard had been peering vainly at Mont Blanc through his telescope for more than three years in search of a route to the summit. When Jacques Balmat approached him with the news of his discovery – also for advice about his sunburn – and the offer of making a joint attempt, Paccard did not hesitate. They agreed to start as soon as the weather cleared. The clouds dissipated in the early hours of 8 August 1786, leaving Mont Blanc outlined in all its glory. Balmat was at Paccard's house before dawn.

In 1832 the novelist Alexandre Dumas was to visit Balmat and persuade him to give his version of what happened next. The resulting narrative owed much to Balmat's sense of self-importance, a great deal to Dumas's journalistic skills and even more to his interviewing technique – he paid for, and Balmat consumed, three bottles of wine – but even so it is worth repeating because it remains the only detailed description of the historic climb.

I went to Paccard and said, 'Well, Doctor, are you determined? Are you afraid of the cold or the snow or the precipices? Speak out like a man.' 'With you I fear nothing,' was his reply. 'Well then, the time has come to climb this molehill.' The Doctor said he was quite ready, but just as he shut the door of his house I think his heart failed him a little, for he could not get

the key out of the lock and kept turning it first one way and
then the other. 'I say, Balmat,' he said, 'if we did the right
thing we should take two guides.' 'No,' I replied, 'either you
and I go together, or you go with the others. I want to be first
not second.' He thought for a moment, drew out the key, put it
in his pocket, and with his head bent down followed me
mechanically. In about a minute he gave himself a shake and
said, 'Well, I must trust to you, Balmat.' . . . He tried, but could
not sing in tune, which annoyed him.

They set off at 5.00 p.m., taking separate routes so as to avoid
drawing attention to themselves, and met up again at the village of La
Côte. 'The same evening we slept on the top of La Côte, between the
glaciers of Bossons and Taconnaz. I carried a rug and used it to muffle
the Doctor up like a baby. Thanks to this precaution he passed a tolerable night. As for me I slept soundly until half past one. At two the
white line appeared, and soon the sun rose without a cloud, brilliant
and beautiful, a promise of a glorious day! I awoke the Doctor and we
began our day's march.'

After quarter of an hour they were crossing the Glacier de
Taconnaz, surmounting crevasses 'whose depth could not be measured by the eye' and snow bridges that 'gave way under our feet'.
'The Doctor's first steps were halting and uncertain,' Balmat
recorded, 'but the sight of my alertness gave him confidence, and we
went on safe and sound.' Up they went to the Grands Mulets where
once again Paccard's confidence waned as Balmat showed him where
he had spent the night. 'He made an expressive grimace, and kept
silent for ten minutes; then, stopping suddenly, said, "Balmat, do you
really think we shall get to the top of Mont Blanc today?" I saw how
his thoughts were drifting, and answered him laughingly.' At the projecting rocks known as the Petits Mulets the wind rose and Paccard's
hat was snatched off his head.

I turned on hearing his cry, and saw the felt hat careering over
the mountain to Courmayeur. With his arms stretched out he

looked after it. 'We must go into mourning for it,' I said, 'you
will never see it again for it has gone to Piedmont, and good
luck be with it.' It seemed my little joke had given offence to
the wind, for my mouth had scarcely closed when a more
violent gust obliged us to lie down on out stomachs to prevent
our following the hat. The wind lashed the mountain sides and
passed whistling over our heads, driving great balls of snow
almost as big as houses before it. The Doctor was dismayed . . .
At the first respite I rose, but the Doctor could only continue
on all fours.

At the Dôme du Goûter, Balmat took out his telescope and looked
back at the town below. He had arranged with a shop woman to look
out for them at this point and, sure enough, there she was with fifty
others. Balmat waved his hat and the villagers waved back. But the
hatless Paccard, who had finally stood up thanks to 'considerations of
self respect', could only be distinguished by his big coat.

At this point Paccard's nerve seems to have gone altogether, if
Balmat is to be believed.

Having used up all his strength in getting on his feet, neither
the encouragement from below, nor my earnest entreaties
could induce him to continue the ascent. My eloquence
exhausted, I told him to keep moving so as not to get
benumbed. He listened, without seeming to understand, and
replied, 'All right.' I saw that he was suffering from the cold,
while I also was nearly frozen. Leaving him the bottle, I went
on alone, saying that I should very soon come back to find him.
He answered, 'Yes! Yes!' and telling him again to be sure not to
stand still, I went off. I had hardly gone thirty paces when, on
turning round, I saw him actually sitting down on the snow,
with his back turned to the wind as some precaution.

From that time onward the route presented no very great
difficulty, but as I rose higher the air became much less easy to
breathe, and I had to stop almost every ten steps and wheeze

like one with consumption. I felt as if my lungs had gone, and my chest was quite empty. I folded my handkerchief over my mouth, which made me a little more comfortable as I breathed through it. The cold got worse and worse, and to go a quarter of a league took an hour. I kept walking upward, with my head bent down, but finding I was on a peak which was new to me, I lifted my head and saw that at last I had reached the summit of Mont Blanc!

I had no longer any strength to go higher; the muscles of my legs seemed only held together by my trousers. But behold I was at the end of my journey . . . I had come alone with no help but my own will and my own strength. Everything around belonged to me! I was the monarch of Mont Blanc! I was the statue on this unique pedestal! Ah, then I turned towards Chamonix and waved my hat on the end of my stick. I could see through my glass the response. My subjects in the valley perceived. The whole village was gathered together in the market place.

Then Balmat remembered Paccard. He shouted for him but received no answer. Alarmed, he retraced his steps and found him rolled up in a ball, 'just like a cat when she makes herself into a muff'. Even the news that Balmat had reached the peak had no effect on him. All he said was 'Where can I lie down and go to sleep?' Balmat hoisted him to his feet and when he complained that his hands were cold gave him one of his hare-skin mittens – 'I would not have parted with both of them even to my brother' – before shoving him up to the summit which they reached shortly after 6.00 p.m.

The sun shone brilliantly and stars could be seen in the deep blue sky. Balmat, who had completely recovered from his previous fatigue, marvelled at the view.

Below was nothing but gaunt peaks, ice, rocks, and snow. The great chain which crosses the Dauphiné and stretches as far as the Tyrol was spread out before us, its four hundred glaciers

shining in the sunlight. Could there be space for any green
ground on the earth? The lakes of Geneva and Neuchâtel were
specks of blue on the horizon. To the left lay the mountains of
my dear country all fleecy with snow, and rising from meadows
of the richest green. To the right was all Piedmont, and
Lombardy as far as Genoa, and Italy was opposite.

They stayed there for an hour. Paccard brought out his thermometer and barometer – despite a temperature of 22°F, which caused his
ink to freeze as he tried to put down the results. Then at 7.00 p.m.,
with only two and a half hours of daylight remaining, Balmat gave one
last wave of his hat to the villagers below and, holding Paccard under
the arms, began the descent. The doctor was 'like a child, no energy
or will. I guided him along the good places and pushed, or carried him,
along the bad'. Every few minutes Paccard would stop, saying he
could go no further, and had to be pushed on by brute force. When
they crossed the snowline at eleven o'clock Paccard announced that
he could no longer feel his hands.

I took off his gloves and found that his hands were dead white,
and my hand also from which I had taken the glove was quite
numb. I said, 'Well, we have three frost-bitten hands between
us.' He did not mind but only wanted to lie down and sleep.
He told me, however, to rub them with snow, and that was
easily done. I began by rubbing his hands and finished by
rubbing my own. Soon sensation returned, but accompanied by
pains as if every vein had been pricked by needles. I rolled my
baby up in his rug and put him to bed under the shelter of a
rock; we ate and drank a little; pressed as close to one another
as possible, and fell fast asleep.

The following morning Paccard was completely snow-blind. 'It is
funny, Balmat,' he said, 'I can hear the birds singing but can see no
daylight.' He wondered if it was because he could not open his eyes.
Yet, according to Balmat, they were 'glaring like those of a horned

owl'. Paccard followed Balmat downhill, holding onto his knapsack until they reached La Côte, where Balmat hurried home, leaving the doctor to feel his way back with a stick.

When Balmat looked in a mirror he was horrified. 'I was quite unrecognisable. My eyes were red, my face black and my lips blue. Every time I laughed or yawned the blood spouted out from my lips and cheeks, and in addition I was half blind.' Within a week, however, he was fit enough to travel to Geneva to claim Saussure's prize. And a month later the story of his ascent was published by the Historian of the Alps himself, the indefatigable Bourrit.

Whereas Saussure was delighted by Paccard and Balmat's success, Bourrit was extremely jealous. In his eyes Paccard had come to public attention in the first place by accompanying the Indefatigable One up the mountain. Now the upstart had stolen his glory. And he had done so with just one guide instead of the tens that the Precentor required merely to steady him across a glacier. If Bourrit could not claim the conquest for himself he would do his best to deny it to Paccard.

Bourrit interviewed Balmat in Geneva while he 'still carried on his face the honourable marks of his intrepidity',[3] and produced an account that broadly accorded with that of Dumas fifty-six years later. Not everything was the same: Balmat was 70 when he spoke to Dumas and was confused by old age as well as an obvious animosity towards Paccard. The humiliating scene on the Dôme du Goûter, for example, was a complete fabrication. They never went there, ascending instead via the Grand Plateau which lies beneath it. Equally, Balmat's claim that he struggled alone to the summit while Paccard sank into hypothermic slumber is open to doubt: Paccard would have frozen to death in the estimated hour and a half it must have taken Balmat after leaving him to reach the summit, wave to his 'subjects' and then rejoin him; and if not dead, Paccard would have been in no condition to record the temperature let alone make observations with his barometer, which he undeniably did. Such details aside, however, the two stories bore a remarkable similarity. According to Bourrit, who published his findings in a public letter on 20 September 1786,

Balmat was the hero and Paccard a feeble tagger-on. Not only had Balmat reached the top before Paccard but he had had to drag the doctor after him. In every respect Balmat had breathed life into the enterprise while Paccard had lagged behind, having to be coaxed, shoved and bullied to the summit. It was a masterful and engaging story – even if it dwelled overlong on Bourrit's own accomplishments the year before – culminating in a typical flourish: 'Chamonix contemplated them, strangers from below saw them through their glasses; they had followed them on their march with inquietude and they rejoiced at the sight of the two little beings upon so lofty a pinnacle of the globe.'[4]

There was more. In Bourrit's view the guide had been grossly underpaid by Paccard. 'Balmat ought to have an honest reward,' he said, ignoring Saussure's prize. 'Strangers have often promised something handsome to the man who first ascended the mountain, but from what I hear they have forgotten it; at present he is without recompense. He has exposed his life or at least his health, and perhaps he is already much altered. His companion has no need of reward, his father is one of the richest men in the valley; besides, it is not the same with an amateur as a guide.'[5]

It was very impressive. But nothing which Bourrit said agreed in the slightest with Paccard's version of events. Having got wind of Bourrit's machinations, Paccard produced a detailed certificate describing the climb. It was signed by Balmat and stated unequivocably that Paccard had proposed the route, had led the ascent, had encouraged Balmat when he was flagging and had helped him with his baggage, and that when he had reached the summit Balmat 'was obliged to run to be nearly as soon as he was on the aforesaid spot'.[6] Balmat stated outright that 'Paccard called me and I followed.'[7] His signature was witnessed by two of his fellow guides. Paccard was perhaps going a little far here, but he gave a more restrained account to Saussure who stated in his diary that as they neared the summit 'they endured great fatigue from the fact that the surface was covered with a thin crust which alternately bore them and gave way under their steps. The guide told him he could not persevere unless he (Paccard) was prepared to take the lead from time to time and to break the snow and he did this all the way to the top.'[8] A brace of German barons, who had been advised by Saussure to watch the climb from a nearby hill, had seen the two men waving from the summit. And every subsequent report from Saussure and others attributed the climb if not solely to Paccard then certainly to both men.

Tempers in Chamonix ran high. When Balmat accused Paccard of forging the certificate, the doctor knocked him to the ground. Eventually, Saussure had to intervene, forcing Bourrit to reword his letter in less antagonistic terms. Bourrit made a number of pale excuses: Paccard hadn't actually reached the summit; his narrative was badly written; it contained information damaging to Saussure's reputation; if he, Bourrit, did not believe what he had written then he would have published it anonymously; and so on. In the end Bourrit made a few reluctant amendments, but even the revised document was damaging. One of Paccard's relatives was imprisoned for a day for using foul language about its author.

Paccard fought back as best he could. He sent two letters to the *Journal de Lausanne* correcting Bourrit's assertions and issued a prospectus inviting people to subscribe to his own forthcoming narrative. His manuscript, which he foolishly gave to Bourrit's editor Bérenger, was never published – or if it was, it was circulated privately; at any rate, no copy of it has ever been found – and in the absence of any solid opposition Bourrit's version therefore became accepted as the true one. After all, was he not the Historian of the Alps? Balmat was accepted as the conqueror of Mont Blanc and Paccard as his accomplice. Balmat received Saussure's reward – Paccard, unwisely, made no claim; he had no need of the money, as Bourrit had pointed out, but it would have strengthened his position – on top of which Balmat was given a gift of 50 Piedmontese pistoles by the King of Sardinia, who also granted him the title 'Balmat *dit* Mont-Blanc'. A public subscription was opened for his benefit, managed rather inefficiently by Bourrit who was suspected for a while of siphoning some of the money into his own pocket, and on the proceeds Balmat built a handsome house for himself. Plaques and statues were erected in his honour, roads were named after him. He was worshipped in Chamonix and became the most sought-after guide in the valley.

So who did conquer Mont Blanc? For two centuries historians throughout Europe have pondered this question. In the wake of Bourrit's letter the laurels were given to Balmat. Then, in the early twentieth century, when Saussure's diaries and other material came to light, they were transferred to Paccard. The truth lies somewhere in between. Paccard was a well-educated man who had no need to lie, but was goaded by Bourrit's account to say that he had led Balmat to the summit. Balmat, meanwhile, had every reason to lie but was unquestionably the fitter of the two and if anyone led it was probably him. The reports which attributed the triumph to Paccard should be taken with a pinch of salt. It was common in those times to ascribe victory of any sort to the man with the highest social standing – several people, including Britain's Lord Palmerston, congratulated Saussure on the conquest even though he took no part in it – and one can imagine Balmat's indignation at having to concede glory to a man simply because he was a doctor. The injustice was underlined by a twentieth-century commentator who said, in Paccard's defence, that Balmat had been paid to do his job and should have been satisfied with the money. On the other hand Paccard was a serious and dedicated mountaineer. The description he gave Saussure of conditions during the climb was far more plausible than Balmat's. And far from being unfit, he was up Mont Blanc within days of his return, seeking an easier route to the top.

From this distance it is impossible to judge the matter fairly. Essentially, the controversy revolved around Bourrit's insecurity and Balmat's desire to get his hands on Saussure's money. That two men had climbed the highest mountain in Europe was almost incidental. If Saussure had put a bounty on any other peak – and there were plenty of them – it would have engendered similar squabbles. One can only agree with the Alpine historian Paul Payot, a recent Mayor of Chamonix, in his decision that 'When climbers rope up they form a team that has to stick together for better or for worse. If Paccard and

Balmat had followed modern methods and used a rope none of these arguments would have taken place. They did not use a rope. Nonetheless, they were still a team.'[9] And so they should be given equal credit.

At the time, people of note attached little significance to the Balmat–Paccard ascent; few were even aware of the sound and fury that accompanied it. For all the Romantic swooning, and for all Bourrit and Saussure's admiration of the views, the overriding purpose of climbing an Alp was to make scientific observations. What these observations would reveal was uncertain – Saussure believed that the Alps were once islands in a primordial sea and hoped, therefore, in a pre-Darwinian way, that they would shed light on humankind's origins – but they had to be made and Paccard's frost-fumbled work with his barometer had revealed nothing. (The instrument, needless to say, had been damaged during the ascent.) In the circles that mattered, Mont Blanc remained a virgin peak. It was up to Saussure to complete the task.

CHAPTER FIVE

While in Geneva Balmat had offered his services to Saussure for a climb the following year. Saussure had accepted them immediately, and in the summer of 1787 he went to Provence to take readings at sea level, leaving instructions for Balmat to contact him as soon as the snows melted. *'Le courageux Balmat,'* as Saussure now called him, reconnoitred the slopes throughout June without any success. Then on 5 July he reached the top accompanied by two other guides, Jean-Michel Cachat and Alexis Tournier. Two days later Saussure was in Chamonix but to his dismay the weather was too bad to make an immediate ascent. For the rest of the month he fretted in the valley, organising his porters and supplies while he waited for the clouds to clear.

He did not fret alone. Breaking one of his cardinal rules, he had invited his wife, his two sons and his two sisters-in-law to observe the great endeavour. Shadowing them closely from Geneva came Bourrit and his son. Paccard, too, arrived from a climbing expedition in Courmayeur. It was an odd mixture. To Saussure's surprise his wife made one or two short climbs and enjoyed the experience enormously: 'Madame de Saussure had never been in such high spirits,'[1] one of her sisters recorded. Bourrit, meanwhile, pestered him with requests that he be allowed to take part in the ascent – he was firmly turned down. And Paccard maintained a wary silence on the outskirts. 'I think he does not want to see me before my expedition,' Saussure commented, noting that 'he seems to have taken pains everywhere to have gone a little further and higher than I have been.'[2]

And so the days passed. Saussure tested his instruments, his shoes and his stamina on the lower slopes – he reckoned 1,500 feet per hour was the best he could do – and when the rain was too heavy for outdoor work he received parcels of books and delicacies from Geneva, talked to travellers who had been drawn to Chamonix by news of his intended climb and began to read the classics. Bourrit rented a chalet and sold his pictures to tourists, now and then visiting the Saussure ménage in the hope of softening the great man's resolve. Bourrit, Jr. presented the women with meadow bouquets to no avail. The weather worsened, and Paccard's father drowned on a perilous river crossing, thereby rendering the doctor even less communicative than usual. On 29 July Saussure recorded streams of stone and dust being blown off the summit. On 30 July he measured the cloud speed at 60 feet per second. Then, on 1 August, by which time he had learned several passages of the *Iliad* by heart, the skies cleared. 'The barometer mounts quickly,' he wrote in his diary. 'I make, therefore, all arrangements for a start, but keep the secret from my wife.'[3]

His proposed route was that followed by Balmat but this time there would be no unseemly final dash for the summit. Saussure wanted as much time to make his observations as possible, to which end he proposed to spend the first night at La Côte and the second on the Grand Plateau below the Dôme du Goûter. It would all be done in as much comfort as possible, a retinue of eighteen guides being hired to carry food, wine and all Saussure's instruments plus an inventory of requisites that included a parasol, several changes of clothes, three pairs of shoes, two nightshirts and a bed with 'mattresses, sheets, coverlet, and a green curtain'. A tent was made which could accommodate the whole party. And Saussure's long-suffering manservant was also enrolled – though what he was meant to do is a bit of a mystery.

Obtaining the guides was at first difficult. 'They imagined that during the night it would be insupportably cold in the high snows,'[4]

Saussure complained. Despite Balmat's evidence to the contrary, 'they seriously feared they would die'.[5] Patiently, Saussure explained that they could dig a hole in the snow, cover it with the tent, and thus protected from the elements, and heated by the warmth of their bodies, they would be quite comfortable no matter how cold it was. 'These arrangements reassured them,' he said, 'and we therefore went ahead.'[6]

To begin with it was almost ludicrously easy. They climbed to the village of La Côte, below the Taconnaz and Bossons glaciers, where Mme Saussure sent up a fresh supply of meat. 'I was really vexed about that which you have, which has been made for two days,' she fussed. 'I shall be better satisfied that you have this as a supplement.' She made a tart remark about Saussure slipping off without telling her but relented at the end: 'I have used rose-coloured paper so that you may have something else than the white of the snows to look at. Will you sleep well under your tent, mon cher ami? I trust so.'[7]

Saussure's first day passed without incident. The second was slightly different. As they crossed the glaciers, Saussure's team began to flag. One of the guides fell through a snow bridge and was only saved because he was roped fore and aft. They were all frightened, especially Saussure.

> We ... found ourselves entangled in a labyrinth of rocks of ice
> separated by large crevasses, in some places opening very
> wide, in others covered either wholly or in part by snow, which
> sometimes forms a sort of arch underneath, and which are
> sometimes the only resources in one's power to get over the
> crevasses; at other times it is an uneven ridge of ice which
> serves as a bridge to cross over. In some places the crevasses
> are quite empty, we had to go down to the bottom and get up
> at the other side by stairs cut with a hatchet in the very ice ...
> and sometimes after having got to the bottom of these abysses,
> you can hardly conceive how you shall get out again.[8]

To cross the deepest crevasses they carried with them a ladder, which

Balmat had previously stored in a cavern at the base of the glacier – he had also stored a long pole, but this had inexplicably been stolen – in places, however, the gap was so wide that the ladder did not suffice. Their only option in these circumstances was to use the snow bridges.

'However narrow and sloping the ice ridges may be,' Saussure wrote, 'these intrepid Chamoniards . . . appear neither afraid nor uneasy; they talk, laugh, and defy each other in jest; but when they pass over these slight roofs suspended over deep abysses, they walk in a most profound silence; the three first tied together by ropes, about five or six feet between them; the others two by two holding their sticks by the ends, their eyes fixed on their feet, each endeavouring to place exactly and lightly his foot in the traces of the one before him.'[9]

They surmounted many such obstacles, each victory being marked by an explosion of relieved chatter. At the brink of one crevasse Saussure's manservant dropped the barometer pedestal. 'It slid with the swiftness of an arrow down the sloping wall of the crevasse and planted itself at a great depth on the opposite side, where it remained fixed and quivering like the lance of Achilles on the bank of the Scamander.'[10] The pedestal was vital because it not only supported the barometer but the compass, telescope and almost every other instrument Saussure possessed. A guide lowered himself down and retrieved it. According to Saussure, 'It took us three hours to cross this redoubtable glacier, although barely a quarter of a league in breadth.'[11]

On reaching the Grand Plateau, where they planned to spend the next night, they were pinched by cold and hunger. But before they could eat or sleep they had to find a place to pitch the tent. This was not as simple as it seemed. They had to choose a spot that would be safe from the avalanches that slid off the Dôme du Goûter. At the same time they had to watch out for crevasses: Saussure had followed a particularly wicked specimen that had sunk out of sight but whose direction led to the Grand Plateau; he had visions of his team digging the tent into a snow bridge and falling to their doom.

Eventually a safe site was found and operations commenced. More than once on his expeditions, Saussure had remarked on the hardiness of Chamonix guides. But when they began to dig the hole for the tent, he was amazed at what happened. 'These robust men, for whom the seven or eight hours march we had just endured were absolutely as nothing, could only shift five or six shovelfuls of snow before declaring the task an impossibility.'[12] Saussure had chosen to camp in an area of the mountain that he later described as one of stagnant air. The men could not breathe properly and the slightest effort became a trial. When one guide went down the mountain to collect water that they had seen running at the bottom of a crevasse he returned empty-handed, wracked by altitude sickness. 'He spent the rest of the night in terrible pain,'[13] Saussure recorded. They all suffered from thirst that was only slightly alleviated by the snow they melted on braziers fuelled by coal which they carried on their backs.

In his published journal Saussure was at pains to point out that he was well accustomed to heights and did not suffer in the slightest from altitude sickness. In his diary, however, he told a different story. 'Immense view . . . but sickness. I eat some bread and frozen beef, raw and nasty, and drink some water which had been carried up to me.'[14] It was not quite the regulated jaunt he had envisaged. That evening, after a meal that none could stomach, the guides crawled into the tent and shut every opening tight, just as their leader had instructed. Saussure was given a corner of the tent in which to lie down. The others crouched as best they could, knee to knee, babbling in terror and occasionally turning aside to vomit. 'Detestable night,' he wrote in his diary, 'sickness, colic, close atmosphere produced by twenty heated and panting inmates.'[15] Eventually he had to go out for air. He was stunned by the view: 'The magnificent basin, glowing in the light of the moon which shone with the greatest brilliancy in an ebony sky, presented a superb spectacle. Jupiter rose radiant behind the Aiguille du Midi, and the glow reflected from the snows was so brilliant that only stars of the first or second magnitude were visible.'[16] The sight was beautiful but also intimidating. 'There were no living beings, no sign of vegetation; it was a realm of frigid silence. When I imagined Paccard and Balmat reaching this desert at the end of the day, without shelter, without the possibility of rescue, without even the knowledge that men could survive where they intended to go, but nevertheless carrying on, I could not help but admire their courage.'[17] Returning to his foetid quarters, he was awoken shortly after midnight by an avalanche that crashed over the slopes he intended to cross the following day. He slept fitfully and was up before dawn to take readings. The temperature was 5°F below zero.

They set off again at 7.00 a.m. with barely 2,500 feet left to climb. Compared to how far they had already come, it was a relatively small distance. But Saussure found it fearsomely hard work, having to stop for breath every thirty paces. After two hours, during which time they had climbed some 1,600 feet, they reached a terrifying crevasse. 'This was one of the worst places,' Saussure wrote in his diary. 'The slope is 39 degrees, the precipice below is frightful, and the snow, hard on the surface, was flour beneath. Steps were cut, but the legs insecurely placed in this flour rested on a lower crust which was often very thin, and then slipped.'[18] He tottered past this obstacle thanks only to a pole that two guides held as a kind of balustrade on the edge of the drop. He became weaker and weaker. Rest stops now occurred every fifteen paces and frequently his legs gave way beneath him. It took the same time to climb the remaining 900 feet as it had the preceding 1,600 – in the nineteenth century the mountaineer Edward Whymper was to reckon on fifty minutes for this last stretch – but finally, at 10.00 a.m. on 3 August 1787, Saussure reached the summit.

In Saussure's first published account he said that his initial thought was of his wife. Unfortunately for Europe's sentimentalists this was not quite correct. True, when he took out his telescope he saw her unfurling a flag, their pre-arranged signal that she could see him on the top. But in later amendments to his journal he revealed that his feelings were of disappointment, even rage. 'Since I had had for the last two hours under my eyes almost all one sees from the summit, the arrival was no coup de théâtre – it did not even give me all the pleasure one might have imagined,' he wrote. 'The length of the struggle, the recollection and the still vivid impresssion of the exertion it had cost me, caused me a kind of irritation. At the moment that I trod the

highest point of the snow that crowned the summit I trampled it with
a feeling of anger rather than pleasure.'[19] Not only was it an anti-
climax but the protracted climb had robbed him of precious time in
which to make 'the observations and experiments which alone gave
value to my venture, and I was very doubtful of being able to carry out
more than a portion of what I had planned'.[20]

Still, he had to admit that the panorama was very grand from a scientific point of view. He did not have the time or the ability to make
a map but the view gave him at last an overall sense of how the Alps
fitted together. 'I could not believe my eyes,' he wrote. 'It seemed as
if it was a dream when I saw beneath my feet these majestic peaks . . .
of which I had found even the bases so difficult and dangerous of
approach. I realised how they were related, how they were connected,
I saw their structure, and a single glance cleared the uncertainties
which years of work had been unable to dispel.'[21] For the next four
and a half hours he toiled away with his instruments, taking a quantity
of readings that he later described as 'prodigious'. Among them was
an attempt to ascertain whether the sky was really darker when seen
from high altitude than when seen from below. Before setting out he
had coloured sixteen cards in deepening shades of blue. While he
flicked through them on Mont Blanc to see which accorded best to
the sky above, scientist friends were by pre-arrangement shuffling
similar swatches in Geneva and Chamonix. The verdict, delivered
with due solemnity, was that the sky did, indeed, appear darker from
Mont Blanc than from below. From certain vantage points one could
see stars during the day. But it was definitely not the stratospheric
black recorded by Leonardo da Vinci and others. According to the
cards, the sky at Geneva was of the seventh shade of blue, at
Chamonix it was between the fifth and sixth and on Mont Blanc it
was almost at the first – a blue *du roi*.

By 3.30 p.m. Saussure had to give up. Clouds were coming in and
he feared that if the descent took anything as long as the ascent he
would be overtaken by night. He left the scene with regret. 'I felt a
painful sense of not being able to draw from it all the profit possible,'
he wrote. 'I counted what I had done but little compared to what I

had hoped to do.' All in all, he declared, he was 'like an epicure invited to a splendid festival and prevented from enjoying it by violent nausea'.[22]

In fact, the descent took just half the time Saussure had expected, allowing him to draw the conclusion that 'it is the pressure on the chest from lifting the knees which causes the enormous fatigue one feels in going uphill'.[23] By 9.30 the following morning they were below the snowline where they were greeted by Bourrit. The distraught Precentor had burst into tears when he saw Saussure on the summit and since then had been fluttering around Mont Blanc like a moth, desperate to find someone to lead him up – 'but the guides refuse,'[24] Saussure wrote. They left Bourrit where they found him. It was a Sunday, and Saussure travelled the remainder of the way on a mule, arriving Christ-like in Chamonix to the peal of church bells.

He was slightly sunburned, a touch snow-blind and a little stiff, but otherwise fine. He embraced his family and then hurried home to write up his journal. On the way to Geneva he met an old correspondent by the name of Wyttenbach. 'Congratulate me!' he cried as he fell into his friend's arms. 'I come from the conquest of Mont Blanc!'[25]

The adulation which greeted Saussure on his return to Geneva was astounding. Paccard and Balmat may not have existed as far as the world was concerned. Saussure was the true victor, and when he published an account of the journey his fame rocketed yet higher. 'We have trembled while following you among precipices and perils,' wrote his daughter's mother-in-law, Mme Necker. 'You have lifted my soul, Monsieur, by showing me these storehouses of the world, and I continually grieve at the weakness which hinders me from following in your footsteps. But my imagination supplies my lack of strength. While I read you I hear the dull roar of avalanches and the palpitations of the electric current . . . I imagine that I could wish to end my days in these quiet retreats beside M. Necker, so as to render a last homage to Nature and to married love, the only things that remain to us in the wreck of all the illusions of life.'[26] This was not the half of it. His account of the climb was translated into English and Italian. A year later he was elected a Fellow of London's Royal

Society. In scientific circles he was considered on a par with Joseph Banks, whose circumnavigation of the globe with Captain James Cook between 1768 and 1771 had made him one of the century's most famous figures.

Meanwhile, Geneva's poets issued screed after terrible screed in honour of Saussure and anything connected with him. One effort, which ran to 112 lines in the classical style, devoted five lines to Mme de Saussure's telescope: 'this tube which brings near the objects removed by distance'.[27] Saussure was fair game for anyone with a pen and a sense of rhyme. Even a convict, serving a life sentence for murder, made his own contribution from 'L'Hôtel de Patience, on the 18th of August, the 129th month of his captivity'.[28] The only discordant note was an ode that eulogised Balmat as the Columbus of the Alps, mispelled Paccard's name, disparaged Saussure as a mere amateur and included several laudatory references to one Marc-Théodore Bourrit. Nobody took much notice.

Poor Bourrit. Having yearned for so long to climb Mont Blanc he was relegated to the position of helpless hanger-on – much the same role, in fact, that he had earlier ascribed to Paccard. The day after Saussure's climb he found guides willing to take him to the summit. But once again his courage failed him. He lost his tinted spectacles and withdrew at the first sign of strong winds on the excuse that dust had blown into his eyes. Four days later, to his utter dismay, a young Briton named Mark Beaufoy found the spectacles and wore them on a successful climb to the summit, during which he walked – according to Paccard – as sturdily as any guide. Bourrit's chagrin was compounded when he rushed forward to ask Beaufoy his impressions of the journey. Had his first thought on the summit, like Saussure before him, been of his wife? (The young woman, to whom Bourrit had taken a shine, was in the room at the time.) Beaufoy's dispiriting reply was, 'Not at all.'[29]

Bourrit's moment came in 1788. In that year he joined an Englishman and a Dutchman to make the fifth successful ascent of Mont Blanc. It was notable for its bad weather and Bourrit wrote it up with all the vim he could muster. Even allowing for his exaggeration, it was clearly an unpleasant climb. The temperature sank to 13°F and the Dutchman turned back, fearing for his life. Groups of exhausted guides scattered the Grand Plateau, gasping the thin air before following his example. When the remainder finally reached the summit they were suffering badly from exposure. By the time they reached their downward bivouac on the Grands Mulets, 'the Englishman Woodley [had] both feet frozen [and] never ceased complaining; Dominique Balmat was almost blind; Cachat le Géant's hands were in a dreadful condition, and the other guides were little better off.'[30] Back in Chamonix, Woodley spent thirteen days with his feet in a bath of ice and salt before he regained their full use; Bourrit did likewise for a whole day. The one snag, and it is a snag that his narrative does its best to obscure, was that Bourrit did not actually reach the top. He dropped behind – or, as he put it, Woodley pressed ahead unreasonably fast – and ground to a halt 400 feet from the summit. Still, it was amazing that he got so far; and had not Saussure said the last stretch revealed little new? In spirit, if not in fact, Bourrit had vanquished Mont Blanc. This was the view he took in his published account and it would be mean now to quibble with it. Whatever his faults, Mont Blanc's most persistent loser should be given credit for its nearest conquest.

CHAPTER SIX

Mont Blanc had been knocked off its pedestal – or, more accurately, it had become a pedestal – but plenty of other challenges loomed in its place and Saussure was keen to face them. The first to attract his attention was the Col du Géant. Not so much a peak as a high pass leading over Mont Blanc from Chamonix to Courmayeur, the Col du Géant had a reputation for inaccessibility stemming from a failed attempt in 1689. But a colleague of Saussure's named Exchaquet had climbed it in 1787, overcoming the glacier that formed the most dangerous part of the route. Bourrit traversed the Col with his son later in the same year. It took him seventeen hours to reach Courmayeur, eleven of which were spent on the ice. He wrote that: 'The difficulties of [Mont Blanc] do not approach those of this expedition . . . The crevasses exceeded those of Mont Blanc in horror as well as in size, and if snow avalanches were to be feared on Mont Blanc, there was [here] no less danger from the fall of séracs.'[1] (Seracs, perilous cliffs of ice that are liable to collapse without warning, are as much a feature of glacial landscapes as are crevasses.) Their clothes froze, as did their shoelaces. Before they reached the top Bourrit's son had lost all feeling in his feet and hands; icicles an inch long hung from his crépe veil. 'The guides . . . ran backwards and forwards like men who, after a shipwreck, avoid the waves by scrambling from rock to rock.'[2] When they arrived in Courmayeur, after a five-and-a-half-hour descent, Bourrit was jubilant. He returned to Geneva 'bringing back from his memorable expedition the most extraordinary pictures and the honour of having crossed in one day . . . through a thousand dangers – dangers which added to his satisfaction by the proof they afforded of what men will do when animated by the love of glory.'[3] It was 'the most audacious expedition which has yet been made in the Alps,'[4] he wrote wildly. (Disappointed to find that he was not the first to climb the Col, as he had believed himself to be, he added a disparaging note about Exchaquet, who had declared that he 'met with no difficulties' in the passage.)

Legend and Bourrit aside, the Col was a relatively easy climb. Saussure knew this and did not care. His main reason for visiting it was to complete the meteorological readings he had been unable to take on Mont Blanc. In many ways, his passage across the Col du Géant was more impressive than his ascent of Mont Blanc: at almost 11,000 feet above sea level the Col was not to be disparaged; the glacier was dangerous; and Saussure did not want just to cross the pass but to stay there for sixteen days. Two years previously it had been considered impossible to survive a night at high altitude. Saussure was proposing more than a fortnight. Nobody had ever done this. Always the diligent second-comer, he was now attempting a first. As he put it, 'It seemed to me it would be interesting.'[5]

The expedition, which set off on 2 July 1788, comprised Saussure, his new manservant (the old one had finally given up), his son Étienne, and a team of guides of whom four, led by Jacques Balmat, were to remain on the Col to carry letters to Chamonix and fetch provisions. For such a prolonged stay the old Mont Blanc tent was deemed useless and Saussure took two more durable versions made of treated canvas. One was for stores the other for accommodation. They came from Widow Tillard in Paris and were 'highly recommended if one does not mind the smell'.[6]

The climb was accomplished without too much trouble – though one guide fell down a crevasse on the glacier, emerging badly scraped – and Saussure was pleased to find that he suffered none of the sickness he had experienced on Mont Blanc. The encampment, however, which had been chosen on Exchaquet's advice, was neither as high nor as spacious as Saussure would have liked. It was a narrow, snow-covered ledge whose uneven surface had to be cleared of boulders to make room for the tents. At one end was a rough stone shelter, barely six feet square, half filled with snow and flanked on two sides by a sheer drop. It was a disappointment for Saussure who, despite constant tramps through the mountains, was a man used to his comforts. Nevertheless, it was a good place from which to take his observations and initially he found the shelter a handy place to spend the night when the sleeping tent became too stuffy.

Despite one or two violent storms, and the unexpected distraction of Exchaquet who made a twenty-four-hour visit to the camp with a group of friends, Saussure was able to conduct most of the experiments he required. Work continued throughout the day, Saussure's son rising at 4.00 a.m. and his father three hours later. They read their barometers, thermometers, electrometers, hygrometers, compasses and pendulums. They gauged the reaction of rocks when placed in different acids. They watched cloud formations and measured their speeds. They observed shooting stars – disappointingly small – and were happy to see that contrary to popular opinion they fell above rather than below them. At 10.00 p.m. Saussure *fils* went to bed while his father spent another two hours with the electrometer before retiring to the hut where, 'on my little mattress which had been laid on the ground next to that of my son, I slept better than I did in my own bed at home'.[7] On good days, they basked in sunshine while down below Chamonix was engulfed in cloud. Showers of puzzled butterflies settled on his camp, blown above the snowline by updraughts from the valley. In their pursuit came flocks of choughs. Saussure revelled in it all even though, come evening, the temperature was minus 4°F and the water froze in his glass.

Saussure was first and foremost a scientist, and his journals reflect that fact. His analyses of rock structure can become unbearably tedious. At times, however, a covert Romantic peeps out. In one passage, written shortly before their departure, he wrote glowingly of the views from the Col:

> These heights have tried their best to make us regret them, we have had the most magnificent evening; all these high peaks that surround us and the snows that separate them were coloured with the most beautiful shades of rose and carmine. The Italian horizon was girdled with a broad belt from which the full moon, of a rich vermillion tint, rose with the majesty of a queen . . . These snows and rocks, of which the brilliancy is unsupportable by sunlight, present a wonderful and delightful spectacle by the soft radiance of the moon. How magnificent is the contrast between these granite crags, shadowed or thrown out with such sharpness and boldness, and the brilliant snows! . . . The soul is uplifted, the powers of intelligence seem to widen and in the midst of this majestic silence, one seems to hear the voice of Nature and to become the confidant of her most secret workings.[8]

But there were bad days too. Saussure was camped just at the height where thunderstorms form. To understand what this entails one should know a little about these fearsome phenomena. Normally the cold air of the upper atmosphere remains separated from the warm air below. Sometimes, however, pockets of warm air can burst through into the cold. Initially they produce harmless puffs of cumulus. But as the clouds build they coalesce into a large mass surmounted by a rapidly cooling head of moisture. When the air freezes it turns the cloud on its head. Plunging earthwards it creates first the wind that commonly precedes a storm and then a deluge of rain. And as the cold air falls, warm air surges up to fill the vacuum at speeds of 100 miles per hour, creating the conditions for yet another downpour. Each such cycle is known as a cell and each cloud can contain as many as five cells. A cell is short-lived – twenty minutes or so – but as the cloud drifts it may be fed by more warm air to produce a storm lasting several hours.

Sometimes a thunderstorm contains hail, frozen droplets of water and dust that form at about 15,000 feet and are then tossed by updraughts until they have collected an irresistibly heavy layer of ice. The ice tilts and then falls, adding a new dimension to the fury. And then there is lightning. As a thundercloud floats along it casts a positively charged electrical shadow on the ground below. The storm itself is negatively charged, and when high ground brings storm and shadow into proximity the result is explosive. Leaping from the ground – contrary to popular belief, lightning does not come from the sky – electricity arcs upwards under stresses of more than 100 million volts in channels that can stretch for five miles yet be only as thick as a pencil. The gases caught in its superheated passage expand to produce the rumble of thunder. Taking the wind and the electricity together, a single thundercloud contains as much energy as ten Hiroshima-sized nuclear bombs.

Throughout 3 July a cloud had been forming over Chamonix and the following morning at 1.00 Saussure became the first man to record life at the centre of a thunderstorm. It was, he said, 'the most terrible [thing] I have ever witnessed'. The wind was so fierce that he and his son huddled together, fearing

at every instant that it would carry away the stone hut in which [we] were sleeping. The gale had this peculiarity, that it was periodically interrupted by intervals of the most perfect calm. In these intervals we heard the wind howling below us . . . while the most absolute tranquility reigned around our cabin. But these calm moments were succeeded by blasts of an indescribable violence; double blows like discharges of artillery. We felt even the mountain shake under our mattresses; the wind penetrated through the cracks in the wall of the hut, it once lifted my sheets and rugs and froze me from head to foot.[9]

At daybreak the wind fell a little allowing them to join the guides in the relative shelter of one of the tents. But the storm soon rose again and all four guides were forced to hold the posts in position lest they topple and the whole tent be blown away with them inside. On two occasions when the wind relented the guides made a dash to their store tent to fetch provisions. Even though it was only a distance of 16 feet they could not make the journey without clinging onto a rock halfway to stop themselves being blown over the edge. They hung there 'for two or three minutes while the wind blew their clothes over their heads and hailstones battered their bodies, before daring at last to resume their mission'.[10] At about 7.00 a.m.,

> continuous hail and thunder were added to the storm; one flash struck so near us that we heard distinctly a spark slide hissing down the wet canvas of the tent just behind the place occupied by my son. The air was so full of electricity that directly I put only the point of my electrometer outside the tent the bubbles separated as far as the threads would allow them, and at almost every explosion of thunder the electricity changed from positive to negative or vice versa.[11]

Towards midday on 4 July the storm blew itself out. They emerged from their twenty-four-hour ordeal badly shaken but with renewed confidence. Flimsy as their tents were, they had been sufficient to protect them from nature's worst and Saussure was relieved to know that he would be able to complete his stay however bad the weather.

In his letters to the valley, Saussure painted a rosy picture of life on the Col. 'I never felt in better health,' he reassured his wife. 'I slept last night in my tent, which had frozen after the rain, so that the canvas crackled like a bracelet, yet I have not had the least indisposition or cold.'[12] In another: 'I am writing to you in the silence of the night; all my companions are asleep, while I, shut up in my tent, buried in my furs, [have] my feet on a hot stone . . . I have just been out to take my observations. What a glorious night!'[13] In another: 'One would think we lived in a forge; as the coal will only burn when blown, our bellows are extremely exhausted and husky. Our guides, who are also ravenous, seize the stove as soon as we have done with it, so that one constantly hears their bellows mixed with the noise of the snow and rock avalanches all around us. We are perfectly sheltered from them; it is one of the chief amusements of [our son] and the guides to set rolling great boulders which, falling on the frozen slopes, produce really magnificent torrents of stones and snow.'[14]

The more glamorous descriptions he sent his wife were later inserted in his journal. But when the book was published, he filled in the details he had felt it prudent to omit. Every day at 5.00 p.m., no matter how good the weather, a bitter wind came from the north-west accompanied by snow and hail that made life 'extremely bothersome. The warmest clothes – even furs – could not protect us: we could scarcely light a fire in our tents; and the hut . . . was hardly warmed at all by our little stoves; the coal only smouldered without the use of bellows and if, finally, we managed to warm our feet and calves our bodies remained constantly frozen thanks to the wind which blew through the hut.'[15] They had to battle the cold for five hours before the wind dropped at 10.00 p.m.

As the days wore on the delightful shelter became '*notre miserable petite cabane*', and Saussure crept into the tent for warmth. Hail and sleet battered them and the gales were capricious. At one moment the tent's guy ropes were stretched to their limit; the next they would be hanging limp; and then, without warning, they would be thrumming with a noise like thunder. In Courmayeur, meanwhile, the villagers were suffering a drought. Its obvious cause was the wizards who had set up camp on the Col du Géant. A posse of strong men was put on standby to bring them down by force.

Saussure's ordeal – and Courmayeur's – came to an end thanks to his guides. For a fortnight they had toiled downhill with Saussure's letters and uphill with loads of coal and food. Their employer's dis-comfort was nothing compared to theirs and they did not have the meagre satisfaction of taking observations. Balmat, who probably resented his role as courier, took increasingly long to deliver Saussure's letters and on one occasion vanished for a week in order to have his portrait painted. Then, on 20 July, Saussure awoke to find that his food supply had run out. It had been gorged by the guides. Horrified by his delight at a particularly beautiful evening, and fearful that he might extend his stay, they had seen deprivation as the only way of driving him back to the valleys. He gave in with good grace and descended to Courmayeur, dizzy from lack of sustenance yet tingling with excitement. His observations had been ground-breaking, even if they led to no scientific breakthrough; paramount, however, was the glow he experienced at having survived for so long at such an altitude and the emotional impact which his stay had had upon him. In his own words he had been a 'neighbour of heaven'.[16]

The first great push at the Alps had ended. After his triumphs on Mont Blanc and the Col du Géant, Saussure extended his researches into the Swiss cantons. He went to the Oberland village of Grindelwald, where he saw the Jungfrau, the immense wall of the Wetterhorn, the precipitous Eiger, and the Schreckhorn – the so-called 'Peak of Terror', then reputedly the next highest Alp after Mont Blanc. In 1789 he explored an undiscovered valley below the Lyssjoch and announced that it did not contain civilisations from a lost age, as the *Journal de Paris* had suggested. He went to Zermatt in the Valais, where he climbed the lower peaks of Monte Rosa and peered at the terrifying rock known as Mont Cervin, or the Matterhorn, of which he remarked only that it looked like a blunted pyramid and, on seeing a river running though Zermatt, wondered where the Matterhorn's debris was washed to. But nothing equalled his two sensational climbs from Chamonix.

Saussure retired to Geneva, his health badly affected by his mountaineering activities – just as his wife had feared. From a mansion, which Bourrit described as without doubt the finest in town, he devoted himself to politics and an unavailing attempt to have geography included in the national curriculum. Eminent people came to visit him and to marvel at his collection of specimens which comprised not only a vast array of rocks but rooms of stuffed birds, sheets of pinned butterflies and a series of fossils that included 'the upper jaw of some species of large crocodile, and a string of elephant bones' as well as a few hippo teeth. His library was 'the biggest and best in private hands'.[17]

Saussure's retirement was disrupted by the French Revolution of 1789. In ten years' time the Revolution would have its foot in the door of every neighbouring state – if it wasn't breaking the door down – and the Alpine regions were no less vulnerable than any other. Its immediate effect, however, was to render him bankrupt. Most of his investments had been in France and by 1793 they were worthless. His wife wrote to her sons, currently studying in England, that 'you must look out for a travelling tutorship, or a wealthy bride; if these fail we shall have to live in our old stuffs and our old green tapestries, with a little maid in a black cap'.[18] Saussure toyed for a while with emigration. Britain, for example, was offering a very attractive package to disaffected Swiss, its Parliament having voted £50,000 for the creation of a New Geneva in Ireland. This model town sited near Waterford was to be built to the finest specifications and, for the benefit of Swiss watchmakers, was to have its own, competitive gold standard.* By 1794 all ideas of travel had to be dropped. For in that year Geneva adopted a radical constitution modelled on that of France, and Saussure had a stroke. The diaries in which he had so precisely annotated his Alpine journeys now took a different slant: 'weaker and thinner' – 'legs giving way' – 'writing difficult'.[19] Instead of visiting the peaks he frequented the spas in a fruitless quest for a cure. He searched for a job, anything 'which would allow me to put aside some five or six hundred louis a year',[20] but it was not forthcoming. He was offered a post as a teacher of Chemistry and Physics in Paris but could not afford the journey and was besides too weak. His wife wrote a romance to try and bring in some money, but although Saussure wept every time she read it aloud it was an ineffective thing. As a friend said, 'In effect to write romances is to be in the local fashion. There is no one who cannot draw from his or her pocket a manuscript sufficient to meet the occasion.'[21]

---

*Some £20,000 was spent on the project before it was cancelled due to lack of interest.

Saussure tried to elaborate what he described as a 'Theory of the Earth' but constrained by ill health and his religious beliefs he managed no more than an outline. (It was a sketchy affair that laid down the precepts of geological investigation but dared not break with the Bible.) He spent his last years preparing the final volumes of *Voyages* for press. He died in 1798, two years after they came out and the same year in which France annexed Geneva. The final editing was left to his son Théodore who preserved Saussure's most memorable utterance in its entirety: 'Placed on this planet since yesterday, and only for a day, we can only hope to glimpse the knowledge that we will probably never attain.'[22]

CHAPTER SEVEN

While Saussure declined the Alps flourished, attracting more tourists than ever before. Nobility from all over Europe came to the mountains: Poles, Russians, Italians, French and Germans struggled to find hotel space amidst the hordes of British aristocrats who had made it their summer home from home. Letters and diaries of the period read like a marriage between *Burke's Peerage* and the *Almanach de Gotha*. Dukes, earls, lords, counts and bishops of every description gathered with their wives and mistresses in popular spas such as Évian and Leukerbad. Each spa boasted its own curative speciality – some were good for scrofula, others for dyspepsia and liver complaints, while the one at Pfäffer, being excellent for sprains, was recommended to those who had recently undergone torture. But it was not a cure that visitors were after so much as an opportunity for socialising. The nobility were accompanied by equal numbers of rakes, swells and ne'er-do-goods. Charles James Fox, a British politician who had been known to gamble non-stop for twenty-four hours losing £10 a minute, was one. William Beckford, author and *bon vivant*, was another, arriving at Neuchâtel in 1792 with such éclat that it left the visiting Lord Cloncurry breathless: he 'made his journey in a style that would astonish the princes of the present degenerate days. His travelling ménage consisted of about thirty horses, with four carriages, and a corresponding train of servants. Immediately upon his arrival, Mr. Beckford set up a fine yacht upon the lake.'[1] Two years later Beckford bought Gibbon's entire library 'to have something to read when I passed through Lausanne'.[2] Then there was Count Joseph Gorani, an adventurer who had been proscribed by every country in Europe and who swept through no less than thirty-one Swiss towns and cities in 1794 pursued by a team of assassins sent after him by the Queen of Naples.

To this glittering and occasionally fly-blown constellation the heights remained as repugnant as ever. Many marvelled at the views and stepped tentatively onto the lower glaciers. But generally they were more interested in the licentious delights of the spas, where it was not unknown for men and women to bathe in the same waters. Such expeditions as they made into the hills were often slightly ludicrous. Take this example, from the journal of one Friedrich Bouterweck, a German traveller who visited the Bernese valley of Lauterbrunnen in 1794:

> An elegant English lady, whose name is not unknown, had come to Grindelwald to see the glaciers, and wanted to hire four men to carry her over the Scheidegg [the pass linking Grindelwald to Lauterbrunnen] for the normal fee of one new gold Louis. The four strongest men in the whole of Grindelwald were searched for. But however keen the Swiss is to earn an honest penny, no-one accepted the task of carrying so important a lady . . . But the lady wished to be carried. Four other men, the next strongest, were sent for and the hire money doubled. The eight stalwarts looked at one another and formed a plan. Divided into two shifts, relieving one another, they lifted the preposterous weight and strode towards the Scheidegg.

Bouterweck noted with awe that when the porters had completed the task they 'slept all night and all next day, and were still exhausted when they woke'.[3]

It was not a new phenomenon. Back in 1786 Saussure, usually the most generous of men, had experienced a feeling of contempt as he climbed Mont Blanc and looked down to see 'travellers struggling across the lower slopes of the Bossons glacier, leaning on their guides and probably composing for their return a pompous account of their courage and the dangers they had faced'.[4] On and on they came, regardless. During the 1780s and 1790s, some 1,200 visitors per year stayed in Chamonix; the track to the Montenvers and the Mer de Glace became so crowded that more illustrious tourists were advised to avoid peak hours. Guides grew old before their time as they shuttled to and fro with their charges.

Other visitors were more discerning. William Wordsworth was deeply moved in 1790:

> We are now . . . upon the point of quitting these most sublime
> and beautiful parts; and you cannot imagine the melancholy
> regret which I feel at the idea . . . I have looked upon, and as it
> were conversed with, the objects which this country has
> presented to my view so long, and with such increasing
> pleasure, that the idea of parting from them oppresses me with
> a similar sadness to what I have always felt in quitting a
> beloved friend . . . At this moment, when many of these
> landscapes are floating before my mind, I feel a high
> enjoyment in reflecting that perhaps scarcely a day of my life
> will pass in which I shall not derive some happiness from these
> images.[5]

Twelve years later Turner was also moved. He did not rhapsodise about the scenery but sketched away silently, producing 400 sketches from which, filling in the colours from memory, he produced a vibrant collection of paintings.

For some people, however, the Alps were dreary, dreadful and dangerous. In 1805, Chateaubriand wrote:

> The grandeur of mountains about which so much fuss is made

is based only on the fatigue which they occasion . . . I was delighted with the shores of the lake [of Geneva], but not at all with Chamonix. High mountains suffocate me. I did not like to feel my puny existence shut in so tightly between those heavy masses . . . Finally, I may have been very unlucky, but I never discovered among those celebrated chalets, made illustrious thanks to J. J. Rousseau's imagination, anything but dirty hovels full of cattle dung or the stink of cheese and fermented milk; they are inhabited only by wretched mountaineers who feel themselves exiled and long for the time when they can go down to the valley.[6]

The mountaineers of whom Chateaubriand spoke were not mountaineers in the modern sense, merely people who lived in the mountains. Those who came to the Alps were known as travellers or *étrangers*. In fact there was no word for mountaineers, and those few who did climb to any height were considered to fall within an unclassified species of idiot. In 1792, a party of four Englishmen decided to climb Mont Blanc just for the fun of it. They went up, according to Bourrit, 'as if on a pleasure excursion . . . Their irresponsibility and carelessness had consequences that were very nearly deplorable.'[7] They set off a rockfall that broke one guide's leg and cracked the skull of another. They returned in disarray, all having suffered injuries of one sort or another. 'Reason and humanity appear to discountenance, except for some definite pupose of utility, expeditions upon this hazardous mountain,' wrote one John Owen the same year. 'Saussure was a philosopher, and his ascension of the Mont Blanc tended to ascertain some points of the moment, respecting the altitudes of the mountains, the rarity of the air, and other physical phenomena. A recent attempt was made, by four English gentlemen, to climb this mountain; and the issue of their expedition ought to render this the last example of similar curiosity.'[8] Bourrit agreed: 'Without some great goal . . . it is pointless to consider such a thing.'[9] These opinions were shared by many. The Alps were there to be marvelled at or swanned around, not trampled underfoot. Climbing was seen as a dangerous, foolhardy, irresponsible and, in some vague way, wicked pastime.

During the Napoleonic Wars of 1799–1815 opportunities for people to visit the Alps, let alone climb them, were drastically reduced. In the first few years they became virtually a no-go zone as French troops marched to and fro across Switzerland, Italy and Austria. British tourists, who had been such a prominent feature of the Alpine scenery, vanished almost completely. Some continued to go there, such as the party who escaped imprisonment by the simple expedient of wearing tricoloured cockades and who crossed the Great St Bernard Pass a few days after Napoleon and his army, noting with interest the number of corpses that scattered the road. For most Britons, however, a trip to the Alps was replaced by a stay at Matlock Bath in the Derbyshire dales, where they could imbibe healthy waters and admire craggy scenery. The crags existed only because Matlock was situated at the bottom of a gorge, and were therefore a slight fraud in terms of altitude. But they looked the part and were easy to get to so nobody minded too much. (Britain's true mountains were eschewed because they were too high and barbarous.) The Peace of Amiens gave the British an opportunity to return to the Alps between 1802 and 1803. During this period Coleridge wrote his 'Hymn before Sunrise in the Vale of Chamouni', which was published on 11 September 1802 in the *Morning Post*. But thereafter it was back to Matlock.

On the continent, where Savoy, Piedmont and the Swiss Confederation all became part of Napoleon's empire, Alpine tourism recovered smoothly after the initial upset. By 1801 everything was more or less back to normal with travellers once more making their way to Chamonix. Bourrit held his habitual court, entertaining audiences with his oratory and leading famous personages on tours of the Mer de Glace. Having climbed the Col du Géant and (almost) Mont Blanc, he had become splendidly authoritative. One devotee whispered to another that '[t]he man must have inherited Rousseau's eyes, for I have never seen such a striking similarity'.[10] Paccard, by now the Mayor of Chamonix, displayed a graver authority, pointing out to visitors on a clear day the route he had taken to the summit. 'Paccard's appearance is one of the most imposing and impressive that I have ever seen,'[11] said a visiting German.

In the meantime, children roamed the streets displaying live marmots, and Saussure's old acquaintance Exchaquet did a busy trade in wooden models of Mont Blanc. Exchaquet's models were about three and a half feet long and were painted to resemble nature, the glaciers being represented by chips of crystal. One such work, measuring twelve feet long, was presented as a gift to Napoleon. (Not to be outdone, the Mayor of Geneva sent a very large trout.) Napoleon, as a military man, did not himself rate the Alps very highly. He crossed the Great St Bernard Pass slightly unsteadily on a mule in 1800 and remained tight-lipped about its beauties. His wife Josephine, however, had a better sense of an occupying power's obligations, importing a Swiss farmer and his wife, plus seven cows and a bull, to live in a mock-Alpine chalet on the outskirts of Paris.

Amidst all the touristic fuss, climbing lingered on as a passion that dared not yet say its name. In 1802 a German named Doorthesen and a M. Forneret from Lausanne made an abortive attempt on Mont Blanc. Taking only seven guides, they set out on 10 August and returned defeated two days later. They described their sufferings at high altitude to Bourrit, who told the world how the low pressure had almost torn their lungs from their bodies. Around the same time a member of the Montgolfier ballooning family tried to go up the mountain without guides – and failed. Then, in 1809 a young girl named Marie Paradis became the first woman to climb Mont Blanc. The story, as related by Jacques Balmat, was that he and two other guides had decided to make an ascent for their own amusement. At the start of the expedition they encountered Marie Paradis, and Balmat persuaded her to accompany them by force of charm, declaring: 'I am an old wolf of the mountains, and even I will not promise to succeed. All I ask of you is to be courageous.'[12] They had then climbed to the Grands Mulets, where they spent the night, and the following day, 14 July 1809, they reached the summit. Balmat proudly, if ungallantly, related that Marie had been unable to keep up with him on the Grand Plateau. 'Go more slowly, Jacques, my heart fails me,' she had begged. 'Go as if you were tired yourself.'[13] But Balmat did not relent. The other two guides took her by the arms and hauled her to the top. On returning to Chamonix on 15 July she was quizzed by other women about her experience. Her only answer was that the marvels she had seen would take too long in the telling and if anyone wanted to know what she had been through, the mountain was there and waiting.

The account of Marie Paradis herself was far less romantic. '"You are a pretty girl and you need to earn money," the guides said. "Come with us. Travellers will ask to see you, and they will tip you well." That decided me, and I went off with them.'[14] On the Grand Plateau, she suffered terribly and, far from asking Balmat to go slower, told him, '*Ficha mé din una cravasse et alla o vo vodra*' – 'Throw me in a crevasse and go where you want.'[15] On her return, there was no grandiose invitation to others to experience for themselves what she had been through. There was simply the stunned recollection: 'I climbed, I could not breathe, I nearly died, they dragged me, carried me, I saw black and white, and then I came down again.'[16]

Taken together the two tales told the same story – that Mont Blanc was a good money-spinner. The climb boosted Balmat's reputation and made Marie Paradis one of the valley's most famous characters. She became known as 'Marie Mont-Blanc', a sort of wife to 'Balmat *dit* Mont-Blanc', and she set up a small tea shop at Les Pèlerins whose remarkable bouncing cascade – long since vanished – was one of Chamonix's tourist attractions. She would spread a cloth beneath a tree and offer visitors a snack of milk, cream and biscuits. As the guides had promised, she was very well tipped.

Bourrit did not especially enjoy being a citizen of the French empire. He took a conservative view of the Revolution and wrote damningly of its adherents. Nevertheless, he was always willing to facilitate peoples' appreciation of the Alps whatever their political hue. His greatest achievement to this end was to create a permanent shelter on the Montenvers from which the Mer de Glace could be explored. There was already a structure in place, a stone shack that had been built in 1779 by an Englishman named Blair, 'whose claret, hounds and fortune had run so fast in Dorsetshire that he himself was obliged to quit England'.[17] It was a rough thing, known locally as 'Blair's Cabin' or the 'Château de Folie', and it was commonly believed that it had been erected as a wine cellar for Blair's trips to the glacier. Whatever its original purpose, it had now become a shelter for tourists and was patently too small to cope with the numbers. In 1792 Bourrit escorted a French diplomat named Sémonville to the glacier and was so expressive about its beauties that the man offered to pay for a new building. Unfortunately, Sémonville was captured by Austrian troops shortly afterwards and Bourrit was forced to find a new benefactor. Help came in the shape of M. Desportes, a friend of Saussure who had been appointed French resident at Geneva and who donated 200 francs for the construction of a 'Temple dedicated to Nature'. Not so much a temple as a slightly larger hut than Blair's, it was nevertheless designed in a grand manner, with a classical pediment and interior arrangements that included hammocks, a fireplace, cooking equipment, medical supplies, a hatchet, alpenstocks, a thermometer and a barometer. There was to be a glazed window and even a mirror fixed to the wall. A padlock was to be fitted to keep undesirables at bay. The site was granted by the Chamonix town council – whose mayor was none other than Bourrit's old foe, Dr Paccard – and throughout the summer of 1795 workmen toiled up the Montenvers on a newly built mule track. Bourrit was delighted with the result – he had even persuaded his daughter to lend a hand – and was so grateful to Paccard that he went to the astonishing length of retracting his statements about the conquest of Mont Blanc. Paccard should share the glory with Balmat, he declared, 'if indeed, as we have reason to believe, he has not the prior claim'.[18] Admittedly, when this was written in 1803, Bourrit seemed to have fallen out with Balmat – whom he now called 'this Chamoniard' – but it was a climb-down all the same.

The Montenvers Temple was picturesquely, if unintentionally, decrepit in the best Romantic tradition. By 1803, however, it had become more ruinous still. The window and mirror had been broken and everything portable had been stolen, including the padlock.

Bourrit applied himself to its reconstruction and with the aid of a new
patron, a prefect of Brussels called Doulcet de Pontécoulant, had the
whole place refurbished in 1806. As well as a new coat of paint it was
given two beds, chairs and the homely touch of tongs and bellows.
Visitors were invited to carve their names on the walls, which Bourrit
did with vigour, and later a guest book was supplied. Empress
Josephine visited the Temple – the page with her comments was
stolen three days afterwards – and so, too, did Napoleon's second
wife, Marie-Louise of Austria.

As Bourrit grew older he abandoned his unsuccessful climbing
career. He still painted, still stayed in Chamonix during the tourist
season and still waxed fulsome on the subject of Alpine splendour,
but the Temple was now his greatest concern. By 1816 it had begun
to crumble and Bourrit once again looked for benefactors. Desportes
came to the rescue. By now exiled to Germany, he instigated an over-
haul that included a cornice on which were to be carved the names of
famous naturalists. The whole thing cost 300 francs, and when it was
finished in 1819 so too was Bourrit. He died that year, leaving the
Temple as a memorial to his life's passion.

Bourrit's death marked the end of an era. After Saussure he had
been the man most linked with Alpine discovery. From those early
days of travail there remained only Paccard and Balmat. Paccard
died in 1827 leaving Balmat as the last participant in the Mont Blanc
saga. For more than fifty years visitors had marvelled at Balmat's
vigour and the genius of his ice craft. 'Balmat is necessary, one could
almost say indispensable, for any journey of discovery,' wrote an
impressed climber in 1813. 'I do not exaggerate when I say we could
have done nothing without him. He has an instinct for glaciers that
lets him choose the right path at a glance . . . The other guides
recognise his superiority and are not jealous.'[19] Unfortunately,
Balmat also possessed an instinct for money. It had first manifested
itself in his dash to claim Saussure's prize and as the years went by it
became increasingly dominant. He refused, for example, to be
accompanied by other guides lest he have to share his employers'
money. 'He does not like to go with other guides across these deserts

of ice,' the same climber remarked innocently. 'He says that he is never happier and more certain of his step than when surrounded by precipices, but that the presence of his fellows makes him nervous and insecure.'[20] Saussure's great-grandson explained his character more precisely: 'It was only the prospect of the large reward offered by [Saussure] which ended in drawing Balmat to the top of Mont Blanc. He several times abandoned his attempt on finding himself followed by other guides. Always greedy of gain, his greatest fear was that of having to share with others, not the glory, but the money.'[21]

Balmat drank heavily and invested unwisely. When his funds ran out, as they often did, he would take off on wild prospecting missions. In 1814, a climber who had looked forward to employing the illustrious Balmat *dit* Mont-Blanc was disappointed. 'We had little hope of meeting him. This extraordinary man darts across the mountains, never following the trodden path but flying like a bird from rock to rock, according to his caprice, in search of precious stones and minerals . . . He has an iron constitution; but although he has abused it heavily he has not yet destroyed it.'[22]

Avarice, rather than alcohol, was Balmat's undoing. In 1834, his fortunes having taken a turn for the worse, he departed for nearby Sixt in search of gold. He fell down a precipice and was never seen again. His death was witnessed by a young boy but was not reported until many years later lest others come in search of the same gold which, ironically, did not exist anyway. Back in Chamonix, amidst rumours that he had been murdered, they slapped yet another commemorative plaque on his house.

CHAPTER EIGHT

The great Napoleonic venture died at Waterloo in 1815, and the Alpine nations which had hitherto been under French control reverted more or less smoothly to their previous status. Britain, however, was left in something of a limbo. It had been at war for almost a generation and with the arrival of peace, and the surprising realisation that it owned most of the globe, it did not quite know how to dispose of itself. John Barrow, Second Secretary to the Admiralty, came up with an answer: exploration. Under his aegis naval expeditions streamed out of the Thames for the next thirty years, seeking now the route of the River Niger, now the North Pole, now the South Pole, now the North-West Passage. A spirit of enquiry pervaded the national consciousness. Not everybody, however, was suited to Barrow's brand of exploration. For these people – who did not have the qualifications, for whom the goal was too frightening or too far, and who had no stomach for pemmican, hardtack, salt beef or, on occasion, human flesh – the next best thing was the Alps.

Britons once again rushed to the mountains, led by a new breed of Romantic poets and writers. In 1816 Byron, Shelley and Shelley's wife Mary made a trip to Geneva that left lasting impressions. The two men applied all their skills to poems in honour of the mountains and Mary Shelley found an infatuation with ice that would later produce, with a bit of help from Barrow's Arctic explorers, the story of Frankenstein. The first likeness between the Alps and the Arctic had been suggested by Bourrit who, after a climb, wrote in 1803: 'Everything was amazing here, no less frightening than were the icy Poles to the bold navigators.'[1] Mary Shelley met similar conditions, finding in the Alps the same wintery emptiness that epitomised the Arctic. She did not climb anything of note, but she would have agreed with Bourrit's view from the Brévent: 'you look [at the mountains] as if they were a wasteland, seeing nothing to suggest that it is a known world . . . You would think yourself on an uninhabited planet.'[2] Into wastes similar to these strode Frankenstein at the end of her hugely influential novel which came out in 1818.

The views were what had inspired Gesner, Haller, Rousseau, Goethe, Wordsworth, Turner and all earlier Romantics who had come to the Alps. And the views, once again, were what most impressed the next generation. 'I never knew – I never imagined – what mountains were before,' Shelley gasped on his first visit to Chamonix. 'The immensity of the aerial summits excited, when they suddenly burst upon my sight, a sentiment of ecstatic wonder not unallied to madness.'[3] As he wrote of his 'Ode to Mont-Blanc', 'it was composed under the immediate impression of the close and powerful feelings excited by the objects which it attempts to describe; and as an undisciplined overflowing of the soul rests its claim to approbation on an attempt to imitate the untameable wildness and inaccessible solemnity from which those feelings sprang.'[4] Byron was similarly moved, as he tried to 'lose my own wretched identity in the majesty, and the power, and the glory, around, above, and beneath me'.[5] The result was some of his most famous works – *Childe Harold's Pilgrimage*, *The Prisoner of Chillon* and *Manfred*.

What the Romantics never did, however, was to look beyond the view. The wildness was tameable, the solemnity was accessible, as Saussure and, perhaps even more so, Bourrit had done their best to show. But this was not desirable. While the Romantics did not hesitate to engage themselves in other areas that caught their fancy, the Alps for some reason had to remain pure and inviolate. Perhaps this was because climbing them was simply too unglamorous. Swimming across the Hellespont, as club-footed Byron did in 1810, was fine; succumbing to consumption in Rome (Keats, 1821) was highly fashionable; being burned on a funeral pyre on the shore at Viareggio (Shelley, 1822) was even better; dying at Missolonghi while supposedly fighting for Greek independence (Byron again, 1824) was outstanding. Such acts mingled modern drama with evocations of classical myth. But where was the glamour, what was there to stir the soul, in being led up and down a big hill at some cost and returning half-frozen, half-burned and snow-blind to a village full of tourists?

One could not find Rousseau's noble savages on the top of Mont Blanc. Nor, for that matter, could one find much noble savagery in the valleys. The prevalence of cretinism and goitre produced whole communities of deformity. 'The people in these exquisite vallies [sic] are without exception the most hideous creatures you can conceive,' wrote one visitor. 'The men are bad enough but the women are fearful, nay perfect hags, and the children wretched little distorted creatures, some without any arms and others half a hand. The women, every second one we saw, had a huge goitre which they appear to consider rather ornamental than other for they never cover them but hang necklaces upon them and crosses &c. Their teeth for the most part fallen out and their skins dark brown, wrinkled & dirty, and horried [sic] expressions make them look perfect Harpies.'[6]* In these circumstances it was not surprising that the Romantics preferred the dream to the reality.

Yet they did encourage a shift in attitude towards the Alps. Their message was part of a trend which Haller and Rousseau had started in the eighteenth century, but the manner in which they delivered it was fresh and vibrant – also, thanks to growing populations and increased prosperity, more people heard it. The Alps entered every literate

*The two diseases secured exemption from military service and as such had acquired a measure of respectability. Cretinous children were treated as omens of good fortune and – the condition being believed to be hereditary – a goitre was the best dowry a young woman could hope for.

person's vocabulary and, if some remained unshaken, there were thousands who were passionately stirred. Thunder-torn banners of freedom flapped against the storm, stars scrawled celestial poetry across the sky, and solitude whispered in quiet, insistent tones amidst the snow. Castle crags, crawling glaciers and moon-freezing crystals tugged at the most moribund of imaginations. Lord Brougham, who travelled through Switzerland in 1816, wrote that: 'It is a country to be in for two hours, or two and a half, if the weather is fine, and no longer. Ennui comes on the third hour, and suicide attacks you before night.'[7] Even he, however, was uplifted when he met the Shelleys. Nobody had encountered imagery or language like this before. The post-Napoleonic poets were the film stars of their time – particularly Byron, who was idolised across the continent – and where they had been so others wished to tread.

Ordinary people came to the Alps in the Romantics' wake, and while admiring the beauty kept a similar distance from the heights. A guidebook of 1818 stated that 'No one ought to expose himself to the dangers, fatigue, and considerable expense, which an excursion to Mont-Blanc renders indispensable, allured by the deceitful expectation of extraordinary magnificence.'[8] Visitors were advised to stay in the valleys and content themselves with hikes from hamlet to hamlet: 'Every young man in the bloom of health and of life must be capable of travelling over distant climes with his knapsack at his back and a stick in his hands,'[9] enthused the book's editor. Twelve months were advised for a full appreciation of the Alps; a youth willing to sleep rough might scamper through them in four. In the back papers of the same volume there appeared this advertisement:

Travellers wishing to proceed direct to Switzerland may hear of Mr. Emery, the agent, at Mr. Recordon's, Cockspurstreet, Charing-cross; or the White Bear, Piccadilly. The journey is performed in sixteen days, allowing two at Paris, and sleeping every night at some town. The proprietors furnish lodgings and provisions. The carriage is roomy and convenient – the passengers are limited to six. One cwt. of luggage is allowed to each, and the charge is only twenty guineas English.[10]

Thousands went to Mr Recordon's or the White Bear every year, and therein lay another reason for the Romantics' ambivalence towards the Alps: they had become too touristy. Shelley was aghast in 1816 when he met the proprietor of Chamonix's nascent Natural History Museum. He was 'the very vilest specimen of that vile species of quack that, together with the whole army of aubergistes and guides, subsist on the weakness and credulity of travellers as leeches subsist on the sick'.[11] Byron was even more dismissive five years later: 'Switzerland is a curst selfish swinish country of brutes, placed in the most romantic region of the world. I never could bear their inhabitants, and still less their English visitors; for which reason, after writing for some information about houses, upon hearing that there was a colony of English all over the cantons of Geneva &c., I immediately gave up the thought.'[12]

Ghastly as the valleys may have been, and however forbidding their surrounding peaks may have appeared, there were still a few who wanted to meet the Alps at close quarters. In 1816 Count de Lusi of the Prussian army made a brave attempt on Mont Blanc. He fell back at the 'derniers rochers' and descended with bad grace, forcing his guides to sign a statement that no Frenchman had got so far. In 1818 the Polish Count Matzewski reached the summit, which was 'sublime beyond everything he had previously conceived'.[13] He asked that he remain anonymous when his account was published in *Blackwood's Magazine*; he was driven not by the need for fame, he said, but by 'curiosity and the pleasure of doing what is not done every day'.[14] In 1819 two Americans named Jeremiah van Rensselear and Howard visited Europe on a tour and decided to give Mont Blanc a go. They drank vinegar and water on the way up – this concoction, a common cure for scurvy, was supposed to counteract altitude sickness – and having reached the top descended in such a state of snow-blindness that they had to return to Geneva in a blacked-out carriage, having 'purchased perhaps too dearly the indulgence of their curiosity'.[15] The same year Captain J. Undrell of the Royal Navy followed suit, carrying with him a modest variety of instruments: 'old Dr. Paccard supplied me with all he had'.[16]* Undrell made his guides drink a toast to 'good old England', and came down 'suffering greatly from inflamed eyes'. Then, in 1820, Dr Hamel instigated Mont Blanc's first disaster.

Hitherto, much had been made of the Alps' dangers but as far as most people were aware they existed only in Bourrit's heated imagination. In 1791, a young Zürich official named Escher had fallen to his death from an unsteady rock on the Col de Balme. Another young man with a similar name, Eschen, had wandered from his guides on 8 August 1800, carrying the third bulky volume of Saussure's *Voyages*, and had dropped 100 feet to his doom on Le Buet. (Bourrit, whose pocket-sized books had been eschewed by Eschen, wrote that it was a 'deplorable death, and one that possibly awaits other travellers imprudent enough to ignore the advice that I have given'.[17]) And one or two people had drowned in the River Arveyron while admiring its source at the base of the Mer de Glace. But these were isolated incidents, few in number and, with the exception of Eschen's fall, occurring below the snowline. Nobody had been entombed in a crevasse, nobody had been crushed by a falling serac, nobody had been swept away by an avalanche, nobody had frozen to death. Generally, therefore, the public remained blasé about Alpine perils. They were wrong to do so.

Those who read of the Alps read mostly the accounts of the scientists who had climbed them. These journals dwelled on the dangers their authors had faced but did not tell the full story. They described neither the scale nor the continuity of Alpine erosion. The extremes of climate which bedevilled travellers were barely hinted at. There was not the slightest suggestion that the Alps were as inhospitable a zone as could be encountered in Europe. Every winter, for example, dozens of people perished on the passes alone. In 1825 the artist

---

*The Americans had broken one of Paccard's thermometers, and one imagines that he was getting tired of acting as a kind of scientific chandler.

William Brockedon discovered a morgue attached to the hospice on the Great St Bernard Pass in which the annual tally of corpses was stored. He was chilled by the sight, especially as it was only a few steps from the room in which he had recently dined.

> Here, the bodies of the unfortunate people who have perished in these mountains have been placed, left with their clothes on, to assist the recognition by their friends, if they have any. In these high regions there is scarcely soil enough to bury them: and it is impossible to break it up when the frosts are so intense. Here they have been placed just as they were found; and upon looking through the grated windows the bodies are seen in the postures in which they have perished. Here they have 'dried up and withered:' for the evaporation is so rapid at this height that the foulness of mortality is less offensive than in warmer situations; and the bodies are long preserved owing to their having dried without decay. Upon some the clothes had remained after eighteen years, though tattered like a gibbet wardrobe. Some of these bodies presented a hideous aspect; part of the bones of the head were exposed and blanched, whilst black integuments were attached to other parts of the face: we particularly remarked this in a sitting peasant. A mother and her child were among the latest victims; several bodies were standing against the wall, upon the accumulated heaps of their miserable predecessors, presenting an appalling scene.[18]

When the bodies finally collapsed their bones were stored in an ossuary that Brockedon could just make out on the far side of the room. 'They might be removed and buried in summer,' he wrote, 'but they are left to their long decay by the monks, probably from a religious feeling, to have before them these memorials of mortality.'[19]

The Great St Bernard Pass killed seven or eight people a year and there were other passes like it. Except in high summer, it was impossible to tell what conditions would be like. You could be walking along in clear sun and then a snowstorm would descend. At these heights the snow was thin and dry, forming not sticky mounds but soft drifts that covered the track in less than an hour. Unwary travellers plunged thigh-deep through the snow, lost their way and stumbled over a cliff. They were mostly smugglers, but sometimes, as Brockedon told, they could be an ordinary family caught unawares. Far more people died every year trying to cross the Alps than ever perished on the high peaks.

And far, far more died in the valleys. In 1618, some 2,430 people were killed when an avalanche hit the town of Pleurs, near Chiavenne. This was the biggest Alpine disaster in history. Since then people had learned not to cut down the protecting forests that over-hung their settlements. But casualties mounted nonetheless. In 1806 the Swiss village of Goldau was eradicated when an entire mountain-side collapsed onto it. According to records, vast chunks of rock bounced like cannonballs through the valley to land in Lake Löwertz, five miles distant, where they created a tidal wave 70 feet high. When the clamour died down, Goldau was covered by a field of rubble measuring five miles long by three wide, dotted with hillocks of rock several hundred feet high, beneath which lay the remains of 300 houses and 450 people. The death toll in the towns alongside Lake Löwertz was not recorded, but it must have been large: one witness recalled seeing clumps of hay hanging from the church steeples.

In 1818 a slice of glacier fell and blocked a river in Bagnes. As the waters mounted, the inhabitants made a desperate attempt to carve a sluice. They bored from either side of the 600-foot-thick barrier, only to find that when they reached the middle, one team of miners was 20 feet higher than the other. A new tunnel was dug, and the sluice was completed just as the waters lapped into it. But their efforts could not halt the build-up. When the dam broke, 530,000 cubic feet of water plunged into the valley at a speed of 33 feet per second, carrying away bridges that were 90 feet above the river's normal level, destroy-ing 400 homes and killing 34 people. The clear-up cost was estimated at one million Swiss livres.

In 1819, some 120 houses were smashed by an avalanche that hit the village of Randa, near Zermatt. Nobody was killed because it was Christmas and they were all at Zermatt to help with the celebrations. But the local priest, whose house was at a distance from the village, was shaken out of his bed by the tremor and on emerging was all but suffocated by the wind that rebounded from the opposite slope.

The Alps were therefore very dangerous. In Hamel's day, however, the dangers were unappreciated and disregarded. None more so than the avalanche. Avalanches occur when fresh snow builds up on a layer of previously frozen snow. In cold weather, when the new snow falls too heavily or, conversely, in warm weather when the accumulation loses its grip on the surface below, the mass slips. Avalanches can be small – clumps of snow tumble constantly from projecting rocks – or they can be large, gathering slabs of snow and ice that plummet downwards until the gradient eases, usually on the upper slopes. Occasionally they can be gigantic, a whole hillside of snow slumping into the valley and washing halfway up the other side. There is nothing that can withstand a serious avalanche and there is little way of telling when or where such an event may occur. 'A stone, or even a hasty expression, rashly dropped, would probably start an avalanche,' wrote one Victorian.[20] Settlements that have been safe for centuries can be smothered in an instant. The sheer displacement of air that an avalanche causes can empty lungs. Its softly pulverising arrival can turn humans to jelly, bags of skin that contain flesh and small pieces of bone.

In August 1820 Hamel became the first climber to be hit by an avalanche. A Russian scientist, and 'Counsellor of State to the Czar', Hamel wanted to climb Mont Blanc to observe the effect of rarefied air upon animal organisms. He took with him M. Selligue, a Swiss engineer from Geneva, and two Englishmen, Mr Joseph Dornford and Mr Gilbert Henderson from Oxford University. Included in his baggage was a cage of homing pigeons that he intended to release at the top to see whether they could fly in such a thin atmosphere and, if they could, to carry home his message of triumph. Twelve guides were hired, three for each member of the party, the leader being Joseph-Marie Couttet. They left Chamonix on the 18 August and by

the evening had reached the Grands Mulets where they pitched camp
on the habitual shelf of rock. The weather worsened and for two
nights and a day they huddled on the cramped site while a thunderstorm crashed around them. When they set off again on the morning
of the 20 August Selligue did not accompany them. He had not been
feeling well, and it was his opinion 'that a married man had a sacred
and imperious call to prudence and caution where his own life
seemed at stake; that he had done enough for glory in passing two
nights in succession perched on a crag like an eagle, and that it now
became him, like a sensible man, to return to Geneva, while return
was still possible'.[21] Three guides were left behind to escort him
down.

Roped in groups of three, the diminished party crossed the Grand
Plateau without incident. The weather was not particularly good, but
it was not particularly bad either – probably a white day, with the sun
shining through cloud cover – and Hamel felt so confident of success
that he decided to save precious time at the summit by preparing
two notes describing his arrival, leaving the exact time to be inserted
later. Behind him, Dornford and Henderson dawdled along discussing
protocol: who should they drink to first when they reached the top:
the King of England, the Tsar of Russia or Saussure? Couttet was
less happy: he pointed out that fresh snow had fallen, and that the
wind was now in the south thereby adding extra encouragement for
unstable layers to slide down the north face, which they were climbing. Hamel dismissed his fears. Was it not sunny? Had not the
thunderstorm passed? They should press on while the weather was
good.

They crossed a crevasse similar to the one that had filled Saussure
with such fear and took off their ropes. In Dornford's words, the things
were 'utterly useless' and occasioned them 'insupportable fatigue'.[22]
Untrammelled, they climbed through the fresh snow. The sun continued to shine and the wind continued to blow from the south.

The three leading guides, who carried Hamel's compass, hygrome-
ter and pigeons, chipped away at the steeper slopes to make steps for
those behind. Possibly it was this steady serration of the crust, possibly

it was the weight of the party treading behind, possibly they were just in the wrong place at the wrong time. One or all of these factors may have contributed to the sinking feeling that Dr Hamel suddenly experienced. It was literally that: a sinking feeling. There was a loud crack and then the entire slope upon which the party stood started to slip downhill. As Hamel felt the ground give way he dug his alpenstock deep into the snow but to no effect. Everything was on the move.

The avalanche was small by Alpine standards, dropping some 600 feet according to Couttet. But it was still strong enough to cover Hamel up to his head, nearly asphyxiating him in the process. Hamel was fortunate in that he was on the edge of the avalanche. When he clawed his way out he could see the hillside still falling and his team being carried with it. The three leaders – Pierre Balmat, Pierre Carrier and Auguste Tairraz – were thrown into the crevasse they had crossed less than an hour previously, followed by tons of snow. Of the next four, one managed to keep his footing, another was tossed across the crevasse and Joseph-Marie Couttet, along with his brother David, disappeared from sight. Henderson, meanwhile, came to a halt on the brink. Only Dornford and three guides remained on their feet, far above, terrified that they too might slide into the depths.

Julien Dévouassoud, who was fourth in line, later gave an account of his experience:

Suddenly I heard a sort of rushing sound, not very loud; but I had no time to think about it; for as I heard the sound, at the same instant the avalanche was upon us. I felt my feet slide from beneath me, and saw the first three men fallen upon the snow with their feet foremost. In falling I cried out loudly, '*Nous sommes tous perdus!*' I tried to support myself by planting the ice-pole below me, but in vain. The weight of snow forced me over the baton, and it slipped out of my hand. I rolled down like a ball, in a mass of loose snow. At the foot of the slope was a yawning chasm, to the edge of which I was rapidly descending. Three times I saw the light as I was rolling down the slope; and, when we were all on the edge of the chasm, I saw the leg of one of my comrades, just as he pitched down into the crevice. I think it must have been poor Auguste; for it looked black and I remember that Auguste had on black gaiters. This was the last I saw of my companions, who fell headlong into the gulf, and were never seen or heard again.[23]

Dévouassoud only just escaped death, thanks to the barometer he was carrying. Its long wooden casing caught on the lip of the crevasse and vaulted him to the other side, where he plunged 50 feet to the bottom of yet another fissure. When he came to he was bruised but alive, lying head down on a slope of fresh snow.

The survivors regrouped and quickly dug out Couttet, whose arms and chest were pinned under the snow and whose face was turning blue. Then they found his brother David, whose arms could be seen waving from a pile of white. After that, they did not know what to do. 'We were all more or less injured,' Couttet recorded.[24] Some guides wandered about aimlessly, crying. One just sat and stared out across the valley, muttering. Dornford became briefly deranged and Henderson 'was in a condition which made one fear for the consequences'.[25] Hamel and Henderson climbed into the crevasse but there was nothing that could be done; the bodies were buried under 100 feet of snow. Henderson later told Couttet that he had been on battlefields, had witnesed the butchery of a surgeon's quarters on a man-of-war, but nothing had horrified him as much as what they had just endured.

The survivors slunk back to Chamonix, in a daze. It was the worst disaster the village had experienced. There was widepread dismay that the bodies would never be recovered; when hunters or crystal-gatherers fell to their deaths there was a prolonged, usually hazardous but ultimately successful effort to retrieve the remains. In this case, however, it was impossible. They blamed Hamel not only for the accident but for the lack of anything to mourn over. The Russian was cold and impassive according to Couttet, and left quickly for Geneva in disgrace. Dornford and Henderson sprinkled money around town before making a similarly swift getaway. 'The English travellers . . .

promised never to forget the families of our friends,' Couttet recalled. 'We haven't heard anything of them since.'[26]

For two years a pall fell over Chamonix. The Hamel tragedy fuelled the arguments of those who believed climbing to be a stupid and foolhardy business. Even the guides began to have doubts about going to the top of Mont Blanc – by the traditional route, at any rate – and contented themselves with shepherding *étrangers* across the lower glaciers. By this time, also, Chamonix was not the only spot on the touristic map. Places like Grindelwald and Lauterbrunnen, in Switzerland's Bernese Oberland, were equally atractive to visitors. In the former one could be carried to a glacier to eat wild strawberries whilst a bearded man blew on an Alpine horn. In the latter one could admire the countless waterfalls that tumbled from the cliffs above, and maybe cross the Kleine Scheidegg as had done the hefty Englishwoman in pre-Napoleonic times. These were the main resorts, but there were hundreds of other places where visitors could commune with God, Nature and that nice couple from Cheltenham Spa.

It was inevitable, however, that somebody would sooner or later banish Hamel's ghost. That man was Frederick Clissold, an abominably fit Englishman who had trained on Mount Snowdon and thought Mont Blanc well within his capabilities. He swept into Chamonix on 2 August 1822 and immediately proved his mettle by climbing the Brévent in an unheard-of time of two and a half hours. That done, he procured two crépe veils, one black and one green, ordered a plaster of Burgundy pitch to protect his chest against sudden changes in temperature, and ordered Joseph-Marie Couttet plus five other guides to lead him to the top of Mont Blanc.

This abrupt visitor took Chamonix completely by surprise. Paccard – who was by now often drunk, according to his enemy Balmat who was himself usually incapacitated – came forward with the offer of scientific instruments. Clissold declined it. He didn't want to take measurements, he didn't want to have extra baggage, all he wanted to do was reach the summit as quickly as possible. Paccard retreated in astonishment. Couttet was similarly taken aback when

Clissold announced that he didn't intend to sleep at the Grands Mulets: he wanted to start before midnight and march through darkness and then day to camp on the summit. There might be another camp on the Grand Plateau as they came down, Clissold conceded, but he was reluctant to commit himself.

Carried along by Clissold's imperious dictats, the team left Chamonix at 10.30 p.m. on 18 August 1822. Their start was necessarily slow, lit by brands, but come daylight Clissold bounded ahead. He amazed his companions, forging glaciers, leaping crevasses, occasionally falling into them yet climbing out with undiminished vigour. He lost his alpenstock, but carried on. Couttet and the others were soon left behind. Seeing this, Clissold turned back, grabbed one of the guide's knapsacks and resumed his assault. Couttet was flabbergasted. '*Diable vous n'êtes pas fatigué du tout*,' he panted.[27] After twenty hours' climbing Couttet suggested they halt. Clissold was having none of such defeatist talk: they had already lost three hours waiting for weary guides to catch up, and he wanted to get to the top before dark. He probably could have achieved his goal had he been on his own. In the end, however, the guides would go no farther then the Rochers Rouges, above the Grand Plateau, and although Clissold dragged Couttet still higher he retreated to spend the night with the others. It was 10.30 p.m. and they had been walking – or Clissold had – for twenty-four hours non-stop.

That night they laid down wooden boards on the snow, wrapped themselves in blankets and went to sleep in temperatures below freezing. Clissold awoke with horrible keenness early next morning. It gave him slight pause when he saw that a bottle of his best Hermitage had turned to ice during the night. But then what was a bit of cold? By 5.30 a.m. on 20 August they stood on the summit; and three hours later they left it, as Clissold resumed his tempestuous journey. They reached the Grands Mulets at 1.30 p.m., pausing only to catch the rumble of an avalanche falling on the slopes they had recently crossed, and at 7.30 p.m. Clissold force-marched them triumphantly back into Chamonix. From start to finish, the climb had taken a record forty-five hours.

Clissold's eyes were dreadful. He had forgone the use of his two veils, 'the scene being too extraordinary to be viewed through the preservative of green crape, or any other medium'.[28] In every other respect, however, he felt fine. 'It was not war,' he wrote casually of the ascent. Truth be told, he thought Mont Blanc rather a let-down – though the views were superb – and wished he had gone up Mt. Chimborazo in Ecuador instead. The guides, wracked with exhaustion, probably wished he had too.

It was hoped that Clissold was an aberration, a one-off madman whose example would not be followed by others. But no. That same year Mrs and Miss Campbell climbed the Col du Géant. And in August 1823 a Mr H. H. Jackson arrived from England in a nankeen jacket and trousers, a small knapsack on his back and a walletful of francs in his pocket. He wanted to climb Mont Blanc, 'from a love of hardy enterprise excusable, as he hoped, in a young man'.[29] He attempted to hire Clissold's guides from the previous year. They immediately said they were booked, so he took a group of five others at a cost of 60 francs apiece. He rushed up the mountain, sleeping under an old sheet at the Grands Mulets and spent ten minutes at the top before rushing down again. The journey was accomplished in a new record of 36 hours.

Whatever the discouragements of the Romantics, the scientists, the guidebooks and even the guides themselves, it was obvious that people were bent on conquering Mont Blanc. Therefore, the Chamonix authorities instituted in 1823 the Compagnie des Guides. It purported to be a guild of professional climbers, but in reality was little more than a list of Chamoniards who were willing to take time off from hunting and crystal-gathering to lead visitors up the hills. Nevertheless, it received royal approval from Savoy, the restored ruler deeming it necessary that some sort of fixed price 'should be applied to those who lead visitors to the glaciers and other remarkable sites in the valley of Chamonix'.[30] The ducal charter was not short, and covered almost every eventuality that the guides might encounter. Article 15, for example, described the difference between ordinary and extraordinary trips. Ordinary was anything below the snowline;

extraordinary was anything above. There was also a separate category
for climbing Mont Blanc. Ordinary cost seven livres per day for one
guide; extraordinary was ten livres per day, two guides per person
being obligatory; Mont Blanc was 40 livres per guide, and required
four guides per person. Another article decreed that the guides be
organised into a quota so that they should have an equal chance,
regardless of merit, of picking the Mont Blanc plum.

For no obvious reason, this system seemed to quieten the
Gadarene rush. When Dr Edmund Clarke and Captain Markham
Sherwill paid their premium to climb Mont Blanc in 1825, they made
the ascent at a moderate pace, sleeping where it was proper to sleep,
feeling nauseous at the correct height, becoming tired when tiredness
was appropriate and displaying suitable appreciation at the top.
Sherwill felt so light-headed that he declared a single slice of the
knife beneath his boots would send him floating into the air. They did
nothing startling except bury a time capsule on the summit: a wide,
glass tube in which they stuffed an olive twig from the Mediterranean
'together with the name of George the Fourth and his deservedly
popular Minister, subjoining the names of some of the most remarkable persons of the age'. The tube was buried deep in the snow in the
hope 'that it might remain unaltered for many centuries like insects
preserved in amber'.[31] (It was found two years later, half filled with
water and containing a pulpy mass of twigs and paper.)

Meanwhile, down below, tourists poured into Chamonix by the
hundred. They left from Geneva, climbing into high coaches whose
springs were adjusted to cope with the poor roads and then trembled
uncertainly, umbrellas at the ready, towards Mont Blanc. (Earlier in
the century, Bourrit had gone to great lengths to have the
Geneva–Chamonix route cleared of stones and resurfaced; but it had
disintegrated over the years.) A large proportion of the tourists were
women, which delighted the Genevans. Crowds gathered at each
departure to marvel at the sight of so many bustles being hoisted
aloft. They nicknamed it 'l'ascension des ballons'.[32]

For a short while everything seemed back to normal. The ordinary
tourists paid their seven livres to be escorted across the glaciers. The

extraordinary ones paid three livres extra to be led above the snow-line. But nobody paid the summit premium. It was not that they were scared of the summit. It was worse than that: they simply had no interest in it. From being anathema, height had become a matter of complete indifference.

The new Alpine *étrangers* were a far cry from the devil-may-cares of pre-war years. The English, who vastly outnumbered all other nation-alities, seemed to have deteriorated particularly badly during the war. Gone were the titled swells, to be replaced by men and women from all classes who were, as the *aubergistes* noted, 'not at all the best of all classes'.[33] They haggled over the prices, drank until midnight, dirtied the linen unduly, overworked their guides and generally behaved far too much as if they were on holiday – which of course they were. In the best tradition of English holidaymakers they wore ghastly cos-tumes that aped the local style. One bemused visitor to Chamonix reported in 1825 that 'we beheld a description of animal rather fre-quent in these mountainous regions – not a chamois nor a lammergeyer but an Alpine dandy. He was fearfully rigged out for daring and desparate exploit, with belt, pole and nicely embroidered jerkin – a costume admirably adapted for exciting female terror, and a reasonable apprehension that some formidable hillocks and rivulets would be encountered during the day, before the thing returned to preside over bread and butter at the vesper tea-table.'[34] In the same year and place another Englishman met a similar apparition, a Londoner 'who somehow had got far out of his road, and wandered, not knowing whither he went . . . He bewailed his miserable lot – he seemed to have lost the log-book of his reckoning, and to be in a per-fect maze. He thought he had lost ten years of his (valuable) life by such an adventure, and doubtless, could he have procured Fortunatus's wishing cap, he would immediately have transported himself to Bond Street. He saw nothing in "Mount Blank", and wondered what others could see there to make such a fuss about.'[35] The English gentility, who considered themselves the only ones capa-ble of appreciating the Alps, were dismayed by the newcomers, a lot of whom for some reason came from London's impoverished East

End. When William Brockedon overheard a family speaking in Cockney accents at a table next to him, he was struck with 'disbelief that such vulgarity could have reached the Great St Bernard. I only record it as a subject of astonishment, how such people ever thought of such a journey. I had no idea that the gentilities of Wapping had ever extended so far from the Thames.'[36]

The class-ridden British sneered at each other. The Europeans took a more egalitarian view: all Britons were equally awful. It wasn't so much their clothes or their accents as their manners. Yes, Britain had won the war, yes Europe was politically unstable, and yes the Alps lacked the amenities of London. But was that a reason to be rude and haughty? The British were known as 'Yes and No Tourists' from their refusal to engage in conversation. The Milords, even more so than the jerkins, were abrupt, dismissive and uncaring of peoples' feelings. 'What an armour of dignity or something else must these singular mortals possess,' wrote an amazed schoolmaster, 'to be able to walk for ten hours in these valleys without . . . giving some sign of greeting, or of politeness, or even of non-ferocity!'[37] George Sand thought she had the answer:

> Albion's Islanders bring with them a peculiar fluid which I shall call the British fluid, enveloped in which they travel, as inaccessible to the atmosphere of the regions which they traverse as is a mouse in the centre of a pneumatic machine. Their eternal unresponsiveness is not solely due to the thousands of precautions which they take. It is not because they wear three pairs of breeches, one over the other, that they reach their destination perfectly dry and clean in spite of rain and mud; nor is it because of their woolen caps that their stiff and metallic coiffure withstands the damp; it is not because they are loaded with sufficient pomades, brushes and soap to convert an entire regiment of Breton conscripts into Adonises that they always have a tidy beard and irreproachable fingernails. It is because the outer air has no hold on them, because they walk, drink, sleep and eat encapsuled in their fluid as in a

bell-jar twenty feet thick, from out of which they look down with pity on riders whose hair is ruffled by the wind, and on foot-travellers whose shoes are damaged by snow.[38]

There were, however, one or two Britons willing to engage more closely with the outside world. Among them was Charles Fellows.

Fellows – later Sir Charles Fellows – was a young man in a hurry. Not for him a four-month ramble through the Alps as recommended by the guidebooks. He was doing Europe, for form's sake, and had no time to waste. He disembarked at Ostend on 20 June 1827 and hurtled across Belgium, Holland, Germany, Italy, Switzerland and France before landing back at Hastings on 11 August, carrying in his slipstream a companion named William Hawes. One of Fellows's stops was Chamonix, where he was disappointed by the 'rank and coarse' vegetation growing in the fields and sneered at the 'sickly green foliage' on the lower slopes. He would have left the valley as rapidly as he left all his other destinations had he not seen Mont Blanc and learned of its reputation. He was told it was impossible to climb the mountain and that so many people had died in the attempt that he may as well abandon all thought of it. The story of Hamel's disaster was not only fresh but flourishing – in the latest version, the avalanche had carried the guides not 600 feet but a full two miles down the hill. Fellows was immediately interested and announced his intention to give it a try. A procession of injured guides came forward to dissuade him; one man whose skull had been fractured in 1792 made him feel the spot where he had been trepanned; but the sight of their shattered limbs acted only as a spur.

Fellows was a man of his age. 'Mad as the attempt was generally deemed, especially as, in proportion to the very few who had succeeded, so many had fallen a sacrifice to their curiosity, we were not to be dismayed.'[39] He had obviously read, and been influenced by, the *Quarterly Review* in which Barrow vented his opinions on the Arctic and on exploration in general. That Barrow's expeditions had largely been failures did not dissuade him. 'If arguments and apprehensions in matters of enterprise were always to carry their discouragements with them,' he reasoned Barrowesquely, 'the boldness of adventure would be checked, and all that field of interest which is opened by the discoveries of the daring, would be closed against the world.'[40]

Normally an ascent of Mont Blanc involved much studying of the weather, collecting of provisions, hiring of guides, saying of farewells to loved ones and other time-consuming details. None of this for Fellows. As he said, 'Our maxim throughout our tour had been to avoid delay.' And so, within a day of their arrival he and Hawes were climbing Mont Blanc accompanied by ten guides and ten porters who carried blankets, sheets, clothes, linen, a change of shoes, candles, wood, straw, a saucepan for melting snow, 'besides an adequate supply of provisions, consisting of eight joints of meat, a dozen fowls, sausages, eight loaves of bread and a cheese, lemons, raisin, prunes and sugar, with forty-two bottles of wine, brandy, capillaire, and syrup of raspberries etc.'[41] Down in Chamonix, the chief magistrate was left holding their wills and the addresses of their next of kin.

Hawes, who was not as keen as Fellows, found the climb arduous and surreal. Struggling over the Glacier des Bossons, he heard the distant conversation of butterfly-catchers on the Aiguille du Midi, who spent their days in a swathe of silk nets, hoping to catch specimens for tourists. Fellows, on the other hand, was impressed by nothing. He described the crossing of snow bridges, when he and Hawes stretched themselves flat as a plank and, attached to a rope on the opposite side, were hauled over by the guides. Before the Napoleonic Wars, such an act would have produced reams of frenzied terror. Fellows dismissed it in a sentence. The snow bridges did not always hold and sometimes he dropped through. Again, where Saussure would have described the situation in several pages, and Bourrit might have squeezed a chapter or even a book out of it, Fellows was unworried: while dangling from his rope he 'had the opportunity of contemplating and admiring the wonders about me. From this novel but awful situation the colours of the snows above me were truly beautiful, varying from a dead whiteness to dark shades of blue and green, while the hanging icicles, some of which were of immense size, glittered with all the prismatic colours.'[42] And that was all he had to say on the subject.

They spent the night on the Grands Mulets. The porters had left by this time and the two Britons and their ten guides slept on two shelves of rock, one of which was four feet square and the other eight feet by four, edged by a 300-foot drop. The temperature was 5°F below freezing. When they awoke the following morning Fellows was slightly taken aback by the provisions the guides allotted for their climb to the summit, 'the forage for the whole party for the day being estimated at little more than I myself had eaten on the preceding'.[43] At first he did not understand it. But after he had experienced the depressing effect altitude had on the appetite, he considered that perhaps they had taken too much. 'A crust of bread,' he later wrote, 'some lemonade and a very few raisins constituted all the sustenance I took in the course of thirty hours.'[44]

They crossed the Grand Plateau safely but found Balmat's old route blocked by avalanche falls. Thereupon Fellows looked for another route and discovered one, after much scouting and peering from hummocks. It led to the east, as opposed to the avalanche-prone western funnel that had been used hitherto. They took it. As they climbed, Fellows began to appreciate some of Mont Blanc's beauties. He could see the stars at midday, and marvelled at the way in which they did not look 'as if studded on the surface of the heavens [but] as if suspended in the air at various distances'.[45] They were smaller than he was used to and gave the impression that he could reach out and touch them. Less beautifully, he experienced Mont Blanc's thin atmosphere: 'I conceive we suffered precisely as we might expect to suffer, had we been placed under the gradually exhausting receiver of an air-pump.'[46] He, Hawes and their guides began to haemorrhage. First came nosebleeds; then they spat blood. After that they vomited blood and finally they urinated blood. (Hawes said he had nothing but a headache.) Bleeding from almost every orifice they reached the summit at 2.20 p.m. on 25 July. Physically, it was unexceptional, being an inclined plane in the shape of an egg, measuring 150 feet long and 30 wide. Hawes felt 'an indescribable feeling of melancholy'[47] but Fellows was moved to brief excitement: 'From the extraordinary brilliancy of the day, and the closeness of the air, it seemed as if we were suspended from heaven itself.'[48]

He stuck his cap on his stick and waved it elatedly in the air. He did not particularly want to make scientific observations – and anyway, he had left his thermometer and barometer at the Grands Mulets – but he made one useful discovery when he invited every-body to join him in 'God Save the King'. (The guides didn't know the words so they settled on a Swiss chant instead.) He found that it was impossible to sing. The sounds came out of their mouths but vanished as soon as they appeared. 'Such was the want of the vibratory power of the atmosphere that we could by no possibility blend or carry one note into another.'[49] It was the musical equivalent of throwing peb-bles into the air.

They did not stay long on the top, to the disappointment of those below for whom an ascent of Mont Blanc was still rare enough to be worthy of attention. (The artist David Wilkie recorded that twenty-five English tourists were clustered in one hotel room, passing a single telescope between them.) Nor did they linger on the descent. The guides seemed to have been infected by Fellows's sense of urgency for instead of climbing carefully down the hill they glissaded on their alpenstocks. This remarkable trick involved leaning back on the alpenstock and sliding feet first down the snow, braking and steering with the heels. Glissading was nothing new: roadmen who maintained the passes traditionally used it as a quick way of getting home in winter, using shovels in place of alpenstocks; Saussure had recorded the practice and so had Bourrit, who declared it was very easy once one got the knack and almost convinced his readers that he had mas-tered the skill himself. Fellows found it very impressive, nonetheless. He did not attempt it personally, but slid down behind one of the guides in a sitting position, 'keeping the eye immoveably fixed upon his hat.' In this manner he descended 'with inconceivable velocity over a space of seven hundred feet at a time'.[50] On one occasion the guide braked too hard and they flew into the air, tumbling chaotically to the bottom of the slope. Fellows spat snow and announced that the incident was rather amusing (in retrospect).

After that, there was very little that could disturb him. They slept at the Grands Mulets and were hit by a thunderstorm. 'No one but those who have experienced it can conceive the extreme irksomeness of passing a night in such a situation,' he complained.[51] He was in the same situation as Saussure had been on the Col du Géant. But whereas Saussure had cowered in his tent, brandishing his electrometer like a cross to a vampire, Fellows observed only that he constantly had to wring out his night cap and that its silk tassle froze when he went to sleep.

Their descent was marked by all kinds of obstacles that Fellows swept aside as mere nothings. The glacier had been transformed by avalanches, and on one occasion they had to cut steps in a fresh crevasse, while a 200-foot block of ice loomed perilously above them. The process took fifteen minutes, during which time the block cracked three times, 'sounding like the report of a pistol echoed through the body of the mountain'.[52] Shortly after they crossed the crevasse, the block collapsed onto the spot where they had been standing. Fellows recorded it with mild interest. The party reached Chamonix at 9.00 a.m. on 26 July, having been on the hill for 48 hours. The Englishmen subsequently went for a two-hour walk through the valley, because they felt the need to stretch their legs, then caroused until midnight and got up at 6.00 the following morning to catch the coach to Geneva.

'The burden,' Fellows wrote, 'of every inquiry was – has the difficulty, labour and danger, been repaid by what you have witnessed? To which I, for myself [Hawes perhaps was of different opinion] replied, and still reply, that I was *amply* recompensed; having witnessed what otherwise I never could have conceived, and in so doing, enlarged my ideas of creation which, with all its magnitude, scarce forms a speck in the universe.'[53] Given the complete absence of any such sentiment hitherto, and the fact that Fellows was the last man on earth to consider himself a speck, this rings with appealing insincerity. Nonetheless, for all his nonchalance he was secretly very proud of his achievement and reproduced in his journal a facsimile of the certificate which Chamonix had awarded him to mark the ascent.

Fellows later went on to become a respected Middle East archaeologist. Hawes sank from sight. In 1828 he published his own account of the climb, in which Fellows appeared as a weakling and he himself as a superman. But his true feelings are best expressed in a closing paragraph in Fellows's journal that one feels can only have been written on Hawes's urging. It reads: 'any one who sets the least value upon his own life, or upon those who must accompany him on such an expedition, hazards a risk which, upon calm consideration, he ought not to venture: and, if it were ever to fall to my lot, to dissuade a friend from attempting what we have gone through, I shall consider that I have saved his life'.[54]

CHAPTER NINE

Eighteen twenty-seven was an interesting year. It was the year in which Fellows opened a new route to the top of Mont Blanc. It was the year in which a Scot named John Auldjo followed the new route and on lighting his pipe made the discovery that 'the rarity of the air rendered the scent of tobacco so powerful and disagreeable that I was obliged to desist'.[1] This finding was 'of profound interest' according to an early nineteenth-century chronicler and earned Auldjo 'the gold medal of civil merit from the late King of Prussia, an autograph letter of approval from the ex-King of Bavaria, and the gift of a valuable diamond ring from the King of Sardinia'.[2] Eighteen twenty-seven was also the year in which Paccard wrote the last entry in his diary of Mont Blanc. It was typically curt: 'Mr. Auldjo, English, arrived at the summit on the ninth [August] at 11 a.m., left again at 11.40, and returned to Chamonix at 8 p.m.'[3]

Paccard died before the year was out. Of the first heroes of Mont Blanc there now remained only Jacques Balmat, and he would go soon. Over the decades Paccard had resided magisterially in Chamonix, offering his barometers and thermometers to those who wanted to follow in his footsteps to the summit. He had been the point of first call for many visitors and in particular for those who wished to climb Europe's highest mountain. During the 1820s, however, he must have felt a sense of disappointment. More often than not his instruments were broken or left unused. Clissold had been so depressingly bold as to reject them altogether, as had Auldjo, who stated that 'I did not much regret the want of them, not professing to make my ascent for any scientific purpose, feeling that I could add very little to the stock of existing knowledge.'[4] Paccard represented an age that did not exist any more. Mont Blanc was no longer a mystery. Chamonix was no longer a quaint hamlet where travellers stayed with the curé. The Alps were no longer the home of dragons – as far as anybody could ascertain, at any rate. In Paccard's youth, science had been all. That thin membrane of academe was now punctured at regular intervals by climbers who went up Mont Blanc for the most unscientific of reasons. Matzewski, for example, had wanted to enhance his poetic skills (the first account of his climb was contained in a lengthy footnote to a poem titled 'Maria'); Rensselear had done it for the hell of it; Auldjo had wanted to get a better view of the mountain's reflection in a lake. Little better were the impulses that spurred subsequent climbers: in 1830 the Hon. Edward Bootle Wilbraham, an army colonel, climbed Mont Blanc because he had been told not to; in 1834 Dr Martin Barry, a Quaker, went up it to broaden his horizons; in the same year Comte Henri de Tilly was depressed by a recent love affair and thought a bit of exercise would do him good; in 1837 H. M. Atkins, a 19-year-old English boy, just wanted something to do; and in 1838 Comtesse Henriette D'Angeville climbed Mont Blanc in men's clothes to prove that she was the equal of George Sand (to make her point she was hoisted onto her guides' shoulders at the summit, thereby reaching a higher altitude than any other human being). Not without reason did Murray's guide of 1851 state that 'It is a somewhat remarkable fact that a large proportion of those who have made this ascent have been persons of unsound mind.'[5] Then there were the dreadful Englishmen who swarmed across the lower slopes in their costumes.

In short, 1827 was the year in which the Alps established themselves beyond redemption as a destination for tourists. The roads were now better than they had ever been – thanks largely to

Napoleon – steamboats puttered across the lakes, and it would not be
very long before the first railway was driven into the mountains. Over
the following decades thousands of Britons came to marvel at the
wonders of 'Switzerland' – a catch-all word used to describe not only
Switzerland but any area of France, Savoy, Piedmont or Italy that
contained mountains. They came for the baths, the glaciers, the views
and the mountains. They came for the exercise, the climate and the
company. They came in hope of finding Byron's signature on a wall
(hoteliers were ever happy to oblige). They came in hope of stealing
famous autographs from hotel ledgers (again, their hosts were at hand;
as soon as a page was removed it would be replaced with another
bearing the same comments and signature of the famous person who
had never been there in the first place). They came in hope of finding a spa cure for whatever ailed them – 'those at least of the bilious,
dyspeptic, hypochondriac, pill-taking class,'[6] as one doctor dismissed
them. And they came because the Alps had become an England
overseas.

In Geneva it was impossible to escape the sound of English. The
Young Switzerland Society adopted the tune of 'God Save the King'
as its national anthem. The best hotels laid on a table d'hôte at
1.00 p.m. and then two more at 5.00 and 8.00 expressly for the
English. Many Britons set up home there, starting a trend that would
continue throughout the century. Among the settlers was a genteel
couple named Arbuthnot. When Mrs Arbuthnot was struck and killed
by lightning, the drama attracted hundreds of British pilgrims.
Eventually, a memorial had to be erected. Less romantic but no less
typical was Lord Vernon who took Swiss citizenship so as to be eligible for the Basle shooting competition and announced that he would
never leave the country until he had won it.

The British liked to go on walking tours and took pride in the fact
that they could travel light. 'A healthy and robust pedestrian
traveller . . . need carry with him only one package, and this in the
shape of a water-proof knapsack of moderate size,' wrote an
enthusiast.[7] They took with them a change of light clothes and wore
small-crowned, wide-brimmed wideawakes on their heads. The

cannier among them packed bars of Windsor soap – 'it is rarely to be met with in the inns'.[8] They walked, rode and steamed through the Alps. Occasionally they climbed some of the lower peaks, an achievement which sent them into ecstasies.

'I can but ill describe what I felt, but I know I felt vividly and strongly,' wrote one man who climbed the no-account Riffelberg from Zermatt and saw the majestic circle of peaks around him. 'Sitting up there in mid-heaven as it were, on the smooth, warm ledge of our rock . . . under a sky of the richest blue, and either cloudless or only here and there gemmed with those aerial and sunbright clouds which but enhance its depth . . . we seemed to feel as if there could be no other mental mood but that of an exquisite yet cheerful serenity – a sort of delicious abstraction or absorption of our powers, in one grand, vague, yet most luxurious perception of Beauty and Loveliness. At another time – nay, it would almost seem at the same time, so rapid was the alternation from mood to mood – the immeasurable vastness of the scene . . . the utter silence, and the absence of every indication of life and living things . . . would excite a tone of mind entirely different – solemn, awful, melancholy.'[9] When he let his mind wander the peaks became 'an awful circle of Titanic Sphynxes'.

Not all the tourists came from Britain, and not all of them were so religiously appreciative of Alpine splendour. On 5 June 1832 Alexandre Dumas attended a funeral in Paris. A few days later he read in the papers that he had been party to a bloody riot in the capital and had been shot, gun in hand, on 6 June. This, coupled with the fact that Paris was in the middle of a cholera epidemic, drove him to the Alps. He had a lively time, during which he interviewed Balmat of Mont Blanc, ate what appeared to be a roast infant but which turned out to be a marmot, was flooded out of one hotel, smoked out the upper floors of another, attended a trial in which live bears were brought as witnesses, and acted as second in a duel between a Frenchman and an Englishman. This last had come about because the Frenchman could not stand the Englishman's behaviour at dinner and so threw a bread roll at him. The Englishman promptly hit him on the head with a bottle of wine. They therefore met the next morning to settle their differences with pistols. The Englishman, who was a renowned shot, fired first. The Frenchman walked towards him. The Englishman fired again. The Frenchman kept on coming. Dumas intervened, and begged the Frenchman to fire into the air. 'It is all very well for you to talk,' said the Frenchman, revealing two holes in his chest. He then strode forward, put his pistol to the Englishman's head and pulled the trigger. Dumas went home shortly aterwards, rather upset, and with little more to say about the Alps' beauties.

More explicitly, in 1837 an exiled French count wrote a description of his stay at the Swiss resort of Interlaken:

> Early in the morning one is awakened by the noise of a cavalcade getting ready for an excursion to the Staubbach or to Grindelwald. Five or six young women on horseback wait while a couple of matrons are hoisted onto donkeys, to cast an air of propriety over the party. A dozen beaux in blouses with long spiked sticks carried as lances curvet round the caravan on their mounts. After much talking, screaming and shouting, and when it is quite certain that nobody has been left undisturbed in the village, they move off in confusion. When the weather is fine, the evening is devoted to walks. But when it rains, it is impossible to escape the torture of hearing detestable music performed by amateurs who take possession of a piano, and murder the pieces which were the rage of Paris during the preceding winter.[10]

In his opinion, people came to Switzerland 'out of pride, fashion, and having nothing better to do; only rarely out of real curiosity . . . one is bored before the tour is half over, and one only finishes it so as not to retrace one's steps'.[11]

Less bilious but equally critical were the reports of a Genevan teacher named Rudolf Töppfer who led an international brigade of schoolchildren through the Alps between 1830 and 1842. His excursions were magnificently shambolic and moved relentlessly from one mishap to the next. He recorded them humorously, but could not hide his dissatisfaction with the area. He found the inns poor, he found the customs officers corrupt, he found the English frankly bizarre, he found the steamers unnerving, he found the tolls extortionate and on the Great St Bernard Pass he found a mouse in his umbrella. He was prone to giddy spells and took no delight in climbing steep hills: 'the heart thumps, the head goes round, the legs shake, and, incapable of going forwards or back, of sitting down or standing up, the most self-assured grenadier in the world is changed into a lump from which one hears, "Come and get me out, come very quickly and get me out!" Ah, the horrid moments! Ah, the detestable recreation!'[12]

Enthusiastic or not, energetic or less so, tourists were now the main category of visitors to the Alps. There were, however, some who still saw the Alps as objects of scientific interest. They were not drawn, as had been Saussure and others, to the peaks. What attracted them were the glaciers. How were they formed? Why and how fast did they move? What caused the moraines that accumulated at their edges and in their middles? Why did they advance and retreat so inexplicably? More importantly, did they have anything to do with so-called 'erratic' rocks, those boulders, alien to the landscape in which they sat, which could be encountered in puzzling lines throughout northern Europe and were concentrated particularly heavily in Switzerland? Various solutions had been offered to most of these problems. Glaciers were formed by a build-up of snow that compacted into ice at high altitude – fine. They moved because the heat of the earth's crust melted the lower layers of a glacier allowing it to slide along like a snail – almost right. The 'erratic' rocks had been dropped by one or more floods that had swept the globe in earlier times; they had been tossed there by volcanic eruptions; or maybe they had been deposited by 'ice rafts', land versions of icebergs, that had been born in the hills and had then wallowed across country, carrying their boulders with them, before dying in a gigantic puddle – completely wrong.

Nowadays geology does not have a reputation for excitement. Back then, however, it was at the cutting edge. In a world where everything rested on the Bible, geology was the one philosophy – to use an archaic term – that dared question Genesis. The De Lucs had been among the first to suggest the possibility that rock formations, so visible in the Alps, offered a clue to Earth's prehistory. Saussure, too, had pondered on the forces that created the Alps. Had they been compressed in some fashion or lifted up by an unknown subterranean energy? (He favoured the former, the De Lucs the latter.) All over Europe, a growing band of gentlemen amateurs were amassing fossil collections that not only indicated the existence of extinct species but provided evidence that the planet had undergone considerable climatic and topographical upheavals.

Orthodox, Bible-based reasoning did its best: fossils were remnants of those creatures which had not been carried on Noah's Ark; the strange vertical rock strata visible in the Alps and other mountains resulted from whatever mechanism God had used to form the continents; and 'erratic' rocks were clearly the debris left by the Deluge. But there were so many holes in orthodox reasoning, so many inexplicable facts that simply could not be explained in biblical terms. When people like Saussure went tapping with their hammers through the Alps, each rock specimen that they retrieved, and then wrapped in the sheets of grey paper that were recommended for the purpose, contributed to an uncomfortable sensation that orthodox reasoning was wrong.

Among the doubters was a vicar's son named Louis Agassiz, who was born on 28 May 1807 in Neuchâtel, a Swiss canton which, by some quirk of history, was part of Prussia. His family was not wealthy and by the time he was a teenager he had learned how to make his own shoes, tailor his own clothes and fashion a watertight barrel. He did, however, have a natural affinity for geology which earned him in 1832 the professorship of Natural History at the University of Neuchâtel. 'Whatever befalls me,' he wrote, 'I feel that I shall never cease to consecrate my whole energy to the study of nature; its all powerful charm has taken such possession of me that I shall always sacrifice everything to it; even the things which men usually value most.'[13] He did sacrifice everything – his own money, his wife's, the university's – and by the 1830s employed a twelve-man research team, an artist and a fossil collector, whose findings were published by the twenty employees of his own private printing press. His speciality was 'Fossil Fishes', which were so easily chiselled from the Alps and whose remains were one of the first, most disturbing signs of a non-biblical prehistory. He corresponded regularly on the subject with his friend Baron Alexander von Humboldt, one of the most influential explorer–scientists of the early nineteenth century. The study of 'Fossil Fishes' obsessed him – colleagues in England called him the 'famous foreign fishmonger'[14] – and it was a topic that he turned to annually when asked to address Neuchâtel's Helvetic Association, a forum that he had set up to discuss matters pertaining to geology. Old bones would have been the stuff of Agassiz's existence had not a friend, Jean de Charpentier, asked him in 1836 to come and inspect a glacier in Bex, Switzerland.

Since the beginning of the century a few, isolated individuals had suggested that the only natural force capable of transporting erratic boulders was a glacier. Britain's Professor John Playfair had proposed the notion in 1802 and it had been seconded by Sir John Leslie in 1804. In later years it received support not only from men of science but from those of relatively humble origins. Jean-Pierre Perraudin, a chamois-hunter from Lourtier, and Marie Deville, a Chamonix guide, both agreed with the theory; so did peasants in places such as Meiringen, Yverdon and Val Ferret. Charpentier had stayed with Perraudin in 1815 and on hearing his host's theory had decided it 'was too fantastic to be worthy of serious consideration'.[15] As the idea gained ground, however, Charpentier concluded that some serious work must be done to set it to rest – particularly as one of his best friends had become a convert, an engineer named Venetz who had been responsible for the Bagnes sluice. Through the late 1820s and 1830s Charpentier made a detailed study of the erratic rocks that littered the Swiss lowlands and was dismayed to find that glaciers did, indeed, seem the most likely agent. He wanted to share the news with a colleague and so, in 1836, Agassiz found himself at Bex.

Agassiz was as much a doubter as Charpentier had been. But when he saw the evidence and heard Charpentier's reasoning, he accepted the theory in its entirety. In fact, the only fault he could find was that it was too limited. For Agassiz the visit to Bex was a road to Damascus: in one of those rare moments that dot scientific history, everything became clear; he suddenly realised that the entire European landscape had been moulded by glaciers.

In the summer of 1837 the students of Neuchâtel gathered at the Helvetic Association to hear the usual sermon on 'Fossil Fishes'. To their astonishment Agassiz started talking about glaciers. He postulated that ice had once been omnipresent, covering the earth from the North Pole to Central Europe. It had killed numerous life forms and had carved the landscape into its recognisable shape. The debris it left was visible in any mountain valley in the form of lateral moraines – the rocks which are carried on a glacier's edge – and terminal moraines – the rocks which a glacier deposits at its snout; central moraines came into being at the Y-junction of two intersecting glaciers. This was so radical as to defy belief. The distinguished geologist Leopold von Buch ran from the room crying '*O sancte de Saussure, ora pro nobis!*'[16] Similar scenes occurred elsewhere. 'Agassiz joined us at Dublin, and read a long paper at our section,' wrote the Revd Adam Sedgwick of the British Association. 'But what think you? Instead of teaching us what we wanted to know, and giving us the overflowing of his abundant ichthyological wealth, he read a long and stupid hypothetical dissertation on geology, drawn from the depths of his ignorance . . . I hope we shall before long be able to get this moonshine out of his head.'[17] But the moonshine was firmly rooted, and it flourished, to the upset of Europe's learned bodies. 'Once grant to Agassiz that his deepest valleys of Switzerland . . . were once filled with snow and ice, and I see no stopping place,'[18] roared Sir Roderick Murchison of the Royal Geographical Society. Using the most friendly language, Humboldt advised Agassiz to stick to 'Fossil Fishes'.

Agassiz did not care. The following year he visited the Alps with his journalist friend Édouard Desor and in 1840 he pitched camp on a glacier in order to refine his theories. The spot he chose was an overhanging rock halfway down the central moraine of the Unteraar Glacier in the Bernese Oberland. A stone wall was erected beneath the overhang, the floor was levelled with flat slabs, and a curtain was hung across the entrance. A niche outside served as a kitchen and a small hole beneath a boulder was used as a larder. Supplies were brought regularly from the nearby hospice of Grimsel. It slept six and became known as the Hôtel des Neuchâtelois. Its first inhabitants were Agassiz, Desor and four fellow scientists: Charles Vogt, Célestin Nicolet, Henri Coulon and François de Pourtales, a 17-year-old pupil from Neuchâtel University.

The gang of six were equipped with a host of scientific instruments – barometers, thermometers, hygrometers, hypsometers and microscopes – as well as a device for boring holes in the glacier. Agassiz organised their responsibilities with care. He and Pourtales were in charge of meteorological observations and taking the temperature of the glacier at various depths; Vogt was ordered to investigate red snow, a bewildering phenomenon that had been noted in the Arctic as well as the Alps; Nicolet was allocated the flora to be found on the glacier and its surrounding rocks; Desor and Coulon were told to study glacial attributes in their widest sense, including moraines and the movement of rocks.

They triangulated the positions of eighteen large rocks resting on the glacier and recorded their movements through the seasons. They measured the annual rate of melt. They drove stakes across the glacier to gauge the speed at which it moved. They poured coloured water onto its surface and dug holes into crevasse walls to see how quickly the dye found its way through the glacier's capillary fissures. And during that year and subsequent ones they climbed all the nearby hills – the Jungfrau and the Finsteraarhorn among them – to get a better picture of the dragon they were dealing with.

For five years, winters excepting, Agassiz lived on the ice. The Hôtel des Neuchâtelois drew scientists and tourists from all over Europe, who were each season rewarded by some novel discovery. In 1841, for example, Agassiz decided to drill down to the bottom of the glacier in order to study striations in the ice. These layers, alternating between clear frozen blue and a frothy white filled with air bubbles, had been brought to his attention by James Forbes, an Edinburgh professor who had visited the Hôtel that August. They were a puzzle that Agassiz wanted to solve. Accordingly, the bore having been sunk, he went down it sitting on a narrow length of plank roped to a tripod above. Desor directed operations, leaning over the hole to catch Agassiz's instructions as they echoed up the shaft. At 80 feet Agassiz encountered a block of ice that divided the shaft into two channels, one wide and one narrow. He chose the wider opening only to find himself faced with a maze of tunnels that led into the very bowels of the glacier. Shouting up to Desor, he was hauled back to the split and then lowered into the narrower channel. Down he went, on his board, past insecure stalactites of ice that theatened at any moment to fall on his head. The layers grew less and less distinct and he was so involved with them that he did not notice, until he was at a depth of 125 feet, that his legs were in freezing water. He yelled up to Desor who mistook his instructions and let out more rope. It took a second cry before Agassiz was rescued, sodden and freezing, from his hole. This was the most dangerous experiment Agassiz ever attempted and one that he described as 'a descent to hell'. He swore never to repeat it: 'Had I known all its dangers perhaps I should not have started on such an adventure. Certainly, unless induced by some powerful scientific motive, I should not advise any one to follow my example.'[19]

Michael Faraday, the electrical pioneer, came to see Agassiz at work, but had no heart for the ice and got no farther than Grimsel. The teacher Rudolf Töpffer was also deterred by the glacier but he met Desor at Grimsel and wrote excitedly that 'they are sinking a pit already 60 feet deep: that glaciers have fleas of their own, like cooks and dogs: and that red snow owes its colour to insects with crimson stomachs'.[20] (Nicolet had indeed found a species of insect that he named the glacier flea; the red snow, however, was caused by microscopic plant life.) More daring were two young British lords, who reached the Hôtel with the intention of using it as a shooting box, and Mr and Mrs Cowan of Edinburgh who arrived in a sedan chair with eleven guides under the impression that the Hôtel really was a hotel. The most important visitor of that season, however, was James Forbes, who was making his own scientific tour of the Alps.

'I here willingly record that I shall never forget the charm of those savage scenes,' Forbes wrote of his stay at the Hôtel. 'The varying effects of sunshine, cloud, and a storm upon the sky, the mountains, and the glacier; the rosy tints of sunset, the cold hues of moonlight, on a scene which included no trace of animation, and of which our party were the sole spectators.'[21] Himself a glacial expert of some standing, he was professionally at odds with Agassiz and stated that 'a multitude of interesting facts had hitherto been overlooked by me . . . Animated and always friendly discussions were the result; and, without admitting in every case the deductions of my zealous and energetic instructor, I readily allowed their ingenuity.'[22] This was a tactful way of saying that a scientific squabble was brewing. For the moment, however, Forbes was enjoying himself too much to develop the matter. The scenery was beautiful, there were endless new things to study, the company was good and he smoked the first cigar of his life.

The weather was generally fine, and if a storm blew up they simply repaired to the hospice at Grimsel and contined their discussions around a roaring fire. On one such occasion Forbes wrote a brief portrait of the group:

M. Agassiz, cheerful, kind, and frank, not much disposed to active exertion within doors, but always ready to contribute to the cheerful companionship of a party, the chief of which he justly considers himself. Dr. Voght, a laughter-loving, and withal shrewd young man of twenty-three, a true German in complexion, phlegm and habits . . . M. Desor, a Frenchman by birth . . . and the journalist of the expedition: like all journalists placed in rather a difficult and dubious position, from which even a certain share of natural quickness and French vivacity did not serve wholly to extricate him. M. Burckhardt, the artist of our Agassian Club, a shrewd sensible man with a sly smile and some dry humour, often successfully used in rebutting the sallies of M. Desor.[23]

At times the hospice bulged with thirty or forty guests, but 'all went

on smoothly, cheerfully and without annoyance or a single unkind or
hasty word . . . Many and pleasant were the evenings we thus spent!'[24]
Forbes arrived at the Hôtel on 8 August and after a fortnight of scientific heaven he regretfully announced that he would have to
continue his tour. He had several other glaciers to explore and the
season was drawing to a close. Full of bonhomie, Agassiz said he
would accompany him part of the way – and why not climb the
Jungfrau while they were at it?

The chain of mountains at the foot of which the Hôtel des
Neuchâtelois lay was renowned not only for its beauty but its impen-
etrability. The north faces of peaks such as the Finsteraarhorn, the
Eiger and the Jungfrau comprised cliffs of granite. To the south, however, they shed glaciers that could be climbed in the traditional
fashion with ropes, crampons and ladders. Of all these hills the
Jungfrau was deemed the most aesthetically pleasing. It was also the
most contentious. It had first been climbed in 1811 by members of
the local Meyer family. Nobody believed they had done it and so
they repeated the climb in 1812 and this time planted a flag on the
top which was seen from all around. Still people did not believe them,
and the guides said that if a flag happened to have been spied from
below, and if it was on the summit, then it had been planted by them
and not the Meyers. From this confusing record, and the fact that in
1828 a scientist named Baumann reached the top without controversy, it can be seen that the Jungfrau's conquest was awarded on a
rather arbitrary basis.

Forbes and Agassiz, who took their own guides, had a hard journey
ahead of them. It involved a twelve-hour hike across several glaciers
before they were even in a position to start the ascent. Success rested
on picking up a ladder for crossing crevasses, which had been hidden at
Märjelen, at the base of the Jungfrau, by an expedition of 1832. Forbes
was physically in bad shape, having sprained his ankle when he slipped
into a crevasse a week before. They set off from Grimsel at 5.00 a.m. on
27 August 1841, to Forbes's mingled delight and apprehension.

As we walked down the slope from the hospice, the less bright stars were vanishing before the dawn, and we thought the situation had never before appeared half so romantic. Scarce a word passed in our numerous company for two hours . . . Each was occupied with his own thoughts of how the expedition might end – which of the objects proposed he might attain – and probably all felt that they were engaging in an enterprise of some danger as well as labour, voluntarily, and on their individual responsibility – a thought which affects for a moment even the most volatile.[25]

The party of twelve – six guides and six scientists – marched through rock, snow and ice, each different terrain leaving its impression in Forbes's journal. He was particularly impressed by the Vietsch Glacier, of which he wrote: 'Red snow was here very abundant; its colour comes out by trampling; our course was marked by footsteps of blood.'[26] On reaching their base camp at the chalets of Märjelen they found the ladder had been stolen so a guide was despatched to the valley to recover it. He returned empty-handed and was sent back with such a barrage of threats that the thief returned the stolen property and they were able to continue. The ladder was 24 feet long and the guide handled it single-handedly with an ease that astonished them. Taking advantage of the delay to sleep for a full twelve hours, they set out again at 6.00 on the morning of 28 August.

The Jungfrau has two main peaks, one a few feet higher than the other. It was the lower of the two that Forbes and Agassiz were aiming for. It was an unexceptional climb save that at the top of the last glacier they met a crevasse of unfathomable depth, over which bulged a near-vertical slope of ice leading to the lower summit. The ladder came into play. Its 24-foot length was just enough to bridge the gap and the guides scrambled up it to chip footholds in the ice above. They then drove an alpenstock into the slope and roped it to the ladder, thereby forming a makeshift balustrade. Even with this aid, however, the prospect of climbing such a terrifying cliff was too much for some. Four of the party refused point blank to attempt it, leaving Forbes, Agassiz, Desor, and five others to continue on their own.

Suddenly, the climb changed character. This was no stolid progression in the Mont Blanc mould, in which tents, barometers and food enough to feed an army were the norm. Instead, it was a perilous hack up inclines that were never less than 43° and sometimes as steep as 60° in which there was only the individual and the mountain. The scientists acquitted themselves respectably, but the experience unnerved them. As Forbes pecked his way up the slope, following the steps which the guides had cut, and constantly aware of the drop below him, he started to despair. 'Our position seemed rather frightful, hanging thus on a slope of unbroken slippery ice, steep as a cathedral roof . . . with precipices at the bottom of the slope of an unknown and dizzy depth.'[27] The higher they climbed the more frightful it seemed. 'We were surrounded with mist,' Forbes wrote, 'so that we occasionally only saw our immediate position, suspended thus, in the middle of the frozen mountain, from which it really appeared as if a gust of wind might have detached our whole party.'[28] When they reached the lower summit an even ghastlier prospect awaited them. To reach the top, to get that little bit higher, they had to cross a long ridge of snow. The ridge was the stuff of nightmares, a knife-edge that dropped hundreds of feet to cliffs on either side. Very carefully, the chief guide lowered himself belly-first onto it and dug his alpenstock into one side; then, teetering on the brink, he dug footholds on the other side. In this manner he slowly inched his way across, and equally slowly his charges followed him.

They finally reached the summit at 4.00 p.m. on 28 August. It was so giddying as to take their breath away. The Jungfrau was not like Mont Blanc, where tens of people could loiter with their scientific instruments – which, interestingly, Agassiz and Forbes had not taken, save for a thermometer. It was a true pinnacle, so pointy as to be near unsurmountable. It was, 'in form almost like a bee-hive of snow piled up, and so small that even when smoothed over and trodden down, scarcely afforded footing for more than one person at a time'.[29] They had to be helped up by their guide, one by one, in order to savour their achievement. The mist had now vanished and the view was magnificent. 'I remained but a few minutes on the summit,' wrote

Desor, 'but it was long enough to make me certain that the view from the Jungfrau would never fade from my memory. After having carefully inspected the most striking aspects of this unique landscape, I hastened towards Agassiz, for I rather dreaded that such an overwhelming emotion would deprive me of my usual composure and I needed to feel the grasp of a friend's hand . . . I think we should both have wept, had we not felt shy.'[30] What awed Forbes more even than the view was the looming presence to one side of a gigantic pile of cumulus, fully 10,000 feet high, whose top was 2,000 feet above their own position. He had never been this close to a cloud, and as it moved closer he swore that he could see crystals of ice glittering in its depths.

They planted a flag, and stayed there for half an hour, despite a thermometer that read 6°F below freezing. Then they began their descent. Back they went over the terrifying ridge, the equally terrifying ice slope and the ladder beneath it. During this time they enjoyed full sunshine. But once they rejoined their companions, night had fallen. Roped together, on the guides' insistence, they made their way through the glaciers by moonlight. In the early hours they heard a distant yodel from across the mountainside. It was a farmer who had been sent up to save them with a bucket of warm milk. The milk was by now cold, but they lapped it up all the same and then 'pursued our way unbound down the glacier with great elasticity, by a splendid moonlight brilliancy, reflected by the crystallised surface of the ice'.[31]

They reached Märjelen at 11.30 p.m. They had been walking and climbing for seventeen and a half hours without rest but were 'by no means over-fatigued'.[32] As for Forbes's twisted ankle: 'I will only add here that the ascent of the Jungfrau proved a sovereign remedy for the sprain.'[33] These extraordinary statements might seem an exaggeration were it not for the fact that they all rose early the following morning, Forbes to spend fourteen days at the north foot of Monte Rosa and Agassiz to walk back to Unteraar with his friends. Their ascent had a sour coda. In 1843 Forbes revisited the region and heard the climb being discussed in an inn. In traditional Jungfrau fashion, everybody agreed that he had not reached the top.

Meanwhile, Agassiz's glacial theories were gaining ground. 'You have made all the geologists glacier-mad around here,' wrote a British marine biologist, 'and they are turning Great Britain into an ice-house. Some amusing and very absurd attempts at opposition to your views have been made by one or two pseudo-geologists.'[34] That year Agassiz went on what he called a 'glacier hunt' through Scotland, North Wales and the north of England, and at every turn he found ancient moraines that proved his point. Charles Darwin, whose theories on evolution would soon become current, was deeply impressed. On visiting several specimens of what he called 'extinct glaciers' he announced that 'they have given me more delight than I almost remember to have experienced since I first saw an extinct volcano'.[35]

In 1842 Agassiz's Hôtel began to disintegrate so he moved into a three-room cabin, framed in wood and covered by canvas. One room was set aside for his guides, another for himself and his friends, and the third was used as a dining room, sitting room and laboratory. There were shelves for books, pegs for coats, a table, two benches and a couple of chairs for any important guests who might stop by. They nicknamed it 'The Ark'. Settled in these relatively comfortable quarters, Agassiz made a number of novel observations. Seeing the way the ice sometimes cracked in crescents, the bulge of which pointed uphill, he came to the conclusion that glaciers moved faster at their sides than at the centre. He also expanded upon a theory of glacial movement which had first been suggested by Scheuchzer – the so-called dilatation theory. According to Agassiz, glaciers remained dormant in winter and then sprang into action during the summer months when they began to melt. The surface water flowed into capillary fissures within the glacier and then froze at night. As the water turned to ice it expanded; and in doing so it squeezed the glacier downhill. He had proof that these capillary fissures existed because he had tested them the previous year with Forbes. They had dug a hole into the side of a crevasse and then poured dye onto the surface above. It wasn't actually dye because they had none, but Agassiz had sacrificed a couple of bottles of wine for the experiment, and it seemed to do the job, trickling obligingly onto the heads of the observers below.

Agassiz also wanted to witness the creation of a crevasse. He was rewarded on the afternoon of 7 August 1842.

> I heard at a little distance a sound like the simultaneous discharge of fire-arms; hurrying in the direction of the noise, it was repeated under my feet with a movement like that of a slight earthquake; the ground seemed to shift and give way under me, but now the sound differed from the preceding, and resembled a crumbling of rocks, without, however, any perceptible sinking of the surface. The glacier actually trembled, nevertheless, for a block of granite three feet in diameter perched on a pedestal two feet high, suddenly fell down. At the same instant a crack opened between my feet and ran rapidly across the glacier in a straight line.[36]

He saw three more such cracks form in the next hour and a half and heard others elsewhere. By the time he went to bed eight new fissures had opened within a space of 125 feet and the splintering continued throughout the night. None of the infant crevasses was more than half an inch wide, but Agassiz reckoned they must be uncommonly deep because they drained a water-filled borehole that was 130 feet deep and six inches in diameter in a matter of minutes.

Agassiz also turned his attention to less dramatic concerns, such as the number of inexplicable half-moon depressions, or meridian holes, that covered the glacier. They invariably faced south, had a steep wall of ice at their upper side, a shallow one at the other, and contained a little heap of debris. After long examination he concluded that they were caused by small collections of dirt that had fallen onto the glacier and had then been warmed by the sun. Dark matter attracted heat, and as the sun was low in the morning, high at midday and low at dusk, the dirt would attract heat in similar measure. The resulting holes were, as Agassiz described them, 'the sun-dials of the glacier'.

In all, 1842 was an exciting year for Agassiz and his team. They watched an eclipse of the sun from the summit of the Siedelhorn.

They made an excursion to Nagerlisgratli and picked up several relics of the battle that had been fought there during the Napoleonic Wars. Desor climbed the Lauteraarhorn and another visitor, Johann Sulger, climbed the Finsteraarhorn. (Agassiz did not accompany them; after his previous exploits his mother had made him promise to abstain from further stunts.) The season ended on a high note. Several workmen had been employed to bore shafts through the ice and before they left they asked permission to bring some friends up to the ice. The guests arrived on a Saturday, and were forced by bad weather to spend the night. On Sunday, since there were so many people, Agassiz decided to hold a ball. A fiddler and a dulcimer player were hired from Oberwald, and from their arrival after Sunday Mass the musicians played their fingers out while the scientists, the guides, the workmen and their guests cavorted on the glacier. The dance floor was uneven, the musicians were mediocre, but when the party ended at sundown Desor announced he had never had a better time in his life.

By 1843 Agassiz's keenness for ice work was wearing a little thin. The romantic Hôtel was gone; the cold was tiresome; and the diet was so unhealthy that he was in real danger of contracting scurvy. 'The greatest privation is the lack of fruit and vegetables,' he wrote to his friend the Prince of Canino. 'Hardly a potato once a fortnight, but always and every day, morning and night, mutton everlasting mutton, and rice soup . . . What a contrast between this life and that of the plain.'[37] In 1843 Agassiz spent less time than usual on the glacier – though the season was not without its moments: they made a nocturnal investigation of a glacial cave, lighting their way with a bowl of flaming eau de cologne; they slid down the glacier on a ladder, stopping at first at crevasses but, on finding that the ladder could leap over them, they tobogganed mercilessly; and Desor climbed more peaks while Agassiz remained obediently below. In 1844 Agassiz did not visit Unteraar at all, relying on others to take measurements and send their reports back to Neuchâtel. In 1845 a M. Dollfus-Ausset built his own hut on the glacier and the Neuchâtelois became his guests. In defiance of his mother Agassiz climbed the Wetterhorn, and Desor made the first ascent of the Galenstock. That was Agassiz's last season on the ice. In 1846 he abandoned the Alps altogether for a more comfortable existence in America. He left behind him one of the most solid blocks of glacial research to date. He carried with him, however, the knowledge that almost every conclusion to which his research had led him was wrong. For this he was indebted to his friend, Professor James Forbes.

CHAPTER TEN

James Forbes was a strange, mercurial man. Born in Edinburgh on 20 April 1809 into a patrician Scottish family, he was, like Agassiz, largely self-taught. Unlike Agassiz, however, he was dour, humourless and fixated. His father had died when he was in his teens, leaving him with a desperate urge to get on in life. Forbes did so thanks to his connections and his intelligence. He published his first scientific paper – on Vesuvius – anonymously, when he was only 19, and followed it with 148 others whose topics ranged from the study of a single boulder in the Pentland Hills to the entire mountain chain of the Alps. He investigated solar rays, magnetic variations, the temperature of hot springs, the colours of the sky, the colours of steam and the colours of dewdrops. He looked into heat, mirages and atmospheric refraction. In 1832 he wrote 'Notice respecting a Vitrified Fort at Carradale in Argyllshire'. In 1833 he lectured on Alpine views. In 1834 he wrote 'On the Horary Oscillations of the Barometer near Edinburgh, deduced from 4,410 Observations', and in the same year spoke about sparks from magnets and delivered an early analysis of ultraviolet rays, following these the next year with a paper on hydraulics which was only a stopgap before he published, in 1836, the results of his experiments on 'The Electricity of Tourmaline and other Minerals when exposed to Heat'. When nothing new came to light, he told people how he hadn't discovered it. 'On the muscular Effort required to ascend Planes of different Inclinations' appeared in the April 1837 edition of the *Philosophical Magazine*.

Forbes was a man of many parts, but he bore them heavily and impatiently. He was unwell for most of his life and in 1839 wrote that 'I yearly feel a greater readiness to die.'[1] What he wanted was to get the job done, and to do it as accurately and as conclusively as was possible in the time he had left. According to one of his relatives, 'he seemed a man too much on the stretch'.[2] This was true. His writings portray him as a Calvinistic figure with little time for anything that was not immediately connected with the task in hand. Science was his life, and he pursued it with a grim and single-minded determination. He did, however, have one solace: the Alps. He had first visited them aged 18 and since then had traversed them widely, finding in their granite solitude the material to satisfy both his intellectual and emotional needs.

'I have crossed the principal chain of Alps twenty seven times, generally on foot, by twenty three different passes,' he wrote in 1843. 'I employed neither draughtsman, surveyor or naturalist; everything that it was possible to do I executed with my own hands, noted the result on the spot, and extended it as speedily as possible afterwards.'[3] Saussure was his hero. Like him he made it a habit to record his impressions immediately in a notebook – use an ineradicable pencil, he warned his readers sternly – before writing them out in full at a later date. Like Saussure, too, he never went anywhere without his geologist's hammer, though in Forbes's case the point was sharpened so that he could use it as an ice axe in case he fell down a crevasse. The only point in which he differed from Saussure was as an employer. He derided the 'uselessness and inconvenience' of large bodies of guides and took only one, or sometimes two, on his journeys. Even this number he sometimes found excessive, particularly at inns, where their 'love of indulgence' coupled to the 'systematic extortion' of the innkeepers caused him unnecessary expense. Let the guides pay for their own board, he grumbled ungenerously.

Forbes detested ordinary Alpine travellers and wrote ascerbically of 'those beaten tracts, along which tourists follow one another, like a flock of sheep, in interminable succession'.[4] In his opinion their outings were 'miracles of rapidity and boldness, from which, if anything were gained, it must have been from a sort of intuition'.[5] What he advocated was a solitary commune with nature in which the individual could revel in his surroundings and then – tellingly – conquer them. 'Happy the traveller,' he wrote, 'who, content to leave to others the glory of counting the thousands of leagues of earth and ocean they have left behind them, established in some mountain shelter with his books, starts his first day's walk amongst the Alps in the tranquil morning of a long July day, brushing the early dew before him, and, armed with his staff makes for the hilltop . . . whence he sees the field of his summer's campaign spread out before him, its wonders, its beauties and its difficulties, to be explained, to be admired, and to be overcome.'[6]

Apart from Saussure – and Professor Playfair, under whom he had studied – Forbes had little time for scientists of the past. He took particular exception to Bourrit – who had pretended many things, but never that he was a scientist – and wrote uncharitably that 'he conveys the simplest fact through a medium of such unmixed bombast as to disgust the reader'.[7] As for everybody else, he dismissed them with a monstrously sweeping judgement: 'It seems very singular that ingenious men, with every facility for establishing themselves, should have relied on conclusions vaguely gathered from uncertain data, or on the hazarded assertions of the peasantry about matters in which they take not the slightest interest.'[8] He had little time for scientists of the present either. In fact he had little time for anybody who did not think and act as he did, and by 1843 he had very little time for Agassiz and his team. It was all very well to play about with rock bivouacs, he wrote, but, 'however amusing such privations are for a time, and however pleasant it may be to laugh over them in good company, such expeditions tend rather to amusement than edification'.[9]

What had happened since 1841 to turn him against Agassiz? It was the ice. When Forbes had pointed out to Agassiz the blue and white striations in the glacier, Agassiz had been taken aback and had said that he had not noticed them before. Shortly afterwards he said that he had noticed them the previous year but was convinced they were mere surface phenomena. Forbes thought differently that they were the very structure of the glacier and was writing up his conclusions in 1841 when Agassiz published a letter to Humboldt in which he described his, Agassiz's, amazing discovery of the alternating ice layers.

Thus began an unimportant but, to Forbes, hugely imperative argument. Who had seen the ice layers first? In the ensuing correspondence, which was published in the *Edinburgh Philosophical Review* and elsewhere, Forbes teetered on slander as he denigrated first Agassiz and then Desor. Agassiz stated that he had previously seen the striations on the Mer de Glace back in 1838. Forbes gathered affidavits to prove this a lie. Agassiz said he had seen them the year before on the Unteraar Glacier, but hadn't understood their importance until 1841. Forbes said this was piffle. Finally, Agassiz gave in and said that his colleague, Arnold Guyot, had first observed them in 1838; but had not he, Agassiz, gone further towards investigating them than anybody else? Forbes said this was entirely by the by. Guyot may have seen the striations – he had – but he had not published the fact and so he, Forbes, was the first person to have publicly announced their presence.

'The dilemma in which M. Agassiz has placed himself,' Forbes wrote to Guyot, 'appears to be this: Either he was acquainted with this structure of the ice on the 9th of August or he was not. If he was not acquainted with it, he learned it from me; for he has never attempted to maintain he showed it to me. If he was acquainted with it he learned it from you. And if he learned it from either of us, how does he claim it as his own in the letter to Humboldt, and in one other private letter at least, not yet published?'[10] The cheerful, optimistic Agassiz was at a loss. He was an intuitive scientist, whose world was smaller, gentler and more gentlemanly than that of Forbes. He probably had no idea that he would cause offence by incorporating Forbes's remarks on the ice into his own annual report. The Unteraar Glacier was Agassiz's private experiment, so surely he had some sovereignty over chance remarks made by guests who came to increase their knowledge at his expense. Had the observation been made by someone he knew – a Swiss, a German or a Frenchman – the business might have been smoothed over quickly and without fuss. Unfortunately, it had been Forbes, and Agassiz was no match for his relentless, granite-like character.

Through the winter and spring of 1842, letters sputtered to and fro, each one leaving Forbes increasingly incensed. That summer he decided to settle it once and for all. Packing a bundle of red and white flags, cans of red and white paint, stakes, brushes and every piece of surveying equipment known to humankind, he departed for Chamonix's Mer de Glace. By this time, Bourrit's Temple had been augmented by a nicely appointed two-storey refuge. It had a large main room, a small kitchen and three bedrooms, below which were quarters for the three servants who lived there for four months of the year. There was only mutton to eat, but otherwise it was all very comfortable and Forbes installed himself in it with much sneering at Agassiz's rough and ready accommodation. (The mutton was excellent, he said, twisting the knife.) Then, with the aid of just one guide, Auguste Balmat, he proceeded to chart the glacier with unprecedented thoroughness. For ten to thirteen hours per day he stalked the ice, planting flags, painting rocks and triangulating their positions. Before long Mont Blanc's hinterland looked like a blasting zone.

Clad in a thin layer of flannels, topped by a suit of chamois leather and wearing a straw hat underneath which lay a velvet cap – or a fur cap if he had to stand still for too long – Forbes became a veritable ice elf. He eschewed artificial climbing aids – 'Of late years I have never habitually used spikes or crampons of any kind for crossing the ice,'[11] he wrote – and relied solely on a good pair of double-soled London shoes with studs. When tourists caught him unawares he sprang to safety over the glacier, picking his way through the crevasses as if he was born to them. The sight must have been arresting, especially in cold weather, when he wrapped himself in a thick Scottish plaid. When the intruders went, he scurried home and wrote up his work in the calm of his cabin. Only once did he have close contact with the public, and that was by accident. On 29 August, while Forbes was squinting through his theodolite, Auguste Balmat arrived in a state of excitement. Accompanying him were two men from Chamonix who supported a dishevelled American tourist between them. The American had apparently been wandering above the Mer de Glace and had slipped, tumbling down a cliff to land on a narrow ledge where he lay for several hours until the two Chamoniards heard his cries. They had been unable to help him until Balmat appeared. Balmat had lowered himself down, grabbed the American's hand and hauled him to safety. The man was a wreck: 'his nervous system was greatly affected,' wrote Forbes, 'and for a time I doubted whether he was not deranged'.[12] He sent the American down to Chamonix where, on recovering from his ordeal, the man promptly fled the town. 'I regretted to learn afterwards that he had not shown himself generously sensible of the great effort used in his preservation,'[13] Forbes recorded.

The next day Forbes visited the shelf from which the American had been rescued and was shocked. The man had fallen from the top of a 210-foot-high precipice. It was sheer and polished save for a tiny ledge, 20 feet down, that was 1 foot wide and a few feet more in length. At one end the ledge narrowed into the cliff and at the other it widened to meet a ten-foot buttress. It was studded with stones and there were one or two juniper bushes whose branches bore scraps of the American's clothes. Below, the glacier was waiting to mangle him; above was a slope 'to which a cat could not have clung'. He would have died on that lonely shelf, salvation tantalisingly beyond his reach, had it not been for the chance passing of the two Chamonix men and Balmat. 'A more astonishing escape, in all its parts, it is impossible to conceive,'[14] wrote Forbes.

He continued his experiments until the end of September when, with the thermometer registering only 6°F above freezing – and that was in his bedroom – he concluded that he done his job. Over the winter he wrote up his findings, made a quick visit to Chamonix to confirm them and then in 1843 published *Travels through the Alps of Savoy*, in which he gave the most comprehensive and accurate account of glacial movement and formation to date. He reported that glaciers moved faster at the centre than at the sides, that they moved by night as well as day and in winter as well as summer. He reported that the striations were caused at the head of the glacier, where cracks in the permanently frozen snow – firn or névé – were filled by melt-water that turned to ice in winter. Above all, he reported that Agassiz was wrong. Glaciers did not move by dilatation. If they did, then objects on their surface would move apart. According to his measurements this did not happen. Moreover, he had found it repeatedly the case that even if the surface water froze in bad weather, the summer melt continued below. Therefore, if the water did not freeze in the fissures, it could not expand.

Having crushed Agassiz completely, he then explained why glaciers did move. They moved because they were plastic: despite their apparent solidity they flowed in the same manner as water, only much more slowly. To prove his point he showed readers how to create their own personal glacier at home by mixing plaster of Paris with glue (to stop it setting) and then pouring the mixture into an inclined trough. Those who followed his instructions – Forbes helpfully supplied diagrams – found that they worked perfectly. And if they sprinkled lines of coloured powder across their 'glacier' they could see the different speeds at which sides and centre progressed.

The home-made glaciers were a masterly conclusion to an irrefutable theory which still holds true today. When Forbes's book came out the scientific community was agog.* Little wonder, then, that Agassiz cut short his 1843 season and did not visit Unteraar at all in 1844. His biographer claims that during this period he shut himself in his study, staying up well past midnight in order to transcribe his discoveries. But one gets a dreadful image of a man covered in plaster dust and glue, watching in misery as, by candlelight, his 'glacier' inched flawlessly to its conclusion. His own countrymen began to

---

*It must be said, however, that when Forbes lectured at the British Association for the Advancement of Science in 1844, his audience was far more taken by one Dr Hodgkin's paper on 'The Dog as Companion to Man'. The *Illustrated London News* squeezed Forbes's findings into a narrow column illustrated with pictures of a bulldog, a husky and a Dalmation.

mock him. 'It is now much the fashion to visit the . . . glacier of the Aar, and a great noise is made about it,' wrote one Professor Chaix. 'Mr. Forbes is a very bold and indefatigable explorer, and not many will dare to follow him everywhere he has been.'[15] Worst of all, Agassiz's own men at Unteraar sent back reports that year that Forbes's theory was undoubtedly correct. So it was not surprising that he climbed into his coach in the early hours of a March morning in 1846, bade farewell to his students – they had come out with torches to see him off – and clattered off for the uncontroversial promise of America. Forbes had destroyed him in Europe.

Agassiz could, however, take some comfort from a little-advertised fact: Forbes's theory had already been formulated by someone else. In 1838 one Bishop Rendu of Annecy had noticed the ice striations and had come to the conclusion that glaciers moved fastest in the centre and were probably plastic. He had then published his conclusions in 1841, two years before Forbes's own book went to press. Forbes said he hadn't known of Rendu's book, had arrived at the theory independently, had provided better proof and so on. 'M. Rendu had the candour not to treat his ingenious speculations as leading to any certain result,' he wrote, 'not being founded on experiments worthy of confidence.'[16] But Rendu *had* made the theory and Forbes was therefore in the same position as Agassiz: he had claimed precedence where he did not deserve it. This humiliating charge hung over him for more than a decade and became the subject of controversy in 1856. Forbes scribbled away, covering twenty pages of small print with reasons why the theory was his alone. The verdict was decided in his favour – but only just, and only because the adjudicators were British.

By that time Forbes was a sick man. Stricken by gastric fever and an ailment of the lungs, he spat blood. As Principal of St Andrews University in Scotland, he coughed his way through a disciplinarian tenure. On the other side of the Atlantic, Agassiz was in good health, had established himself on the East Coast, had taken a new wife and was planning a trip to Brazil. His father had once described him as having 'a mania for rushing full gallop into the future',[17] and in this case the future was a happy one. He became one of America's most eminent scientists and although he preserved a penchant for taking the wrong side – such as a tortuous attempt to refute Darwin's theories – he was generally hailed as a brilliant addition to the New World intelligentsia.

Forbes was a scientist, and his expeditions were made for scientific purposes. During his travels he did, however, open a whole new area of the Alps to the world. The Dauphiné, or Massif des Ecrins, was a virtually unexplored sector that lay to the south-west of the Mont Blanc chain. Forbes walked all over it and, in between geological observations, gave his readers the best yet description of life off the beaten track. Not only that, but in his odd, critical way he provided an image of noble savagery better even than Rousseau's. He was fascinated, for example, by the chalets, the rough stone shacks in which cattle-herders lived during the summer months and which were often used as stopovers by climbers such as himself. Each herdsman had two huts, one hut for day and one for night. The day hut was where they made cheese. It had an earth floor, no windows, no chimney and a fireplace in a hole near the door. The only furniture was a one-legged milking stool, the only cooking equipment a wide copper dish in which the milk was heated and the only utensil a six-inch wooden spoon for skimming the milk. 'Morning, noon and night, the inhabitants think but of milk,' Forbes wrote. 'It is their first, last and only care; they eat exclusively preparations of it; their only companions are the cattle which yield it; money can procure for them *here* no luxuries; they count their wealth by cheeses.'[18] Next door was a night hut, that again had neither chimney or window; nor did it have a fire. What it did have was a door, three feet high, through which travellers crawled to make their bed on a pile of grass, covering themselves with a blanket of hay.

Forbes was overcome. The chalets were picturesque beyond his imagination – noticeably, there was no sneering about lack of comforts – and when he emerged in the mornings he was greeted by the sight of several hundred cows tethered on a terrace, being milked by their owners. Here was the isolated existence he hankered after.

'There is an indescribable unity and monotony of idea which fills the minds of these men,' he wrote of his hosts, 'who live during all of the finest and stirring part of the year in the fastnesses of their sublimest mountains, seeing scarcely any strange faces, and but few familiar ones, and these always the same; living on friendly terms with their dumb herds, so accustomed to privation as to dream of no luxury, and utterly careless of the fate of empires, or the change of dynasties.'[19] He found them shy, gentle and impeccably mannered.

The purity of these people was reinforced for him by his encounters with civilisation. In the valley of Evolène he met villagers so rude and inhospitable that he could only agree with historians that they were a sept of Hun, who had been stranded there in the fifth century. On a high pass he encountered a couple of Piedmontese customs officers, huddling in a shelter.

The absolute discomfort in which this class of men live is greater than in almost any other profession. Hard diet, constant exposure, sleepless nights, combined with personal risk, and still more galling unpopularity, great fatigue, and perpetual surveillance, are the ordinary accidents of their life . . . posted for hours together on a glacier 9,000 feet above the sea, and, like animals of prey, taking repose in some deserted hovel in their wet clothes – one cannot but conclude the smuggler's lot to be luxury compared to the protracted sufferings of their detectors.[20]

Man was vile and nature sublime. Forbes saw more spirituality in a glacier than he did in his fellow humans, a view he explained to his readers in a laboured comparison between the movement of ice and the passage of a soul to heaven. He did his best to dispel the idea, so popular in that age of Arctic exploration, that ice was still and deadly. Glaciers had a life of their own: 'All is on the eve of motion. Let him sit awhile, as I did, on the moraine of Miage, and watch the silent energy of the ice and the sun. No animal ever passes but yet the stillness of death is not there; the ice is cracking and straining onwards.'[21] Nature, however, was not consistently sublime, as he was honest enough to admit. He was terrified by rockfalls, which he described as 'dry avalanches . . . the most terrible of the ammunition with which the genius of these mountain solitudes repels the approach of curious man'.[22] He also witnessed, with some awe, the price an Alpine snowstorm could exact on the unwary.

Crossing just one pass Forbes found the corpses of three men in varying stages of decomposition. The freshest was on a slope of scree and lay face down, its hands still in its pockets. It was so well preserved that Forbes thought it must be a recent casualty until he turned it over and saw how its face had been rubbed off as the thaw carried it downhill. The second comprised a little pile of bones surrounding a backpack. The third was the strangest of them all. It lay on a glacier and its flesh had long since vanished. Its skeleton, however, was still intact and was strung out in an extraordinary, yet anatomically correct, fashion: from head to foot it measured five yards. Had Forbes found this earlier he might have been tempted to agree with Agassiz's theory of dilatation. As it was, he was at a loss. He could only put it down to a glacial property that he had yet to fathom.

The experience upset him deeply, and in a rare moment of non-scientific reflection he wrote that 'We surveyed with a stronger sense of sublimity than before the desolation by which we were surrounded and became still more sensible to our isolation from human dwellings, human help, and human sympathy – our loneliness with nature and, as it were, the more immediate presence of God.'[23] Scurrying to the other side of the pass, he learned that a group of twelve had tried to cross it the previous winter and had been driven back by snow, leaving three of their number behind. Two bodies had already been recovered and the survivors were grateful to him for having found the third. They had no clue as to the identity of the other skeletons. Forbes understood completely. 'We are men,' he wrote, 'and we stand in the chamber of death.'[24]

When Forbes's *Travels through the Alps of Savoy* came out in 1843 it caused a stir. First there was his glacier theory, then there was his exploration of the Dauphiné. From Switzerland, Professor Chaix wrote to London's Royal Geographical Society that Forbes's *Travels* was 'by far the best thing that has been written on our Alps either by natives or foreigners. Mr. Forbes has proved himself a worthy successor of Saussure by his modesty, his keenness of observation, his absence of charlatanry, and his laborious researches.'[25] It was true. In his travels and his scientific work, Forbes *was* the spiritual heir of Saussure. Both men were devoted to science and both had incidentally broadened the scope of Alpine exploration. Both, too, were pivotal characters who stood on the brink of a new age. Saussure had set in motion the rush of climbers to Mont Blanc. During the 1850s Forbes prompted a similar wave of explorers. Saussure's disciples had followed his example, taking hordes of guides on their ascents. Forbes's followers approached the hills in a leaner fashion, employing one or two guides and sometimes not even that. A new attitude was afoot.

When Sir John Barrow, father of Arctic exploration and founder of the Royal Geographical Society, read Forbes's book he was excited and angry. The excitement came from the fact that he had another icy world to contend with. The anger came from the fact that this world, so close to home, was still unmapped and was likely to remain so during his lifetime. (He was then 79, and died five years later.) Forbes had acknowledged in his book the merit of a few three-dimensional models made by Exchaquet and others, but he had denigrated in no uncertain terms the Alpine maps that were available. 'Now, it is not creditable to European geographers,' Barrow wrote, 'that at a time when every day adds to our intimate knowledge of the Ural and Caucasus, of the Bolor-tag, the Altai, and the Himmalaya, and of the mountain masses of America, such ignorance and confusion should prevail regarding the mountain mass which may be regarded as the central knot of the upheaving of the European continent.'[26] He was all for further investigation. 'It is in the Alpine regions of Europe that the European geographer . . . can rightly understand and turn to account . . . the important facts gleaned by travellers in more remote regions. The account given by Professor Forbes of the wretchedly deficient knowledge of a portion of the European Alps . . . show[s] that this maxim has been entirely disregarded.'[27] Barrow ended on a strident note: 'It is to be hoped, the ground having been fairly broken for an improved geography of the Alps, that the region will not much longer be allowed to remain a reproach to modern geographical knowledge.'[28]

The Alps would not remain a reproach for long. In the 1850s the Swiss government instigated a thorough topographical survey of the region, its progress being reported to the Royal Geographical Society at regular intervals by Professor Chaix – seemingly a rather obsequious Anglophile. But it was a time-consuming affair and before it was completed several individuals from Britain had already done the job to their own satisfaction. Anyway, even before the survey started, the very notion of such a prosaic venture was being questioned by the century's most prominent aesthete, John Ruskin. Ruskin did not want the Alps to be mapped. He wanted them to be understood.

CHAPTER ELEVEN

It is hard to categorise Ruskin. Born in 1819, the son of a London wine merchant, he was a writer, artist, architect, designer, critic and social opinionator the like of which had never been seen before. He espoused so many different ideas, spanned such a wide field and was so absolute in his judgements that people did not know whether to mock him or stand in awe. Usually they did both. One of Ruskin's most heartfelt beliefs was that humankind had deviated from its natural state. He spoke not as a Luddite but as a reformer, espousing a form of Christian socialiam with a back-to-basics, self-help dogma of the kind that would later be put into practice by the Arts and Crafts movement.

One can see why he felt the way he did. By 1850 industrialism was entrenched in Britain and wherever Ruskin looked he saw evidence of how nature was being degraded. In Lancashire valleys it was impossible to walk 1,000 yards without meeting a mill or furnace. Not only was industrialisation ruining the countryside, it was ruining the very nature of the goods it produced: beer was flavoured with sulphuric acid; white bread contained alum powder; wholemeal bread was adulterated with potatoes, chalk and pipeclay; tea was made from used leaves and hedgerow clippings; pepper was augmented with floor sweepings; and milk was diluted with water. As Ralph

Waldo Emerson wrote in 1856, 'In true England all is faked or forged.'[1]

What Ruskin wanted was a society in which people could make honest, healthy products in an honest, healthy environment. He also believed that the best work – in which he included art – could only be done in surroundings of maximum beauty. His was an economy of aesthetics, and there was no spot in Europe he found so aesthetically pleasing as the Alps. He visited them first in 1832 when he was 13, and continued to do so for much of his life. Mountains, to him, were 'the beginning and end of all natural scenery'.[2] Oddly, though, he rarely climbed them and when he did he restricted himself to passes and the most accessible of low peaks. In 1844 he went up Le Buet with Joseph-Marie Couttet, Dr Hamel's old guide. It was foggy and stormy and he saw nothing of the fabled view. The most memorable moment of the whole day was when Couttet remarked, 'Poor child! He doesn't know how to live!'[3] Ruskin thought he was making a joke but it was, in fact, the truth. In thrall to his domineering parents until he was middle-aged, Ruskin was many things but he was rarely a partaker. He approached the high peaks in the same manner as he did his strange, unconsummated marriage: look but do not touch – according to one biographer, he likened his wife's body to a mountain slope full of terrifying ravines. Understandably, perhaps, his aesthetic economy came to nothing. The Alps remained as they always had been, very beautiful and very poor.

To his credit, however, Ruskin did do a lot of very perceptive looking, even if he preferred his perception to the reality. He painted what he saw, and he wrote about it too, becoming the successor of the Romantics. His influence was enormous and there are few people today who have read of the Alps without being touched in some fashion by Ruskin's works.

Among his many accomplishments Ruskin was an amateur geologist – one of his ambitions was to become president of the Geological Society of London – and he admired the work done by Saussure and Forbes. He met the latter in 1844 when (with his father) he crossed the Simplon Pass. He showed Forbes some sketches he had done of the Matterhorn. 'His eyes grew keen and his face attentive as he examined the drawings,' Ruskin wrote, 'and he turned instantly to me as to a recognised fellow-workman – though yet young, no less faithful than himself. He heard kindly what I had to ask about the chain I had been drawing; only saying with a slightly proud smile, of my peak supposed to be the Matterhorn: "No, and when once you have seen the Matterhorn, you will never take anything else for it!" He told me as much as I was able to learn at that time . . . but I knew nothing of glaciers then, and he had his evening's work to finish. And I never saw him again.'[4] Ruskin was eternally proud of this interview and became in later years a fervent supporter of Forbes. But he was less generous to other geologists. In his view the Alps 'formed a background not merely to one particular set of experiments but to all worthwhile existence'.[5] He disapproved of 'those worthless and ugly bits of chucky stones which, dignified by the name of "specimens", become in the eyes of a certain class of people, of such inestimable value',[6] and he could not understand how men could be so single-minded in their appreciation of landscape. 'Many an Alpine traveller, many a busy man of science, volubly represent to us their pleasures in the Alps,' he wrote, 'but I scarcely recognise one who would not willingly see them all ground down into gravel, on his being the first to exhibit a pebble of it at the Royal Institution.'[7] He satirised them in a semi-fictitious encounter between two Englishmen:

A few rosy clouds were scattered on the heaven, or wrapped about their bases, but their summits rose pure and glorious, just beginning to get rosy in the afternoon sun and here and there a red peak of bare rock rose up into the blue out of the snowy mantle.

'How beautiful,' I said to my companion, 'those peaks of rock rise into the heavens like promontories running out into the deep blue of some transparent ocean.'

'Ah – yes, brown, limestone – strata vertical, or nearly so, dip eight-five and a half,' replied the geologist.[8]

It was not an inaccurate picture – though few geologists went so far as Ruskin, who was portrayed chipping specimens from gravestones. It must be said, however, that the scientists whom Ruskin abhorred had a much closer acquaintance with the Alps than he did himself. True, they did not 'love crag and glacier for their own sake's sake [or] . . . question their secrets in reverend and solemn thirst',[9] but they did actually climb mountains. Ruskin did nothing of the sort. In 1858 he spent whole weeks in Turin, reporting to his father on the various moods the Alps presented, cursing when they were obscured by cloud, rhapsodising when he could see their tops and being transformed when the range showed itself in its entirety. Later he would inspect them at close quarters but shrank from climbing them. When he visited Chamonix in 1859 he paid more attention to a ghost that was rumoured to live in the woods, and a story of buried treasure, than he did to Mont Blanc. (The ghost proved illusory and when he used divining rods to find the treasure his excavations unearthed nothing but an old key.) He did climb a few passes but found them disappointing – 'I thought the top of the St. Gotthard very dull and stupid.'[10] His happiest moments were when he could stand on the flat and take in the scenery around. From Chamonix he calibrated some twenty pleasing lines on the Aiguille Blaitière. He categorised them alphabetically, line a–b running across the top of the hillside – 'the most beautiful single curve I have ever seen in my life'[11] – and so on until he reached lines s–t and u–w which were mere flat-chested bulges at an indistinct point on the lower slopes.

Ultimately, Ruskin was a ground-level man. 'All the best views of hills are at the bottom of them,'[12] he wrote. Everything that was worthwhile in the Alps should be available, in his opinion, to everybody. As he explained: 'the real beauty of the Alps is to be seen, and seen only, where all may see it, the child, the cripple, and the man of grey hairs'.[13] Hundreds of Britons agreed with him, migrating south in the summer to visit Chamonix's Mer de Glace on a mule, traverse the lower slopes of the Glacier des Bossons with a guide – in exactly the same manner as tourists had done in Saussure's time – to stare at the peaks and then to go home with the news that they had done the

Alps. An equal number, however, went to the mountains for higher purposes. For them Ruskin had made the Alps the embodiment of the sublime.

Ruskin's thoughts on the Alps gestated over a long period and were brought to the public in *Modern Painters*, a five-volume work whose publication was spread between 1843 and 1860. Its message was that of insight. 'The greatest thing a human soul ever does in this world is to *see* something, and tell what it *saw* in a plain way. Hundreds of people can talk for one who can think, but thousands can think for one who can see. To see clearly is poetry, prophecy and religion – all in one.'[14] Ruskin reckoned that Turner had been a man with insight and his advocacy of the painter's vision was passionate. He had a premonition that all the worthwhile things that were to be seen in nature – in which he included the Alps – would very soon be gone, either swept away by industry or contaminated by materialism. He did not subscribe to dragons, witches and demons – well, not publicly: his search for the Chamonix ghost was only mentioned in his wife's diaries – but he did find a spiritual element in the Alps and all other mountains which was no longer to be found in more accessible areas. He implored and, at times, commanded people to make the most of what they had while it was still there.

This was fighting talk in mid-nineteenth century Britain, whose industry and ingenuity brought 'improvements' by the day. Writing in the *Quarterly Review*, Lady Eastlake condemned *Modern Painters* for its 'false assumptions, futile speculations, contradictory argument, crotchety views and romantic rubbish'.[15] Ruskin did not care. He was contradictory, he was crotchety and at times he may have been more romantic than was currently fashionable. But his assumptions and speculations were valid and he pressed them to the hilt. Presciently, he felt he was working against time. Could people see before it was too late? So many things had already been tarred with the brush of progress. Would the little that survived be worth seeing in a few years? Would it, like real beer, real bread, real milk, real tea and the real Lancashire valleys, be consigned to history? What part did truth – of any sort, other than that of profit – play in modern society?

Ruskin fountained his opinions indiscriminately, personally and rudely. On one occasion he had to defend them in court. His values, however, remained sacrosanct and he refused to deviate from them, particularly when it came to the Alps. His writings, combined with those of the Romantic poets before him – for whom he acted, in a way, as interpreter – inspired people to think of mountains in semi-religious, transcendent terms. Any rugged rock would do for his acolytes. They found solace in Wales's Snowdonia, England's Lake District and, to a lesser extent (because farther away), the Scottish Highlands. The Pyrenees and the Eastern Alps in due course entered the sphere of Ruskin's high priestdom. But it was the Central Alps, from Mont Blanc in the west, to the Wetterhorn in the east and the Matterhorn in the south, on which he spread his altar cloth. This region which had been an obstacle to early pilgrims now became an object of pilgrimage in itself. Writers and painters sought inspiration there. Mendelssohn, Liszt and Wagner composed in the shadow of the hills. 'Let me create more works like those I conceived in that serene and glorious Switzerland, with my eyes on the beautiful gold-crowned mountains,' wrote Wagner in 1859, having just included alphorns in the score for *Tristan und Isolde*. 'They are masterpieces and nowhere else could I have conceived them.'[16] Ruskin influenced Christians, agnostics and explorers alike. Sir Leslie Stephen, who was at various times all three, fell under the Alpine spell, 'woven in a great degree by the eloquence of *Modern Painters*'.

Adults of the time and schoolchildren of all subsequent generations felt the blast of Ruskin's rhetoric. As the Alpine historian Ronald Clark has said, 'He wrote copiously, at times pompously, at times magnificently, but across whole oceans of prose there sails the message that mountains provide fine, uplifting, thought-provoking sights. For nearly half a century Ruskin used this message to erode the slowly disappearing belief that mountain areas were areas of horror and ugliness and danger. For that, all men are perpetually in his debt.'[17]

Ruskin's message did get through and it did drive men and women to the Alps. When they got there, however, some tended to forget

Two of Scheuchzer's dragons

(© THE ALPINE CLUB COLLECTION, LONDON)

Horace Benedict de Saussure

(© THE ALPINE CLUB COLLECTION, LONDON)

Marc-Théodore Bourrit
(© THE ALPINE CLUB COLLECTION, LONDON)

Jacques Balmat
(© THE ALPINE CLUB COLLECTION, LONDON)

Michel-Gabriel Paccard
(© THE ALPINE CLUB COLLECTION, LONDON)

The ascent of Mont Blanc by Fellows and Hawes, 1827
(© ROYAL GEOGRAPHICAL SOCIETY, LONDON)

Glissading down Mont Blanc, 1827

(© ROYAL GEOGRAPHICAL SOCIETY, LONDON)

Louis Agassiz

(BY COURTESY OF THE NATIONAL PORTRAIT GALLERY, LONDON)

James Forbes

(© THE ALPINE CLUB COLLECTION, LONDON)

Forbes on the Mer de Glace

(© The Alpine Club Collection, London)

The Hotel Neuchâtelois

(© Royal Geographical Society, London)

Smith's ascent of Mont Blanc

(© ROYAL GEOGRAPHICAL SOCIETY, LONDON)

what the message was. They may have looked on the hills as objects of beauty – they all said they did – but what many craved was drama to match the breath-catching scenery, a moment of action to bring the backdrop to life. They wanted to see avalanches like the one that had hit the Hamel expedition, and if they were lucky they got them. In 1848 John Forbes, Queen Victoria's personal doctor (no relation to James Forbes), visited the Alps and witnessed an avalanche. It slid off a shelf in a V shape that preceded a 100-foot column of snow and ice. The whole stream hung in the air for several seconds before crashing into the trees. Of his companions' reaction to the spectacle, Forbes remarked: 'It is like that [state] which accompanies and follows the triumphant close of some elaborate and difficult air by an accomplished singer at the opera . . . it would hardly have astonished me if, on the present occasion, the spectators . . . after their pause of fearful delight, had clapped their hands in ecstasy and ended with "Bravo!"'[18]

Cheap applause was not what Ruskin liked. Had he heard the 'Bravo', he would probably have taken the cheerers to a distance and counselled them. It was, however, bread and butter to the Alps' next most prominent propagandist. While Ruskin elaborated on Alpine splendours, a misfit medical student cantered onto the scene, bearing behind him a cart. It contained nothing but cheap canvas, on which was painted scenes of Mont Blanc, a number of poles to hold the canvas up, and a box of candles – for effect. Nonetheless, he toured England's home counties to such acclaim that it changed both his career and the world's view of the Alps. His name was Albert Smith.

CHAPTER TWELVE

If Saussure found his heir in Forbes, the mantle of Bourrit fell on the shoulders of Albert Smith. Like Bourrit, Smith was not a particularly successful climber, but he had an unquenchable urge to tell the world just how wonderful the Alps were. Whereas Bourrit, however, had only been able to express his enthusiasm through mediocre paintings and overblown prose, Smith had the whole arsenal of mid-nineteenth-century ingenuity at his disposal. It was largely thanks to him that, during the 1850s, word of the Alps spread beyond the small worlds of scientific travellers, gentlemen adventurers and vacationing tourists. Over the course of eight years he promoted them so successfully that hardly a soul in Britain remained unaware of their beauties and their hazards. For Smith was that most colourful, dubious, entertaining and ephemeral of characters: he was a Victorian showman.

Albert Smith was born on 24 May 1816, the son of a doctor in the Thameside town of Chertsey. It was a provincial place, where nothing of excitement happened and whose topographic high point was a small rise 'from which it was fabled that the dome of St. Paul's had once been seen with a telescope'.[1] Smith loved it. In 1825, however, he was given a book called *The Peasants of Chamouni*, which contained a harrowing description of the Hamel disaster. This, and the discovery that he had a good voice – as a boy he got up at a dinner party and 'sung two songs in the style of Matthews, with a genius and versatility that astonished everybody'[2] – changed his life. It was understood by his father that he would become a doctor, but Smith's inclinations lay elsewhere. He wanted to be an entertainer and, if possible, to become involved with the Alps. Aged 11, he frightened his younger sister with, 'a small moving panorama of the horrors pertaining to Mont Blanc from Mr. Auldjo's narrative',[3] and a few years later he learned French for the sole purpose of translating Saussure's *Voyages*. He did eventually go to medical school in Paris, in 1838. But its only attraction was that it was nearer Mont Blanc than London was. In his first year he went to Chamonix on the cheap, carrying everything he owned in a second-hand French army rucksack and twelve pounds' worth of French currency stored in five-franc pieces in a money belt.

To begin with he was amazed at Europe's differing rates of exchange. On entering Savoy he tendered a French ten-sous piece to a fruit-seller and received six pears and twelve Savoyard sous in change. But the sense of wonder soon wore off and he trundled into Chamonix atop a pile of hay on a *banquette*, the cheapest mode of coach travel, congratulating himself on having reached his destination at a quarter of the cost to most other travellers. Like everybody else he went to the Montenvers and viewed its glacier. He was unimpressed. 'The story that the Mer de Glace resembles the sea suddenly frozen in a storm is all nonsense,' he recorded in his diary. 'From Montenvers it looks rather like a magnified ploughed field.'[4] He observed that others felt the same. Having walked on the glacier, he spent four hours in Bourrit's Temple where he met 'someone from almost every nation on earth, and with scarcely an exception, each one told the rest that they could see something in his country quite as good'.[5] But he loved the climate, loved the atmosphere, was stupefied by his first view of Mont Blanc and, having been hauled off the streets to drink a glass of champagne in celebration of a fellow Englishman's birthday, declared that 'Chamouni is the nicest place in Europe'.[6] He offered to act as porter to any party attempting Mont Blanc, but he had no takers and was very disappointed to learn that Henriette D'Angeville made her ascent the day after he left. His only regret on coming home was that he hadn't done the trip even more cheaply. As one Parisian had told him, 'With a knife, a bit of string and a walking stick I would go from here to the source of the Niger.'[7]

In 1841 Smith began a desultory career as a doctor in England. But his heart was not in it – he described his certificate as 'a license to kill human game by powder and ball, in the shape of calomel and bolus'.[8] Mont Blanc hung constantly in his imagination and so, in his free time, he dug out his childhood panorama, repainted the pictures on a larger scale and with the aid of a carpenter contrived a mechanism to make them roll smoothly. His first professional show was in the making. This was the age of the Literary and Philosophical Society, an age in which every British citizen with pretensions to knowledge could be found on Saturday afternoons, usually in the town hall, listening to lectures on the physiology of the eye or watching charcoal being burned in a bottle of oxygen. Into this stultifying world burst Albert Smith with 'a grand lecture about the Alps'.[9] His show comprised excerpts from Auldjo's narrative, interspersed with his own observations on the movement of glaciers and the dangers of the Grand Plateau about which he knew nothing. Meanwhile, by the light of oil lamps, Smith's brother Arthur wound the handle to provide an ever-changing backdrop of Alpine scenes. One of the best-loved moments came when Arthur ducked behind the pictures and held up a candle to illuminate the moon on the Grands Mulets. It was rickety in the extreme, and there were several near disasters with the oil lamps and candles, but it was very popular. For three years they toured Richmond, Brentford, Guildford, Staines, Hammersmith, Southwark and most of London's outlying towns, with Mont Blanc packed on the back of a wagon. Smith said it was the finest time of his life.

When the tour was over Smith gave his spare hours to journalism. He started at the hard end, narrowly escaping death when a balloon flight from Vauxhall Gardens went horribly wrong. But he soon found an aptitude for the slight, less taxing subjects that absorbed early Victorian society. 'Confession of Jasper Buddle, a Dissecting-room Porter' did very well, as did 'Physiology of the London Medical Student' and a 'History of Evening Parties'. These were followed by a series of sketches and pantomimes that made him, according to a friend, 'one of the most popular and prolific writers of the day'.[10] So he quit medicine and set himself up as a writer. He became the mainstay of *Bentley's Miscellany*, was one of the earliest contributors to *Punch* and was dramatic critic for the *Illustrated London News*. He wrote in instalments a novel called *Christopher Tadpole* that might have earned him fame were it not a thinly disguised imitation of a more accomplished novel called *Dombey and Son* which Charles Dickens was publishing in instalments at the same time. He founded a paper for new writers called *The Man in the Moon* which he edited with energy if not finesse until 1849, when he suddenly dropped everything and went on a journey to Constantinople and Cairo. He wrote a good book about his exploits in the Levant and then, for no discernible reason, translated his travels into a show called 'The Overland Trail' describing a trip to India. Smith talked and sang, and the panorama was painted by a capable artist called William Beverley. Once again, audiences loved it. As Smith put it, 'There is no nation of the world so great in distant enterprise and love of wandering as the English – none which ever turns with such deeply-rooted and constant affection, unchanged by any time or distance, to its HOME.'[11] With shows such as 'The Overland Trail,' Smith hoped to tap both these loves at the same time. And, as his till receipts showed, he succeeded admirably.

An interesting picture of Smith in his *Man in the Moon* days was given by one of his contemporaries:

I can recall him as a sturdy-looking, broad-shouldered, short-necked man, with grey eyes and flowing locks of light brown, and large side-whiskers; later in life he wore a beard; and, on the whole, he bore a most striking resemblance to Mr. Comyns Carr. His voice was a high treble; his study was like a curiosity shop; although the 'curios' were not highly remarkable from the standpoint of high art, and were not very antique. Littered about the room, which was on the ground floor, were piles of French novels, in yellow paper covers, dolls, caricatures, toys of every conceivable kind, a *debardeuse* silk shirt, crimson sash, and velvet trousers, the white linen raiment of a Pierrot, cakes of soap from Vienna, made in the simulitude of fruit, iron jewellery from Berlin of the historic *Ich gab Gold für Essen* pattern, miniature Swiss chalets, porcelain and meerschaum pipes – although Albert was no smoker – and the model of a French *diligence*.[12]

Another friend remembered him for his shabby clothes, his gaudy neckerchiefs, his watch chain festooned with charms and the skeleton that stood in his hallway and which sometimes sat at the dinner table when there were 13 guests.

Many people disliked this strange, chirping man of eclectic tastes and curious costumes. His sense of self-importance was legendary and even his friends called him Albert the Great, or Lord Smith. He had the gift of the gab with a laugh like 'the clatter of a steam shovel',[13] and 'was hail-fellow-well-met, Christian-name calling, hand-shaking with hundreds'[14] – qualities that did not go down well in middle-class Victorian Britain. According to the historian of *Punch* he 'was usually the butt of jokers'.[15] Thackeray detested him. Dickens sighed wearily that 'we all have our Smiths'.[16] On seeing Smith's initials under a magazine article, the editor Douglas Jerrold said they represented only two-thirds of the truth.* A fellow member of the Garrick Club described him 'in such offensive language that Smith's friends were sorely perplexed as to the way it could best be resented'.[17]

Yet many people loved him, and reading his works on the Alps it is hard not to like him too – as, for instance, when describing Mont Blanc he told of a 'traveller of rather full habit of body, who went up, and whose head flew off with a bang, by reason of the rarefied air',[18] or, confidentially, 'I believe they show you, somewhere on the glacier, an entire boys' school from Geneva, shut up in the ice like . . . strawberries in a mould of jelly.'[19] He was so patently who he was, a man

*Jerrold's calculations were incorrect. Although Smith signed himself A. S., he did in fact have a middle name. It was Richard.

without airs, determined to get the best deal, the finest view, the biggest audience, a man who was prepared to live on nothing, but when he had something was equally prepared to spend it. He was a showman and made no claim to be anything else. Even Dickens realised this and, regretting his previous slight, later asked him for advice on public speaking. It was nice, therefore, that in 1851 Smith achieved his greatest ambition – to climb Mont Blanc.

Since his first visit in 1838 Smith had spent at least three weeks of every year in Chamonix. He had never had the money to climb Mont Blanc – guides' charges went up and up – but in 1851, flush with the success of 'The Overland Trail', he thought it worth a try. His friends tried to dissuade him, pointing out that he was far from fit. 'Pluck will serve me instead of training,'[20] Smith replied grandly, climbing to the attic in search of his old French army backpack. He may now have become a wealthy man but he was going to do the trip on the cheap and carrying the minimum of equipment just as he had done in his youth. From the very outset it filled him with glee. 'I found my old knapsack in a store-room,' he wrote, 'and I beat out the moths and spiders, and filled it as of old, and on the first of August, 1851, I left London Bridge in the mail-train of the South-Eastern Railway, with my Lord Mayor and other distinguished members of the corporation, who were going to the *fêtes* at Paris in honour of the Exhibition, and who, not having a knapsack under their seat, lost all their luggage, as is no doubt chronicled in the City archives.'[21]

At Chamonix, however, a disappointment awaited. On summoning the chief guide, Jean Tairraz, and informing him that he was now able to make the ascent, he was told that he couldn't. He was too fat, his health was bad, and anyway the weather was turning. But Tairraz had a soft spot for Smith, and promised to call a meeting of the guides the following morning and see what they thought about it. As it happened, Smith was in luck; not because the guides thought he was capable but because he was able to tag along with a party of three Oxford undergraduates who had noticed Mont Banc while on a reading tour the month before and had set their caps at it. As one member said, 'Richards of Trinity ascended last year, why should not we?'[22] So,

while Smith was sweating his way pluckily southwards, the three
youths – whose names were Floyd, Philips and Sackville-West – went
into thorough training in Chamonix. They arrived in the first week of
August and booked their guides. While waiting for the weather to
clear they received a note saying that 'a Mr. Smith of London' wished
to accompany them. They ignored it at first, on the stout British principle that one should not speak to someone one does not know. But
on learning that it was *the* Mr. Smith, the well-known comic author,
they introduced themselves. Hands were shaken, Smith did his usual
back-slapping routine, and it was agreed by all that he was 'a tremendous brick'[23] and would make an excellent climbing companion.
Smith was so excited that for several nights he could not sleep.

Such was Smith's personality that he leaped from being latecomer
to leader. The expedition which departed on Tuesday, 12 August was
the largest and most extravagant Chamonix had ever witnessed.
According to regulations, each climber had to take four guides; on top
of that Smith hired some twenty porters to carry the provisions he
thought appropriate for the occasion. His inventory from the Hôtel de
Londres, where he was staying, ran as follows:

60 bottles of Vin Ordinaire
6 bottles of Bordeaux
10 bottles of St. George
15 bottles of St. Jean
3 bottles of Cognac
1 bottle of syrup of raspberries
6 bottles of lemonade
2 bottles of champagne
20 loaves
10 small cheeses
6 packets of chocolate
6 packets of sugar
4 packets of prunes
4 packets of raisins
2 packets of salt

4 wax candles
6 lemons
4 legs of mutton
6 pieces of veal
1 piece of beef
11 large fowls
35 small fowls.

The whole lot cost 456 francs, approximately £45, which to put it in perspective was more than seven times the amount Smith had allowed himself for his entire trip in 1838. Having travelled cheap, he clearly didn't intend to climb cheap.

Smith, however, wanted to do more than climb Mont Blanc. He wanted to crush its myth. In all the years he had spent at Chamonix he had wondered not only at Mont Blanc's beauty but at its apparent accessibility. From the valley, it didn't look half the monolith it was made out to be. It still doesn't, and modern visitors who scramble to the top of the Brévent must scratch their heads at the thought of Mont Blanc being considered a difficult climb, or even very high. With its smooth, dromedary humps of snow it looks absurdly easy. Smith was of the modern cast and he decided, therefore, that its difficulties and dangers had been exaggerated so that the guides could demand a higher fee – as was commonplace on the Mer de Glace – and it was down to him, straightforward people's man that he was, to 'expose the whole affair as an imposition'.[24] And he wanted to expose it in as dramatic a fashion as possible, with every possible comfort to hand and champagne to crack at the summit. One can see why some people disliked him. In a very recognisable fashion he wanted to have his own dream and shatter those of others. Luckily, it didn't work out that way.

Smith's caravan set out at 7.30 a.m., its general leading the way on a mule, and a crowd of friends, family and sweethearts cavorting in its wake. At 4.00 p.m., Smith having dismounted and the camp followers having gone home, they reached the Grands Mulets. It was not cold; if anything it was rather sultry, and they draped their wet clothes to dry on the rock which was radiating heat like a natural storage heater. They then had a sumptuous banquet, which they concluded with a competition to see who could throw the empty bottles farthest downhill. The only discordant note came when they were joined by an Irishman who had followed their trail with his guide. They banished him indignantly to rocks farther uphill. When a second follower, a well-known American adventurer and balloonist called Vanstittart, also arrived with a guide, he too was invited to sleep elsewhere. Such annoyances aside, it was exactly the kind of climb Smith had anticipated and he was so happy with the way things were going that he did not bother with a tent that night. They slept under the sky, Smith resting his head on his old knapsack, spellbound by the scenery. As the sun went down, Smith thought the peaks 'looked like islands rising from a filmy ocean – an archipelago of gold'. The sight was 'more than the realisation of the most gorgeous visions that opium or *hasheesh* could evoke'.[25] And to all of them it seemed as if Mont Blanc *was* an imposture. They had completed the first stage without the slightest mishap, wearing only cricket flannels in the case of the Oxford men, and the way ahead looked 'as smooth as a racecourse'.[26] Smith reckoned he could reach the top in two hours. They were so sanguine that they got up at midnight to continue the climb by lamplight. As they passed the Irishman's camp they could hear him enjoying himself 'in a most convivial fashion' and teaching his guide to sing 'God Save the Queen'.

Their euphoria did not last. Smith began to feel cold shortly after leaving the Grands Mulets. He also began to feel a bit sick. When they reached the Grand Plateau and his guides pointed out the Hamel crevasse he noted it half-heartedly. The Irishman, who had overtaken them, was shortly discovered on his face, vomiting into the snow while simultaneously bleeding from his nose. He was sent back to the Grands Mulets. Floyd was disturbed. 'It gave us some idea of the horrors of a forced march and the pluck needed to endure it,'[27] he wrote. Meanwhile, Smith's mind took on a life of its own. 'Every step we took was gained from the chance of a horrible death,'[28] he wrote, exaggeratedly. It got colder. He sat down and refused to continue.

The guides dragged him on. An hour later, on the steep but relatively untaxing Mur de la Côte, he was reeling like a drunkard and said he just wanted to be left alone to sleep. Again, they hauled him on. 'It is an all but perpendicular iceberg,' Smith lied in his journal. 'You begin to ascend it obliquely; there is nothing below but a chasm in the ice, more frightful than anything yet passed. Should the foot slip or the baton give way there is no chance for life. You would glide like lightning from one frozen crag to another, and finally be dashed to pieces hundreds and hundreds of feet below, in the horrible depths of the glacier.'[29] For a while the horrors overcame him. 'He looked very ill indeed,' said Floyd, 'and was quite insensible when I poured a glass of champagne down his throat.'[30] Thus restored, Smith continued his ever more lurid litany. 'Placed fourteen thousand feet above the level of the sea, terminating in an icy abyss so deep that the bottom is lost in obscurity; exposed, in a highly rarefied atmosphere, to a wind cold and violent beyond all conception; assailed, with muscular powers already taxed far beyond their strength, and nerves shaken by constantly increasing excitement and want of rest – with bloodshot eyes and a raging thirst, and a pulse leaping rather than beating – with all this, it may be imagined that the frightful Mur de la Côte calls for more than ordinary determination to mount it.'[31] He was hauled up by rope, a couple of guides hacking steps in the ice, and at 9.00 a.m. on 13 August, crawling on his hands and knees, he finally reached the summit. It had happened at last: Albert Smith had climbed Mont Blanc. He immediately fell asleep.

They stayed there for only half an hour, during which time Smith recovered sufficiently to enjoy the view and drink several glasses of champagne, then they hurried back to the Grands Mulets where they finished off the last of their provisions, collected the Irishman and marched down to Chamonix. The manner of their arrival more than compensated Smith for any discomfiture he had experienced on the ascent. Forming themselves into a line, they walked through the fields, attracting as they went the same camp followers who had started out with them. Tourists and locals alike crowded the streets of Chamonix, waving handkerchiefs and cheering the procession as if it had returned from a military campaign. Bands played and, to complete the picture, volleys of artillery fire rumbled through the valley in what had become the traditional salute of a successful assault. (A small cannon was by now de rigueur for any self-respecting Chamonix hotelier.) In the courtyard of the Hôtel de Londres a table strewn with flowers and champagne bottles awaited the conquerors. And that evening Floyd's cousin Sir Robert Peel invited the entire Company of Guides to a boisterous celebration.

If Smith had not destroyed Mont Blanc's reputation he had done the next best thing: he had reinforced it. When he left for London he carried in his head a piece of copy that had money written all over it. The public's first inkling of what was to come appeared in *The Times* on 20 August 1851, when Smith wrote a short letter alerting Britain to his achievement. Then came the full journal. He told the tale in dramatic fashion, exaggerating the dangers and omitting the names of the Irishman or the American, whom he described as mere 'followers'. He also omitted the fact that he had been last to the summit and made great play of the frostbite he claimed to have suffered in one hand: 'even as I now write, my little finger is without sensation, and on the approach of cold, it becomes very painful'.[32]

People wrote in to complain. They complained firstly about the value of such risky expeditions. This was, after all, the year in which Britain was at last becoming aware that its explorer hero Sir John Franklin, who had departed in search of the North-West Passage in 1845, was never going to return, nor were the two ships and 135 men he had taken with him. In the ensuing backlash, snow, ice and death became indivisible. Futility was the word that cropped up whenever anyone mentioned risk, and Smith had most definitely mentioned risk. Secondly, they complained about Smith himself. 'Saussure's observations and his reflections on Mont Blanc live in his poetical philosophy,' said a writer in the *Daily News*. 'Those of Mr. Albert Smith will be appropriately recorded in a tissue of indifferent puns and stale, fast witticisms with an incessant straining after smartness. The aimless scramble of four pedestrians to the top of Mont Blanc, with the accompaniment of Sir Robert Peel's orgies at the bottom, will not go far to redeem the somewhat equivocal reputation of the herd of English tourists in Switzerland, for a mindless and rather vulgar redundance of mere animal spirits.'[33]

It was all perfectly true in Smith's case, and he retorted mildly that 'those who chose to attack me, in print, on my return from [this] achievement, in such a wanton and perfectly uncalled-for manner, knew nothing at all about the matter'.[34] But the same writer made the mistake of slighting Smith's second 'follower', Vanstittart, who unlike the Irishman, had made it to the summit. In a diatribe on pointless exploits, he jeered at 'aeronauts who peril their lives for the purpose of earning a few shillings as showmen, or to gratify an idle vanity'.[35] Balloonists were stupid enough he said, but at least they risked only their own worthless necks; climbers, however, were grossly idiotic because they also risked the lives of their guides. Vanstittart was the wrong man to pick on. He was widely travelled, very intelligent and had a good idea of the risks – if any – that he undertook. He crushed his antagonist in a frosty reply: 'Having walked under the sea in a diving apparatus at a depth of more than a hundred feet, having descended into the bowels of the earth both in the iron mines of Dannemora in Sweden and the salt mines in Poland, having made balloon ascents and climbed many high mountains, I can safely assert that there is a pleasure in such enterprises altogether unknown to those who have not experienced them.'[36] Floyd also wrote to the *Daily News* in defence of the climb, and the man soon shrank into his slippers.

The controversy was delightful as far as Smith was concerned because it drew his climb to the attention of armchair travellers, the very people he had targeted as a potential audience. And he had a show in the pipeline that he thought such people would like very much. 'The Ascent of Mont Blanc' opened on 15 March 1852 at the Egyptian Hall, Piccadilly. It comprised two parts: the first was a description of the journey from London to Chamonix, taking in anything else that was not exactly en route but which was in the slightest sensational, such as the charnel house on the Great St Bernard Pass; the second was a portrayal of Chamonix and Mont Blanc. It followed

Smith's usual routine, in which he stood on stage and sang and talked his way through a series of illustrations drawn by William Beverley. He exaggerated unashamedly: every slope was a precipice, every snowball an avalanche, every rock a cliff, every crevasse an abyss. He feared on the first night that Mont Blanc might not be sufficiently attractive to Londoners. But as he wrote delightedly, 'I have found, to my infinite delight, that a large proportion of the public have appeared to be, with me, interested in the subject.'[37] Audiences were spellbound, and for a run of six years Smith's 'Ascent' was the most popular show in town. He milked it with consummate professionalism. Every year the route to Chamonix would be changed – he researched it himself, taking an annual six weeks' holiday to do so – and whenever possible a novelty was introduced. One year St Bernard dogs panted through the stalls, little boxes of chocolate slung around their necks for children to pick at.* Another year, two Alpine milkmaids paraded on stage in traditional costume. (Actually, they were a pair of Chamonix barmaids who had been persuaded to play the part.) And on one occasion four chamois made a nervous appearance. He fiddled with the pictures to make them look like photographs. At the close of each season he personally presented a bouquet of flowers to every woman in the audience.

People still laughed at Smith – he was was forever flourishing his Mont Blanc certificate at them – and the press poured scorn on him and his mountain. 'Mont Blanc has become a positive nuisance,'[38] said *The Times*, describing it as 'a mere theatrical gimcrack . . . about as tremendous as the mysteries of the Thames Tunnel . . . really, the world in general cares very little about the matter'.[39] Ruskin, who had been present at Smith's champagne-popping descent from Mont Blanc and had been disgusted by its showiness, pointed out that the money Smith earned from his 'Ascent' could have set up the Alpine economy forever – forgetting that by his reasoning geographical

---

*They were not true St Bernards. The original, leaner breed had been wiped out earlier in the century when the St Bernard hospice kennels were hit by disease. The mastiffs which Smith hired were the closest the monks could get by breeding back. They did not at all resemble the over-furred animals we now recognise.

beauty, rather than cash, was the most powerful stimulus to material success. But Smith laughed back at them. After only three months he gave a private morning performance for Queen Victoria's husband, Prince Albert, and their two sons Prince Edward and Prince Alfred. He gave another, two years later, at Osborne, after which Queen Victoria presented him with a diamond scarf pin. (He gave her two St Bernards in return.) And two years after that he was once again entertaining the royal family, this time at Windsor and in the presence of the whole court plus King Leopold I of Belgium. In 1857 he escorted the Prince of Wales to Chamonix. He was known to thousands as 'the man of Mont Blanc'. A board game was issued called 'The New Game of Mont Blanc', and thousands of children across the realm prayed with each throw of the dice that they would land on the Mur de la Côte – to receive two counters from each player for their extraordinary bravery in climbing it. In London, their parents danced to the 'Mont Blanc Quadrille' and the 'Chamonix Polka', or, at the Baker Street Glaciarium, skated year-round on 3,000 square feet of ice amidst Alpine scenery, covered with snow and hoar frost. The country was gripped by what *The Times* described as 'a perfect Mont Blanc mania'.[40] Smith let his beard grow and posed ruggedly for photographs. When the 'Ascent' closed in 1858 it, had earned him an estimated £30,000.

Among those who saw Smith's show was a nine-year-old boy called Douglas Freshfield. In later years Freshfield would become Saussure's biographer and one of Britain's foremost Alpine climbers. He was a 'grim, behind-the-stockades figure',[41] according to one historian, and Smith's vulgarities were the last thing he wanted to be associated with. But, as Freshfield admitted, '[Smith] came forward just at the psychical moment when railways across France had brought the Alps within the Englishman's long vacation. And, strange to say, he had a genuine passion for Mont Blanc, which fortune or rather his own enthusiasm enabled him to put to profit.'[42]

Enthusiasm and profit were just fine as far as Chamonix's hoteliers were concerned. In 1848 the continent had been convulsed by a series of revolutions that affected it almost as profoundly as the Napoleonic

Wars. For a few months every European state was in flux and the Alpine duchies, kingdoms and confederacies were no exception. The ensuing autocratic backlash had only put a lid on a pot that was still boiling. Normality was needed and Smith helped provide it. He became a local hero, not only for the crowds he drew to Chamonix but for the time and money he spent on the place. He contributed to several public projects and organised relief funds when the village was hit by fire and floods in the 1850s. His annual return was greeted with cannonades; he was given his own suite in the Hôtel de Londres, complete with brass nameplate; fêtes and holidays were proclaimed in his honour; and during his stay he was treated as the lion of Alpine society.

Thanks to Smith, so many people wanted to climb Mont Blanc that in the winter of 1853–4 the guides built a hut on the Grands Mulets. It measured fourteen feet by seven, had two glazed windows, a door 'that fitted tolerably well', and was equipped with benches, tables, shelves and an iron stove. Naturally, Albert Smith was among the fifty-strong group of swells and guides who attended its opening. He was delighted to note that it was the biggest party ever to have climbed to the Grands Mulets. He was even happier when they arrived too late and had to spend the night in the hut – the distress of grand people always amused him. One by one the notables sat down against the wall, their knees drawn up, then another line of people sat in front of them, and so on until all fifty people had somehow crammed themselves inside. The guides shut the windows, fired up the stove and lit their pipes. It reeked and stank and reminded Smith nostalgically of the diligences he had travelled in when he was younger. A fellow inmate took it less well: 'The spasmodic and quick repeated sound "ppahh," "ppahh," of fifty smokers on Mont Blanc – could anybody sleep under it?'[43] Then there was what he called 'the malicious revelry' of Albert Smith, who started a round of joke-telling, each person raising his hand for attention when he remembered something good. So it continued through the night, Smith darting out for the occasional breath of fresh air, until dawn arrived and they all went home.

A later Alpinist, Edward Whymper, said that the 'Ascent' could have played forever. But fickle Smith deserted Chamonix in 1859 and went to China, returning from there with yet another profitable show. It ran for only a year before he had a stroke. In the spring of 1860 he contracted bronchitis and on 23 May he died. The funeral was held five days later in Brompton Cemetery, and on Smith's instruction that it cost no more than £20 was attended only by a few relatives. 'Poor, dear Albert is gone!' wept a friend. 'The joyous voice, the merry laugh, the droll remark, the quaint anecdote, will be heard no more.'[44] Or, as another friend put it, they would never again see his big, red face grinning out of the cab window as he went home with the takings.

Chapter Thirteen

'The Ascent of Mont Blanc' was watched by hundreds of thousands. Many went home with the memory of a good evening's banter and left it at that. Some, however, decided to follow Smith's example and climb to the summit. They made their presence felt. Between 1786 and 1853 there had been forty-five ascents of Mont Blanc. In 1854 alone there were sixteen, mostly by Britons. Many more made the less perilous climb to the hut on the Grands Mulets which had now become an attraction in itself. Smith had brought people to the Alps, without a doubt. But the influx of British visitors was not due solely to him.

In the 1850s Britain was on a high. This was the decade of the Great Exhibition, the decade when British supremacy in almost every area was acknowledged across the globe. Britain was the most prosperous, most technologically advanced nation in Europe. It was the stablest one too, having been spared the revolutions which swept Europe in 1848. Its furnaces flamed into the night, its gas-lit mills spewed roll upon roll of cotton and worsted, and the air at Wigan and other mining centres was black with coal dust for miles around. Locomotives charged across viaducts, through 100-foot-deep cuttings and long, lightless tunnels. Energy was everywhere. The popular mood was expressed by Queen Victoria after a visit to the Great

Exhibition. 'We are capable,' she wrote in her diary on 29 April 1851, 'of doing anything.'[1]

Not only was it thought that Britons could do anything, but that they *should*. It was an age when success was seen as a gift from above. Whatever some radicals said, it was widely believed that the poor were poor and the rich were rich because God had decreed it so. Expanding this philosophy, it was therefore obvious that Britain had done well because it was naturally, divinely better than all other nations. It was the right – nay, it was the duty – for Britain to stamp its mark on the world, and for more than half a century British soldiers, engineers and industrialists did just that, their success serving only to prove the theory.

In the 1850s this brand of chauvinism had yet to become dogma, but Britons – Englishmen especially – felt it in their bones neverthe-less. Some people expressed their superiority by conquering distant territories or becoming missionaries in Africa, others by building sewage systems and gasworks in foreign cities, yet others by selling machine tools to developing economies. A select band exercised their divine right – and themselves – by conquering the Alps. 'I unhesitat-ingly maintain,' wrote one climber, 'that there is a joy in these measurings of strength with Nature in her wildest moods, a quiet sense of work done, and success won in the teeth of opposition.'[2] He did not know whether he owed this aggressive impulse 'to our Anglo-Saxon blood, as some may hold, or whether it be only one of the modes in which the "contrariness" of human nature crops out in cer-tain individuals'.[3] Wherever it came from, it was there, and for a decade and a half British climbers swamped the Alps, crossing off peaks like partners on a dance card. They called it the Golden Age of Mountaineering.

The Golden Age was a godsend to the lawyers, doctors, clergymen and others who made up Britain's middle class. Their jobs prevented them indulging in great adventure. But they had money, and a good six weeks' summer holiday in which to do some exploring. Thanks to the marvels of modern rail travel, Mont Blanc could be reached in twenty-four hours and the Swiss Alps in little over fifty-six. So they went, conquered and came home. At London Bridge station, on a late August morning when the sky was smogging over, groups of travellers were to be seen brandishing their alpenstocks, hoisting their rucksacks and comparing notes about climbs, the Channel ferry and the excellence of French railways compared to British. Then the cabs came and they dispersed excitedly to their various callings. The thrill was palpable. Hundreds of criminals were prosecuted, hundreds of patients attended and hundreds of sermons given by men who had scarcely washed their socks since Chamonix.

By common agreement, the Golden Age began with the ascent of the Wetterhorn by Alfred Wills. Wills – later Sir Alfred Wills, the man who tried Oscar Wilde – was a well-to-do barrister with nothing much on his books. In 1854 he made the journey to Grindelwald. He had been to the Alps before, but this trip was something special. He was on his honeymoon and he wanted to climb a major peak to show his wife how it was done – also to see if he could actually do it. As he wrote, 'I had crossed many a lofty col, and wound my way among many a labyrinth of profound and yawning crevasses. I had slept on the moraine of a glacier, and on the rugged mountainside, but I had never yet scaled any of those snowy peaks which rise in tempting grandeur above the crests of cols and the summits of the loftier passes.'[4] Ideally, he wanted to climb the Jungfrau, failing that the Finsteraarhorn or the Schreckhorn. But he found himself on the wrong side of the chain and did not have time to go round to the approachable faces. So he settled instead for the Wetterhorn, a mountain of 12,143 feet that could be reached from Grindelwald and had yet to be climbed (or so he was told).

He set out from Grindelwald at 1.30 p.m. on 17 September 1854 with four guides: Auguste Balmat, to whom he had been introduced by Forbes in London the previous year; a second Chamoniard, named Auguste 'Samson' Simond, who could lift a grown man off the ground at arm's length; a Grindelwald guide called Peter Bohren, who had made three attempts already that season; and the leader, Ulrich Lauener, a 'tall, straight, active, knowing-looking fellow, with a cock's feather stuck jauntily in his high-crowned hat'.[5] They travelled reasonably light, taking just one porter to carry their food and wine. There was one exceptional piece of luggage, however. Perhaps bearing in mind the squabbles over the Meyers' ascents of the Jungfrau, Lauener had decided to take a flag that would not easily blow away or perish. It comprised a sheet of iron measuring three feet by two, attached to a twelve-foot-long metal mast.

They spent their first night on the mountain in a cave used by chamois-hunters. Wills found it a dreadful experience. The cold, clammy roof was only six inches from his head, Lauener used his feet as a pillow, the atmosphere was stifling, their blankets had fleas and he was kept awake by the sound of 'a foaming glacier torrent brawling past my head, not six feet from me'.[6] On top of it all he was very hungry, having been unable to eat their evening meal because the mutton was flavoured with garlic, which he detested. 'I must say,' he wrote, 'I was desperately uncomfortable.'[7] Balmat, too, could not sleep and the two of them wormed their way out of the cave and into the moonlight. 'Oh! how grateful was that cool night air! how refreshing that draught at the mountain torrent!' Wills wrote. 'The stars were shining as I never saw them shine before, like so many balls of fire in the black concave; the glaciers were sparkling in the soft light of the waning moon . . . a bracing air blew briskly, yet pleasantly, from the north-west . . . so beautiful a nocturnal view as this I never had yet beheld.'[8] Wills was so refreshed that he decided to take a bath. Thus, at 2.00 a.m., halfway up a very high snow-covered mountain, he stripped naked and immersed himself in the nearby glacial stream. It 'was icy-cold, but did me more good than a weary night in the hole'.[9]*

At 4.30 a.m. they resumed their climb, Lauener carrying the 'flag' on his back and using its pole as an alpenstock. They held lanterns to help them over the ice and rubble, and by 10.00 a.m. they were on the

---

*It is an old cliché that Englishmen are addicted to cold baths. In the mid-nineteenth century it was a truth. Whether for reasons of hygiene, toughness or perversity, they would sluice themselves under any pump, waterfall or stream that availed. Even Smith was devoted to the practice. They could not understand why others did not follow their example and saw it as one more instance of Anglo-Saxon superiority. Continentals thought they were mad.

main plateau from which the Wetterhorn's three peaks sprang. Here they took a rest. But as they admired the scenery they spied two figures on the mountainside above them. Bizarrely, one of them was carrying a fir tree. After much shouting they discovered that the men were Christian Almer and Ulrich Kaufmann, two chamois-hunters who had heard of the ascent and had determined to reach the summit first. The fir tree was an impromptu version of Lauener's iron flag, which they intended to plant at the top for the honour of their valley. Wills was outraged. Balmat had to be restrained from going up to fight them. In the end, however, the two teams joined forces and Balmat was so impressed with the opposition that he declared them '*bons enfants*' and gave them a slab of chocolate apiece.

Roped together, the enlarged party struggled on, hacking their way over a glacier that was 45° to begin with, but which soon reached a terrifying 70°. As the guides chopped their way upwards, clumps of ice showered onto those below. Wills dodged valiantly but was nevertheless hit on the head by a lump of debris, 'which made me keep a better look out for its successors'.[10] From where he was Wills could only see a steep slope of ice, above which hung an impenetrable cornice. He was sure that the summit, presumably a dome like so many other summits, lay beyond the cornice. But how were they to overcome the overhang? It 'curled over towards us, like the crest of a wave, breaking at irregular intervals along the line into pendants and inverted pinnacles of ice, many of which hung down to the full length of a tall man's height'.[11]

After a brief parley, Lauener was given an axe and told to do his best. If he could bring the cornice down, the way would be open to the summit. They clung nervously to the ice while Lauener swung the axe. 'It depended upon this assault,' Wills wrote, 'whether that impregnable fortress was to be ours, or whether we were to return, slowly and sadly, foiled by its calm and massive strength.'[12] Lauener chopped; a large block of ice bounced down from the cornice and rolled onto the glacier below. Then came one of the most memorable statements in Alpine history: 'I see blue sky!'[13]

There was no dome. The cornice was the last obstacle. It was the peak. Lauener thrashed away with his axe and soon he had made an opening wide enough for him to slither through. One moment Wills was facing a blank wall of ice, the next a hand reached down and grabbed him. 'I stepped across, and had passed the ridge of the Wetterhorn! . . . The whole world seemed to lie at my feet. The next moment I was almost appalled by the awfulness of our situation. The side we had come up was steep; but it was a gentle slope, compared with that which fell away from where I stood. A few yards of glittering ice at our feet, and then, nothing between us and the green slopes of Grindelwald, nine thousand feet beneath.'[14]

Wills gasped, not from the altitude – they were nearly the height of Mount Snowdon beneath the summit of Mont Blanc – but from sheer, dumbstruck amazement. He experienced a sense of upliftment: 'We felt as in the more immediate presence of Him who had reared this tremendous pinnacle, and beneath the "majestical roof" of whose deep blue Heaven we stood, poised, as it seemed, half-way between the earth and the sky.'[15] Balmat was similarly struck. '[He] told me repeatedly, afterwards, that it was the most awful and startling moment he had known in the course of his long mountain experience.'[16] Even Lauener trembled 'like a child'. They soon had more cause to tremble. When Lauener and Samson cut away the dangerous overhang, the party was straddling a ridge only four inches wide. Wills was petrified. Although surrounded by scenery of 'indescribable sublimity . . . it was impossible long to turn the eye from the fearful slope at the top of which we stood. For twenty or thirty yards beneath us, the glacier curved away steeper and steeper, until its rounded form limited our view . . . Nothing else broke the terrific void, and the next objects on which the eye rested were . . . nearly two miles of absolute depth below us.'[17] Eventually he mustered the courage to stand upright and, 'where there was not room to place my two feet side by side', waved his hat in the direction of Grindelwald. At the same time the guides 'began an unearthly series of yells, which . . . produced a strange and unpleasant effect on the nerves'.[18] Reading between the lines it appears that Wills almost lost his balance. Certainly he lost his glove, which slithered down the ice towards Grindelwald and was later rescued by Bohren despite Wills's commands to the contrary.

They planted their two incongruous flags and were just about to leave when they noticed another flag, underneath and to one end of the cornice, which had been placed there earlier in the year by a team that had failed to reach the top. 'No better comment could be devised on the reality and greatness of the difficulty we had overcome in passing the cornice,' Wills wrote. 'These explorers had actually arrived within ten feet of the summit; but had been arrested by that frowning barrier of overhanging ice.'[19] Balmat made him crawl along and give it a contemptuous kick. 'In doing so,' Wills recorded, 'I caught a glimpse of the arête below, ending in the glacier of Schwarzwald, which made me shudder.'[20]

Down in the valley, Grindelwalders were puzzled by what they saw. There was the flag, there was Wills – recognisable by his white flannel trousers – and there were his four guides. But who were the other two men? And what was that thing next to the flag; was it a tree? The landlord of Wills's hotel telegraphed Berne, where the great observatory telescope swung round to focus on the Wetterhorn. Yes, the observatory telegraphed back, there were seven men on the summit and they were standing next to a black flag and a fir tree.

Lauener had broken through the cornice at 11.20 a.m. and by 11.40 Wills's team was beginning its descent. Once the ice slope was out of the way they moved at astonishing and at times incautious speed. They slid down scree slopes where each step carried them 12 feet at a time. When the snow permitted they glissaded 'at railroad pace'. If the ground was firm they ran. At 2.50 p.m. they reached the cave where they had spent the previous night and paused only to drink the last of their wine before careering off again. By the time they reached the lower pastures they were almost flying, hurdling fences and hedges alike with enormous strides. Wills and Lauener were in the lead, racing and laughing like a pair of schoolboys. At one point Wills gained the advantage but Lauener soon caught up and they took a hedge together only to come to an abrupt halt when 'suddenly, and very much to our mutual astonishment',[21] they discovered themselves within ten paces of Mrs Wills taking a stroll with her brother.

Mrs Wills looked at her husband and his guide with bemusement. Their faces were both suffused with a deep purple and they seemed practically deaf. Wills, meanwhile, looked at his watch. It had taken them twenty-two hours to climb the hill; they had come down it in six. The whole party moved off to Grindelwald where they entered the village in procession, their hats decorated with red berries, to the accompaniment of rifle and cannon discharges. For days afterwards Wills was pointed out in the streets as '*Der Wetterhörner Herr*', which gave him such pleasure that when he discovered he was not the first to reach the top – two of Desor's guides had reached the summit in the 1840s – he forgave Lauener entirely for charging the fee that was normally reserved for a first ascent and declared that he had earned every centime. He was a little put out, however, when people began to query whether he had reached the top. The flag was there, Wills said. They could see it and the Berne observatory had seen it. Yes, said the townsfolk, but from where they stood it seemed as if a higher section of the ridge lay to the west. Wills argued it as best he could but eventually gave up. 'I never saw such a race of unbelievers as the people at Grindelwald,'[22] he said despairingly.

Wills was by no means the only British climber loose in the Alps that season. He was, however, one of the first to write about his experiences and, like Smith, he found a ready audience. Where Smith had told people where to go, Wills told them what to do when they got there. He told them of blue ice walls and perilous cornices, of tumbling rocks and the couloirs or chutes down which they fell, of starlit nights and dawn winds that swept streams of 'smoke' from the peaks; and then he told them to go out and experience it all for themselves – for the fun of it, for the exhilaration of reaching the top and for the chance, in the grubby industrial world in which they lived, of reaching a true rapport with God and Nature. What he did was to reconcile all the disparate tenets of the Victorian age – national duty, physical exercise, spiritual reward, self-improvement – and channel them into a small piece of Europe known as the Alps. In short, he was the first person to advocate mountaineering as a pursuit worthwhile in itself. This was news.

The exploits of Auldjo, Fellows and all the others who had 'done' Mont Blanc paled beside Wills's philosophy. They had been adventurers. Wills was a teacher. Throughout the 1850s Britons followed his example, climbing peak after undiscovered peak and glorying in every minute of it. Continental climbers – of whom there were several very successful examples – were brushed aside as irritants. Like so many other parts of the world, the Alps now belonged to Albion.

Collectively, the newcomers might have been driven by a subconscious jingoism. Individually, however, each climber had his own motives for visiting the Alps. Some wanted exercise, others excitement, others enlightenment. Doctors considered an Alpine holiday the best medicine there was. Clergymen saw the peaks as natural steeples, leading them ever closer to God. Agnostics saw them as an answer to religion. Lawyers relished the clear-cut simplicity of a mountain. Aesthetes were enraptured by the shapes they encountered. Geologists were in primordial paradise. Explorers had the satisfaction of knowing that the rocks with which they grappled had never before been touched by human hand. And historians could tell them that they were wrong when, in a brief respite from arguing over Hannibal's route, they learned that a Bronze Age arrowhead had been found at the top of a mountain by American tourists. The Alps were everything to everybody. And they had the further attraction, in an age of progress, that they led forwards and up.

Inevitably the new mountaineers felt the need of a forum in which they could discuss their ideas and experiences. It took the shape of that quintessentially Victorian institution, the club. The notion was first mooted by an Alpine enthusiast named William Mathews, who wrote on 1 February 1857 to a climbing companion, the Revd Fenton John Anthony Hort, Fellow of Trinity College, asking him 'to consider whether it would not be possible to establish an Alpine Club'.[23] Mathews envisaged something basic: an annual dinner, say, at which mountaineers could get together and swap stories about their climbs.

Possibly their experiences could be published in an annual or bi-annual volume. There would be a President, of course, but otherwise it would be pretty informal. Hort replied damply that the idea was fair enough so long as the dinner didn't cost too much. Undeterred, Mathews went on a climbing expedition to Switzerland that summer and asked his companions – a cousin, Benjamin Mathews, a friend, Edward Shirley Kennedy, and two others, a Mr Ellis and the Revd J. F. Hardy – what they thought of an Alpine Club. They thought it a splendid suggestion and when, on 13 August 1857, they became the first Britons to climb the Finsteraarhorn, they thought it more splendid still. On returning home they gathered at Mathews's house on the outskirts of Birmingham and drew up a list of who should be invited to join.

Kennedy took the lead in rousting up subscribers, a task which suited him to perfection. He was a man who should have been born fifty years earlier, when blue swallowtail coats were the rage and every man worth his salt carried a rapier to give the nightwatchman a prod. He had come into a fortune when he was 16 and since then had devoted himself to life. For a while he lived with thieves and garrotters and once walked from London to Brighton with a mob of tramps. He was famous for his catchphrase 'Is it right?' which he applied to every situation in which he found himself. The Alps were 'right' in his eyes and he persuaded many people to take this view. He also plumped up Mathews's proposal into something much more to his liking. There would be not one but two dinners per annum, famous names would be invited to speak and everybody should pay a guinea for a year's membership. Hort was disturbed. It was quite right that the club should be select, he told Kennedy, but 'Is it not rather much to ask a guinea a year, besides *two* dinners and (for all except Londoners) two double journeys to town?'[24] There were also one or two other clauses in Kennedy's outline that Hort disagreed with: 'What idea lurks under "geographical explorers" and "other guests of celebrity"?' he asked. 'Surely we do not want speeches from Dr. Livingstone or Sir Robert Murchison?'[25] In fact, the more he thought about it, the more worried he became – 'The guinea subscription should be reconsidered as possibly showy,' he said, adding a desperate postscript: 'Lightfoot, who left me this morning, begs me to say the same thing.'[26]

Kennedy ignored Hort's quibbles, added his name to the list and told Mathews that everything was in order. On 22 December 1857, therefore, the Alpine Club was formally inaugurated at Astley's Hotel, Covent Garden, its declared aim being 'the promotion of good fellowship among mountaineers, of mountain climbing and mountain exploration throughout the world, and of better knowledge of the mountains through literature, science and art'.[27] There was a slight flurry when Albert Smith, one of the first invitees, told everybody that he had discussed just such a club several years earlier with Auldjo and was very pleased that his idea had now been taken up. But otherwise the Alpine Club got off to an easy start. John Ball, the Irish politician and scientist, Under-Secretary for the Colonies in 1855, who had spent the last twenty years climbing the Alps, took the chair as President, while the publisher William Longman was elected Vice-President.

Initially it was decided that all members should have climbed to a height of at least 13,000 feet. Later, however, this was toned down to to include people who had written about the Alps, performed 'mountain exploits' or simply shown an interest in the region. 'It was at first assumed,' Longman wrote, 'that the Club would take the character rather of a social gathering of a few mountaineers rather than of a really important society.'[28] This, and the relaxed qualifications for membership, proved very attractive. In the first year 80 people joined; by 1861 there were 158 members; and two years later the club's list contained 281 names who had paid their annual guinea. The composition of the 1863 list was interesting. It included 57 barristers, 34 clergymen, 23 solicitors, 19 landed gentry and 15 university dons. This was to be expected: these types, 148 of them in all, enjoyed good incomes and long holidays. More intriguing, however, was the fact that 133 members – nearly half the total – were not so blessed yet still devoted what spare time they had to the pursuit of mountaineering. The Alpine Club was open to all, regardless of class or income, and as such was a *rara avis* in the world of Victorian clubmanship. As the club grew it attracted its share of non-climbers: Wilfrid Scawen Blunt, for example, who was primarily a diplomat and breeder of Arab horses; Richard Burton, who scraped in on the count of 'General travel; mountain ranges in all parts of the world'; Thomas Atkinson, a bricklayer's assistant who travelled across Russia as a spy for the Tsar and then returned to Britain to become a prominent architect with two wives; and on a very basic level, the poet Matthew Arnold who declared that 'everyone should see the Alps once, to know what they are'.[29] On the whole, however, everybody had a genuine enthusiasm for the Alps as well as a desire to climb them. They had, as one journal put it, been 'bitten by the tarantula of sport'.[30]

In 1859 the Alpine Club published its first volume of climbers' tales to huge public acclaim. *Peaks, Passes and Glaciers* was edited by John Ball and contained a selection of the most important climbs made in the last few years by club members. Wills contributed a story and so did many other big names. The entries were well written, well illustrated and stirring in the extreme. Wills told readers what it was like to shelter in a grotto on the back slopes of Mont Blanc; another member, John Tyndall, described the horrors of a rockfall amidst the seracs of the Col du Géant, where lumps of stone weighing half a ton bounced from pillar to pillar streaming contrails of ice in their wake; and Kennedy described in nail-biting terms his ascent – the first ever – of the Bristenstock when he and a companion reached the peak without guides and then made the mistake of coming down by a different route.

Of all the chapters in *Peaks, Passes and Glaciers*, Kennedy's was the most thrilling. He told how he and his friend had been assured by their innkeeper that the Bristenstock was an easy climb: everybody had done it; several guides had been up and down in less than six hours. So the two Britons went up it. They reached the top without any trouble, then decided to descend by the easiest-looking slope rather than the ridge by which they had ascended. The easy slope gradually became a difficult one and then turned into a rock precipice lined with shelves. They slipped from shelf to shelf in the confidence that they would soon reach the bottom. But, having descended 2,000 feet, they came to a halt. Below them was a 5,000-foot drop of sheer rock. There was no way round it. They could only go back the way they had come. It was late afternoon and they had just a few hours to reach safety before darkness fell. When slithering from shelf to shelf they had given no thought to climbing back up; often they had dropped more than a man's height. Kennedy described the return journey in which he balanced himself on narrow outcrops a few inches wide, his fingers gripping any available crevice, while his companion climbed on his shoulders to reach the outcrop above. Shelf by shelf they laboured back to the summit. Incredibly, they then chose another short cut down. It was as hopeless as the first, and when night fell they were stuck on a ledge measuring four feet by eight with cliffs above and below. They built a small wall to stop themselves rolling over the edge and then fell asleep in each other's arms. When either of them turned, lumps of wall tumbled into the valley below. The next day they worked their way back to safe ground and started on a new short cut. This time they were lucky and got below the snowline. They were battling their way through the pine trees when, to their relief, they met a woodcutter from whom they asked directions. Surprised, he told them that most people came down the hill by the track. It was over there, a few yards away.

When Kennedy reached the bottom, after an absence of thirty-six hours, he learned that, in fact, his innkeeper had exaggerated when he had said that it was an easy climb; and when he said everybody had done it he really meant that nobody had: 'He admitted that neither he, nor any one else, knew anything about the mountain, that the professed guides had never reached the summit, and that, so far as was aware, only one man had ever been there, and he was killed.'[31] Later on in their travels, Kennedy and his companion heard that two young men had perished miserably on the Bristenstock: 'nothing was found of their mangled corpses,' they were told, 'save some small particles of blood-stained clothing'. Kennedy replied, in an example of the most ponderous Victorian humour, that he had slid down some rough patches and that 'I afterwards found myself minus a portion of my nether integuments, and these, no doubt, are the portions of raiment, the discovery of which you relate.'[32]

Stories like this appealed enormously to the British public. *Peaks, Passes and Glaciers* went into its second edition after only six weeks and received rapturous notices. Forbes, Smith and Wills had done their bit to acquaint people with the Alps; the Alpine Club now placed them irrevocably on the map. 'The aim and end of the Alpine Club is a noble one,' cheered a reviewer in *Blackwood's Magazine*, who went on to explain, in rather appalling terms, why this was so. 'The sporting passion exists to a greater or lesser degree, in some shape or other, in the breast of every genuine British man,' he announced. 'It is a remnant of barbarism, we are willing to allow, which has clung to us through the whole course of our progressive civilisation and which we hope, indeed, will be the last to leave us.'[33] Sport was defined as 'physical exercise combined with hazard', and hitherto had been confined in English eyes to fox-hunting or, at a pinch, lion-stalking and buffalo-shooting. It was something that Britons did and which other nationalities were only dimly capable of understanding – they went to war instead, sniffed the reviewer, ignoring Britain's recent fracas in the Crimea. But not everybody could afford to 'gratify the national longing' in the time-honoured fashion. What then were they to do, these 'hundreds of high-spirited Britons, well educated, well mannered, with high tastes and sympathies, blest with abundant vigour, but moderate means'?[34] Why, they were to go to the Alps. Not to the usual watering holes – 'none but a degenerate Briton would be found among the *habitués* of a German spa,'[35] the reviewer warned – but to the high tops because, 'the great discovery of the day is a species of sport to which its devotees give the not unapt name of Mountaineering'.[36]

It was out. Mountaineering had a name, a purpose and a following. Moreover, given that the Alps were for the most part undiscovered, it was considered as valid a means of exploration as any other. The Royal Geographical Society, which was Britain's prime mover in the field of exploration, had paid scant attention to the Alps. Apart from Barrow's brief blast in 1844, the only notice it took of the region was when Professor Chaix of Geneva sent the odd communication relating Switzerland's efforts to map the range. The Alpine Club could therefore claim the opening of a new part of Europe as its own. 'It is to be esteemed a national honour,' *Blackwood's* concluded, 'that most of these peaks hitherto considered inaccessible, and many of those passes hitherto considered impassable, have yielded to the courage and perseverance of those islanders, whose still more daring and enduring countrymen have passed the continuous night of the Arctic winter in darkness and suffering, to solve problems not much more important; or endured the torture of thirst in the burning deserts of Central Africa, with an end and purpose avowedly and really higher, but in no dissimilar spirit.'[37] Neither comparison was exact but it was a welcome announcement that the Alps were worthy of exploration. Suddenly, people realised that in the middle of Europe there lay a zone with its own flora and fauna, its own climate and its own hundreds of unclimbed peaks. This was not news: scientists had known that the Alps were a unique environment for more than 150 years. What was news, however, was that virtually anybody could go out there and climb them. And who knew what they might find? Dragons were probably too much to hope for – although one could never be sure – but there was the prospect of limitless discovery on a smaller scale. All they had to do was join the Alpine Club.

'We prophesy,' said *Blackwood's*, 'that, amongst men of intelligence as well as spirit, this will soon be one of the most popular of all the clubs.'[38] It was.

CHAPTER FOURTEEN

John Tyndall was a pale, highly intelligent, very aggressive, Irish scientist who worked his way from obscurity to fame by sheer force of intellect. Born on 2 August 1820, he received a rudimentary education from a local priest and went on to work as a surveyor in England before studying in various European universities. To say he was quick would have been an understatement. In 1854 he wrote: 'I am . . . sadly bewildered. I know nothing of magnetism. The experiments which everybody seems to understand are those which puzzle me most.'[1] The following year he was lecturing on magnetism to the Royal Society. His forte, however, was gases, and he coughed himself sick over them as long as he lived. He later became one of Britain's most famous physicists. He was a populariser rather than an innovator, but he gave his name to numerous discoveries – such as 'Tyndall's Scattering', an analysis of light rays that explains why the sky looks blue. After Faraday he was the world's most successful promoter of science: his books sold in thousands and his lectures were attended by as many.

Tyndall was thin but possessed huge hands and an enormous head on which were perched exaggerated features that betrayed humour and irritation in equal measure. He wore an under-the-chin beard in an attempt to make his long face look shorter – the style was known as a Newgate fringe, after the notorious London gallows – and he was usually seen in a tall hat which he hoped would achieve the same effect. Neither device worked; indeed, they made him look even stranger than he already did. He was probably aware of this, which may have fuelled his notoriously short temper. He instantaneously loathed anybody who disagreed with his views – once he offered to fight a man who spoke slightingly of his favourite poet, Carlyle – and he held strong views about the Alps.

He first visited the mountains in 1849 when, like Smith and so many others, he went on a walking tour as a student. He was very poor: 'Trusting to my legs and stick, repudiating guides, eating bread and milk, and sleeping where possible in the country villages where nobody could detect my accent, I got through amazingly cheap.'[2] He was more interested in the people he met and in the novelty of travelling alone than he was in the Alps themselves. The celebrated tourist peak of the Rigi, the view from which at sunrise and sunset was reckoned the most magnificent in the world, he described merely as 'a cloudy mountain, famous for its guzzling and its noise'.[3] When he came home he declared in Ruskinesque fashion that 'the distant aspect of the Alps appeared to be far more glorious than the nearer view'.[4] He would probably have continued to hold this opinion forever were it not for slaty cleavage.

Slaty cleavage, by which was meant a particular result of pressure upon mineral bodies, was the subject of a lecture that Tyndall gave to the Royal Institution on 10 June 1856. By this time he was a well-known and respected scientist – in 1853 he had been offered one of the Royal Society's two annual medals but had turned it down in a fit of purism; the other one was accepted by Charles Darwin – and he and his fellow scientist and friend T. H. Huxley, both of whom had read Forbes's *Travels*, wondered if the theory of slaty cleavage might be applicable to the laminations Forbes had found in the glaciers. That summer they went to the Alps to investigate. Scientifically, the only interesting outcome of this visit was a furious spat that turned on an emendation suggested by Tyndall of the way in which glaciers moved and a query as to who had first formulated the idea of glaciers being plastic. Tyndall said it was Rendu via Agassiz, Forbes said it was himself. Tempers rose: 'Forbes is *not* a great man,'[5] Tyndall wrote in his journal. A colleague went further, declaring that Forbes was 'self-ish, uncandid and ungenerous minded',[6] and that his reasonings were 'contemptible from beginning to end'.[7] Both men were about equal in scientific respectability, intransigence, temper and health – Forbes suffered from gastric problems, Tyndall from chronic indigestion and insomnia – and they enjoyed a choleric correspondence from which Forbes emerged, narrowly, as the victor. This was was quite some victory for, as one man said, Tyndall was 'in debate a terribly rough and unconquerable antagonist . . . he enjoys an intellectual fence for its own sake, and I am not sure that his own dexterity in inflicting sharp lashes is not a source of amusement to him'.[8] Amongst Tyndall's peers there was a quiet joy that he had met his match.

On a secondary but more lasting level, Tyndall fell in love with the Alps. 'By and by,' he had written in 1855, 'when the mind has grown too large for its mansion, it often finds difficulty in breaking down the walls of what has become its prison instead of its home.'[9] A troubled agnostic, he wanted something more emotive than science and more tangible than religion: 'My power over science is, I think, increasing greatly; but the power and vigour of what I call my soul is not com-mensurate,'[10] he wrote in the same year. The Alps offered the physical and spiritual release he craved. Relaxing after a climb with Huxley he ate a meal of mutton and fried potatoes, washed down with cool, fizzy Sallenches beer. 'I can hardly think it possible for [anyone] to be more happy than we then were,' he wrote.[11] In a letter to Michael Faraday dated 27 August 1856 he said little about science and much about the view to be had from the Bernese Oberland glaciers:

A scene of indescribable magnificence opened before us. Right in front was the mighty mass of the Finsteraarhorn, further towards the horizon was the grand peak of the Weisshorn, more to the left we had the snowy summits of Monte Rosa, by the side of which the cone of the Matterhorn rose like a black savage tattooed with streaks of snow. Still further to the left

the chain of the Furca, with shoulders of snow as smooth as
chiselled Carrara marble, completed the picture; and over all
this the glorious sun poured his undimmed radiance. It was a
scene calculated to stir the heart of man, and to carve for itself
an everlasting place in his memory.[12]

Against this, slaty cleavage seemed a trifle dull.

Tyndall continued to make forays into the Alps, and reiterated constantly that he was doing so only for scientific purposes.
Simultaneously, he announced that there was nothing he liked so
much as a difficult climb over undiscovered slopes. Bit by bit, and
without for a moment admitting it, he mutated from scientist to
explorer – a move that reflected the overall trend. With the great
glacier question more or less solved, the Alps were of diminishing
interest to scientists. This did not mean that they had nothing to
offer. Quite the contrary: geologists, botanists, astronomers, meteo-
rologists, glaciologists and geographers still found plenty to occupy
them. But in relative terms science no longer held sway as it had
done. The great game for modern explorers was to cover new ground,
to scale unclimbed peaks and – though it would be a while before
anyone expressed it in so many words – to examine the inner, spiritual
benefits which mountaineering conferred.

Within a few years Tyndall was climbing for the sheer pleasure of
it. Reading the journals of his climbing years one gets an idea of the
forces that drove him. At home, in London, his health was appalling:
he was plagued by constant headaches; every month he was wracked
by some new pain in other parts of his body; his digestion was so
dreadful that once, having eaten some bread and butter for breakfast
and a bowl of soup for lunch, he had to go for a three-hour walk to
relieve the discomfort. The heaviest he ever weighed was ten stone,
and that with his clothes on. Worst of all was his insomnia: perhaps
one night in thirty he managed six hours' sleep; for the rest he got by
with five minutes and the odd doze. He tried to combat his condition
with a careful, but ineffective, combination of plain food, brandy,
cigars, chloroform and exercise. Every day he went for an hour's walk

around Kensington Gardens; sometimes he would run instead of walk. He wanted desperately to find a wife but feared that his age, physical oddness and devotion to science were against him. His loneliness was exacerbated by an extraordinary fondness for children. His scientific mind forbade him any comfort in religion and he was outspoken on that other Victorian solace, spiritualism.

In the Alps, Tyndall forgot his pains. His digestion improved, he slept better and he was able to forget his matrimonial disappointments. He also found there a source of comfort which he was hard pressed to define but which seemed to fill a void. 'There are certain aspects of nature,' he wrote, 'which . . . *utter* or make manifest the human soul.'[13] In similar vein: 'The soul is a form into which those masses pour themselves thus imparting to it their mass and vigour.'[14] From being a catalogue of woes and doubts his journal became, during the months of July, August and September, a model of positive thinking. 'Hail to the Alps!'[15] began a typical entry, as he embarked on a new spree of mountaineering. Infused with the strength of the hills, he went up them in a maniacal display of toughness. In 1858 he climbed the Finsteraarhorn once and Monte Rosa twice – on the second occasion he did so with no guides, no porters and no provisions save a bottle of tea and a ham sandwich. At the top he dropped his axe without which he would have been unable to make his descent. It slid towards the edge of the precipice and came to a rest 30 yards from the brink. He regained it and made light of the incident in his journal. But as he told a friend towards the end of his life, it had been the worst moment of his life. Later that season he climbed Mont Blanc with Wills and Auguste Balmat in conditions so appalling that Balmat nearly lost both hands to frostbite and the porters looked 'like worn old men, their hair and clothing white with snow, and their faces blue, withered, and anxious-looking'.[16] The following year he took Balmat to Mont Blanc again for the purpose of erecting a chain of permanent thermometers up and down its slopes. He felt ill when he started, and became sicker as he went on. But he refused to give up – 'had I faltered my party would have melted away'[17] – and proceeded to spend a record twenty hours on the summit at 5°F below freezing, firing pistols to test the transmission of sound waves, lighting candles to see how fast they burned, sending rockets up to check on the speed and extent of their combustion and making careful observations of transmitted and reflected light at sunrise. Then he returned to Chamonix having lost his temper only once and presumably – although he did not mention it – still feeling sick.

Describing his lust for hardship, he wrote that 'Vague and deep combinations organised in barbarous times, have come down with considerable force to me.'[18] It was almost as if he was trying to re-define himself as one of Rousseau's noble savages. If he succeeded in doing so it was as a particularly aggressive Victorian savage. He attacked mountains with ferocity, ambitious to conquer, keen to break new ground – scientific, geographical or spiritual, it did not matter which – determined to succeed, to free his mind from its mansion and his soul from its fetters. He quickly gained a reputation. 'One of the best mountaineers is one of the foremost Engish scientists,' wrote the Belgian economist Émile de Laveleye, 'all through the Swiss Alpine districts people know of him . . . [as] a hardy and dauntless mountaineer . . . Guides never mention him . . . save with the utmost respect.'[19] His friend Huxley was so struck by his tenacity that he nicknamed him 'Cat'. No longer was Tyndall an odd man with a long face, silly beard and narrow shoulders. He may still have possessed all these physical attributes – his shoulders did fill out with time – yet such was his presence that he came across as a giant. A Genevan climber named Thioly, who had a temper to match Tyndall's, recalled meeting him. 'Mr. Tyndall . . . stared me up and down from head to foot (I was wearing white canvas gaiters), just as a member of the Jockey Club might look at the legs of a racehorse. As I was not com-pletely arrayed in wools and furs, I was to him only an amateur, a meddler attempting to defy the giant of the Alps, erected by God himself for the exclusive use of English mountaineers.'[20] In the la-boratory Tyndall was a diligent practitioner. In the mountains he was the lord of all creation.

As a mountaineer Tyndall was among the first to realise that if people wished to reach the unknown they had better refine their technique for doing so. Mountaineering skills had reached a certain level in the sixteenth century and since then had hardly advanced at all. Climbers went to the hills equipped with an alpenstock and crampons but little else. In Chamonix, the typical alpenstock was seven or eight feet long, tipped with an iron ferrule; it was good for surmounting steep glaciers, it was a magnificent glissading pole and, turned horizontally, it made a good trapeze when snow bridges disintegrated beneath your feet. But it was unwieldy; and its length was so smooth that unless you gripped the top it was all but useless as a stay. Oberlanders were slightly more sophisticated, favouring shorter poles equipped with a small axehead that could be hooked into crevices to give the user extra purchase. Both Chamoniards and Oberlanders carried a small hatchet for cutting ice steps. The modern ice axe with a pick and a blade was in its infancy. Crampons were only slightly more advanced. In the late eighteenth century Chamonix hunters had used crampons that consisted of a single bar of iron strapped beneath the instep of each foot; Saussure had found this incredibly uncomfortable and had suggested a better device comprising a human horseshoe studded with nails at the front and sides. It was adopted without question – it was anyway already commonplace in the Oberland. Trusting nobody in the matter of footwear, Britons eschewed crampons altogether and drove two rows of triple-headed tacks around their double-soled 'London' boots. (Continental tacks were acceptable in an emergency, but travellers were advised to purchase the genuine item from a reputable bootmaker in the Strand.) When it came to ropes, however, Chamoniards, Oberlanders and Britons were equally obtuse. Throughout the first half of the nineteenth century the use of ropes was considered unmanly and unprofessional – dangerous, even: it was universally held that if a party was roped on a steep slope and one member slipped, then everybody else would be dragged to their doom with him. No, ropes were not for serious climbers, they were a placebo for the faint-hearted. Guides would string a line of tourists together and lead them over the glaciers holding onto either end of the rope as if it were a dog's lead. When ropes were deemed necessary on major ascents, the same philosophy prevailed: stout hessian and good knots gave the *étrangers* a sense of security, but the guides still preferred just to hold on, or, at a pinch, to loop the rope around a free arm.

The first suggestion that ropes could save lives had come in the aftermath of the Hamel disaster. Dornford, however, had quashed the idea. As a survivor he could state confidently that ropes were a hindrance to climbing and the lack of them had probably saved his life. In that particular case he may have been right for the counter-weight of one man, two men or even 20 men would have been as nothing against the force of an avalanche. There were other cases, however, where he was wrong and this was quickly spotted by members of the Alpine Club – among them Tyndall.

The weather in 1860 was as bad as the Alps had experienced in years. Nevertheless, two Britons accompanied by three guides, decided to climb the Col du Géant. They reached the top without any trouble but on the way down the Britons felt tired: they opted for a short cut via a treacherous snow slope rather than take the longer but safer route over rocks. (This was another realisation that was slowly dawning on the mountaineering community: rocks, although harder and apparently less sure than snow, held fewer perils because they were avalanche-free and their solidity was not so dependent on the weather. Tyndall, ahead of his time, was a rock man.) The Britons were roped together with one guide, Frédéric Tairraz, on the rope between them. The other two guides, as was customary, held the rope at either end. Exhausted, one of the Britons slipped. He dragged first Tairraz and then his companion off their feet. All three slid through the fresh snow, precipitating an avalanche that swept them to their deaths. The guides who should have been supporting them, either had the rope pulled from their hands or let go. Tyndall was in the area at the time and, being a member of the Alpine Club and therefore a sort of Honorary Consul to the state of mountaineering, he decided to investigate the accident. His findings were grim.

Accompanied by one guide from Courmayeur, he climbed the slopes down which the climbers had fallen. It was not hard to follow their route. At regular intervals his hand grasped for a rock only to find traces of the dead men's passage – a penknife, a compass, scraps of cloth, a brand-new axe. On reaching the col he was deeply depressed: 'As I stood there and scanned the line of my ascent a feeling of augmented sadness took possession of me. There seemed no sufficient reason for this terrible catastrophe. With ordinary care the slip might in the first instance have been avoided, and with a moderate amount of skill and vigour the motion, I am persuaded, might have been arrested soon after it had begun.'[21]

Meticulously, Tyndall reconstructed the disaster. The weather had been foggy and by the time they reached the top everybody was in a state of fatigue. Even on the gentler slopes one of the Britons had slipped repeatedly. Coming down, the guides should have been alert to the danger of letting weary men enter difficult ground. But they weren't. The first man slipped and the others came down after him. They slid, gathering momentum as the snow crust separated from the ice below, and flew over a ridge of rocks that marked the top of a precipice. The ridge gave them an upward lift which carried them over a steep slope of rocks leading to the brink of a second precipice. They bounced over this and hurtled towards a third. One Briton stopped at the bottom of the second precipice, another stuck on the edge of the third and the last dangled over the lip, still attached to his companion by the rope. Tyndall did not say exactly where Tairraz landed, but it was much lower down and in consequence the body 'was much more broken'.[22]

Tyndall was certain that they all died painlessly: 'I do not think a single second's suffering could have been endured. During the wild rush downwards the bewilderment was too great to permit even of fear, and at the base of the precipice life and feeling suddenly ended together.'[23] He was also certain that the Britons died as Britons should. 'Tairraz screamed,' he recorded, 'but, like Englishmen, the others met their doom without a word of exclamation.'[24] And he was even more certain that the two other guides had been derelict in their duties: 'What efforts were made to check their fearful rush, at what point the two guides relinquished the rope, which of them gave way first, the public does not know, though this ought to be known. All that is known to the public is that the two men who led and followed the party let go the rope and escaped, while the three Englishmen and Tairraz went to their destruction.'[25]

Tyndall's verdict was that inadequate use had been made of the rope. 'Each man as he fell ought to have turned promptly on his face, pierced with his armed staff the superficial layer of soft snow, and pressed with both hands the spike into the consolidated mass beneath. He would thus have applied a brake, sufficient not only to ring himself to rest, but, if well done, sufficient, I believe, to stop a second person.'[26] The fallers had been unable to do so, for some reason – a note of reproof enters Tyndall's analysis at this point – but the guides on either end could have, had they been roped around the waist leaving both hands free to deploy the alpenstock. 'I do not lightly express this opinion,' Tyndall concluded, 'it is founded on various experience upon slopes at least as steep as that under consideration.'[27]

An enquiry exonerated the surviving guides of all blame, sending Tyndall into paroxysms of outrage. 'A catastrophe of this kind ought not to be suffered to be skimmed over by a mere judicial acquittal,' he wrote to *The Times*. 'What can an ordinary Government official know of the power or the duty of a guide under such circumstances? Cast such an official upon such a slope; he will infallibly go to smash, and he naturally concludes that all others must do so in similar circumstances. But little weight is to be attached to the opinion of any man unpractised in such matters . . . The guides of Chamonix ought to regard this terrible disaster as a stain upon their order which it will require years of service faithfully and wisely rendered to wipe away.'[28]

Tyndall's letter was printed on 8 September 1860. Four days later a correspondent gave the following reply: 'I would . . . inquire what right we wealthy strangers have, making Switzerland our playground, thus to thrust ourselves in sheer wantonness into all manner of dangerous positions, bribing the poor people of the country to aid and protect us in doing so at the peril of their own lives.' He asked Tyndall to imagine what might happen if the Swiss descended on the Highlands of Scotland, sending 'their overfed and plethoric men of

pleasure and their wan and jaded lawyers' to climb a hill accompanied
by whatever locals were willing to accept their money. What then, if
they slipped and fell? Would the Highlanders be to blame? Or would
the Swiss be responsible, for having lured them with their bottomless
moneybags to try feats they had never attempted before? 'And then
imagine,' he concluded, 'a Swiss Mr. Tyndall writing to *The Times* to
denounce and censure the uneducated peasants who had been
enticed into the foolish and deadly undertaking by educated men
like himself who ought to have known better.'[29] The writer signed
himself COMMON SENSE.

The Alpine Club hastened to Tyndall's rescue. A flock of letters
landed on the editor's desk – most of them anonymous, most of then
published – rebutting all of COMMON SENSE's arguments. The guides
knew what they were doing; guiding was the best chance they had of
making money; they earned little enough as it was; and the risks were
minimal compared to their usual occupation, chamois-hunting.
Tyndall's was the one absent voice. But he had never been prone to
argument in the press.

Unlike many of his fellow climbers, Tyndall did not lose sight of
the dangers inherent in mountaineering. 'The perils of wandering in
the High Alps are terribly real,' he warned, 'and are only to be met by
knowledge, caution, skill and strength.'[30] This was the right attitude
and he was supported in it by many fellow members of the Alpine
Club. Strangely, however, there were some who thought the dangers
exaggerated. 'With tolerable training and proper precaution, nothing
serious need be apprehended,'[31] stated the climber Thomas
Hinchliff. More extraordinarily, Kennedy announced after ascending
Mont Blanc that 'the risk of serious accident was but little greater than
that incurred by the pedestrian in the streets of London'.[32] The very
clothes of some climbers suggested insouciance: back in 1787 Beaufoy
had conquered Europe's highest mountain in what he described as
little more than a pair of pyjamas; Wills went up the Wetterhorn wearing elastic-sided boots and cricketing flannels; Smith's Cambridge
companions climbed Mont Blanc in 'a light boating attire'.[33] It was not
that these people underrated the hazards of the Alps, simply that

they thought they knew how to handle them. Their judgement was clouded by familiarity. They needed a shake-up and they got it in 1861 when the glaciers of Mont Blanc oozed forth a timely reminder.

In the spring of 1861, Tyndall invited Auguste Balmat to speak at a meeting in the British Museum. The occasion started uneventfully but, halfway through, Balmat was interrupted by an old man in the audience. Was he from Chamonix, the man wanted to know? Balmat admitted that he was. 'Then when are you going to recover the bodies of my three guides?' the man snapped. 'I am Dr. Hamel.' Balmat could only stutter that he was sure they would surface sooner or later. 'Yes, yes, I think so too, and it'll be a happy day for Chamonix,' sneered Hamel. 'They'll make very interesting museum exhibits and lots of tourists will come to see them.'[34] In the commotion that ensued, Balmat sat down and said nothing more. For forty-one years, ever since the disaster of 1820, Chamoniards had execrated the Russian doctor who, they believed, had brought about the deaths of three brave men; his name had become legendary, the stuff of cautionary tales and childhood admonishments. Meeting Hamel was, for Balmat, like meeting the tiger under the bed.

Hamel's acerbic reappearance was not coincidental. In 1858, during his last visit to Chamonix, Professor James Forbes had calculated that if his measurements of the various glaciers' speeds was correct, the bodies of Hamel's guides would emerge between thirty-eight and forty years after the accident. He was only a year out. On 12 August 1861 a panting guide arrived at the Chamonix town hall with a sack on his back. It contained a number of items he had found in a crevasse at the bottom of the Glacier des Bossons. The sack was opened and its contents spread across a table for inspection by M. Million, the local doctor. Million closed the doors and began his examination. His findings, which were delivered in the subsequent *procès-verbal* and later published under a pseudonym by the chief of police, read as follows:

More than three-quarters of two skulls with flesh attached.
Several tufts of blond and black hair adhering to the scalps.

An entire jaw bone displaying good, white teeth.

A fore-arm with the hand attached, the latter missing only one finger. Both displaying undecayed, white flesh, with traces of blood at the stump of the ring finger, and retaining a degree of flexibility at the joints.

One left foot, severed at the calf, the flesh undecayed and white, the bones firm but slightly darkened.

Several ribs, intact and broken, two sections of spinal column, and a number of other anatomical fragments shattered to a greater or lesser degree but all recognisable as being of human origin.

Alongside the remains lie several other items: several pieces of cloth – wool or linen; part of a waistcoat; half of a black felt hat, some lengths of woven straw, part of another hat; a hobnailed boot, its crampon still attached by a strap; the rim and the top of a white felt hat lined in yellow silk; a pigeon wing with black feathers; a length of dark pine attached to a rusted ferrule, and a piece of sharpened iron, also rusted, measuring 0.12 metres in length and 0.03 metres in diameter; a tin lantern, its base circular and flat; a gigot of cooked mutton, the only item amongst the remains that smells foul. The guide swears that on the glacier it was as odour-free as the rest . . .[35]

And so Million went on, detailing with clinical precision the relics arrayed before him, while outside the town hall a crowd of locals waited for news. Million ordered the doors to be opened only once, to admit Hamel's two surviving guides: the octogenarian Julien Dévouassoud and Joseph-Marie Couttet, aged 72. Dévouassoud was now in his dotage and seemed to recognise or remember nothing. Couttet, however, identified everything with precision. The blond-haired skull belonged to Pierre Balmat. The other was that of Pierre Carrier. The silk-lined hat had been worn by Auguste Tairraz; and there was a wing from one of the pigeons he had been carrying. The iron segment had come from Couttet's own alpenstock. As the litany went on, Couttet lost his composure and tried to shake the hand that

lay on the table – 'That is Balmat's hand, I know it well!'[36] he cried –
but no further confirmation was needed. What Dr Million had before
him was the split, mangled yet horribly fresh remains of three men
who had fallen into a crevasse forty-one years before.

When Million was through, a search party was sent to the glacier to
look for more remains. It was driven back by bad weather and not
until the following year, a little lower down, was more debris recovered. Amongst the gruesome finds was a forearm that protruded
horizontally from the wall of a crevasse, its hand offering itself as if to
be shaken. The man who found it, one Francis Wey, did actually
shake it. He noted that although the flesh was white the fingernails
were pink and the knuckle joints were perfectly mobile. When he
pulled it free there was no body attached, and as he held it in the sun
its flesh began to wither and its nails faded to an opaque alabaster. Bit
by bit, and lower with each passing season, more body parts seeped
out. Another hand was recovered, which had gripped its alpenstock so
tightly that splinters of wood were embedded in its palm. In 1863, to
everybody's distress, a portion of somebody's back became visible in
the ice.

Exactly as Hamel had predicted, the relics were handed to the
great-niece of one of the guides, in whose home they were displayed
in a coffin to be gawped at by tourists. Such was the demand that her
door was open twenty-four hours a day. The remains were finally
buried in a communal grave – except the foot, which was immured in
a glass case by the Department of Museums at Annecy. The grave was
opened eight times in the next two years to accommodate additional
pieces of body. Meanwhile, the simplest articles retrieved from the
glacier sold for a phenomenal sum. Little scraps of cloth fetched ten
francs; larger rolls of material went for 100 francs a metre. An iron
crampon and part of a tin lantern fetched almost their weight in gold.
Back in London, the Alpine Club railed against such commercialism:
'It is sincerely to be hoped that a degrading trade in these relics will
not be allowed to spring up at Chamonix.'[37] It had no effect. An
Englishman paid one pound sterling for a trouser button.

If anything gave mountaineers a jolt, it was the discovery of these

remains. Having witnessed the hideous results of a process that shredded men, very slowly, limb from limb and then ejected them in as
pristine a state as if they had died the day before, they became more
subdued in their estimates of the Alps' dangers. There was no more
talk of the risks involved in crossing a London street, nor was there a
great deal of support for cricketing flannels as the ideal climbing
trouser. In succeeding years most mountaineers wore plus fours made
of tweed (now considered out of date, but an excellent material in
damp conditions) and were very cautious in the vicinity of glaciers.
They also roped up properly – some of the time.

CHAPTER FIFTEEN

Normally, Edward Shirley Kennedy knew how to write. On occasion, however, he could produce blisteringly awful prose. In 1855, when he climbed Mont Blanc with the Revd Charles Hudson – one of the Golden Age's most talented climbers – he wondered why they should try such a tired old hill on which so many scientific experiments had been made: 'May we add yet another drop to that mountain cup of knowledge, which is about to overflow?' Kennedy asked purply. 'The knapsack of Alpine lore is closing; and can we venture to assert that they who pack it leave one small corner unoccupied?'[1] His answer was that 'the ascent of this monarch of mountains gave us unbounded gratification'.[2] In other words, they did it just for the fun – and for the satisfaction of attacking it from such a direction as to avoid the iniquitous charges levied by the Chamonix Compagnie des Guides. But he was right in one respect: the knapsack was closing, and as the throng of Alpine Club members picked off more and more peaks there remained only one that ranked alongside Mont Blanc as the ultimate challenge: the Matterhorn.

Travellers and scientists had seen the Matterhorn from afar. But they had never dared dream of climbing it. Why not? Because it wasn't a mountain, it was a rock, the biggest rock in the known world, a rock that defied humankind with its absolute grandeur and its sheer faces. It was a decaying rock, and centuries of erosion had created an embankment of smaller rocks around its base. Twenty-four hours a day boulders dribbled down its flanks before smashing into the debris below. In winter its faces were covered with unstable snow; in summer the snow became a varnish of black ice. There was no clear way up it and its slopes were so impenetrably awful that nobody had ever thought of finding one. Anyway, dragons lived there.

Tyndall did not believe in dragons. He believed in what he saw, and what he saw was beauty. 'The summit seemed to smoke sometimes like a burning mountain,' he wrote, 'for immediately after its generation, the fog was drawn away in long filaments by the wind. As the sun sank lower the ruddiness of his light augmented, until these filaments resembled streamers of flame.'[3] In 1860 he and a friend named Vaughan Hawkins decided to climb the Matterhorn with the Oberland guide Johann Bennen. Everybody in the Alpine Club had a favourite guide, and Bennen was Tyndall's. Tyndall had an uncomfortable relationship with his guides. In 1857, when he made his first ascent of Mont Blanc, he refused the services of Auguste Balmat – 'the cunning of the boy did not please me'[4] – and chose a guide called Simond who was apparently even more unsatisfactory: 'Had a disaster occurred he certainly would have been clear of blame, for from beginning to end a word of encouragement never crossed his lips . . . Simond "fears" – his fears are perpetual. He is forever anticipating difficulty.'[5] Having accomplished the climb, Tyndall met again 'that grasping little Balmat . . . [he] put me on the whole in a humour which would have found pleasure in kicking him'.[6] Later, of another respected guide named Christian Lauener, he wrote that he did not like him because his trousers were too baggy: 'you prefer a machine whose parts work more easily, and do not expend their work in friction at the places of contact'.[7]

In Bennen, however, Tyndall found the man he wanted. When he first met him in 1858 he described him thus:

His round shoulders were bent forward, and set firmly upon them was a thick pedestal of a neck, which bore a massive

round head. He wore earrings. His trunk was of the same
width throughout: his pelvis was broad, which set his legs
rather far apart, but a slight bow neutralised this to some
extent. His limbs were massive but moved with alacrity and
firmness. The man's countenance was firm and straightforward
looking while a light of good nature broke from his eye and
made his face pleasant to look upon. In short, the whole man
gives the impression of great physical strength combined with
great decision of character.[8]

Hawkins was equally enthusiastic, describing Bennen as 'remarkable'. He belonged to

a type of mountain race having many of the simple heroic
qualities which we associate, whether justly or unjustly, with
Teutonic blood, and essentially different from – to my mind,
infinitely superior to – the French-speaking, versatile, wily
Chamoniard . . . he surpasses all the rest in the qualities which
fit a man for a leader in hazardous expeditions, combining
boldness and prudence with an ease and power peculiar to
himself, so he has a faculty of conceiving and planning his
achievements, a way of concentrating his mind upon an idea,
and working out his idea with clearness and decision, which I
never observed in any man of the kind . . . any one who has
watched Bennen skimming along through the mazes of a
crevassed glacier, or running like a chamois along the side of
slippery ice-covered crags, axe and foot keeping time together,
will think that nothing could bring him to grief but an
avalanche.[9]

When Tyndall called him the Garibaldi of mountaineering, Bennen
replied, 'Am I not?'[10]

In fact, Bennen was far less remarkable than Tyndall and Hawkins
thought. He was hesitant, sometimes nervous, and wanted not so
much to lead as to be told where to lead. Having lost his wife he

shunned society and moved homes with odd regularity on the grounds that the people did not suit him. In 1860 he was living at Laax with his mother and three sisters where, as Hawkins surmised, 'I guess him to be not perhaps altogether at home.'[11]

Not often at this date did Alpine Club members give much thought to their guides' characters. With one or two exceptions they preferred them to be stereotypes and portrayed them as such. In almost every journal the guide comes across as a simple, manly type with lungs like bellows, legs of steel, a hearty laugh, a keen eye and manners as perfect as any to be found in London society. Occasionally they were allowed wit, as in the case of Wills's guide Franz Andermatten whose favourite, and oft-quoted, expression with regard to difficult ascents was '*Es muss gehen*!' – 'It must be done!' or literally, 'It must go!' (It sprang from a mildly risqué joke that involved a priest, a lecherous old man and the latter's chances of getting into heaven.) On one memorable occasion an Englishman pointed at a difficult peak and tried to cajole Andermatten into climbing it with the words 'It must go!' Andermatten replied that it might well go but he wasn't.

When it came to Bennen the picture shimmered. He was agile yet recalcitrant, determined yet timorous, at one moment bold at another frightened. He was hearty when heartiness was required but had a disturbing tendency to burst into tears. In private he was almost a misanthrope. Out of season he worked on his own as a carpenter and went chamois-hunting with a silent friend named Bortis. One gets the impression that he climbed for the same reason as did his employers: he sought release. Whatever demons might lurk on the peaks, they were imps against those that bedevilled him in the valleys.

The Matterhorn, up which Bennen was to lead Tyndall, lay on the boundary between Switzerland and Italy and could be approached from two different directions. One was from the north, from Zermatt. This was considered beyond the bounds of human capability. A single glance was enough to dissuade people from climbing it. Like most north faces in the Alps it was sheer rock and seemed to offer not the smallest handhold. The other approach was from the south, from Breuil in Italy, where glaciers and a series of minor peaks presented a

better chance of reaching the summit. Hawkins and Bennen had surveyed the Matterhorn in 1859 and had decided that they could reach
the top from Breuil – 'almost', according to Bennen – and so, with
Tyndall (whom Hawkins had met by chance on the train to Basle),
they set about conquering the giant.

Tyndall may have not believed in dragons, but Hawkins did – or if
not dragons, then something similar. 'The mountain has a sort of
prestige of invincibility,' he wrote, 'which is not without its influence
on the mind, and almost leads one to expect to encounter some new
and unheard-of source of peril upon it.'[12] In 1860 the perils included
not only falling rocks but a shroud of snow that obliterated the terraces up which they had planned their route. Even before they started
they realised that they had little chance of reaching the top. But they
went ahead anyway, if only to show that the mountain could be
approached. They took with them a shaggy-haired, easy-going porter
named César Carrel who was said to be the best man for the job. He
was 40 or 50 – it was hard to tell – and had a sense of humour as well
as a sense of what was possible. He was willing to go wherever he was
directed but, as Hawkins wrote, 'I don't think his ideas of our success
were ever very sanguine.'[13]

The group left their hotel at Breuil at 3.00 a.m. on Monday, 20
August, Carrel carrying a lantern to see them over the rough patches.
Beyond its light the Matterhorn's outline beckoned against a nascent
dawn. 'Measuring with the eye the distance subtended by the height
we have to climb, it seems as if success *must* be possible,'[14] Hawkins
recorded. It was a climb unlike any other that had been attempted
before. Mont Blanc, the Jungfrau, the Wetterhorn and even the
Breithorn were by and large snow mountains. The Matterhorn was
rock – except that in this year it was also ice with a thin covering of
snow. Up they hacked, Tyndall shouting down constantly to remind
Hawkins of what he called 'the conditions'. The conditions were
that Hawkins should turn on his face if he slipped and drive his
alpenstock into the snow. If he did not do so, or if he rolled onto his
back, it 'is all over, unless others can save you: you have lost all
chance of helping yourself'.[15] Soon, however, they found themselves

free of snow and were onto a plateau. 'We are immersed in a wilderness of blocks, roofed and festooned with huge plates and stalactites of ice,' Hawkins wrote, 'so large that one is half disposed to seize hold and clamber up them.'[16] Bennen searched for an escape from this surreal landscape and eventually found one: it was a narrow ledge, above which rose a cliff that lacked any handholds and below which the mountain dropped sheer to the glacier below. The ledge was 1 foot wide and had a pronounced slope. They inched their way along it. Hawkins was scared: 'if the nails in our boots hold not, down we shall go'.[17] At one point they rounded a jutting rock to find themselves under a waterfall. They strode through it. On the other side the ledge stopped.

Dripping, they surveyed their options. The only possible way up was via a chimney of rock. But Tyndall and Hawkins could not imagine how anybody could climb it. Its sides were covered with an inch of black ice; the top was out of their sight; and the bottom opened onto space. Neither of the two Britons could explain what Bennen did next. One moment he was standing on the ledge, the next he had rolled 'like a cat'[18] to the top of the chimney and was lowering a rope to help the others up. Tyndall went first, followed by Hawkins, who tried to brace himself against the walls but dropped, only to be saved by the rope. Carrel was hauled up afterwards.

Three hours later, after they had climbed an endless succession of ridges and snow slopes, Hawkins got fed up. 'There is a tide in the affairs of such expeditions,' he wrote, 'and the impression had been gaining ground with me that the tide on the present occasion had turned against us.'[19] Bennen thought there was still a chance and Tyndall ventured no opinion; he would do whatever the guide thought right. When Bennen reached 'a mighty knob, huger and uglier than its fellows, to which a little *arête* of snow served as a sort of drawbridge'[20] and insisted on climbing it, with Tyndall pushing on his heels, Hawkins let go the rope and sat down with Carrel to await the outcome.

As silence descended, and Carrel took out his pipe, Hawkins began to revise his opinion both of the climb's practicability and the beauties of mountain scenery. 'The air was preternaturally still,' he wrote, 'an occasional gust came eddying round the corner of the mountain, but all else seemed strangely rigid and motionless, and out of keeping with the beating hearts and moving limbs, the life and activity of man. These stones and ice have no mercy in them, no sympathy with human adventure; they submit passively to what man can do; but let him go a step too far, let heart or hand fail, mist gather or sun go down, and they will exact the penalty to the uttermost. The feeling of "the sublime" in such cases depends very much, I think, on a certain balance between the forces of nature and man's ability to cope with them: if they are too strong for him, what was sublime becomes only terrible.' Had he been offered at that moment the finest Alpine sunset he would have seen not the vision of unearthly loveliness which so many had described so often, but only 'the angry eye of the setting sun fixed on dark rocks and dead-white snow'.[21]

Shouting up to Tyndall, he asked how long he intended to be. 'An hour and a half,' came the reply. Hawkins felt lonelier than ever. As if the Matterhorn was aware of his despair, it hurled down a boulder. It fell from the crags above, bounced down the rock face and then careered along a nearby couloir, narrowly missing Hawkins. Along its way it shed a splinter that hit Tyndall in the throat, nearly choking him. This shot across their bows, plus the fact that time was running out, persuaded Tyndall and Bennen to retreat. 'I was glad he had not gone on as long as he chose,'[22] Hawkins recorded plaintively, as he heard the clatter of nails on rock grow louder.

The way down, in which Bennen repeated his mysterious trick with the ice chimney, was, in Hawkins's opinion, as bad as the way up. Tyndall, however, seemed impervious to all perils. 'Splendid practice for us, this!'[23] he cried as he clambered across each successive difficulty. Roped between Tyndall and Carrel, who was now in such a haze of relaxedness that he had to be reminded constantly not to let go of the rope, Hawkins felt a touch queasy. After two hours they had overcome most of the major obstacles and were faced with the choice of continuing by the way they had come up or taking a short cut via a funnel of snow which issued onto the glacier below.

Bennen was all for the snow: it was now afternoon and the rocks would be slippery with melting ice. But the funnel was 'portentously steep, deeply lined with fresh snow, which glistens and melts in the sun'.[24] It was perfect for an avalanche, as well as an obvious conduit for rocks falling from above. After a brief discussion, they opted to go down it.

Tyndall must have been either touched by the sun or very tired. Already he had relaxed his rules to allow Carrel – the last in the line, an important position – to hold the rope rather than tie it round himself. Now, instead of sticking to the hard ground as was his wont, he decided to go down the snow – precisely the same decision that killed the four men on the Col du Géant. There were a few small outcrops at the bottom of the funnel which he persuaded himself would halt them in the event of a slide – a strange theory, given his knowledge to the contrary, but one which he often used to justify a dangerous move. Hawkins was less sure: 'Their tender mercies seem to me doubtful,'[25] he wrote. The four men spreadeagled themselves and began to climb down the funnel following a zigzag course set by Brennen. No rocks fell but, sure enough, there was an avalanche. It fell to their right just after they had zagged to the left. It was a small one, but it slid with terrible speed. Hawkins, who was nearest, said it was like being in the carriage of a provincial train as the London express passed by. Luckily – incredibly luckily – that was their only bad moment. They reached the bottom without further adventure and floundered waist-deep over the glacier, heedless of crevasses. Above them, storm clouds gathered over the Matterhorn.

On reaching dry ground Tyndall ran as fast as he could for Breuil, leaving Hawkins, Brennen and Carrel to follow. They did so with a degree of dignity, stopping off at a chalet for a drink of milk for which they offered the cowherd 40 centimes. He refused the payment, saying it was too much. Hawkins was bewildered and humbled. Like Forbes and other climbers, he could not help reflecting on the difference between his world and the one inhabited by these simple, hospitable people. In the industrial age it seemed as if the ancient projections were true: the Alps did harbour an alien race.

Bennen, Tyndall, Hawkins and Carrel had achieved something quite impressive. They had climbed to a height of 13,000 feet on what was never intended to be more than a reconnaissance mission – despite Hawkins's earlier hopes – and on their final burst Tyndall and Bennen had spied a relatively easy route to a peak that seemed to be a stepping stone to the summit itself. But Tyndall was discontented. 'Had I felt we had done our best on this occasion,' he wrote, 'I should have relinquished all further thought of the mountain; but, unhappily, I felt the reverse, and thus a little cloud of dissatisfaction hung round the memory of the attempt.'[26] He never stated explicitly what caused his dissatisfaction, but it may have been Bennen's behaviour. On the final stretch, while he and Bennen were scrambling up the rocks in just the hazardous fashion that Tyndall liked best, Bennen had announced excitedly 'I will lead you to the top!' Tyndall was equally excited and would have shouted 'Bravo!' had he not been squashed like a frog against the rock, in such a position that filling his lungs for a shout would have dislodged him. Later, however, Bennen dithered, became doubtful and – one of the worst crimes a guide could commit, in Tyndall's view – asked his employer what to do. Tyndall offered no opinion, and after further deliberation Bennen decided to retreat.

Tyndall was willing to be beaten by a mountain but he was not going to be beaten by a guide's nervousness. In 1861 he arrived at Breuil, primed for a second attempt. Alas, Bennen announced it was not to happen. On inspection he found the mountain more difficult and dangerous than he had imagined. It was impossible to reach the top in a day and if they tried to spend the night on the slopes they would freeze to death. Tyndall was puzzled: people had slept on Mont Blanc without dying. Might they, he wondered, reach a lower peak, which was a long way below the main one but only 400–500 feet above where they had turned back the previous year? To this Bennen replied, 'Even that is difficult. But when you have reached it, what then? The peak has neither name nor fame.'[27] Tyndall did his best to keep an even temper. While listening to Bennen's speech he stroked his beard thoughtfully; once the guide had gone he kicked the ground in anger, grinding his hobnails into the grass. Not being able to climb even one portion of the Matterhorn was 'like the removal of a pleasant drug or the breaking down of a religious faith. I hardly knew what to do with myself. One thing was certain . . . the mountains alone could restore what I had lost.'[28]

That year Tyndall embarked on a ferocious campaign of mountaineering. From Grimsel he climbed the Eggishorn. From the Eggishorn he descended to the Aletsch Glacier and fell in love with the views to be had from the hotel at Bel Alp. He discovered a pine tree growing horizontally from the gorge at the end of the glacier and climbed along its trunk to bathe his frustrations in the cold breath that came from below: 'I hugged its stem, and looked down into the gorge. It required several minutes to chase away my timidity, and as the wind blew more forcibly against me I clung with greater fixity to the tree. In this wild spot, and alone, I watched the dying fires of the day, until the latest glow had vanished from the mountains.'[29]

From Bel Alp he saw the grey pinnacle of the Sparrenhorn. He went up it. Later he went up the Monte Moro and after that the Old Weissthor too, during which he and Bennen were caught in a rockfall. They had risked a traverse across a gulley when a single boulder rumbled down on them. They ducked behind an outcrop and it sprang over their heads. In its wake, however, came a shoal of smaller rocks each of which was 'quite competent to crack a human life'.[30] At that moment they hung on a horribly steep slope of ice, which could only be crossed by hacking steps. A single slip would have meant death. '"Schnell!" with its metallic clang rang from the throat of Bennen; and never before had I seen his axe so promptly and vigorously applied.'[31] Bennen chopped footholds and handholds – mere scratches, according to Tyndall – and led his party on a fingernail escape to the other side of the couloir. It was an astonishing display of coordination: while carving steps Bennen also had to dodge the cannonade of stones and at the same time protect his employer. 'He once caught upon the handle of his axe,' Tyndall wrote, 'as a cricketer catches a ball upon his bat, a lump which might have finished my climbing.'[32] Hacking, ducking and batting, Bennen led them with a final jump to an embankment that was out of the line of fire, 'and we thus escaped a danger extremely exciting to us all'.[33] Tyndall may have found it exciting but the others did not. The experienced guide Franz Andermatten, who was part of the team, was so shaken that he slipped on the next traverse, knocked Bennen off his legs and might have dragged everybody with him had he not halted his fall. Had he heard Tyndall's later opinion that the rope 'was not made in England, and was perhaps lighter than it should have been',[34] he would have been more shaken still. Eventually they reached the summit and had a bite of cold mutton washed down with champagne.

The Old Weissthor aside, Tyndall's greatest achievement that year was the first ascent of the Weisshorn, a mountain that was 14,780 feet high and which was the most impressive thing to be seen from Zermatt other than the Matterhorn and Monte Rosa. 'I have always regarded [it] as the noblest mountain in the Alps,'[35] he wrote semi-truthfully to Faraday. He set out for it at 4.30 a.m. on Friday, 16 August 1861, leaving Bel Alp for Randa, near Zermatt, while 'the eastern heaven was hot with the glow of the rising sun'.[36] He had instructed Bennen to reconnoitre the Weisshorn – for once, the prognostication was favourable – and he had two pairs of rugs sewn together and forwarded to Randa in case sleeping bags were needed during the ascent.

Tyndall, Bennen and a guide named Wenger started for the Weisshorn from Randa at 1.00 p.m. on 18 August. Tyndall, as usual, had neither eaten well nor slept well but was fortified by a draught of milk at a chalet. 'The effect . . . was astonishing,' he wrote. 'It seemed to lubricate every atom of my body, and to exhilarate with its fragrance my brain.'[37] The sleeping bags were needed, and the team spent their first night in the open. Come sunset, Tyndall was agog. 'An intensely illuminated geranium flower seems to swim in its own colour, which apparently surrounds the petals like a layer, and defeats by its lustre any attempt of the eye to seize upon the sharp outline of the leaves. A similar effect was observed upon the mountains . . . the crown of the Weisshorn was imbedded in this magnificent light.'[38] He watched the stars wheeling over him and at length he covered his eyes with a handkerchief for fear he be blinded by the sight. He did not sleep.

At 3.35 a.m. the climb resumed. Tyndall shed his tweed jacket – 'The sunbeams and my own exertion would keep me only too warm during the day'[39] – and stowed it against his return. After three hours of slow progress they glimpsed the peak of the Weisshorn for the first time since leaving Randa. It looked as if it was within their grasp. When Tyndall remarked on this, Bennen replied grandly, 'I do not allow myself to entertain the idea of failure.'[40] Down below they could see the figures of two Randa guides who had set out with the idea of following them – maybe even beating them – to the summit. Tyndall was not worried: let the poor fools do their best; they were no match for Bennen, Wenger and himself; anyway, it could only be a short time before they were at the top.

Six hours later, however, the summit seemed no nearer and Tyndall was feeling unaccustomedly tired. 'There is scarcely a position possible to my body into which it was not folded up at one time or another during the day,' he wrote. 'Sometimes it was a fair pull upwards, sometimes an oblique twist round the corner of a rock tower; sometimes it was the grip of the finger ends in a fissure and lateral shifting of the whole body in a line parallel to the crack. Many times I found myself with my feet highest and my head lowest.'[41] The worst moment came when they reached a 20-yard ridge that spanned two sets of rocks. It was topped by a ridge of snow, and precipices sloped away on either side. Tyndall balked: 'How to cross this snow catenary I knew not, for I did not think a human foot could trust itself upon so frail a support.'[42] Bennen looked at it, trod the snow down and then walked across it on a path that was little wider than a hand's breadth. Tyndall 'followed him, exactly as a boy walking along a horizontal pole, with toes turned outwards. Right and left the precipices were appalling.'[43] At the other side Tyndall could only marvel at Bennen's sagacity. Ever the scientist, he wondered how Bennen knew that the snowy molecules would compress into 'a semi-solid rather than a mass of powder'.[44] Bennen replied that he'd given it a tread and it seemed firm enough.

By this time they were all flagging and Tyndall feared they would never make it: 'Wenger complained of his lungs, an expression of deep weariness shaded Bennen's face, while I was half bewildered and stupefied by the incessant knocking about.'[45] The summit, once so attainable, now seemed 'hopelessly distant'.[46] Wenger and Bennen fortified themselves with food and wine. Tyndall, for whom this was not an option, steeled himself with patriotic sentiment: 'I thought of Englishmen in battle, of the qualities which had made them famous: it was mainly the quality of not knowing when to yield – of fighting for duty even after they had ceased to be animated by hope. Such thoughts helped to lift me over the rocks.'[47] These selfsame qualities had also driven many British explorers and soldiers to their deaths, but this he did not dwell upon. The team struggled on, over false horizon after false horizon, until, four hours later, they met a knife-edge of pure snow that ran up to a little point. At first Tyndall refused to believe it was the summit, but when he slithered along the ridge and stood, shakily, on the peak he realised that at last the Weisshorn was his.

'Bennen shook his arms in the air and shouted as a Valaisian,' he recorded, 'while Wenger yelled the shriller cry of the Oberland.'[48] Some 3,000 feet below, the rival Randa climbers heard the shouts. 'Again and again the roar of triumph was sent down to them,'[49] until they acknowledged defeat and turned for home. Bennen then stripped the head from one of their axes and stuck the shaft in the snow with a red handkerchief tied to it. Tyndall was too awestruck to share in the enthusiasm. All he could do was stare. He could not even bring himself to make scientific notes. 'I had never before witnessed a view which affected me like this one,' he wrote. 'I opened my note-book to make a few observations, but soon relinquished the attempt. There was something incongruous, if not profane, in allowing the scientific faculty to interfere where silent worship seemed the "reasonable service".'[50] What gave him greatest happiness was not the view, however, but the contemplation that nobody in Randa had believed the Weisshorn could be climbed, least of all by a puny bean-pole who couldn't even eat the food he was served. Tyndall had proved them all wrong and had done so on nothing more substantial than twelve meat lozenges.

The descent was hazardous. As Kennedy had on the Bristenstock, Bennen chose a different route from the one they had taken going up, and at one point Tyndall, now weary beyond belief having eaten little and slept not at all for more than forty-eight hours, feared they had climbed themselves into a dead end. 'I felt desperately blank,'[51] he recorded, as he stared at the cliffs in front of them. But Bennen found a way down. As they descended, the Weisshorn gave a dramatic display of contempt: a single boulder fell from the summit; it bounced down, raising clouds of dust and bringing hundreds of smaller rocks in its wake, each of which puffed more dust into the air. Within seconds a major rockfall was under way. 'The clatter was stunning,' Tyndall wrote. 'Black masses of rock emerged here and there from the cloud, and sped through the air like flying fiends. Their motion was not one of translation merely, but they whizzed and vibrated in their flight as if urged by wings. The echoes resounded from side to side, from the Schallenberg to the Weisshorn and back, until finally, after many a deep-sounding thud in the snow, the whole troop came to rest at the bottom of the mountain.'[52] The rocks came nowhere near them but, after his experience on the Old Weissthor, Tyndall was shaken. It was 'one of the most extraordinary things I had ever witnessed'.[53]

They reached Breuil at 11.00 p.m., when Tyndall managed to swallow a bowl of broth and a piece of boiled mutton. Then he had a hot footbath and slept for a whole six hours. It was a welcome climax to a season of unparalleled triumph and hardship. When he woke, however, the Matterhorn still niggled at his mind. He was determined to conquer it, and told Bennen so. By 1862, he declared, the 'savage' would be his.

CHAPTER SIXTEEN

'As the strokes of midnight were clanging from the Campanile at Sondrio, a carriage rolled heavily into the courtyard of the Hotel della Maddelena.'[1] With these evocative words, Edward Shirley Kennedy opened his account of the first ascent of Monte della Disgrazia in August 1862. It was not an exceptionally high mountain nor an outstandingly difficult one to climb. But the account of its conquest was memorable because it was written with such style and because it was the first article in the first edition of the *Alpine Journal*. The direct successor of *Peaks, Passes and Glaciers*, the *Alpine Journal* was the truest yardstick to date of how popular the Alps had become. The first number was published in 1864 and positively fizzed with energy. Like its predecessor it gave accounts of new climbs; but it also contained a plethora of fascinating minutiae. Readers wrote in to ask whether such-and-such a man had climbed such-and-such a mountain, and whether anybody knew if the mountain even existed. They recommended Swiss inns, warned about incompetent guides, inveighed against banditry, and discussed boots, ropes and alpenstocks. Extraordinary images filled its pages: one man told how on Mont Blanc, just before dawn, he had cast a shadow that was completely green; another described phosphorescent snow sparkling from his companion's boots with each step that he took; a third related how his hair stood on end – as did his companions' crêpe veils – and how his upraised hands sang like a kettle in the electrical discharge of a thunderstorm. And booming from page to page came the echoes of Kennedy's declaration on the peak of Monte della Disgrazia: 'I am therefore justified in claiming for Alpine climbing the first rank among athletic sports, as the nourisher of those varied elements that go to form all that is commendable in the constitution of the Anglo-Saxon character.'[2]

The excitement was overwhelming – reminiscent, in a way, of that felt by citizens of a newly founded republic. Here was a group of men, unfettered by any rules save those they laid down, in thrall to no sovereign or governmental body, who were charged with opening a new world in a manner of their own choosing. Best of all, theirs was a republic without political or territorial responsibility, one that ignored boundaries (could one say that a precipice was intrinsically French, Italian or Swiss?), whose message was supranational (the Swiss and Italian Alpine Clubs were founded in 1863, the German and Austrian in 1869, the French in 1874 and the American soon after; a Carpathian Club sprang up in Poland) and whose scope was limitless – in the first number of the *Alpine Journal* a man described a climb in Sinai; soon reports would pour in from Norway, Greenland, Spitsbergen, Turkey, the Andes, the Rockies, the Caucasus, the Himalayas, anywhere, in fact, where there was a mountain. Theirs was a republic of the mind and the body. What did a man think of when he reached the top? Kennedy asked himself on Monte della Disgrazia. Was it 'How do I get down?' or 'Where's the wine?' or 'What a view!' or 'Give me my barometer!' No, he said, what men thought of was 'the exhilarating consciousness of difficulty overcome, and of success obtained by per-severance'.[3] He described the headiness of his return in words that had readers scrabbling for their boots: 'We had thus made a day of twenty-four hours, but whether it was the same day, or the next day, or the day after that day, or the same week, or the next week, that that day ended, is one of those things that a fellow never could tell.'[4]

Kennedy was the Alpine Club's prime propagandist. He told mem-bers what they wanted to hear, in tones that combined drama with confidentiality. When he clattered into the courtyard of the Hotel della Maddelena he had every intention of elucidating 'matters of antiquarian and geological interest' on the slopes of Disgrazia. But, as he added with a nod and a wink, 'another and a mightier attraction existed; we had an unascended peak in contemplation, and what mountaineer can resist the charms which such an object presents?'[5] Unascended peaks drew people like a magnet. There were still plenty of them: by 1862 barely half the peaks of the main Alpine range surrounding Mont Blanc, Grindelwald and Zermatt had been climbed, and there were scores of others in other areas. Even if a hill had been climbed there was the prospect of finding new, more testing routes up it. Members responded avidly.

The Alpine Club swelled in stature and numbers, gathering a hectic selection of madmen as it did so. There was, for example, Francis Fox Tuckett, who fled from mountain top to mountain top in an almost unblemished record of near disasters. (In 1863 he escaped by a hair's breadth one of the most monstrous avalanches ever known on the Eiger.) There was Lucy Walker – not a man and therefore not a member of the male-only Alpine Club, but nevertheless part of the circle – whose normal pastimes were needlework and polite conversation until shown an Alp, whereupon she would don a sturdy dress and spring to its summit. And what was one to make of a man like James Benjamin Redford Bulwer, who was simultaneously a barrister, musician, artist, actor, cricketer, skater, soldier, Conservative MP and a Master of Lunacy? Then there was Leslie Stephen.

Stephen, who had been Kennedy's partner on Monte della Disgrazia, protruded like a rock of sanity amid the torrent of Alpine enthusiasm. He was a man of letters, best remembered today as the editor of the *Dictionary of National Biography* and as the father of Virginia Woolf and Vanessa Bell. There was something of the Tyndall in him, in that he had been unhealthy and shy as a child, had overcome his weaknesses by exercise and had grown into a long, thin, bearded adult with a keen mind, an abhorrence of idleness and a capacity for overwork. He walked long distances at a steady four miles an hour and once covered the 50 miles between Cambridge and

London in twelve hours to attend an Alpine Club dinner. He had taken holy orders but had renounced Christianity to follow the same vaguely agnostic path as Tyndall. He lacked Tyndall's temper but had a knack of making people dislike him. This stemmed not from any particular unpleasantness in his character, but from an overwhelming desire to be left alone. 'I am the most easily bored of men,'[6] he once said. If a visitor outstayed his welcome, Stephen became visibly agitated, twisting his hair and finally muttering, to himself but quite audibly, 'Why can't he go? Why can't he go?'[7] His avowed opinion was that 'Life would be more tolerable if it were not for our fellow-creatures. They come about us like bees, and, as we cannot well destroy them, we are driven to some safe asylum. The Alps, as yet, remain.'[8] To the Alps, therefore, he went.

Year after year he stalked across Switzerland like a pair of dividers over a map, clad in a long tweed coat that became his hallmark. Virginia Woolf remembered how he wore it proudly in London, its waist stained yellow from ropes. He liked the companionship of other mountaineers, in whose company 'little adventures might be congenial to more intellectual intercourse and help the formation of permanent friendship,'[9] but he generally preferred a long, slow, meditative slog accompanied only by guides. His meditations gave him no greater belief in the Almighty, but they led, as in the case of almost every mountaineer – including Tyndall – to a sense of wonderment. On top of the Schreckhorn he said, 'One felt as if some immortal being, with no particular duties on his hands, might be calmly sitting upon these desolate rocks and watching the little shadowy wrinkles of the plain, that were real mountain ranges, rise and fall through slow geological epochs.'[10]

For Stephen the Alps were the only worthwhile place on the globe. 'You poor Yankees,' he wrote to an American friend, 'are to be pitied in many things, but for nothing as much as your distance from Switzerland.'[11] In another letter: 'Poor son of a degraded race, thinking I dare say of a trip to the White Mountains or some such second-rate substitute for the genuine article, don't you envy me?'[12] He loped on voraciously, as happy to climb old peaks as he was to

tread new, finding beauty wherever he went. Of one sunset from
Mont Blanc he wrote:

> The snow, at our feet was glowing with rich light, and the
> shadows in our footsteps a vivid green by the contrast. Beneath
> us was a vast horizontal floor of thin level mists suspended in
> mid air, spread like canopy over the whole boundless
> landscape, and tinged with every hue of sunset. Through its
> rents and gaps we could see the lower mountains, the distant
> plains, and a fragment of the Lake of Geneva lying in a more
> sombre purple. Above us rose the solemn mass of Mont Blanc
> in the richest glow of an Alpine sunset. The sense of lonely
> sublimity was almost oppressive.[13]

Stephen did not give a hoot for those who wanted to climb an Alp
simply because it was higher than another, and sided somewhat with
Ruskin in his condemnation of mountaineering excess: 'The mere dry
statement that a mountain is so many feet in vertical height above the
sea, and contains so many tons of granite, is nothing. Mont Blanc is
about three miles high. What of that? Three miles is an hour's walk for
a lady – an eightpenny cab fare – the distance from Hyde Park Corner
to the Bank – an express train could do it in three minutes, or a racehorse in five.'[14] Contrarily, however, he recognised (and shared) the
urge of his fellow club members not only to climb but to climb as high
as was possible. 'I am a fanatic,' he wrote. 'I believe that the ascent of
mountains forms an essential chapter in the complete duty of man,
and that it is wrong to leave any district without setting foot on its
highest peak.'[15]

As Chairman, Vice-President and then President (and as Editor of
the *Alpine Journal*), Stephen was the Alpine Club's intellectual
mentor. He criticised guideless climbing, stating famously – and
incorrectly and to many people's annoyance – that the best amateur
was no match for even a third-rate guide. He was also a stickler for
safety. And he was dismissive of scientists, declaring that 'true Alpine
travellers loved the mountains for their own sake, and considered

scientific intruders with their barometers and their theorising to be a simple nuisance'.[16] This last view was fair enough, given that the age of Alpine scientific exploration was fading fast, but he was unwise to state it so openly when there remained some climbers for whom science was all. As he later put it, 'My first contact with Tyndall was not altogether satisfactory . . .'[17]

Tyndall had never enjoyed an easy relationship with the Alpine Club. Mathews had invited him to become a member shortly after the club's inauguration but he had turned the offer down. Why he did so is uncertain, as Mathews seemed willing to disregard the 13,000-foot qualification. (Tyndall had not yet reached that height.) Perhaps it was pressure of work; perhaps it was pique that he had not been included in the list of founding members; perhaps it was annoyance that the club should not have science as its foremost object. At any rate, he joined in 1858 when the 13,000-foot entry had been discarded, and with the offer of the presidency dangled as a bait. But when John Ball resigned in 1860, Tyndall was embroiled in his glacier argument with Forbes. Ball did not care either way about the debate – 'be hanged to it,'[18] he wrote – but he feared that Tyndall's appointment 'might interfere with the thorough cordiality'[19] of proceedings. Kennedy was considered a safer choice for, as Ball explained to Tyndall, he 'does not care, so long as he has glaciers and peaks to climb, whether the ice moves up hill or down'.[20] Tyndall promptly offered his resignation, noting privately in his journal that Ball was 'amiable and cultivated, but without distinct purpose and direction'.[21] Ball responded with mild asperity: 'I quite understand that the Alpine Club and its affairs are of infinitesimal importance to you, but . . . I still think it a pity that you should separate from it . . . If you are fixed on so doing, let me suggest that it would be a graceful thing for you – if not too inconvenient – to come to the dinner on the 13th and propose Kennedy's health. If you can do so I think it would be well whether you remain or leave the club especially in the latter case.'[22] Once again a future presidency was hinted at. Tyndall withdrew his resignation and on 7 November 1861 it was voted that a second Vice-President might be desirable, and that Tyndall was the man for the job. He accepted, and took his place at the winter dinner that December with some pride.

Unfortunately, Stephen was one of the speakers. In his address, which described an ascent of the Rothorn, he made mock of scientists: '"And what philosophical observations did you make?" will be the enquiry of one of those fanatics who, by a reasoning process to me utterly inscrutable, have somehow associated alpine travelling with science. To them I answer, that the temperature was approximately (I had no thermometer) 212 [Fahrenheit] below freezing point. As for ozone, if any existed in the atmosphere, it was a greater fool than I take it for.'[23] Once again Tyndall resigned, this time for good. 'It is utterly impossible for me to attend your meetings or to do anything which could practicably promote the interests of your body,' he told the Honorary Secretary. 'Do not therefore ask me to correspond further on this matter.'[24]

Tyndall's response was curious. He was still a scientist but he had long since forsaken measurements on the Alps. As early as 1859 he was complaining that he had to attend a Royal Society meeting to hear 'a tedious paper on the tedious subject of ice'.[25] A year later, he wrote to Ball that if one more person queried his observations – one man had apparently done so – 'I shall be inclined . . . to damn the whole Alps if they get me into many more of these botherations'.[26] What may have been the problem was that the Matterhorn was on his mind and there was a new member of the club who wanted to climb it as badly as did he. Moreover, he was the very type who might succeed. His name was Edward Whymper and Tyndall did not like him at all. For once Tyndall was not being quarrelsome: Whymper was, indeed, an exceptionally unlikeable man.

Edward Whymper was born in 1840. His father ran a wood-engraving business in Southwark and when he was a teenager Edward Whymper joined the family firm as an apprentice. During his apprenticeship he wrote a diary that was admittedly adolescent but which revealed nevertheless the development of a strange mind. He was a conventional moralist. He could carve competently but had little interest in the trade except to worry about finance. He spent his spare time watching fires – whenever there was a major conflagration he would be there – and scouring the newspapers for murder stories. He played cricket but had few friends, none at least that he mentioned, preferring of an evening to go for long walks or to note the times at which garrotters frequented the parks. He was ambitious, solitary, sour and unforgiving. What he really wanted was to be an Arctic explorer – which would have suited him down to the ground – but this was impossible so he made do instead with wood engraving, a dead-end trade which would soon be superseded by modern printing methods and which he plied with increasing disinterest. When the Whymper household moved briefly to Haslemere, he escaped drudgery by walking, sometimes covering forty-five miles in a day. He was a well-educated, striking youth with fair hair, glaring eyes and a precise mind. He was destined for something greater than printing, but he did not know what that something was or how it was to be found.

His break came in 1860. In that year, while Whymper was recovering from a broken romance, Longman, one of the firm's last customers, sent him to make preliminary drawings for a series of woodcuts to illustrate a book on the Alps. As soon as he arrived, Whymper discovered his true vocation. There stood the mountains, fierce, white, unapproachable and largely undiscovered – just like the Arctic. His immediate instinct was to climb them. Almost uniquely among Alpinists, however, he felt little sense of awe, either spiritual or physical. Where other visitors exuded sentiment by the libraryful, Whymper remained cold, indifferent and judgemental. His diary for August and September 1860 reads as a litany of disappointment.

At Zermatt: 'Saw of course the Matterhorn repeatedly; what precious stuff Ruskin has written about this, as well as many other things. When one has a fair view of the mountain, as I had, it may be compared to a sugar loaf set up on a table; the sugar loaf should have its head knocked on one side. Grand it is, but beautiful I think it is not.'[27]

Of the Mischabel range: 'I do not believe in the pretty views in which Switzerland is represented in the conventional manner. Everything here is *fine*, but I have not seen any *pretty* views.'

At the Giessbach Falls: 'I had the misery of hearing that horrid noise the *ranz de vache* squalled by a couple of mealy-faced girls. There is a precious piece of humbug in relation to this in Murray.'

At Lauterbrunnen: 'there are some echoes which are exhibited by idiots blowing on horns.'

At Thun: 'I am put here into the most absurd bedroom I have ever been in, which I expect I shall have to pay for heavily.'

At Martigny: 'Martigny by daylight looks worse than Martigny by moonlight.'

Climbing the St Bernard Pass: 'I have not had any day so devoid of interest and barren of incident, neither have I walked over so un-interesting a road.'

Descending the St Bernard Pass: 'The scenery is very common-place, and the people on the whole very stupid and somewhat uncivil.'

At Chamonix: 'The place is mad, yes, perfectly insane! Today at a quarter-past ten the Emperor of the French (called here simply Napoleon) made his entry with the Empress. The weather was still bad but what did that matter? The mud, which was filthy, was per-fectly hidden by the crowds of people who flocked in from every part. Rows of young fir-trees had been inserted in the ground to give the idea that the place was flourishing, and I was amused to see that a number of small ones had been placed in front of some pig-stys.'

At the Colo de Viso: 'The rant about the awful grandeur and sub-limity etc., is to one who has crossed it perfectly absurd.'

At the Dauphiné: 'Let no one stop [here], the uncivility of the people combined with the bad fare was an almost unique specimen to me.'

On the way home: 'Had a most uncomfortable and tedious journey of 18 1/2 hours and got to Paris to find that it was not possible to leave by the Brighton route before six o'clock in the evening.'[28]

Everything seemed to revolt or anger him. The hotels were

'stinking', the chalets 'wretched', the villages 'miserable and squalid', the guides 'abominable'. When he found nothing to carp about, as on the 'admirable' road to Briançon, he made do with a discourse on the deficiencies of England's Eastern Counties Railway. Luckily, Briançon turned up trumps: 'I went to the diligence office and to my intense disgust found that all the places were taken so, as there remained nothing for me but to walk to Grenoble, I set about it at once . . . passing several rather wretched villages on the way [and spending] the last half-hour in nasty rain.'[29] The only occasions on which he expressed the slightest satisfaction with the Swiss was when he found a bargain – as, for instance, when he was given a meal of bread and cheese at a chalet above Val Tournanche; 'the cheese was uncommonly like paste beginning to turn bad. Unto what shall I liken the bread?'[30] But it cost only one franc and he therefore declared the people very hospitable.

What could have persuaded such a person to return to the Alps? The answer was that Whymper saw them as a challenge; he must climb them, strip them of their mystery and tread them underfoot. During that introductory season his enthusiasm was stoked by several members of the Alpine Club. Hinchliff offered to coach him on the Riffelberg; Horace Walker (Lucy Walker's father) took him on the Trift Glacier; he went over the Eggishorn Pass with a party that included Leslie Stephen and wrote admiringly that 'our pace was much too slow to suit Mr. Stephen who bolted away and got to the hotel an hour before us'.[31] He was delighted by the constant passage of big names. On 12 August he wrote: 'Just after dinner, Stephen, Hinchliff and another came into the *salon* as wet as water-dogs, having just come from the Riffel for a walk. They did it in 35 minutes. Rather a contrast with my four hours of last night. I hear that Professor Tyndall is at the Eggishorn with Mr. Hawkins, having just accomplished some wonderful climbs at Lauterbrunnen. Professor Hall of King's College is here to-day and a fresh batch of Alpine men have arrived, so the table talk is continually interesting.'[32] At home, Whymper was a humble wood engraver who spoke with a a London accent and tended to drop his aitches. He would have doffed his cap to people like Stephen, Tyndall, Hall and Hinchliff. Here, however, he could watch them in action, eat meals with them, talk shop and share their wine. It was heady.

Whymper was soon acting the sage. Of an unsuccessful attempt on the Weisshorn he wrote that it was bound to fail because of the amount of snow and that 'I should think it will not be done this year, in spite of several A.C.s somewhat boastfully asserting at the commencement of the season that they were going out to *do it*.'[33] He wrote those words on 13 August, having never seen a mountain until he arrived in the Alps five days before. On 16 August, he made his first Alpine expedition, taking two English tourists and one guide across the Grimsel Pass. It was something that had been done a hundred times before, but Whymper thought it impressive, and his diary entry is worth recording because it reveals the essence of his character.

About 3 p.m. we started. We had hired a man to show us the way and carry our packs, but the said man found carrying the two knapsacks quite enough, so I carried mine the whole way. He, of course, after the manner of the people of this country, had an umbrella, we had none, and although hired to show the way he evidently did not care to take the lead, so we did. There is about 2,600 feet of ascent from Obergestelen to the summit of the pass, and by the time we had got half-way we came to one of the formidable torrents that we had heard of. It did not present any difficulty at all, that was supposing we did not object to wetting ourselves at once completely; this, however, we did, and after a few minutes of looking for the best place to cross jumped two-thirds across with our batons; a splash, and the formidable torrent was crossed. Our dismal guide, however, assured us that the next one was something like a torrent, the first being a mere bagatelle. On we went, still raining; presently looking back I saw that the valley of the Rhône was fast getting under water and floating down I saw some black specks in the torrent which were doubtless beams of a bridge or chalet. Still higher up it began to rain very hard, accompanied with very strong lightning and thunder, and just before the summit was reached the heaviest storm of hail that I have ever seen fall. This completed our guide's discomfiture. He rushed behind a piece of rock, crouched down and beckoned us to do the same. We waited a few seconds but what was the use, we were thoroughly wet. So by and by we again went on and, after crossing at different places a great deal of snow, we came to the torrent that was to shut us up entirely. We, however, had no more difficulty with this than with the other. After having accomplished this, the man pulled up to demand more than had been agreed, alleging, which I think was true, that he had agreed to go to the summit only. Again we went on, plunging through pools of water and patches of snow, with hail blown on to our faces and hands, feeling as if we were being whipped with knotted small cords. At last the guide could stand it no longer and went behind a piece of rock and refused to move. He looked the picture of woe, with two knapsacks on his back, an umbrella it was impossible to hold up, water streaming down his face and all over him, and he was gasping and making the most extraordinary indiarubber-like faces that I have ever seen. I believe this time the money-element of his character again turned up, and if he had been promised an extra franc he would have come on at once. However, we rightly imagined if we moved on, he would be sure to follow; so he did. Presently coming in sight of the hospice, the hail laving off and the wind moderating, he got again in the front and tried to make himself look smart and go into the place cocky. I was after him, and putting on a spurt got in first, leaving him in the rear with his umbrella turned inside out.[34]

Whymper hoped that his description was amusing. Perhaps it was by the standards of the time. But to the modern eye it portrays an immature, inexperienced man making the most of an easy pass by sneering at a guide who in all likelihood never pretended to be more than a porter. Climb, conquer, leave weaklings to their fate: that was Whymper's mountaineering philosophy. Alas, it served him well.

In 1860 he had been shown the as yet unclimbed Mont Pelvoux, in the Dauphiné. In 1861 he came back and went up it. This gave him admission to the prestigious Alpine Club and from that date he ground his way around the Alps for weeks on end. He had little time for mountains that had been previously climbed, and saw every other mountaineer as a competitor. His record of new climbs was impressive and his stamina without parallel. Now and then he broke out in moments of genuine passion but, on the whole, his attitude was severe. Again and again he berated porters and guides: they could not keep up with him or they had cheated him in some fashion. The entire Alpine climbing community had tales to tell of untrustworthy porters and unsatisfactory inns. Whymper told how he made the porters suffer and how he bent innkeepers to his will. On one occasion, when a porter had eaten all the party's provisons save for a small crust, Whymper force-marched the man until he was almost dead. He was impressive but implacable. As Stephen later wrote, 'To Mr. Whymper belongs the credit of having had no weak spot at all.'[35]

Whymper did, however, have one weak spot: the Matterhorn. In 1861, following his success on Mont Pelvoux, he turned to the Matterhorn, reaching Breuil shortly after Tyndall's departure. He at once tried to do what Bennen had declared impracticable: to climb as far as possible with a guide, bivouac on the rocks and make for the summit the following day. He failed. The tent threatened to blow away and had to be dismantled, leaving Whymper and his guide to sleep in the open. Whymper made no complaint, but his guide 'passed the remainder of the night in a state of shudder, ejaculating "terrible" and other adjectives'.[36] On reaching the chimney up which Bennen had rolled so effortlessly, Whymper managed to climb it but the guide refused to follow, unroped himself and said he was going home. A ludicrous exchange ensued, Whymper blustering from above and the guide replying happily from below. Eventually, Whymper lost his temper. Go, he told the man, go back to Breuil and tell everyone how he had left his 'monsieur' on the mountain. The guide picked up his knapsack and prepared to do as he was told, at which point Whymper realised that, unlike Bennen, he could not get down the chimney without help from below. So, with enormous loss of face, he recalled the guide, begged his aid and followed him thunderously back to Breuil.

Whymper was enraged. His first season's climbing had been ruined. No matter how many peaks he climbed in succeeding years – and there were many – the Matterhorn taunted him with its inaccessibility. It was no longer a sugar loaf whose head needed knocking off. It was something bigger and more terrible, something that might well harbour dragons. As he explained, 'There seemed to be a cordon drawn around it, up to which one might go, but no farther. Within that invisible line gins and effreets were supposed to exist – the Wandering Jew and the spirits of the damned. The superstitious natives . . . spoke of a ruined city on its summit wherein the spirits dwelt; and if you laughed, they gravely shook their heads; told you to look yourself to see the castles and the walls, and warned one against rash approach, lest the infuriated demons from their impregnable heights might hurl down vengeance for one's derision.'

Whymper could not sleep while the Matterhorn stood inviolate. He had to attack it 'until one or the other was vanquished'.[37]

CHAPTER SEVENTEEN

Both Tyndall and Whymper were obsessed with the Matterhorn, and by 1862 the race was on. If the Alpine Club had seen fit to make wagers, Tyndall would have been the favourite: he had years of mountaineering experience, was a lover of risks, knew how to deal with rock faces, knew the hill and was primed for a conquest. Whymper was a dark horse: he had only started climbing seriously in 1861, had shown poor form on his single attempt at the Matterhorn, and was notoriously suspicious of guides, describing them collectively as 'pointers out of paths, and large consumers of meat and drink',[1] and on one specific occasion as men whose faces 'expressed malice, pride, envy, hatred and roguery of every description'.[2] On the positive side there was his sturdy physique, his steeplejack ability and his nut-cracking approach to anything that stood in his path. A gambling man would have put his money on Tyndall; but he would also have put something on Whymper, a guinea or two at high odds, just in case.

Whymper beat Tyndall to the Matterhorn in the season of 1862, arriving at Breuil on 5 July accompanied by a man named MacDonald with whom he had climbed Mont Pelvoux the previous year. They brought with them a tent of Whymper's own design which they hoped would withstand the winds. The tent held up but they did not.

Whymper, MacDonald, their two guides and their porter, an in-experienced hunchback named Luc Meynet, survived a night of tremendous storms on the mountain. When they woke, however, the storm was still raging. 'We clutched our hardest when we saw stones as big as a man's fist blown away horizontally into space,' Whymper wrote. 'We dared not attempt to stand upright, and remained station-ary, on all fours, glued as it were to the rocks . . . Our warmth and courage soon evaporated.'[3] They packed up the tent and came down as quickly as they could.

Undaunted, they regrouped for a second attempt. Once again they took a porter and two guides but this time they were fortunate enough to be able to hire as chief guide a man named Jean-Antoine Carrel. The cousin of César Carrel who had accompanied Tyndall and Brennen, Jean-Antoine Carrel had more experience of the Matterhorn than anyone else. He had been scouting its slopes for some four years in a quiet, unobtrusive fashion – purely for his own benefit, not as part of a group – and his record for the highest climb had only recently been beaten by Tyndall. Whymper was delighted to have him. 'We thought ourselves fortunate,' he wrote, 'for Carrel clearly considered the mountain a kind of *preserve*, and regarded our late attempt as an act of *poaching*.'[4] Starting from Breuil on 9 July, they pitched camp below the chimney at a height of 12,550 feet and the following day made a reconnaissance of the slopes above. Everything seemed fine; the only impediment to success would be bad weather. They returned to the tent full of optimism and were greeted the next morn-ing by a perfect, cloudless sky. But once again Whymper was to be disappointed. The second guide felt ill and refused to continue. Carrel, likewise, refused to continue without his companion. MacDonald, 'the coolest of the cool',[5] took Whymper aside and mur-mured that they could leave both guides behind and attack the mountain on their own. It was now Whymper's turn to refuse, not from any compassion for the sick guide but from a suspicion that MacDonald's skills were not equal to his own. Fuming, he returned to Breuil for the second time that season, not even bothering to take down his tent. On 12 July MacDonald left for home.

Whymper had now been up the Matterhorn three times and on every occasion save one he had been forced to retreat by the weakness of his companions. He suspected that Carrel had deliberately sabotaged the last attempt out of pique. This may well have been correct: Carrel did resent outsiders poaching on his mountain. More to the point, though, Carrel was a patriot and if anyone was to climb the Matterhorn he wanted it to be an Italian. This never entered Whymper's mind. Secure in their island stability, Britons had fallen into the habit of viewing continental Europe as a mishmash of squabbling kingdoms in thrall either to France or the Austrian or Russian empires. After the revolutions of 1848, however, Europe had changed. Nations had expanded and solidified into culturally distinct blocks. Savoy became part of France in 1861. That same year the Risorgimento turned Piedmont and the rest of the Italian peninsula into a unified state. In 1871, Prussia and its neighbouring German principalities would coalesce into a single entity. It was important for the new states to prove themselves, and short of military expansion – to which they would soon resort – mountaineering was as good an expression of national pride as any other. Germany would later prove this in the 1930s with its obsession with the north face of the Eiger. In the 1860s, however, Italy had its eyes on the Matterhorn. Without realising it, Whymper was battling the covert forces of nationalism.

Whymper's last attempt left him helpless. 'Want of men made the difficulty, not the mountain,'[6] he raged. He left Breuil and walked to Zermatt to drum up some enthusiasm amongst the Swiss. It was no good. Whereas the Italians believed the Matterhorn was surmountable, the Swiss were resolute that it was not. They had a point: from the Italian side the Matterhorn offered a series of shoulders and plateaux; from Zermatt it was a sheer rock face. Unable to find a guide, Whymper vented his fury by climbing Monte Rosa, from which he was able to scowl at the Matterhorn. Then, on 17 July, he returned to Breuil for a fourth attempt. Carrel either could not or would not help him, so Whymper resigned himself to the tedious task of climbing back to the chimney to retrieve his tent.

Whymper had never made a solo climb before and he found he

rather liked it. He wandered up the lower slopes collecting plants – something he had never done before in his life – and when he reached the tent he did not dismantle it but decided to spend the night, watching the sun go down until 'the earth seemed to become less earthly and almost sublime; the world seemed dead, and I its sole inhabitant'.[7] This sentiment had been repeated ever since Saussure first slept on Mont Blanc, but for Whymper, all alone, it now had some meaning. Solitude suited him. When he awoke he felt so good that he decided to climb a little bit higher.

Whymper was the most practical of all Alpine men. His tent was an example of his handicraft: its endpieces comprised two pairs of iron-tipped wooden stakes, bolted at the top, which could find purchase on most surfaces; its covering was of canvas, sheeted over with mackintosh, thus protecting the occupants while giving them room to breathe; the guy ropes were held down by stones; and the whole thing could be dismantled in minutes to make a bundle which one man could carry with ease. On this ascent Whymper also carried another of his inventions: a grapnel. Based on the maritime model, it was a metal claw to which was attached a length of rope. The claw could be hoisted on top of an alpenstock or it could be thrown to give purchase beyond the normal reach, and it was fitted with an innovatory iron ring which allowed the rope to be pulled free during a descent. Armed with his grapnel, Whymper went up the chimney.

He reached his highest point yet with little difficulty and was so charmed by the ease of it all that he went on. 'When I got to the foot of the tower it certainly seemed a pity to turn back,' he wrote, 'so I went a little further to see what was round the corner, and when I got round the mountain seemed more interesting than ever; the pinnacles behind it were wagging in the wind. Without exaggeration, one could take hold of huge Egyptian-like blocks, ten or more feet high, and rock them backwards and forwards.'[8] This surreal spot was nicknamed 'the coxcomb' by valley-dwellers. 'Strangely fascinated,' Whymper wrote, 'on I went . . .'[9]

Leaving 'the coxcomb', he clung to tiny ledges and manoeuvred across precipitous faces. Occasionally he glanced upwards and saw rocks that seemed to leer at him with demonic faces from the ridge above. Finally he reached a point where the cliffs became even steeper and at this point he gave up. He had cause for satisfaction: he had come within 1,400 feet of the summit and had climbed higher than anyone before him. 'Some amiable critics [he meant Tyndall] have announced that I was endeavouring to make an ascent by myself,' he later smirked. 'I should be the first to laugh at any idea so absurd; it was a combination of accidental circumstances that caused me to get alone on that day higher than any other person.'[10] On any other mountain he would have had to plant a flag so that the world could see what he had done. Not here. Simply being able to describe where he had been was enough on the Matterhorn, whose features were soon to be spoken of in capital letters – the Chimney, the Col du Lion where he had pitched his tent and, the face he had just climbed, the Great Tower.

He climbed back to his tent, left it where it was, fixed a rope to the top of the Chimney and started down for Breuil. He was rightly thrilled by what he had done. But as he later wrote, his 'exultation was a little premature'.[11] He had reached easy ground and was heading as hard as he could for the hotel at Breuil where he could tell the world what he had done, when he slipped. The slip would have been nothing had he not been wearing a heavy knapsack and had it not happened at the head of a 200-foot couloir that ended in a precipice, below which lay the Glacier du Lion 800 feet below.

Whymper fell twelve feet, head first, onto rocks and bounced into the couloir. Carried by the weight of his knapsack he ricocheted from side to side, crashing from stone to ice to snow. He later wrote:

I was perfectly conscious of what was happening, and felt each blow; but, like a patient under chloroform, experienced no pain. Each blow was, naturally, more severe than that which preceded it, and I distinctly remember thinking, 'Well, if the next is harder still, that will be the end!' Like persons who have been rescued from drowning, I remember that the recollection of a multitude of things rushed through my head, many of them trivialities or absurdities, which had been forgotten long before; and, more remarkable, this bounding through space did not feel disagreeable. But I think that in no very great distance more, consciousness, as well as sensation would have been lost, and upon that I base my belief, improbable as it seems, that death by a fall from a great height is as painless an end as can be experienced.[12]

While Whymper's mind resigned itself to extinction, his body made a final leap of 60 feet and lodged momentarily on some rocks on the side of the couloir. He landed head up and by reflex scrabbled at the snow as he began his final slide. He stopped himself ten feet from the precipice, while his hat, his alpenstock and his tinted veil flew past him, pursued by a shower of rocks. For the moment he was safe, but 'The situation was still suffcently serious. The rocks could not be left go for a moment, and the blood was spirting out of more than twenty cuts. The most serious ones were in the head, and I vainly tried to close them with one hand, while holding on with the other. It was useless; the blood jerking out in blinding jets at each pulsation. At last, in a moment of inspiration, I kicked out a big lump of snow and stuck it as a plaster on my head. The idea was a happy one, and the flow of blood diminished.[13]

He had just the strength to drag himself up the couloir – that had a gradient of at least 60° – and wedge himself behind some boulders before he fainted. When he came to the sun was setting. As night fell, he took stock:

The battering was rough, yet no bones were broken. The most severe cuts were one of four inches long on the top of the head, and another of three inches on the right temple: this latter bled frightfully. There was a formidable-looking cut, of about the same size as the last, on the palm of the left hand, and every limb was grazed, or cut, more or less seriously. The tips of the ears were taken off, and a sharp rock cut a circular bit out of the side of the left boot, sock, and ankle, at one stroke. The loss of blood, although so great, did not seem to be permanently injurious.[14]

Superhumanly, Whymper climbed up the couloir – despite his injuries and the lack of an alpenstock – and then came down 4,800 feet in pitch blackness to Breuil, 'without a slip, or once missing the way'.[15] He slunk past the first cow sheds, 'utterly ashamed of the state to which I had been brought by my imbecility',[16] and managed not to alert the inhabitants whom he could hear talking and laughing within. But he was detected as soon as he tried to sneak into his inn unnoticed. The landlord appeared with a lamp and yelled with fright when he saw Whymper's condition. Soon there were two dozen people clustered over him and, protest as he might, he was unable to prevent them administering an immediate remedy. His journal does not say whether he screamed when the Breuil folk rubbed his wounds with salt and vinegar; but it is hard to believe that he did not.

Whether because of the cure or his own stubbornness, Whymper was back on his feet within days. He must have been a terrible sight, limping through the village, his face covered in black scabs. Yet for all his wounds he managed to persuade Carrel to take him up the Matterhorn again. He, Carrel and one of Carrel's cousins set off on 23 July, spent a night in the tent and were at 12,992 feet when the weather turned. Whymper argued that it was a local snowfall and that they should wait another night for it to clear, 'but my leader would not endure contradiction, grew more positive, and insisted that we must go down'.[17] They did so, and discovered to Whymper's despair that the cloud was indeed a passing affair and below 3,000 feet the mountain basked in sunshine.

Whymper was becoming tired of Carrel.

[He] was not an easy man to manage. He was perfectly aware that he was the cock of the Val Tournanche, and he commanded the other men as by right. He was equally conscious that he was indispensable to me, and took no pains to conceal the knowledge . . . It seemed to me that he was

spinning out the ascent for his own purposes, and that
although he wished very much to be the first man to the top,
and did not object to be accompanied by any one else who had
the same wish, he had no intention of letting one succeed too
soon – perhaps to give a greater appearance of *éclat* when the
thing was accomplished. As he feared no rival, he may have
supposed that the more difficulties he made the more valuable
he would be estimated.[18]

Whymper's assessment was largely correct. Carrel, on the other hand, must have thought his employer a lunatic. His suspicions were confirmed on the night of 24 July when Whymper ordered him to make ready for another ascent the next morning.

Carrel obviously did not think it a serious proposition. When Whymper woke at dawn on 25 July he found a note to the effect that it was a beautiful day for marmot-hunting and Carrel would not be available. It was the ultimate insult. 'These men clearly could not be relied upon,'[19] Whymper wrote. He hired the hunchback porter Luc Meynet and left Carrel to his marmots. They slept that night in the tent and early on the morning of 26 July had passed Whymper's highest point and were struggling with the Great Tower. 'Little by little we fought our way up,' Whymper wrote, 'but at length we were both spread-eagled on the all but perpendicular face, unable to advance and barely able to descend.'[20] Clinging to the rock, Whymper saw smooth walls seven or eight feet high in every direction. In such a situation it was impossible for one man to help another up them. The only recourse was a ladder. Back he went for the fifth time that year, Meynet consoling him at every difficult patch with the news that, '"We can only die once," which thought seemed to afford him infinite satisfaction.'[21] But when Whymper reached Breuil he 'found [his] projects summarily and unexpectedly knocked on the head'.[22] Tyndall was there.

It was unreasonable for Whymper to imagine that he had sole rights to the Matterhorn but one can sympathise with his disappointment. Tyndall had mustered an incredibly strong team consisting of the

mighty Bennen, a 'powerful and active'[23] Valaisian guide named
Anton Walter and, to Whymper's undying disgust, Jean-Antoine and
César Carrel. He had acquired a ladder, was stocking up with provisions and was planning to leave the following evening. It was almost
as if he had been watching Whymper's progress through a crystal ball,
had seen the path, had seen the problems and had chosen the perfect
time to intervene. As for the turncoat Carrel, Whymper could only
attribute his behaviour to anger at his temerity in daring to try the
Matterhorn without him – in which he was probably correct. If it was
an insult to Whymper that Carrel should go marmot-hunting, it was an
even greater insult to Carrel that Whymper should think so lightly of
his abilities as to take a twisted little porter in his place. 'It was useless
to compete with the Professor and his four men,' Whymper wrote, 'so
I waited to see what would become of their attempt.'[24]

If Whymper was surprised by Tyndall's presence, Tyndall was even
more horrified by his. Far from watching Whymper through a crystal
ball, Tyndall had been killing time at Visp, as he wrote to Huxley, 'not
dreaming that the enemy would be so soon upon myself. Well, here
he is: and I write not through love of you but through hate of him.'[25]
Publicly, of course, he remained polite, and when Whymper offered
him the use of his tent which was still pitched on the mountain,
Tyndall professed delight at the clubman-like spirit in which the offer
was made. In return, he asked if Whymper would like to come with
them.

'It certainly would have enhanced the pleasure of my excursion if
Mr. Whymper could have accompanied me,' he wrote stiffly, long
after the event.

> I admired his courage and devotion; he had manifestly set his
> heart upon the Matterhorn, and it was my earnest desire that
> he should not be disappointed. I consulted with Bennen, who
> had heard many accounts – probably exaggerated ones – of Mr.
> Whymper's rashness, He shook his head, but finally agreed
> that Mr. Whymper could be invited 'provided he proved
> reasonable.' I thereupon asked Mr. Whymper to join us. His

reply was, 'If I go up the Matterhorn, I must lead the way.' Considering my own experience at the time as compared with his; considering, still more, the renown and power of my guide, I thought the response the reverse of 'reasonable', and so went on my way alone.[26]

Whymper could only look on impotently as Tyndall's group set out in high spirits for a cloudless mountain. He was 'tormented with envy and all uncharitableness. If they succeeded, they carried off the prize for which I had been so long struggling; and if they failed, there was no time to make another attempt, for I was due in a few days more for London.'[27] He began to pack his bags.

Tyndall had not, in fact, been merely killing time in Visp, as he told Huxley. For the past three weeks he had been training on the Bernese and Valaisian Alps. He had climbed the Wetterhorn, the Galenstock and the Great Aletsch Glacier, 'burning up the effete matter which nine months' work in London had lodged in my muscles . . . each succeeding day added to my strength'.[28] When he was completely fit and thought that further delay would be counterproductive, he decided it was time to move. More even than Whymper, Tyndall was wedded to the mountain. 'The Matterhorn,' he wrote, as he crossed the pass from Zermatt, 'was our temple, and we approached it with feelings not unworthy of so great a shrine.'[29]

Tyndall, like Whymper, was not beyond a few technical tricks. His ladder had not been acquired at Breuil, as Whymper had supposed, but was a collapsible model that he himself had devised, comprising two poles and a sack containing rungs, nails and a hammer. The poles could be used as huge alpenstocks but when the need arose the rungs could be hammered into them to create a ladder. He also carried a rope, made to his own specifications in London, which was guaranteed to have a greater breaking strain than anything available in Switzerland. Armed with these tools, Tyndall was certain that the Matterhorn would be his – or, failing that, that he would go as high as was humanly possible.

While Tyndall was climbing ever higher, crossing with ease the couloir in which Whymper had nearly lost his life – Tyndall noted this specifically in his journal – Whymper was assembling his luggage. As he did so, he noticed that he had left one or two essentials in the tent. He therefore went back up the Matterhorn to get them. It is hard to imagine what he might have left that was so essential: he would have taken his climbing equipment for the descent with Meynet; likewise, other valuables such as his knapsack and his tea caddy – a novel gadget that comprised a cylindrical tube containing furnace, cup and kettle as well as a compartment for storing food and tea – would have been brought back for refilling. In all likelihood it was just an excuse, metaphorically speaking, to cock his leg on the mountain.

Climbing fast and skilfully, he passed Tyndall's party as they were having lunch, and soon reached the tent. Then a strange thing happened. Down below, Tyndall and his men were gathering up their bits and pieces, 'when suddenly an explosion occurred overhead'.[30] A boulder cracked down from above, shattering into a spray of fragments slightly wide of them, 'but still near enough to compel a sharp look-out'.[31] Two or three similar explosions occurred, each of them leaving a strong smell of sulphur as the rocks split and cascaded down the hill. It would be wrong to suggest that Whymper dislodged the rocks; he had a fondness for boulder-tumbling like many other climbers of the time, but whatever his faults he would not endanger another person's life; besides, the mountain was notorious for the way in which it shed its rocks. Nonetheless, it was uncanny that the Matterhorn should give such a violent display of its power on the only occasion when the two men were on the mountain simultaneously. It was almost as if it had sensed their rivalry and decided to join in.

Whymper waited at the tent until Tyndall arrived, gave him his double-edged congratulations, then returned to Breuil. Back in his hotel he packed and repacked his bag. Although he was meant to be travelling for London he could not tear himself from the Matterhorn while Tyndall was still on it. Soon, the first reports came in. A flag had been seen on the summit. Whymper quailed, but to his relief the sighting was false. Then Tyndall was seen to have passed Whymper's highest point – of this there could be no question. 'I had now no doubt of their final success,'[32] Whymper wrote in despair.

On the Matterhorn, Tyndall was less confident. 'The mountain is a gigantic ruin,'[33] he recorded, as Bennen led the way from crevice to crumbling shelf. Up the Great Tower they went, Walter scrabbling his way from ledge to ledge under Bennen's direction, then lowering a hand for the next person. 'It was manifest that for some time our fight must be severe,'[34] Tyndall wrote. But he rejoiced in the struggle: 'we worked up bit by bit, holding on almost by our eyelids,' he told Huxley. 'It was the best and hardest piece of rock climbing that I have ever known man to accomplish. It was these precipices that stopped Whymper. Well, we scaled them.'[35] Soon he was standing on a ridge that led upwards to a conical peak. It was not the summit, but it was something to aim at. Tyndall said as much to Bennen, only to be told, 'That will not satisfy us.'[36] Then Bennen pointed to the Matterhorn's pyramidical apex, looming against the sky: 'In an hour the people at Zermatt shall see our flag planted yonder.'[37] The Carrels gave a laugh of scorn, which Tyndall assumed was aimed at the Matterhorn rather than at Bennen. He wrote: 'We felt perfectly certain of success; not one amongst us harboured a thought of failure . . . Up we went in this spirit, with a forestalled triumph making our ascent a jubilee.'[38] They planted a flag on the lower summit then surveyed the path to the peak itself. It was a ragged, narrow ridge flanked by 'ghastly abysses'[39] and ending at a sheer cliff. Walters voiced his doubts: 'We may still find difficulty there.'[40] The Carrels were of similar opinion. Tyndall very nearly lost his temper: 'The same thought had probably brooded in other minds; still it angered me slightly to hear misgiving obtain audible expression.'[41] The only one not to speak was Bennen.

Tyndall drove Bennen and the others forward, following them as they edged towards the last face. Once they reached it the Matterhorn would be theirs. As he told Huxley, 'We were as sure of it as you are of your dinner.'[42] At the end of the ridge, however, they met an unexpected obstacle: between them and the cliff was a sheer-sided notch, several hundred feet deep. 'So savage a spot I had never seen,' Tyndall wrote, 'and I sat down upon it with the sickness of disappointed hope. The summit was within almost a stone's throw of us, and the thought of retreat was bitter in the extreme.'[43] Bennen could see no obvious way over it, so Tyndall asked the Carrels what they thought. The Carrells were not happy. They had been hired as guides but had been treated as porters throughout. Now, when Bennen was stuck, and their expertise was required, they saw no reason to give it. Their answer was frank: 'Ask your guides.'[44] Tyndall did so. Bennen pondered the notch for thirty minutes and then gave up. 'Our occupation was clearly gone,'[45] Tyndall recorded. It only remained to plant a marker to show how far they had come – a six-foot length of ladder was used – then to go home. Smirking, Jean-Antoine Carrel offered to take Bennen's place in front. Tyndall refused: Bennen had led them up and he would lead them down.

This was the difference between Tyndall and Whymper: whereas Whymper was willing to lead, Tyndall trusted always in his guide. When Bennen asked him what he thought, Tyndall would ask him what *he* thought, and kept on asking until Bennen came up with an answer. If there was no answer, Tyndall was satisfied. 'Where you go I will follow, be it up or down,'[46] was his refrain.

Shakily, Bennen took them down the mountain. They had to use the remains of the ladder at one point, lowering it by rope and then sliding down it one by one. Unable to retrieve it, they left it dangling. The weather worsened and their retreat became more miserable. 'A tempest of hail was here hurled against us,' Tyndall wrote, as they reached the camp, 'as if the Matterhorn, not content with shutting its door in our faces, meant to add an equivalent to the process of kicking us downstairs. The ice-pellets certainly hit us as bitterly as if they had been thrown in spite, and in the midst of this malicious cannonade we . . . returned to Breuil.'[47]

Whymper had hung around until the last moment, and was drinking a farewell glass of wine with his landlord, when Tyndall's group came into view. 'There was no spring in their steps – they, too, were defeated,' he crowed. 'The Carrels hid their heads, but the others said, as men will do when they have been beaten, that the mountain was horrible, impossible, and so forth.'[48] Tyndall was so exhausted that he greeted Whymper like an old friend, wrung his hand, 'and in the most earnest and impassioned manner abjured me to have nothing more to do with the Matterhorn'.[49] He stated that he had come within a stone's throw of the summit but the thing was totally impossible. The notch could never be crossed, and he himself was not going to make another attempt. In Tyndall's view, 'the Matterhorn is inaccessible and may raise its head defiant as it has hitherto done – the only unconquered and unconquerable peak in the Alps'.[50] Whymper was relieved. He too was 'almost inclined to believe that the mountain was inaccessible',[51] but he could not have left it if Tyndall was going to have another go. He said goodbye to Breuil, depositing his equipment with the landlord for the use of whoever needed it. The gesture was made 'more, I am afraid, out of irony than for generosity. There may have been those who believed that the Matterhorn could be ascended, but, anyhow, their faith did not bring forth works.'

Nothing Whymper ever did was free from controversy, and the same could be said to a lesser degree of Tyndall. It was inevitable, therefore, that when both men published their accounts of that year's mountaineering they disagreed violently. Tyndall, who published last, said that Whymper had lied by omission – he had not mentioned, for example, his refusal to join the climb unless he was its leader – and that he had denigrated Bennen by suggesting that Carrel had shown him a route to the top but had been ignored. 'Regarding other inaccuracies,' Tyndall concluded, 'and touching Mr. Whymper's general tone towards myself, I do not feel called upon to make any observations.'[52]

Whymper responded greedily: 'My account . . . of the Professor's defeat is not perhaps so clear as it might have been, because I did not wish to lay too much stress upon it, and condensed it to a few lines [ninety-five lines, to be precise, accompanied by a diagram of Tyndall's route up the Matterhorn]. I willingly take the opportunity to refer to it at greater length.'[53] On the matter of his insisting to be leader he explained that Tyndall had requested him to follow Bennen's instructions implicitly and that he had naturally refused. 'You will remember, Dr. Tyndall,' he had said, 'that I have been much higher than Bennen, and have been eleven days on the mountain, whilst he has been on it for a single day; you will not expect me to follow him if he is evidently wrong.'[54] As for Carrel's willingness to carry on, Whymper had said no such thing, but he was very willing to say it now: 'I have no doubt that he *could* have pointed out a way, and have led the party to the top.'[55] Moreover, Tyndall had been utterly mistaken in declaring that he had come within a stone's throw of the summit: there was indeed a notch that fitted Tyndall's description but there was also a second one, a good deal higher than the one he had reached – as any fool could see, Whymper all but said – and there remained at least another 800 feet of rock unclimbed between the two. Having quashed Tyndall's assertions, Whymper delivered the *coup de grâce*. Tyndall had deliberately told him that the hill was unclimbable and had insinuated that he was not going to try it again; but as soon as Whymper was out of sight he had asked Bennen to prepare for another assault; Bennen's refusal – whether through good judgement or weakness – was all that saved Tyndall from being a blackguard.

Whymper smashed people as he did mountains. Tyndall did not respond, or if he did his response has been lost. He abandoned the Matterhorn for the time being, leaving Whymper to solve the problem of the final notch. 'This defeat has fallen upon us like the chill of age,' he explained to Huxley, 'and I must "mix myself with action" to shake it off . . . The mountain is one of the most savage grandeur . . . certainly on the whole – both near and far – the grimmest and grandest object in the Alps. Well, goodbye to him and goodbye to you and goodbye to my climbing. For there is nothing else in the Alps that I should care to do.'[56]

CHAPTER EIGHTEEN

'Although there have been fools before, and very big ones, Mr. Whymper is the biggest of the lot.'[1] This oddly personal criticism appeared in the British press in 1862, and caused Whymper a degree of annoyance. Had he learned of an acquaintance's patronising comment that '[he] always put in a little visit to me on this hopeless quest of his',[2] he might have been even more annoyed. But the opinions of others were not enough to put him off. On 29 July 1863 he crossed the English Channel for his sixth attempt at the Matterhorn. With him he carried what he hoped would be a solution to the final notch (or notches) – a fireman's ladder that extended to 24 feet but which could be compressed to half that length for ease of transportation. It was a good idea: the ladder was tried and tested whereas the grapnel – which Whymper also took, along with several lengths of rope and other climbing equipment – was still an uncertain novelty. Unfortunately, Swiss customs officers did not look favourably upon the ladder. When Whymper staggered with his load to the border, he was greeted not as a mountaineer but as a potential housebreaker. Not knowing what to do with him, and unsure as to his intent, they hemmed and hawed until they arrived at a satisfactory conclusion. He was a circus turn, one man said, who was going to balance on top of his ladder in Turin. Yes, agreed another, and he would light his pipe, put his alpenstock in it, and then swivel round. The rope might be used to keep spectators at a distance, put in a third. 'Monsieur is an acrobat then?'[3] they asked. Philosophically, Whymper admitted that he might be; he was passed without hesitation. After many similar tribulations, the ladder became 'the source of endless trouble'.[4] It fitted awkwardly on a mule; many hoteliers turned him away on account of it; and it was generally more bother than it was worth. Still, having dragged it all this way, Whymper was not going to relinquish it.

He reached Breuil on 1 August only to find that fresh snow covered the Matterhorn and that he would have to wait until it cleared. He also learned that MacDonald, with whom he had tentatively agreed to make the ascent, was not going to join him after all. 'I get a letter from MacDonald,' he wrote in his diary, 'by which I plainly see that *he* means to have nothing to do with it; a reliable companion!'[5] Irritably, Whymper took Jean-Antoine Carrel on a seven-day jaunt over the Matterhorn's surrounding peaks and passes in order to study the mountain from every possible angle. Along the way, to compensate for the Matterhorn's graceless unavailability, he tackled the virgin summit of the Dent d'Hérens. The experience did nothing to improve his temper. Whereas Whymper favoured an approach via snow slopes which lay above the Glacier de Za de Zan, Carrel insisted on leading him up the rocky west ridge. At 12,500 feet it looked as if Carrel had made the right choice: to all appearances it was at most an hour before they stood on the summit. An hour later, however, they were balanced on a narrow slice of snow that trembled underfoot; before them loomed a massive boulder that teetered as precariously on the precipice as they did themselves. Had they been able to surmount the boulder – which they could not; it was more than twelve feet high and after all Whymper's efforts they had forgotten the ladder – they would still have had to climb for another hour, by Whymper's revised estimate, before they reached the top. He rebelled. 'There was no honour to be gained by persevering,' he wrote, 'or dishonour in turning from a place which was dangerous on account of its excessive difficulty.'[6] On returning, however, he noted that 'This is the only mountain which I have essayed to ascend, that has not, sooner or later, fallen to me. Our failure was mortifying.'[7] It was all the more mortifying when, four days later, the mountain was climbed by MacDonald following exactly the route which Whymper had advocated in the first place.

The Dent d'Hérens aside, Whymper's reconnaissance satisfied him in one respect: the Matterhorn could only be climbed from Breuil. He and Carrel had crossed the Zmutt Glacier which lay below the Matterhorn's western flank and had decided that an approach from that direction was impossible. 'Nothing can be more inaccessible than the Matterhorn upon this side,' Whymper wrote, 'even in cold blood one holds the breath when looking at its stupendous cliffs. There are few but equal to them in size in the Alps, and there are none which can more truly be termed *precipices* . . . Stones which drop from the top of that amazing wall fall for about 1500 feet before they touch anything; and those which roll down from above, and bound over it, fall to a much greater depth, and leap well nigh 1000 feet beyond its base. This side of the mountain has always seemed sombre – sad – terrible; it is painfully suggestive of decay, ruin, and death.'[8]

Ruskin had written that, 'There is no aspect of destruction about the Matterhorn cliffs.'[9] When Whymper saw the western face, he exploded in derision: 'But approach, and sit down by the side of the Z'muttgletscher [the Zmutt Glacier], and you will hear that their piecemeal destruction is proceeding ceaselessly – incessantly. You will *hear*, but, probably, you will not *see*; for even when the descending masses thunder as loudly as heavy guns, and the echoes roll back from the Ebihorn opposite, they will still be as pin-points against this grand old face, so vast is its scale!'[10] From the west and the north, Zermatt had nothing to offer. Far better to attack the Matterhorn from its gentler, southern slopes.

Just before dawn, on 10 August 1863, Whymper and Carrel left Breuil with four porters including Carrel's cousin César and Luc Meynet. They were well equipped, carrying tent, blankets, provisions, 450 feet of rope and the extending ladder. The sky was still and cloudless. The men were keen and confident – particularly Meynet, who was pathetically pleased to have been chosen. 'Pay me nothing, only let me go with you,' he had begged earlier. 'I shall want but a little bread and cheese and I won't eat much.'[11] Everything in fact, in Whymper's opinion, 'seemed to promise a happy termination to our enterprise'.[12] He felt so cheerful that he passed some time during the walk estimating the value of Meynet's clothes. He decided that if they were sold by weight as rags they might fetch just under one and a half shillings.

They were at the Col du Lion by 9.00 a.m. and Whymper found things very much changed since last he was there. Familiar ledges had vanished; the platform on which he had pitched his tent in 1862 had half disappeared; the summit of the Col, which had been a respectably broad and easy mound of snow was now sheer ice and 'sharper than the ridge of any church-roof'.[13] The rocks were glazed and treacherous: Whymper and Carrel both slipped, with potentially fatal consequences. And the party was hampered by loose snow which poured over them like flour, obscuring ice steps as soon as they were cut. Yet they were not deterred. 'The weather was superb,' Whymper recorded, 'the men made light of the toil, and shouted to raise the echoes from the Dent d'Hérens. We went on gaily, passed the second tent platform, the Chimney and the other well-remembered points, and reckoned, confidently, on sleeping that night upon the top of "the shoulder"'.[14]

Before they reached the Great Tower, however, the Matterhorn hit them with one of its temperamental moods. Their first inkling of what lay in store was a sudden gust of cold air. It did not blow as a normal wind, Whymper noted with amazement, but simply dropped from above, as if they had walked under a cold shower. They looked around, but saw only clear skies. 'There was a dead calm,' Whymper wrote, 'and not a speck of cloud to be seen anywhere. But we did not remain very long in this state. The cold air came again, and this time it was difficult to say where it did not come from. We jammed down our hats as it beat against the ridge, and screamed amongst the crags.'[15] Small patches of mist formed above and below. With incredible rapidity the patches united until 'the whole heavens were filled with whirling, boiling clouds'.[16] Seconds later, a blizzard blew in from the east. In the time it took for them to unshoulder their packs the ridge was inches deep in snow.

For two hours they worked against wind and snow to construct a platform capable of supporting their tent. Hardly had they put up the canvas and crawled inside than the blizzard turned into a thunderstorm. Whymper was horrified: 'Forked lightning shot out at the turrets above and the crags below. It was so close that we quailed at its darts. It seemed to scorch us – we were in the very focus of the storm. The thunder was simultaneous with the flashes; short and sharp, and more like the noise of a door that is violently slammed, multiplied a thousand-fold, than any noise to which I can compare it.'[17] The wind was so fierce that they crawled out between blasts to erect a wall of rocks. Without this protection, Whymper was certain, the tent and they within it would have been blown over the edge.

The storm raged through the night, its riot augmented by the crash of tumbling boulders. Having recovered from his initial shock, Whymper tried to make light of it: 'We passed the night comfortably – even luxuriously – in our blanket bags, but there was little chance of sleeping, between the noise of the wind, the thunder, and of the falling rocks. I forgave the thunder for the sake of the lightning. A more splendid spectacle than its illumination of the Matterhorn crags I do not expect to see.'[18] Certainly it must have been an impressive sight, but it was also a dismaying one. When Whymper turned out at 3.30 the following morning he was forced back into the tent by driving snow. It was another six hours before a feeble glimmer of light penetrated the clouds and they felt secure enough to continue.

By 11.00 a.m. they had climbed a paltry 300 feet and the snow had started to fall again. By Whymper's reckoning it would be another four or five hours before they reached Tyndall's abandoned rope and were in a position to cross the first notch. And if they did get that far, there yet remained several hundred feet of ice-plastered rock before they reached the second notch; and beyond the second notch lay the summit which harboured God knew what perils and where the weather might be more awful still. Possibly they could have waited out the storm in their tent, but they did not have the provisions and Whymper did not have the time; he was due in London by the end of the week. He decided to retreat.

Their descent was as rapid as their advance had been slow. They were in Breuil that same afternoon, where their story was greeted with mild derision. As they recounted the difficulties of the climb, their innkeeper raised an eyebrow. 'Why,' he said, '*we* have had no snow; it has been fine all the time you have been absent, and there has been only that small cloud on the mountain.'[19] Nothing could persuade him that the small cloud had contained terrors beyond his ken. Whymper paid his men and left for home, 'defeated and disconsolate; but like a gambler who loses each throw, only the more eager to have another try, to see if the luck would change . . . ready to devise fresh combinations, and to form new plans'.[20] His last act before quitting Breuil was to weigh Meynet's clothes; they were worth 1*s*. 5*d*.

Whymper returned to the attack in 1864. He did not immediately head for the Matterhorn, however, but chose to warm up with a few other unclimbed peaks. First in his sights was the Pointe des Écrins, one of the highest mountains in the Dauphiné. He had first spotted it from the top of Mont Pelvoux, at the beginning of his climbing career, and it had niggled at him ever since, like a childhood memory of a lost toy. 'I was troubled in spirit about this mountain,' he admitted, 'and my thoughts often reverted to the great wall-sided peak, second in apparent inaccessibility only to the Matterhorn.'[21] Two parties had tried to climb it – one of them led by the disaster-prone Tuckett – but both had failed, leaving Whymper with just the situation he liked: the chance to climb a new peak and prove himself better than others.

He took two fellow Alpine Club members – A. W. Moore and Horace Walker – plus two of the best guides on offer: Christian Almer and Michel Croz. Almer was a sturdy, unflappable Oberlander who had already proved himself on the Wetterhorn and other heights. Croz was a bold, risk-taking Chamoniard, who had yet to carve himself a reputation. Of the two, Whymper was most impressed by Croz:

Places where you and I would 'toil and sweat, and yet be freezing cold', were bagatelles to him, and it was only when he got above the range of ordinary mortals, and was required to

employ his magnifient strength, and to draw upon his
unsurpassed knowledge of ice and snow, that he could be said
to be really and truly happy. Of all the guides with whom I
have travelled, Michel Croz was the man most after my own
heart. He did not work like a blunt razor, and take to his toil
unkindly. He did not need urging, or to be told a second time
to do anything. You had but to say *what* was to be done, and
how it was to be done, and the work *was* done, if it was
possible. Such men are not common, and when they are known
they are valued.[22]

Whymper had planned a circuitous approach to the Pointe des
Écrins to stiffen them for the climb and, importantly, to spy out the
terrain from as many angles as possible. 'All mountaineers know how
invaluable it is to study beforehand an intended route over new
ground from a height at some distance,' he said, sniping at Tyndall's
confusion over the Matterhorn's notches. 'None but blunderers fail to
do so.'[23]

His route took them over as much unconquered territory as possible. On 21 June 1864 they attempted, but failed, to climb the central
pinnacle of the Aiguilles d'Arves. After that they made for the Meije,
an impressive mountain of 13,067 feet, the very sight of which sent
Whymper into raptures. 'One can hardly speak in exaggerated terms
of its jagged ridges, torrential glaciers, and tremendous precipices . . .
were I to discourse upon these things without the aid of pictures, or to
endeavour to convey in *words* a sense of the lovelines of *curves*, or the
beauty of colour, or the harmonies of *sound*, I should try to accomplish
that which is impossible.'[24] Whymper had no plans to take the Meije
this season, but he did consider its western shoulder, the Brèche de la
Meije, a possibility. The great guide Melchior Anderegg had stated
that it was difficult but not impracticable, and Whymper took this as
an invitation. Anderegg, an Oberlander, was one of the most respected
figures in the Alps, renowned for his surety of foot, his uncanny,
instinctive knowledge of what was climbable and what was not, and
for the fact that he had led countless parties to success without the

loss of a single life. As Whymper wrote, he was 'a very prince among guides. His empire is among the "eternal snows" – his sceptre is an ice-axe.'[25]

Unlike Anderegg, the locals of La Grave, a village below the northern face of the Meije – 'noted equally for the splendour of its view and for the infinity and voracity of its flies'[26] – believed an ascent of the Brèche impossible. Undeterred, Whymper left La Grave early on the morning of 22 June, and scaled 6,500 feet in five and a quarter hours to reach the top of the pass, where the whole party screamed in triumph. Their success was not enough for Whymper. Peak-bagger that he was, he had no patience for the Brèche once he had climbed it. The Pointe des Écrins still beckoned and he became increasingly irritable as he walked down the other side of the Meije. The scenery was 'a howling wilderness, the abomination of desolation; destitute alike of animal or vegetable life; pathless, of course; suggestive of chaos but little else; covered almost throughout its entire length with debris from the size of a walnut to that of a house . . . Our tempers were soured by constant pitfalls . . . There was no end to it, and we became more savage at every step.'[27]

Whymper's temper deteriorated as they made their way towards the Pointe des Écrins. Bivouacking on the Glacier de Bonne Pierre on 24 June, he discovered that their porter had smoked all their cigars. The man denied it, but as Whymper discovered, 'he is reported to be the greatest liar in Dauphiné.'[28] That night the porter drank most of their wine. 'It was clear that there was no explanation of the phenomenon, but in the dryness of the air,' Whymper wrote caustically. 'Still, it is remarkable that the dryness of the air (or the evaporation of wine) is always greatest when a stranger is in one's party – the dryness caused by the presence of even a single Chamonix porter is sometimes so great . . . that the entire quantity disappears. For a time I found difficulty in combating this phenomenon, but at last discovered that if I used the wine-flask as a pillow during the night, the evaporation was completely stopped.'[29] Even the simple act of making soup elicited a sour note: 'Fortnum and Mason's portable soup was sliced up and brewed, and was excellent; but it should be said that before it *was* excellent, three times the quantity named in the directions had to be used.'[30] When making this soup, he noted, always offer it to your friends first: it tended to burn the mouth on first sip and, besides, all the goodness was to be found at the bottom of the cup.

The Pointe des Écrins was surrounded by three faces: the Glacier Noir, one of the sheerest ice slopes in the Alps; the slightly shallower Glacier du Vallon; and the more amenable Glacier de l'Encula. They approached via the third, and easiest, face. But easy was a relative description. 'Imagine a triangular plane, 700 or 800 feet high, set at an angle exceeding 50°,' Whymper wrote, 'let it be smooth and glassy; let the uppermost edges be cut into spikes and teeth, and let them be bent, some one way, some another. Let the glassy face be covered with minute fragments of rock, scarcely attached, but varnished with ice; imagine this, and then you will have a very faint idea of the face of the Écrins on which we stood.'[31]

Before they began, Whymper was feeling tired and cross. As they went on he became tireder and crosser and his mood infected the others. Each yard of progress took an age. Loose stones were dislodged by the leaders, causing oaths to rise from below. When one member complained about the time it was taking, Croz lost his temper and had to be restrained. Later, Almer slipped and very nearly lost his life. They advanced, retreated, changed course, hacked up dangerous couloirs, struggled along treacherous ridges and, in Whymper's words, became, 'I am afraid, well-nigh worn out.'[32] When, by 12.30 p.m., victory seemed within their grasp they were almost too tired to seize it: 'Small, ridiculously small, as the distance was to the summit, we were occupied another hour before it was gained.'[33]

At the top Whymper pocketed a small piece of rock, as was his custom – such mementoes had the curious habit of replicating the shape of the mountain they came from, he observed – and wrote four, hackneyed sentences describing the view. Then, at 1.45 p.m. he wondered how they were to get down. Everybody refused to set another foot on the slopes they had ascended, so they opted for a descent via a series of arêtes, 'so narrow, so thin that it was often a matter of

speculation on which side an unstable rock would fall'.[34] Whymper
was unaccustomedly nervous:

> Had any one then said to me, 'You are a great fool for coming
> here,' I should have answered with humility, 'It is too true.'
> And had my monitor gone on to say, 'Swear you will never
> ascend another mountain if you get down safely,' I am inclined
> to think I should have taken the oath. The guides felt it as well
> as ourselves, and Almer remarked, with more piety than logic,
> 'The good God has brought us up, and he will take us down in
> safety,' which showed pretty well what he was thinking
> about.[35]

They were right to be nervous, for the rocks were rotten and the
precipices on either side sheer. Moore froze with vertigo as he strad-
dled a knife edge of rock 4,000 feet above the Glacier du Vallon and
only with difficulty could he be persuaded to move. It was a 'fiendish
place,' he wrote. 'We had, for half an hour, without exception the
most perilous climbing I ever did.'[36] At one particular point, the arête
was split by a deep chasm which could only be crossed by jumping an
eight-foot gap from one unstable boulder to another. Interestingly, it
was the reticent Almer rather than daredevil Croz who made the leap.
Although the rock teetered, Almer got a secure handhold and was able
to help his companions across the gap. Whymper found that if he
ignored the drop below it was easy enough. Croz, who had been muttering that they were all doomed, said nothing. By 4.45 p.m., they
were on the relative safety of a glacier and four hours later they were
on solid ground. With the appetite of stress, they cut up and ate the
last item of food they possessed – a strip of pig fat they had been
using to waterproof their boots.

Whymper considered it the ugliest climb he had ever made. His
journal contained a notable lack of self-congratulation, and the single
positive thing he had to say about the experience was that the summit
had been snow-free. 'So far am I from desiring to tempt any one to
repeat the expedition,' he warned, 'that I put it on record as my belief,

however sad or miserable a man may have been, if he is found on the summit of the Pointe des Écrins after a fall of new snow, he is likely to experience misery far deeper than anything with which he has been hitherto acquainted.'[37]

He continued through the Dauphiné, never achieving anything so memorable as the conquest of the Pointe des Écrins* but nevertheless forging new passes and crossing unknown, unnamed glaciers. He also scrounged up a bit of humour to compensate for his nervousness on the Écrins. The butt was a Frenchman named Reynaud, whom he had invited to accompany him up the unclimbed Col de Pilate. Reynaud carried a pocketful of books, a knapsack of scientfic instruments and a small larder of food, all of which Whymper considered derisory. 'His shoulders were ornamented with a huge nimbus of bread,' he wrote, 'and a leg of mutton swung behind from his knapsack, looking like an overgrown tail. Like a good-hearted fellow, he had brought this food, thinking we might be in need of it.'[38] The unfortunate Reynaud was sniggered at all the way up the Col and all the way down. Whymper found him particularly amusing when they reached a bergschrund (the first, huge crack that a glacier makes when it tears away from the mountain) whose upper lip drooped pendulously, and dangerously, over its lower.

As on the Écrins, a leap was necessary. Croz went first, then Whymper. Reynaud, however, dithered. 'He came to the edge and made declarations,' Whymper wrote. 'I do not believe he was a whit more reluctant to pass the place than we others, but he was infinitely more demonstrative – in a word, he was French. He wrung his hands, "Oh what a diable of a place!" – "It is nothing, Reynaud," I said, "it is nothing." – "Jump," cried the others, "jump." But he turned round, as far as one can do such a thing on an ice-step, and covered his face with his hands, ejaculating, "Upon my word, it is not possible. No! no!! no!!! it is not possible."'[39]

What happened next was recorded only by Whymper:

*Seven years later it had been climbed by only one other, a Frenchman named Vincent.

How he came over I scarcely know. We saw a toe . . . we saw
Reynaud a flying body, coming down as if taking a header into
water – with arms and legs all abroad, his leg of mutton flying
in the air, his baton escaped from his grasp; and then we heard
a thud as if a bundle of carpets had been pitched out of a
window. When set upon his feet he was a sorry spectacle; his
head was a great snowball; brandy was trickling out of one side
of the knapsack, chartreuse out of the other – we bemoaned its
loss, but we roared with laughter.[40]

The Col de Pilate was Whymper's last conquest in the Dauphiné.
From there he walked to Chamonix where he had agreed to assist the
Irish cartographer Anthony Adams-Reilly in mapping the Mont Blanc
chain. It was now some twenty years since Sir John Barrow had first
railed against the deficiencies of Alpine maps, and the Swiss government had gone a long way to remedy the problem. Four-fifths of the
Mont Blanc range, however, lay within France and the various restora-
tions which had clung to power since 1816 had more pressing
concerns than mapping the Alps. Forbes's survey of the Mer de Glace
remained an oasis of sanity in an atlas where mountains were misplaced, mismeasured and, at times, invented or omitted. When
Adams-Reilly's first map of the region came out in 1863, Whymper
was deeply impressed. Here was a 'man of wonderful determination
and perseverance'.[41] Here, too, was a man whose presence would be
invaluable on the top of the Matterhorn.

Whymper, despite his accomplishments, was still regarded as something of a johnny-come-lately. The Alpine Club may have been a
brotherhood of equals but some members were more equal than
others, however well they climbed. Compared to people like the eru-
dite Leslie Stephen, Whymper was still a printer's son who dropped
his aitches. He was aware of this. He was aware, too, that he was ill-
qualified to explain Alpine phenomena in anything but the most basic
terms – he made a few brave forays into the field, but produced only
bland, long-winded tracts on the progress of glaciers and the configur-
ation of mountains. He had none of the sensitivity of Leslie Stephen

and none of the scientific clout of John Tyndall. He was a peak-bagger, pure and simple. But if he could bag the Matterhorn and at the same time show that he had done so in a good cause his standing would soar. Adams-Reilly was the answer. Conveniently, he disliked Tyndall, being a protégé of Forbes and, in due course, his biographer. Whymper offered to help him map the remaining portions of the Mont Blanc range if, in return, he would climb the Matterhorn. Adams-Reilly was initially doubtful: 'When I found Whymper just arrived from Dauphiné with a great bag of peaks and passes, I confess my feelings towards him were a compound of envy, malice, and all uncharitableness – unchristian but sincere.'[42] When Adams-Reilly finally agreed, Whymper was delighted. 'The unwritten contract,' he wrote, 'took this form: – I will help you to carry out your desires, and you shall assist me to carry out mine. I eagerly closed with an arrangement in which all the advantages were upon my side.'[43]

Whymper was not overly fond of the Mont Blanc range. 'It has neitther the beauty of the Oberland nor the sublimity of Dauphiné,' he wrote. 'But it attracts the vulgar by possession of the highest summit in the Alps.'[44] Vulgar was a word which he used with revealing frequency in his diaries and journals. Fearing that in the eyes of some his background might place him on the fringes of vulgarity, he saw more that was vulgar and condemned it with greater disgust – another favourite word – than most of his fellows. Mont Blanc's perceived vulgarity, however, could be endured for the opportunity of getting Adams-Reilly to climb the Matterhorn. In addition, several peaks in the chain had yet to be climbed, and Whymper was able to forgive a mountain anything if he was the first up it. (Many of these peaks were also very beautiful, but this was an adjective that Whymper did not use much; he preferred his hills to be terrifying, fierce, jagged, difficult and, in general, to reflect upon his achievement in climbing them.)

Whymper had Croz as his guide, Adams-Reilly a Chamoniard named François Couttet. For a brief period they were also accompanied by Moore and Almer. Their first target was the Aiguille d'Argentière, which they approached on 6 July. They were

unsuccessful. On their initial attempt they were driven back by a
wind so strong that they were barely able to stand upright; and on a
second try – during which Couttet cut no less than 700 steps up an
ice slope – conditions were so bad that they had to retreat within less
than 30 yards of the summit. Two days later, however, they became
the first people to cross the Col de Triolet and on 9 July they conquered Mont Dolent. On 12 July they added the Aiguille de
Trélatête to their tally of firsts. Finally, on 15 July, they returned to
their starting point and completed the Aiguille d'Argentière. It was a
tour de force both in the number of new peaks taken in so short a
time, and in the amount of cartographic work completed. A likeable
man with a dry sense of humour, Adams-Reilly presented an idle face
on the mountain. At rest stops he was usually to be seen lying against
a rock, smoking his pipe and reading a yellow-backed thriller.
Belying this casual veneer was the quantity of sketches and measurements he made. They were fast, accurate and incontestably
authoritative. Whymper was impressed:

> Under the most adverse conditions, and in the most trying
> situations, Mr. Reilly's brain and fingers were always at work,'
> he wrote. 'Throughout all he was ever alike; the same, genial,
> equable-tempered companon, whether victorious or defeated;
> always ready to sacrifice his own desires to suit our comfort and
> convenience. By a happy union of audacity and prudence,
> combined with untiring perseverance, he eventually
> completed his self-imposed task – a work which would have
> been intolerable except as a labour of love – and which, for a
> single individual might well-nigh be termed Herculean.[45]

Whymper was also slightly relieved: Adams-Reilly was not sufficiently
intrepid to climb the Matterhorn without his assistance; when the
moment came, therefore, the credit would be mostly his.

CHAPTER NINETEEN

Whymper left Adams-Reilly to make his own way to the Matterhorn, and strode off to Zermatt via the Moming Pass – another first – with Croz, Moore and Almer. As so often, he was disgusted. Of the Col de Forclaz, which he crossed en route, he wrote that 'it is not creditable to Switzerland . . . mendicants permanently disfigure it'.[1] The more vulgarity he saw the more disgusted he became.

We passed many tired pedestrians toiling up this oven, persecuted by trains of parasitic children. These children swarm there like maggots in a rotten cheese. They carry baskets of fruit with which to plague the weary tourist. They flit around him like flies; they thrust the fruit in his face; they pester him with their pertinacity. Beware of them! – taste, touch not their fruit. In the eyes of these children, each peach, each grape is worth a prince's ransom. It is to no purpose to be angry; it is like flapping wasps – they only buzz the more. Whatever you do, or whatever you say, the end will be the same. 'Give me something,' is the alpha and the omega of all their addresses. They learn the phrase, it is said, before they are taught the alphabet. It is in all their mouths. From the tiny toddler up to the maiden of sixteen, there is nothing heard but one universal chorus of – 'Give me something.[2]

Whymper's vitriol was all-encompassing. On leaving the masses he sought refuge in a chalet – 'surrounded by quagmires of ordure, and dirt of every description. A foul native invited us to enter . . .'[3] – and forthwith found more to criticise. Others had been charmed by chalet life. Not Whymper. His palace, as he ironically described it, was 15 feet by 20, with a ceiling height that varied between five and seven feet. In one corner his host smoked a pipe and blew, in between puffs, into a vat of milk. 'It accounts, perhaps, for the flavour possessed by certain Swiss cheeses,'[4] he wrote pettishly. Others, too, found the area unpleasant but nobody went out of his way to condemn it so forcibly as Whymper.

To atone for his xenophobia – or perhaps to purge the incident from his mind – he flung himself at the Moming Pass, deliberately, it would seem, leading his party up the most dangerous slopes available. The following morning they climbed across an unstable ice face on the Schallhorn. 'It was executing a flank movement in the face of an enemy by whom we might be attacked at any moment,' he wrote. 'The peril was obvious. It was monstrous folly. It was foolhardiness.'[5] Moore was horrified: 'I am not ashamed to confess that during the whole time we were crossing this slope my heart was in my mouth, and I never felt relieved from such a load of care as when . . . after, I suppose, a passage of about twenty minutes, we got onto the rocks and were in safety.'[6] Almer, who had never been known to swear, ran a commentary of the strongest oaths Moore had ever heard. They had barely crossed the face when an ice tower 'at least as great as that of the Monument at London Bridge'[7] heeled over as if on a hinge and collapsed on the slope they had just traversed, obliterating every atom of their track and turning the snow face into a sheet of glassy ice. The excuse Whymper offered for taking such a route was that the alternative would have involved spending another night in a chalet.

He then directed them along a horrible knife-edge between two crevasses. As Croz said, 'Where snow lies fast, there man can go; where ice exists, a way may be cut; it is a question of power; I have the power – all you have to do is follow me.'[8] They did follow Croz and none but Whymper was pleased to have done so. The passage was 'one of the most nervous I have ever made,' wrote Moore. '[It] was as bad a piece of ice-work as it is possible to imagine.'[9] At length, however, they completed the first crossing of the Moming Pass and limped into Zermatt. Their journey had taken them twelve hours and had proved that, although the Moming Pass was the most direct route to Zermatt, it was easier, safer and not much slower to take a coach.

Zermatt had changed very little since its 'discovery' by Saussure more than seventy years before. It was rather like Chamonix, being a small village tucked into a tight valley. Unlike Chamonix, however, which had grown into a major tourist resort, Zermatt remained a simple place. Smallholders eked out a living on terraces that lay below the snowline. It had a church and two hotels: the Mont Cervin for tourists, which had a view of the Matterhorn; and the less expensive Monte Rosa for climbers which didn't. Yet above Zermatt rose some of the most majestic mountains in the Alps: Monte Rosa, the Weisshorn and, of course, the Matterhorn. Free of the valley, climbers could see some of the most stunning Alpine vistas on offer.

Whymper painted a vivid picture of the scene that greeted new arrivals:

Two dozen guides – good, bad, and indifferent; French, Swiss and Italian – can commonly be seen sitting on the wall on the front of the Monte Rosa hotel: waiting on their employers, and looking for employers; watching new arrivals, and speculating on the number of francs that can be extricated from their pockets. The *Messieurs* – sometimes strangely and wonderfully dressed – stand about in groups, or lean back in chairs, or lounge on the benches which are placed by the door. They wear extraordinary boots, and still more remarkable head-dresses. Their peeled, blistered, and swollen faces are worth studying. Some, by the exercise of watchfulness and unremitting care, have been fortunate enough to acquire a raw sienna complexion. But most of them have not been so happy. They have been scorched on rocks, and roasted on glaciers. Their cheeks – first puffed, then cracked – have exuded a turpentine-like matter, which has coursed down their faces, and has dried in patches like the resin on the trunks of pines. They have removed it, and at the same time have pulled off large flakes of their skin. They have gone from bad to worse – their case has become hopeless – knives and scissors have been called into play; tenderly, and daintily, they have endeavoured to reduce their cheeks to one, uniform hue. It is not to be done. But they have gone on, fascinated, and at last have brought their unhappy countenances to a state of helpless and complete ruin. Their lips are cracked; their cheeks are swollen; their noses are peeled and indescribable.

Such are the pleasures of the mountaineer! Scornfully and derisively the last comer compares the sight with his own flaccid face and dainty hands; unconscious that he too, perhaps, will be numbered with those whom he now ridicules.

There is a frankness of manner about these strangely-apparelled and queer-faced men, which does not remind one of drawing-room, or city life; and it is good to see – in this club-room of Zermatt – those cold bodies, our too frigid countrymen, regale together when brought into contact; and it is pleasant to witness the hearty welcome given to the new-comers by the host [Herr Seiler of the Monte Rosa] and his excellent wife.[10]

This was the world Whymper relished, a world where everyday cares were left behind, where social pretensions were subsumed in an equality of weeping flesh and knobbly boots, where greatness was measured by physical ability, and where, by that reckoning, he was one of the greatest alive. When he strode into town he knew what he was worth. And he knew that other people knew it too. As Whymper entered Zermatt with yet another clutch of firsts to his name, he was aware that the assembled *Messieurs* eyed him with respect – more so, perhaps, because he was there to conquer the Matterhorn.

Whymper could not climb the Matterhorn that year. On visiting the post office he was handed a letter that demanded his immediate presence in London for business matters. He offered Croz and the Matterhorn to Adams-Reilly, who was at that moment travelling to Zermatt with their supplies. As Whymper had suspected, Adams-Reilly declined: he was not up to the challenge, even with Croz. Whymper was annoyed that he could not make an ascent that year with such a strong party to hand: 'Our career in 1864 had been one of unbroken success, but the great ascent upon which I had set my heart was not attempted, and, until it was accomplished, I was unsatisfied.'[11] But he was happy on two counts: nobody else was trying the Matterhorn; and his arch-rival Tyndall was, by all accounts, out of the game.

The Matterhorn fiasco of 1862 almost ended Tyndall's Alpine career. He climbed mountains for as long as he was able, but he was getting old. The new generation of Alpine Clubbers were young men – Whymper, for example, was still in his twenties. Moreover, from 1864 Tyndall no longer had Bennen to guide him. In that year, on a March morning, Tyndall was travelling by train from Chislehurst to London. A fellow passenger drew his attention to a notice in *The Times* giving details of a new avalanche disaster in the Alps. Such notices were by now rather common, and Tyndall commented severely that nobody in their right minds would trust the snow so early in the year. The next day he learned that Bennen had been one of the victims.

Bennen had been hired to take two climbers up the Haut de Cry – a Frenchman named Boissonnet and an Englishman named Gossett who was attached to the Swiss Topographical Survey. The Haut de Cry was not a big hill, nor was it a dificult one. But, like many hills in March, it was covered with fresh snow. Bennen had doubts. On approaching a couloir he asked whether it was free of avalanches.

The three local guides whom Gossett had hired assured him it was perfectly safe. Bennen didn't believe them. While the three locals ploughed through the snow, creating a furrow of exactly the kind that had caused the Hamel disaster, Bennen picked a higher route over firmer ground, beckoning his employers to follow. Gossett and Boisonnet did as they were instructed, and all three roped themselves together, Gossett taking middle position between Bennen and Boissonnet. There was a short stretch of soft snow to cross – perhaps 12 feet in all – but it was deep, rising above their elbows. They had gone only a few steps when they heard a deep cutting sound. 'The snow-field split in two about fourteen or fifteen feet above us,' Gossett recorded. 'The cleft was at first quite narrow, not more than an inch broad. An awful silence ensued; it lasted but a few seconds, and then it was broken by Bennen's voice, *Wir sind alle verloren*." His words were slow and solemn, and those who knew him felt what they really meant when spoken by such a man as Bennen. They were his last words.'[12] Gossett drove his alpenstock into the snow as far as it would go – three inches protruded when it finally reached ice – and braced himself for the avalanche. In the remaining seconds of calm he looked up to see if Bennen had taken the same precaution. To his astonishment, Bennen dropped his alpenstock, turned to face the valley and spread his arms wide. Slowly at first, but with increasing momentum, the ground began to move.

Gossett had blurred memories of what followed. At one moment he was almost suffocated by snow; then, as a body to which he was roped caught on a rock, he was jerked to the surface and found himself riding the crest of the avalanche: 'It was the most awful sight I ever witnessed.'[13] Then he was back under the snow, swimming against the flow with his arms until, suddenly, the avalanche halted with a deep, creaking noise. Gossett was encased in hard-set snow, unable to move any part of his body save his hands, which were still above the surface. He was beginning to freeze, the pressure on his chest was intense and his air supply was limited. Using the tips of his fingers he scrabbled at the snow above his face. Soon he saw a glimmer of light. But his fingers could not reach far enough to remove the last crust.

His only recourse was to blow hard and hope that his breath either melted the snow or blew it away. He was lucky. After several efforts, the crust collapsed – 'it was time, for I could not have held out much longer'[14] – leaving a little round hole through which he could see the sky. 'A dead silence reigned around me,' Gossett wrote. 'I was so surprised to be alive, and so persuaded at the first moment that none of my fellow-sufferers had survived, that I did not even think of shouting for them. I then made vain efforts to extricate my arms, but found it impossible; the most I could do was join the ends of my fingers.'[15]

Minutes later he heard shouts. The three local guides were alive, one of them having escaped the avalanche completely, the others having come to rest on the surface. It took them almost an hour to dig Gossett out, during which time he could see, and actually touch, Boissonnet's foot protruding from the snow near his head. Tantalisingly, Boissonnet might still have been alive at that time. Once Gossett had been freed it took minutes to clear his companion, but by then he was dead. As for Bennen, there was no hope. The rope led vertically down from the bottom of Gossett's hole, 'and showed us that there was the grave of the bravest guide the Valais ever had, and ever will have'.[16] Five hours later the survivors hobbled to safety, their feet frostbitten and their bodies covered in bruises. Gossett was a broken man and never went climbing again.

It was three days before the bodies were recovered. The rescuers found Bennen lying horizontally under eight feet of snow, his head facing the valley. Remarkably, the body was intact. Avalanches are notorious for the way they mangle their victims but despite having carried Bennen 1,900 feet, according to Gossett's estimate, this one had done nothing but tear his watch off its chain. It was recovered in October by a shepherd who had been amongst the rescuers. It worked perfectly.

Gossett sent Tyndall a letter of commiseration: 'I know you were very much attached to Bennen; the same was the case with him in regard to you. An hour before his death the Matterhorn showed its black head over one of the *arêtes* of the Haut de Cry. I asked Bennen whether it would ever be ascended. His answer was a decided,

"Yes!"'[17] Tyndall, who knew that the Matterhorn could never be climbed, was impervious to posthumous encouragement. Strangely, he also seemed untouched by Bennen's death. His journal – unusually threadbare for this year and the next – made no mention of the disaster. He subscribed to a monument but he did not write an obituary for the *Alpine Journal*, as was becoming increasingly common when favourite guides died, and it was not until 1871 that he published a small paragraph to Bennen's memory. Blindly loyal to his old guide – but not extravagantly so; the paragraph occupied four and a half lines – he maintained that Bennen was unaccustomed to spring snow and had been misled by the advice of inferior, local guides. That was all.

Had Tyndall been a superstitious man he might have pondered on the odd coincidence of what happened next. On 30 July 1864 he left Pontresina to climb the Piz Morterasch with two companions, a Mr Hutchinson and a Mr Lee-Warner from Rugby. Their guides were Walter, Bennen's erstwhile second-in-command on the Matterhorn, and a huge, stolid man called Jenni. Tyndall was impressed by Jenni. '[He] is the most daring man and powerful character among the guides of Pontresina,' he wrote. 'The manner in which he bears down on all the others in conversation, and imposes his own will upon them, shows that he is the dictator of the place. He is a large and rather an ugly man, and his progress up hill, though resistless, is slow.'[18] He seemed keen to impress Tyndall with his abilities. Maybe he was angling for the position Bennen had left vacant. If so, he went about it the wrong way. 'He accomplished two daring things,' Tyndall wrote, 'the one successfully, while the other was within a hair's-breadth of a very shocking issue.'[19]

In Tyndall's opinion the Piz Morterasch was 'a very noble mountain, and, as we thought, safe and easy to ascend'.[20] So it was. Having left Pontresina at 4.00 a.m., they were toasting their conquest with glasses of champagne mixed with snow at 12.30 p.m. Tyndall spent an hour admiring the clouds as they drifted opalescently across the peaks. 'Clouds differ widely,' he recorded, 'but I had hardly seen

them more beautiful than they appeared to-day, while their succession of surprises experienced through their changes were such as
rarely fall to the lot even of an experienced mountaineer.'[21] It was so
splendid that Tyndall was transported to scientific delight, rhapsodising on the nature of vapour and the particles contained therein.
Then he began the descent.

Coming down, they reached a bergschrund. It was the same kind of
thing that Forbes had crossed with a ladder on his ascent of the
Jungfrau. But in this case they had no ladder. Walter, who was in the
lead, hesitated when he saw the crevasse. Jenni, however, offered an
easy solution. He 'came forward, and half by expostulation, half by
command, caused him to sit down on the snow at some height above
the fissure. I think, moreover, he helped him with a shove.'[22] As soon
as he sat, Walter slid down the slope, travelling so fast that he flew
over the bergschrund and landed on the other side. One by one the
others followed him until Jenni was the only one remaining.
Contemptuously, Jenni manoeuvred himself until he was over the
widest portion of crevasse and then slid over it, 'lumbering like a
behemoth down the snow-slope at the other side. It was an illustration
of that practical knowledge which long residence in the mountains
can alone impart, and in the possession of which our best English
climbers fall far behind their guides.'[23]

That was Jenni's first daring thing. His second was less fortunate.
Having glissaded to the top of the Morterasch Glacier, the party was
faced with a broad gully filled with snow that had melted and then
refrozen to create a steep wall of ice. Jenni wanted them to cross it.
Tyndall wanted them to take the safer option of climbing down the
rocks. Jenni affected not to hear him and made for the couloir. At its
brink, Tyndall remonstrated. 'Jenni, you know where you are going,'
he said, 'the slope is pure ice.'[24] Jenni replied that he knew what he
was doing: there were only one or two yards of ice, in which he would
cut steps; beyond that there was snow. The snow would be safe.

Of all men Tyndall should have known that a slope covered with
freshly frozen snow which had not firmed onto its underlying surface
was an invitation to disaster. But he trusted in his guide. They roped

up. 'Keep carefully in the steps, gentlemen,' Jenni called as they stepped across the ice, 'a false step here might detach an avalanche.'[25] The avalanche happpened without a false step being taken. There was no warning, no crack from above, just a sudden rush of snow and bodies that swept Tyndall off his feet. He tried to drive his alpenstock down but it bounced off rock, tossing him into the air. At that moment he was hit by Jenni and both of them lost their alpenstocks. They were driven down, striking the lower lip of a crevasse and bouncing over it. Tyndall and Jenni tried to right themselves. For a second it looked as if they might regain control, then they were swept across a second crevasse. Tyndall was carried over but Jenni, who weighed 13 stone, dropped deliberately into the fissure to halt the slide. The rope nearly squeezed him to death before he was plucked out again.

As they crashed down, and as Jenni tried repeatedly to slow their progress, crying, '*Halt, Herr Jesus, halt!*',[26] Tyndall's mind became free: 'A kind of condensed memory, such as that described by people who have narrowly escaped drowning, took possession of me, and my power of reasoning remained intact. I thought of Bennen on the Haut de Cry, and muttered, "It is now my turn." . . . I experienced no intolerable dread. In fact, the start was too sudden and the excitement of the rush too great to permit the development of terror.'[27] He saw their destination clearly: a gentler ledge, on which they would slow down, followed by a cliff that promised death. He tried to detach himself from the rope but was unable to do so. Dispassionately, he watched Hutchinson clutch Lee-Warner as they approached the final drop.

Then, on the lower gradient, Jenni's scrabbling slowed their speed. Tyndall stood up and added his weight to the rope. The avalanche poured over the cliff but, thanks to Jenni and Tyndall, the others did not. It was close – three seconds more, by Tyndall's calculation, and they would all have been dead. Hutchinson had a bleeding forehead, Jenni had lost a chunk of his hand, Tyndall had rope welts up his arm and they all 'experienced a tingling sensation over the hands, like that induced by incipient frostbite, which continued for several days'.[28] But they had survived.

Fresh snow, a treacherous slope, an avalanche . . . it could have been a refrain of Bennen's accident except that this time everyone was alive. And there was one other thing: a strand of watch chain was wrapped around Tyndall's neck; a few more links lay in his pocket; but the watch itself was lost. On 16 August Tyndall went back for it, accompanied by five friends. Tyndall had a theory that if the watch had fallen face down its back, being made of gold, would reflect the sun's rays and therefore prevent it sinking into the snow as happened with darker objects. His theory was proved correct. Twenty minutes into the search the watch was spotted. It was dry, unbroken and like Bennen's it worked perfectly. Tyndall treated it like a fellow survivor: 'The little creature had continued to beat underneath the snow,' he wrote. 'I have put it in an inner pocket near my heart so that its present warmth may make amends for the tremendous cold it must have endured.'[29] His sentimentality may have reflected a deep loneliness and a sense of despair that his climbing days were almost at an end.

Tyndall might not have considered the coincidence on the Morterasch of any importance, but it fitted into an odd current that was flowing through Switzerland that year. Richard Wagner, who had composed most of his operas within sight of the Alps and who had not visited them for five years, suddenly found himself thrown back there as a political fugitive. Johannes Brahms, likewise, was drawn to Basle, where he gave his first solo recital. Elizabeth Gaskell, who had never been to Switzerland before, inexplicably decided to write *Wives and Daughters* in a hotel at Pontresina. At Morzine, troops were summoned to put down an epidemic of insanity which had overtaken a congregation of a hundred young women. There was an air of expectancy which unnerved even the most seasoned and precise of Alpinists – while waiting for the weather to clear at Zinal, Leslie Stephen broke a chapel window playing street cricket. Something was about to happen.

Over it all, brooded the Matterhorn. 'Magnificent rock,' wrote a visitor to Zermatt that year, 'with his broad breast fronting you, his back and loins covered with pure snow, and a glacier issuing from between his outstretched paws. There he reposes, standing out clear against

the sky, like a colossal sphinx, calmly looking down on the world . . .
I have seen the glories of the Indies, the bright calm beauty of inland
China, the blue skies and rich landscapes of Italy, the purple hills and
ruined temples of Greece, the virgin forests and park-like lands of
Tartary, the wild grandeur of iceberg and glacier in Arctic seas, but
[this] . . . outstrips them all.'[30]

CHAPTER TWENTY

Leslie Stephen described Whymper as the Robespierre of mountaineering: 'he was clearly the most advanced, and would, but for one melancholy tragedy, have been the most triumphant of us all'.[1] The tragedy to which he referred had its roots in a series of tiny mistakes, insignificant on their own but culminating in a disaster that shook the Alpine fraternity to its foundations. It stemmed from Whymper's decision to make 1865 the year in which he conquered the Matterhorn.

Whymper's first mistake was not to ensure he had a good guide when he wanted one. In 1864 he had verbally engaged Croz for an attempt at the Matterhorn in July the following year. He had neglected to put this in writing and when he did so, in April 1865, Croz was already engaged at Chamonix from 27 June. His employer was John Birkbeck, an Englishman who had won fame a few years previously when he slid more than 1,000 feet down an ice slope, flaying the skin from his back and legs and nearly killing himself in the process. Birkbeck's plan was to climb Mont Blanc and then to proceed to the Matterhorn. When Whymper arrived in Switzerland in mid-June, he therefore had Croz's services for barely ten days. He made the most of them.

Accompanied by Croz, Almer and another guide, Franz Biener,

Whymper embarked on an orgy of mountaineering. The Ebenefluhjoch eluded him on 13 June, but the Grand Cornier fell on the 16th – 'an awful piece of work'[2] – the south-west face of the Dent Blanche on the 17th, and the Col d'Hérens on the 19th – almost as bad as the Écrins. On 20 June he crossed the Théodule Pass from Zermatt to Breuil and on the 21st he went up the Matterhorn by a new route: a gully leading to the Furggen ridge, separating the south and east faces. It was an odd choice – Whymper knew very well that the Matterhorn shed more stones than most mountains, and that gullies were natural conduits for stones. The guides were rebellious: they were tired, they were equally aware of the dangers, and Croz for one was certain that the Matterhorn was unclimbable from any direction, let alone via this unpleasant gully. The only person to have implicit faith in Whymper's decision was Luc Meynet, who had once again been hired as a porter. Whymper quelled their doubts, but was soon defeated by the absurdity of his own decision. At 10.00 a.m., while they were eating lunch, a ferocious stonefall swept the gully, forcing them to abandon their knapsacks and run for cover. Whymper insisted that it was still possible to climb up the gully's edges, but only Meynet was willing to follow. 'Come down, come down,' shouted Croz, scrambling after them. 'It is useless.'[3] One hundred feet below, Almer sat on a rock, his head in his hands. Biener was out of sight, not having bothered to move an inch. Whymper conceded with ill grace, but refused to give up just yet. His second plan was to cross the Furggjoch and have a stab at the supposedly impossible north-east ridge. This time the guides refused outright: Biener said it could not be done; Almer asked 'Why don't you try to go up a mountain which can be ascended?'[4]; and Whymper recorded that 'I then had a small wrangle with Croz in which he came out bumptious.'[5] The question of whose will would prevail became academic when, in mid-argument, snow started to fall. They had now no option but to retreat.

Whymper had, in fact, been perfectly sensible in advocating an ascent of the north-east ridge, and had the weather been kinder they might have conquered the Matterhorn the next day. Compared with the snow slopes and rugged ridges that led from Breuil, the north face seemed steep, smooth and unclimbable. Yet Whymper had noticed one or two new facts: on the Italian side the rock formations dipped outwards, therefore it was likely that on the Swiss side they dipped inwards and might prove climbable; further, he had observed how patches of snow clung permanently to the face even on the hottest summer's day, indicating that the angle was unlikely to be more than 45°; and, when one climbed above the Zmutt Glacier, as he had done, the face looked much shallower than it did from below.

The idea had been mooted as early as 1858, when a contributor to the *Illustrated London News* had declared: 'If ever this vast crag is climbed by Hudson, Kennedy or other brave hand, it will be from the Zermatt side; but it will require a perfectly calm day.'[6] This had been echoed by the Parker brothers in 1860, who had climbed to a height of 12,000 feet from Zermatt, and were driven back only by bad weather and lack of time. But Whymper had been loath to attempt the north-east face until all the other, simpler-seeming options had been exhausted. Only the snow and his guides prevented him from trying it now. Still, he consoled himself, there would be better weather and maybe better guides – Carrel, for instance – later in the season.

Disconsolately, he trudged with Croz over the passes to Chamonix. Along the way he climbed Mont Saxe above Courmayeur and nearly lost his life in an avalanche – 'the solitary incident of a long day'[7] – and then endured a terrible passage of the Col Dolent, in which the party was forced to hack its way down a 1,000-foot slope of ice with a gradient of 50° where 'one slip would have been finish'.[8] In his journal he did not make light of the descent, and with good reason according to his biographer Frank Smythe, himself an eminent mountaineer. 'To-day,' wrote Smythe in 1940, 'the traverse of the Col Dolent ranks as an ice expedition of the first order, and the first traverse in 1865 was one of the finest, perhaps the finest, ice expeditions of that time.'[9] It was all the finer given that Whymper's fingers were still frostbitten from the Dent Blanche.

At Chamonix, Whymper, Almer and Biener climbed the Aiguille Verte – the first to do so – a peak of great beauty which everyone said was impossible and which stuck in Whymper's mind mainly on account of his porter. Instructed to wait on the glacier at the bottom with their provisions, the man had got fed up. He knew very well that the Aiguille could not be climbed and that his employers were dead. So he ate the food. When Whymper came down, famished, there remained nothing but a crust of bread. Whymper loaded him with all the baggage he could muster and drove him viciously across the ice. 'He streamed with perspiration,' he wrote with satisfaction. 'The mutton and cheese oozed out in big drops – he larded the glacier.'[10] The porter was soon avenged, however. When Whymper reached Chamonix the local guides were incensed that the Aiguille should have been climbed without their assistance and harassed Whymper's men remorselessly. They did not believe that it had been done: 'They were liars, yes, liars, they had not climbed the Aiguille Verte.'[11] When Almer and Biener complained to Whymper he sent them back out to meet the mob, and strolled after them to watch the fun. A small riot began, which was only ended by the intervention of the police and a fellow Alpine Clubber, T. S. Kennedy, who confronted the ringleader and 'thrust back his absurdities in his teeth'.[12] Whymper was too tired to contribute to the scene. 'These days are mixed up in my head in an inextricable jumble,' he wrote in his diary. 'I know that I had my watch mended, my hair cut and that innumerable people talked endless rubbish to me. I know that the weather was abominable and that I was very like the weather. The first day was almost entirely occupied by the Verte row. The second partly so. I was waited on by the Commissary of Police.'[13]

On 3 July, while Chamonix was still in a state of unrest, he crossed the Col de Talèfre – again, it was a first – and on 6 July he climbed the Ruinette – another first – where, amidst fields of unending snow and rock, he at last felt free from the pressures of Chamonix. He then made the first passage of the Portons Pass to the Otemma Glacier, crossed the Col d'Oren and then the Col de Valvournera to the Val Tournanche and Breuil. All the time he was heading towards his ultimate goal. '*Anything* but the Matterhorn, dear sir!' wept Almer, when he realised what was happening, '*anything* but the Matterhorn.'[14]

Fortunately for Almer, he was not needed on the dreaded mountain. Jean-Antoine Carrel had just returned from an unsuccessful attempt on the Italian ridge and Whymper was able to persuade him to have a stab at the other side on 9 July, camping first on the Col Théodule, with the proviso – insisted upon by Carrel – that in the event of a fail-ure they would try once again the Italian ridge. Whymper paid off Almer and Biener, 'with much regret, for no two men ever served me more faithfully or more willingly',[15] and thus ended an eighteen-day marathon during which he had climbed up more than 100,000 feet of mountainside. According to Smythe it was an epic 'that stands unique in the annals of mountaineering'.[16]

In Alpine literature Whymper comes across as a species of super-man, a climbing machine for whom height and hardship were nothing. Now and then, however, from journals and archives one gets a glimpse of his weaker, human side: betting Moore two francs that they would not reach the Écrins within thirteen hours; struggling so long to squeeze his feet into ill-fitting boots that his companions almost left him behind; being bedridden for two days after the Écrins, while his fellows continued easily onwards; losing four francs to Moore and Adams-Reilly on a bet that he and they would never climb one mountain; being crippled for a day and a night after climbing another; imploring the guides to stop and wait for him on the Dent Blanche; marvelling at Croz's anecdotes, around a fire of rhododen-dron branches. These little snatches are brought to life when one considers Whymper's age. In the season of 1865 he had only just cel-ebrated his 25th birthday. He was terribly young.

Whymper's second mistake of that season was to place such implicit trust in Carrel. He had already had some experience of the man's unre-liability. He knew, too, of his proprietorial attitude to the Matterhorn and, in particular, the Italian ridge. What he did not know, however, was the depth of Carrel's patriotism: Carrel wanted the Matterhorn to be conquered by an Italian, led by an Italian guide (himself), via the Italian ridge. Although willing to go with Whymper on 9 July, Carrel had already accepted an offer for 11 July from a man who was much more to his liking. Felice Giordano was an engineer and geologist

who, in concert with Italy's Finance Minister, Quintino Sella, had
determined to take the Matterhorn by stealth. On 7 July Giordano
was ready to make his move, and wrote to his sponsor from Turin:
'Let us, then, set out to attack this Devil's mountain, and let us see that
we succeed, if only Whymper has not been beforehand with us.'[17]

On 8 July, as Whymper was preparing for the following day's climb,
news arrived that an Englishman was ill at Val Tournanche. He felt
honour-bound to help him, so set aside his preparations and walked
off to get medicine. This was his third mistake inasmuch as, that
although it was the decent thing to do, it meant delaying his climb.
While engaged in his third mistake, Whymper became aware of the
extent of his second. En route to Val Tournanche he met the two
Carrels leading an Italian gentleman towards Breuil – only in the
capacity of porters, they assured him. Suspiciously, he reminded them
of their agreement. Ah yes, Jean-Antoine Carrel remarked, there was
a small problem. They were engaged to travel in the Aosta valley
with 'a family of distinction'[18] from 11 July. It was most unfortunate,
but there was nothing to be done, the arrangement being of long
standing and precise details having been confirmed only that day.
Whymper was annoyed but not too worried. The family of distinction
was obviously a group of ladies who wanted to potter over the lower
glaciers. 'That work is not for *you*,'[19] he chided, pointing out that he
had dismissed two first-rate guides in the expectation of having
Carrel's services for some time. Carrel made no comment, but smiled
apologetically to indicate that the matter was out of his hands. Honour
applied as much to guides, he implied, as to English milords with
stricken countrymen.

Whymper gave the sick man medicine and dragged him back to
Breuil, from where he hoped an ascent with Carrel might yet be possible. The weather was too bad on 10 July and worsened on the 11
July, giving Whymper the consolation that even had Carrel been free
they could have done nothing – certainly they could not have walked
to Zermatt and gone up from there. Meanwhile, Giordano fretted
anxiously. 'I have tried to keep everything secret,' he wrote to Sella,
'but that fellow, whose life seems to depend on the Matterhorn, is

here, suspiciously prying into everything. I have taken all the competent men away from him, and yet he is so enamoured of this mountain that he may go up with others, and make a scene. He is here, in this hotel, and I try to avoid speaking to him.'[20]

The Italian conspiracy got off to a flying start. On the morning of 12 July Whymper's patient – who was the Revd A. Girdlestone, a dubious exponent of guideless climbing – rose early and seeing that the clouds had thinned a bit, woke him with the news that a party had left in the early hours for the Matterhorn. It comprised the two Carrels, several porters and a mule-load of provisions. By strange coincidence it was directed by one of his fellow guests, a man called Giordano – though he, apparently, had not accompanied the party.

Whymper was furious. He had been 'bamboozled and humbugged'.[21] On complaining to the innkeeper he was greeted with a smile like Carrel's: a conquest from Breuil would make his hotel famous. Whymper snatched a telescope and peered through it. Yes, there was Carrel and his party, making their way up the lower slopes. He returned to his room and paced up and down, smoking cigar after cigar. Carrel had stolen a lead. But his group was large and unwieldy. It would take them three days to reach a position from which they could tackle the summit. If he moved fast Whymper could be in Zermatt inside a day and, conditions willing, could be at the Col Théodule on the next and on the summit the day after. It was just possible. But he had no guide. Almer and Biener were gone, and Carrel had taken every able-bodied man in Breuil with him. Even Luc Meynet was unavailable, being busy with his cheese-making – or bribed by Carrel as Whymper interpreted it. If, by some chance, a guide did appear there were no porters. Giordano had planned with foresight.

Miraculously, Whymper was saved by the arrival of Lord Francis Douglas, an 'exceedingly amiable and talented' 18-year-old whose brother, the Marquess of Queensberry, would later instigate the Wilde trial over which Wills was to preside. Douglas was no stranger to daring exploits: he had scaled the walls of Edinburgh Castle aged 14, and had swum the Hellespont aged 16. Although not an experienced mountaineer he had done some fine climbing that season – Whymper was very impressed by his account of the Ober Gabelhorn, on which he had nearly killed himself – and had in tow young Peter Taugwalder, son of old Peter Taugwalder from Zermatt. Old Peter was a well-known figure, described by one visitor in 1861 thus: 'hard as nails, brown as a pet meerschaum, about 5ft. 6in., with head and shoulders like a Highland Bull'.[22] He and his son had carved themselves a reputation for leading tourists up the easier slopes. They were second-echelon guides – 'Rather eccentric in his ways,'[23] was the entry Old Peter merited in one guidebook – with none of the flair or knowledge of a Croz or an Almer, and several Alpine Clubbers had been disappointed by their performances on difficult slopes. But they did have some interesting opinions regarding the Matterhorn. Old Peter had reconnoitred the north-east ridge and was convinced, like Whymper, that it was surmountable. Casually, Douglas mentioned that he had hired Old Peter for an attempt.

Whymper was immediately interested. Did Douglas truly want to climb the Matterhorn? Yes. Did he want to do so from Zermatt? Yes. Could young Taugwalder carry their gear there? Yes. Then Whymper would be very happy to join them, and could they leave as soon as possible? Douglas agreed – or, as Whymper put it, 'it was determined he should take part in my expedition'[24] – and the next day he and Douglas crossed the Théodule and went down to Zermatt where they instructed old Peter Taugwalder to prepare for an immediate attack on the Matterhorn.

Then Croz turned up. Birkbeck had fallen ill in Geneva, so he had allied himself to the Revd Charles Hudson and his protégé Douglas Hadow. Hudson too was planning to climb the Matterhorn and was staying at the same hotel as Whymper – the Monte Rosa. That evening, while Whymper was finishing his dinner, Hudson strode in from a reconnaissance. Whymper sized him up, and then took him aside. They talked for a while and decided that it would be wasteful for two separate teams to go up the Matterhorn. It would be much better if they joined forces. This was Whymper's fourth mistake.

Hudson, vicar of Skillington in Lincolnshire, was the glamourous face of British mountaineering. Unlike many of his fellows who were not only odd but, to be frank, looked odd, Hudson was a handsome, cheerful man without a problem in the world. Young women stuck his photograph in their albums, from where it smiled out romantically above a dashing signature. No other man seemed so about to give a wink as Hudson. At the same time – and this doubtless contributed to his charm – he was entirely self-effacing. 'He would have been overlooked in a crowd,' Whymper wrote, 'and although he had done the greatest mountaineering feats which have been done, he was the last to speak of his own doings.'[25] Leslie Stephen described him as 'the strongest and most active mountaineer I ever met'.[26] Others said he was as skilful as a guide. He had incredible stamina, considering a 50-mile hike a fair day's exercise – Whymper thought 30 miles was reasonable – and he had been known to walk from St Gervais near Chamonix to Geneva and back, a distance of 86 miles, within twenty-four hours. He had been climbing in the Alps since 1853, had made with Kennedy the first guideless ascent of Mont Blanc by a new route in 1855 and was, in short, the best companion Whymper could have asked for.

Hadow was a different proposition altogether. He was 19 years old and, as Whymper tactfully put it, 'had the looks and manners of a greater age'.[27] It was his first season in the Alps and although he was a rapid walker he had spent very little time in the Alps. Whymper quizzed Hudson about him and received the answer that Hadow 'has done Mont Blanc in less time than most men'.[28] Hudson then mentioned a number of other exploits and concluded that 'I consider he is a sufficiently good man to go with us.'[29] Here, Hudson was being generous. Hadow was young, inexperienced and exhausted. But what else could Hudson say, in the circumstances? He had taken Hadow on, had planned to climb the Matterhorn with him, and it would have been churlish to drop him for no reason other than he did not suit the new situation.*

Whymper's fourth mistake was therefore not only to combine the

---

*Hudson was generous to a fault. During the season he had extended the same invitation to Birkbeck, T. S. Kennedy, the Revd J. Robertson, the Revd A. Girdlestone, the Revd J. McCormick and a bewildered cleric, the Revd R. Wood, who had hardly seen a mountain, let alone climbed one.

two parties into one – whatever the merits of the individuals, small, agile groups are more effective than large ones – but to include Hadow in the party. In such a large expedition, the largest ever to attack the Matterhorn, the group was dependent on its weakest member. If they were all roped together and one man fell on a treacherous slope he might drag one, then two and, as the weight increased, the whole party in his wake. Hadow was indisputably the weakest member. He had visited Birkbeck the previous summer at his home in Settle, where he had been taken up a nearby hill and had displayed unfortunate incompetence. 'On one side there is a small piece of rock which has to be descended with care,' wrote Mrs Birkbeck. 'but most of our party could walk down it with ease. Poor Mr. Hadow found it very difficult and had to be helped down.' Mrs Birkbeck opined that if Birkbeck had not been taken ill in Geneva and had continued to Zermatt with Croz and Hudson, 'Mr. Hadow would *not* have been of the party; he was no mountaineer.[30]

On Thursday, 13 July, Hudson wrote a quick note to a friend, the Revd Joseph McCormick, who had planned to join him and Hadow for the Matterhorn but had been delayed.

MONTE ROSA HOTEL, Thursday, 5 a.m.

MY DEAR M'C,
We and Whymper are just off to try the Cervin [the French name for the Matterhorn]. You can hear about our movements from the landlord of the Monte Rosa Hotel. Follow us, if you like. We expect to sleep out tonight, and to make the attempt to-morrow . . . We expect to be back to-morrow. It is possible we might be out a second night, but not likely.
Ever yours affectionately,
C. HUDSON[31]

Hudson might have been a surgeon reassuring a patient: a short while and it will all be over.

He and Whymper pranced up the Matterhorn. It was so much easier than they had expected that they led the way, taking it in turns to hack steps in the ice while the guides hung behind. When they made camp on a ledge at 11,000 feet they were almost delirious. Compared to the Italian route, the north-east ridge, which appeared so daunting from below, was simplicity itself. Croz and young Peter Taugwalder scouted ahead and returned with the news that there 'was not a difficulty, not a single difficulty! We could have gone to the summit and returned to-day easily!'[32] Everybody went to bed in good spirits. 'Long after dusk,' Whymper wrote, 'the cliffs above echoed with our laughter and with the songs of our guides, for we were happy that night in camp, and feared no evil.'[33] He and the Taugwalders slept in the tent and the others made do as best they could outside. (Privately, Whymper noted that the Taugwalders snored so badly that he did not get any sleep and wished he had chosen to camp out.) In Breuil, meanwhile, Giordano had heard of Whymper's movements and though he thought them ridiculous had sent messages to Carrel telling him that he must 'climb the mountain at all costs, without wasting time, and must make the route practicable'.[34]

The following day, the rocks were more difficult and Whymper handed the lead to Croz. 'Now,' said the Chamonix guide, 'now for something altogether different.'[35] In fact it wasn't that much different. All Croz had to do was extend an occasional hand to his employers. The rocks were testing in places, and extremely exposed, but Whymper thought it a lot easier than the Pointe des Écrins. He was worried, however, by Hadow, who 'was not accustomed to this kind of work and required continual assistance'.[36] They went up and up, crossing 400 feet horizontally here, ascending 60 feet vertically there, then doubling back to a convenient ridge when their way was blocked. There was an awkward corner and finally they were there, separated from the summit by 200 feet of snow. 'The last doubt vanished!' Whymper wrote, 'The Matterhorn was ours!'[37]

Or was it? All the way up there had been a succession of alarms in which one or other of the party thought he had seen figures on the summit. It was not impossible that Carrel's party had beaten them and

were already on their way down. Croz and Whymper raced neck and
neck up the final stretch and discovered to their delight that no footsteps could be seen in the snow. 'At 1.40 p.m. the world was at our
feet,' wrote Whymper, 'and the Matterhorn was conquered.'[38]

There yet remained a faint possibility that Carrel had got there
first: the summit comprised a ridge some 350 feet long, and there
was a chance that the Italians had left traces elsewhere. Whymper ran
along the ridge. Again nothing. Peering over the edge, he saw his
rivals some 1,250 feet below, crawling like ants up the hillside. He and
Croz yelled and waved their arms, to no apparent effect. 'We *must*
make them hear us; they *shall* hear us,'[39] Whymper cried. He seized
a block of stone and hurled it down. Croz joined him and together
they wrestled lumps of crag down the cliff. 'There was no doubt
about it this time,' Whymper crowed. 'The Italians turned and fled.'[40]

Then came the flag-planting. One of the tent poles had been
removed that morning – against Whymper's protestation that they
were tempting providence – and it was now embedded on the northern end of the ridge with Croz's shirt tied to it as a flag. The day was
superlatively calm and clear, and they marvelled at a view which read
like a roll-call of Alpine exploration. 'All were revealed,' Whymper
wrote:

> [N]ot one of the principal peaks of the Alps were hidden. I see
> them clearly now – the great inner circles of giants, backed by
> the ranges, chains and massifs. First came the Dent Blanche,
> hoary and grand; the Gabelhorn and pointed Rothorn; and
> then the peerless Weisshorn; the towering Mischabelhorn,
> flanked by the Allaleinhorn, Strahlhorn and Rimpfischhorn;
> then Monte Rosa – with its many Spitzes – the Lyskamm and
> the Breithorn. Behind were the Bernese Oberland, governed
> by the Finsteraarhorn; the Simplon and St. Gotthard groups;
> the Disgrazia and the Orteler. Towards the south we looked
> down to Chivasso on the plain of Piedmont, and far beyond.
> The Viso – one hundred miles away – seemed close upon us;
> the Maritime Alps – one hundred and thirty miles distant –

Storm on the Matterhorn, 1862

(© Royal Geographical Society, London)

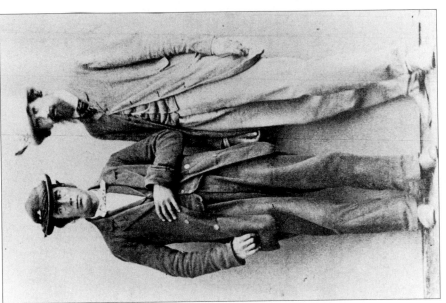

Leslie Stephen (right) with
Melchior Anderegg

(© THE ALPINE CLUB COLLECTION, LONDON)

Albert Smith

(BY COURTESY OF THE NATIONAL PORTRAIT GALLERY, LONDON)

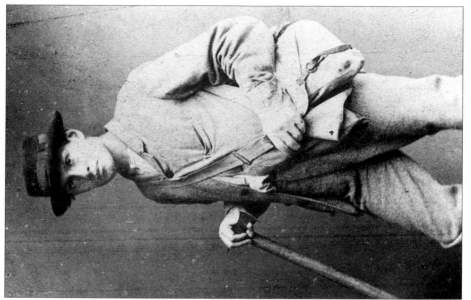

Edward Whymper, 1865

(© THE ALPINE CLUB COLLECTION, LONDON)

John Tyndall

(BY COURTESY OF THE NATIONAL PORTRAIT GALLERY, LONDON)

Almer's leap

(© Royal Geographical Society, London)

Whymper on the Matterhorn

(© Royal Geographical Society, London)

*The apparition which followed
the Matterhorn disaster*

(© Royal Geographical Society, London)

MICHEL A CROZ.

Hadow.

Charles Hudson 1828-1865

Lord F. Douglas 1847-

Peter Taugwalder Vater

1865 (22)
Peter Taugwalder Sohn

Whymper's companions on the Matterhorn ascent, 1865

(© THE ALPINE CLUB COLLECTION, LONDON)

Sir Edward Davidson (centre) with guides

(© The Alpine Club Collection, London)

William Coolidge
(© THE ALPINE CLUB COLLECTION, LONDON)

Edward Whymper in old age
(© THE ALPINE CLUB COLLECTION, LONDON)

were free from haze. Then came my first love – the Pelvoux;
the Écrins and the Meije; the clusters of the Graians; and
lastly, in the west, gorgeous in the full sunlight, rose the
monarch of all – Mont Blanc. Ten thousand feet below us were
the green fields of Zermatt, dotted with chalets, from which
blue smoke rose lazily. Eight thousand feet below, on the other
side, were the pastures of Breuil. There were forests black and
gloomy, and meadows bright and lively; bounding waterfalls
and tranquil lakes; fertile lands and savage wastes; sunny
plains and frigid *plateaux*. There were the most rugged forms,
and the most graceful outlines – bold, perpendicular cliffs, and
gentle, undulating slopes; rocky mountains and snowy
mountains, sombre and solemn, or glittering and white, with
walls – turrets – pinnacles – pyramids – domes – cones – and
spires! There was every combination that the world can give,
and every contrast that the heart could desire.[41]

Such a sight might be visible one day in a hundred, Whymper
reckoned. They stared at it for a long hour before starting on the
descent.

The flag they left behind was not an impressive thing; nor was
there any wind to make it float; but it was visible from all directions.
Down in Breuil, convinced that their group had succeeded, the inhabitants came out *en fête*, toasting Carrel, Italy and the Matterhorn. It was
only when the dejected team arrived home that they learned their
mistake. 'It is true,' said the men. 'We saw them ourselves – they
hurled stones at us! The old traditions *are* true – there are spirits on
the top of the Matterhorn!'[42]

CHAPTER TWENTY-ONE

Eighteen sixty-five was the year in which *Alice in Wonderland* was published and the year in which the American Civil War came to an end. It was the year in which the first complete dodo skeleton was discovered and the year in which Abraham Lincoln was assassinated. It was also the year in which, shortly after 3.00 p.m. on 14 July, a small boy rushed into the Monte Rosa Hotel with the news that he'd seen an avalanche on the north face of the Matterhorn. He was given a clip round the ear and told not to be so silly. No avalanche had fallen, or they would have heard it. But the boy wasn't entirely silly. Something had fallen down the Matterhorn.

Twenty minutes before the boy's report, Hudson and Whymper had agreed on their order of descent. Croz would go first, with Hadow after him. Hudson, who had an eye out for his boy, would go next, then Douglas, old Peter Taugwalder, Whymper and, finally, young Peter Taugwalder. They had plenty of rope: there were two 100-foot lengths of standard Manilla, another 150 feet of a stronger variety and more than 200 feet of a much slighter brand, all of which Whymper had brought from London, home suppliers being infinitely preferable to Swiss ones in his opinion. While they were roping up, Whymper spent a last few minutes sketching the summit and then, darting back up to put their names in a bottle, he took his place in the chain.

The adrenalin which had carried them to the top was gone, leaving them shaky-legged and exhausted. They knew this and acted accordingly, taking exaggerated care on the rocks they had bounded up so eagerly that morning. Only one man moved at a time and not until he was safely anchored would the next in line leave his position. On ice slopes, the more experienced helped the less. Hadow, who was the weariest of them all, had his feet guided into position by Croz. Their precautions were standard practice for any well-guided party coming home after a new conquest save for one important difference – although the leaders were tied to one of the stronger ropes, Old Peter and Douglas were linked by the weakest of the lot.

At 3.00 p.m. Croz put his axe to one side so that he could assist Hadow on a tricky slope. What occurred next could only be guessed at. Whymper's theory was that Croz had helped Hadow into a safe position and had then turned round to pick up his ice axe. As he did so, Hadow slipped and knocked Croz over. Whymper did not see it happen, his view being blocked momentarily by a rock, but he witnessed every moment of the subsequent tragedy.

I heard one startled exclamation from Croz, then saw him and Mr. Hadow flying downwards; in another moment Hudson was dragged from his steps, and Lord F. Douglas immediately after him. All this was the work of a moment. Immediately we heard Croz's exclamation, old Peter and I planted ourselves as firmly as the rocks would permit: the rope was taut between us and the jerk came on us both as one man. We held; but the rope broke midway between Taugwalder and Lord Francis Douglas. For a few seconds we saw our unfortunate companions sliding downwards on their backs, and spreading out their hands, endeavouring to save themselves. They passed from our sight uninjured, disappeared one by one, and fell from precipice to precipice on to the Matterhorngletscher below, a distance of nearly 4,000 feet in height. From the moment the rope broke it was impossible to help them.[1]

Whymper and the two Taugwalders did not move for half an hour. Old Peter burst into tears. Young Peter cried, 'We are lost! We are lost!'[2] Young Peter's despair infected Old Peter and soon he too was crying that they were lost. Caught between the two, Whymper stared down the slope, helpless. Of the three, only Whymper was in control of himself. Neither Taugwalder was willing to move. With difficulty the 25-year-old Londoner broke the stasis. He persuaded Young Peter to leave his perch – they were still roped together and unless he moved they were stuck – then guided father and son back to Zermatt. They went down slowly and carefully, searching for their companions' bodies as they went, sometimes calling out in the vain hope that one of them might have survived. No voices came in return; instead the Matterhorn offered a silent reply of its own. At 6.30 p.m., when they had cleared the most dangerous part of the descent, an enormous arc of light rose in the sky. 'Pale, colourless and noiseless, but perfectly sharp and defined, except where it was lost in the clouds, this unearthly apparition seemed like a vision from another world; and, almost appalled, we watched with amazement the gradual development of two vast crosses, one on either side. If the Taugwalders had not been the first to perceive it,' wrote Whymper, 'I should have doubted my senses.'[3] He recognised it as a solar fogbow, a rare but not unheard-of phenomenon. The Taugwalders, however, saw it as a heavenly manifestation and despite his knowledge to the contrary Whymper was also touched by superstition. 'It was a fearful and wonderful sight; unique in my experience, and impressive beyond description, coming at such a moment.'[4]

Until then the Taugwalders had been in a state of shock, Old Peter crying 'I cannot! I cannot!'[5] as Whymper coaxed him over the rocks. 'Very seldom indeed in my life have I experienced so vividly what it is to have a step between myself and death as I did on this most terrible occasion,' Whymper later wrote to a friend. 'For two hours after the accident I thought every moment that the next would be my last . . . the two guides were unnerved to such an extent that I suspected every minute one or the other would have slipped, and then it would have been all over.'[6] Oddly, however, the sight of the crosses

seemed to restore their senses. The Taugwalders now began to talk
about their wages. Who would pay them, they wondered, now that
Douglas was dead? Whymper retorted that he would pay them, of
course. After a brief consultation, Young Peter said that they would
prefer it if Whymper paid them nothing and to put the fact in writing,
both in his journal and in the hotel book. Astonished, Whymper asked
why. Because, Young Peter explained, next year there would be lots of
visitors to Zermatt and they would get more work if it was felt they
had been poorly treated. Whymper was appalled by their attitude. He
made no reply, nor did he speak to them afterwards, unless it was
absolutely necessary, but 'tore down the cliff, madly and recklessly, in
a way that caused them, more than once, to inquire if I wished to kill
them'.[7]

Now it was Whymper who was the person in shock. His body still
functioned but his mind began to swirl. At 9.30 p.m. he chose 'a
wretched slab, barely large enough to hold the three',[8] on which to
spend the night. Dismayed, the Taugwalders suggested they continue by moonlight. Whymper saw this as a deliberate attempt to
force him into a fatal accident, after which the only account of the disaster would be the one the Taugwalders concocted between them.
Later, when they urged him to go to sleep, he feared they might
murder him. Little of this made its way into his journal, but in a
memorandum to the Alpine Club he later described how Young Peter
'broke out into frightful levity, displaying the most brutal insensitiv-
ity – eating – drinking – smoking – laughing – vociferating . . . that
their demeanour gradually became, and continued to be, suggestive of
personal danger'.[9] According to another account, Whymper did not
sleep but spent the night with his back against the cliff, axe at the
ready, as the Taugwalders leered ghoulishly, waiting for their chance,
on a slip of rock thousands of feet above home.

Six hours later there was enough light for them to continue the
descent and the danger passed. They went down in silence, met the
first chalets, and then ran all the way to Zermatt. Whymper burst into
the Monte Rosa Hotel and made for his room, pursued by an inquisi-
tive landlord. As he closed the door he announced 'The Taugwalders

and I have returned.'[10] The landlord understood perfectly. Within the hour he had roused the village and twenty men were on their way to spy out the terrain. They returned, having spotted the bodies at the base of the north face.

Hudson's friend McCormick had ignored the offer to join the Matterhorn team and instead had climbed the nearby Gornergrat. On Saturday, 15 July, Whymper sent a note alerting him to Hudson's death: 'A party of guides has been sent immediately from here to search for him, and I follow them; but I wish particularly to have an Englishmen with me, and I therefore beg, if you can possibly return here by 4.30 p.m., to do so, in order to go with me.'[11] McCormick received the message too late to be of any assistance that day, but joined Whymper in a rescue mission on Sunday, 16 July. The Zermatt guides could not help, having been threatened with excommunication if they missed early Mass, but there were plenty of others willing to join the team. The Revd J. Robertson and J. Philpotts enlisted with their guide Franz Andermatten. Another English visitor offered his guides Joseph and Alexandre Lochmatter. Two Chamoniards, Frédéric Payot and Jean Tairraz, made up the party. They left Zermatt at 2.00 a.m. on the 16th and by 8.30 were within sight of the bodies. 'As we saw one weatherbeaten man after another raise the telescope, turn deadly pale, and pass it on without a word to the next,' wrote Whymper, 'we knew that all hope was lost.'[12]

The view from afar was nothing compared to what awaited. When they reached the scene they found Croz and Hadow lying next to each other on the snow, with Hudson some 50 yards distant. The bodies had been stripped almost naked during the fall and were so battered that they were barely recognisable – Croz, for example, was missing the top half of his head and was identified only by his beard and by a rosary cross which the Revd Robertson dug out of his jaw with a penknife. Their boots, the last items to be torn off, lay next to them alongside a pathetic collection of personal belongings. 'I have never seen anything like it before or since,' Whymper wrote, 'and do not wish to see such a sight again.'[13] Of Douglas there was no trace, save a pair of gloves, a belt and a boot. His body had either caught on a ledge or had been shredded as it bounced from rock to rock. Apart from a single coat sleeve, nothing more was ever found of him.

They buried the bodies where they found them. McCormick tried to read the funeral service from Hudson's prayer book, which had survived the fall and lay a short distance from his boots, but it was an abridged version so he had to make do with reciting Psalm 90. 'Imagine us standing,' he later wrote, 'with our bronze-faced guides, leaning on our axes or alpenstocks around that newly-made and singular grave, in the centre of a snow-field, perhaps never trodden by man, with that awful mountain frowning above us, under a cloudless sky.'[14] Then they returned to Zermatt where the authorities insisted the bodies be disinterred and brought back for a Christian burial. On 19 July, twenty-one local guides went back to the site and dug the corpses out. As they were doing so, a Rugby schoolmaster named Knyvett Wilson fell off the Riffelhorn and died.

Hudson, Hadow and Wilson were shovelled into a joint grave, covered by two, bland, Victorian coffin stones. Croz was given an upstanding, granite memorial. Hudson was later removed and laid to rest in Zermatt's English church.

The news broke slowly, inaccurately and piecemeal. Whymper wrote a description of the tragedy in the visitors' book of the Monte Rosa Hotel, which was stolen almost immediately, but it was 8 August before he published a definitive account in *The Times*. Until then, wild rumours circulated that made Zermatt, briefly, the most famous place in Europe. Climbers from every nation rushed to the village, impelled by the desire to help, to offer condolences or simply to gawp. The greatest attraction for ghouls was the story – put about by the Zermatt guides – that Old Peter had cut the rope. Whymper dismissed this firmly: the piece of rope was in his possession and it had clearly not been cut either before or during the accident; indeed, given the circumstances, it was plainly impossible for Old Peter to have done so. But the tale persisted, and Taugwalder was reduced to the status of a medieval flagellant, displaying to all and sundry the wounds he had suffered as he took the strain. 'Mr. Robertson,' he beseeched the vicar, 'they say I *cut* the rope! Look at my fingers!'[15] One arrival, a German student named Güssfeldt, went so far as to try and persuade old Peter Taugwalder to guide him to the scene of the disaster: 'But he was terrified, and tried to dissuade me, showing me the scars which the rope had left on the wrist round which the broken rope had been wound.'[16]* On 19 July the British Consul in Geneva sent his chaplain to conduct a private inquiry and on 21 July Zermatt opened its own inquest. Midway through its deliberations a wrenchingly ignorant telegram arrived from Douglas's mother, Lady Queensbury: 'Is it not possible to seek in the rocks above or to let down food?'[17]

As all this was happening, Tyndall was making his way to the Matterhorn for a final try via Breuil. The first he knew of the disaster was when a traveller stopped him on a pass and asked if he'd heard the news. Professor Tyndall was no more. He had tried to climb the unclimbable and had fallen to his death. Tyndall hastened to Zermatt to see what was going on.

When he learned the truth he immediately started a rescue operation to recover Douglas's remains. 'The idea of leaving the body to bleach upon the crags of the Matterhorn was abhorrent to me. Many people deemed it a noble resting place. *I* did not and I cannot explain why I did not.'[18] On his way he had been struck by the abilities of Swiss road-makers, who could drill a foot-deep hole in solid granite within an hour. It occurred to him that a few metal pegs driven into the cliff could support him as he climbed down the track of the falling bodies. None of the Zermatt guides would accompany him, so he hired one of the Lochmatters from St Nicholas and then sent him to Geneva to pick up 3,000 feet of rope. Lochmatter returned with the rope, straggled over a team of mules, plus hammers, steel punches and a tent. The cargo was hauled up to a suitable depot where it waited until the weather was right. Alas, the weather was never right. For twenty days the Matterhorn was hidden by clouds and, eventually, Tyndall gave up. A contemporary put it in a slightly different

---

*They did make an unsuccessful attempt from Breuil, in great secrecy, on 18 September.

fashion: 'the Syndic of Zermatt fortunately found out what was going on, and sent him and his ropes away; they had had plenty of Englishmen killed there; they did not want any more.'[19] Whatever the reason for Tyndall's withdrawal, he left in the comforting knowledge that Douglas had died painlessly. 'No death,' he wrote, 'has probably less of agony in it than that caused by a fall upon a mountain. *Expected* it would be terrible, but unexpected, not.'[20]

(This opinion, which might not have been shared by those who saw the bodies, was given pseudo-scientific validation in 1892. In one of the first examinations of near-death experiences, an Austrian named Albert von St Gallen Heim interviewed a number of people who had survived falls in the Alps.

In nearly 95 per cent of the victims there occurred, independent of the degree of their education, thoroughly similar phenomena experienced with only slight differences. In practically all individuals who faced death through accidental falls a similar mental state developed. It represented quite a different state than that experienced in the face of less suddenly occurring mortal dangers. It may be briefly characterised in the following way: no grief was felt, nor was there paralyzing fright of the sort that can happen in instances of lesser danger (e.g. outbreak of fire). There was no anxiety, no trace of despair, no pain; but rather calm seriousness, profound acceptance, and a dominant mental quickness and sense of surety. Mental activity became enormous, rising to a hundredfold velocity or intensity. The relationship of events and their probable outcomes were overviewed with objective clarity. No confusion entered at all. Time became greatly expanded. The individual acted with lightning quickness in accord with his accurate judgement of his situation. In many cases there followed a sudden review of the individual's entire past; and finally, the person falling often heard beautiful music and fell in a superbly blue heaven containing roseate cloudlets. Then consciousness was permanently extinguished, usually at the moment of impact, and the impact was at most heard but never painfully felt. Apparently hearing is the last of the senses to be extinguished.[21]

St Gallen Heim had himself fallen off an Alp, and the music and roseate clouds were probably extrapolated from his own experience. But the numbing immediacy of shock was exactly as he described. When one of his interviewees, an eight-year-old boy, fell off a cliff he worried only that the penknife his father had given him might slip out of his pocket. St Gallen Heim offered no explanation for his findings. He used them only to comfort the bereaved.)

Meanwhile, Whymper was giving his deposition to the local court. He told everything as it had happened – omitting the Taugwalders' subsequent behaviour – and blamed the fall entirely on the use of the weak rope. Looking at the piece he had retained as evidence, the officials accepted his deposition without question. It had clearly snapped and no wonder – it was flimsy beyond belief.* The verdict was accidental death.

What was not explained (or asked), however, was why the weak rope had been used in the first place. Croz and Old Peter may have paid the matter no attention, guides being notoriously dismissive of such unmanly aids. Hadow and Douglas might have been too inexperienced to know or care what they were tied to. But surely Hudson, one of Europe's most experienced climbers, would have noticed what was going on. The possibility emerged that Old Peter, nominally their head guide, had deliberately sanctioned the use of the weak rope so that if the lower members fell he would not be dragged after them. 'The rumour is absolutely without foundation,'[22] Whymper said. In his denial of Taugwalder's culpability, however, he may also have been trying to save his own neck.

According to Whymper the weak rope was employed only between Old Peter and Douglas; he had been 100 feet distant when the group roped up and had been unaware of the precarious arrangement. Yet,

---

*Sections of all three ropes are preserved in Zermatt's Alpine Museum. The one that broke is little thicker than a washing line.

by his own admission, there were 250 feet of good rope free as they started the descent. This indicated that the leading members had been joined by 100 feet of Manilla, with the other 100 feet plus the 150 feet of the stronger make being wound round the shoulders of either Croz or Young Peter. That at least one stretch of good rope was in Young Peter's possession was confirmed by Whymper's statement that they had tied sections of it to the rocks to help them during their descent. The implication, therefore, is that Douglas, Old Peter, Whymper and Young Peter were all linked by the weaker rope. Even had Whymper not been tied to the weaker rope, he must have been blind not to see that it linked Old Peter and Douglas. Maybe it was nerves, maybe it was confusion, maybe it was the excitement of having conquered the Matterhorn, but one thing is certain: Whymper had to have known that the poorest rope was being used, did nothing about it and was therefore partially to blame. The one mitigating factor was ignorance: contrary to his later statements Whymper did not at the time think the rope was too weak; until the creation of new ropes woven to Alpine Club specifications, he had always used the weak variety on his climbs; Taugwalder also stated that he had considered the rope strong enough, adding in his evidence to the court that had he not thought so he would never have let it be taken up the mountain in the first place. Taugwalder's opinion may not have been valid: most guides thought a rope was simply a rope, whatever its strength; as one British climber wrote, 'I have absolutely known a man propose to take the line from the laundry ground at the Riffelberg.'[23] All the same, the incident did not show Whymper in a good light. Nor did the fact that all the ropes subsequently vanished except for the piece he retained as evidence.

He threw out diversionary leads, blaming Hudson for having allowed Hadow to be a member of the party and hinting at a conspiracy within Zermatt's judicial system. 'I handed in a number of questions which were framed so as to afford old Peter an opportunity of exculpating himself from the grave suspicions which at once fell upon him,' he wrote in 1871. 'The questions, I was told, were put and answered; but the answers, although promised, have never reached me.'[24] He had a go at M. Clemenz, the presiding official – 'It is greatly to be regretted that he does not feel that the suppression of the truth is equally against the interests of travellers and of the guides.'[25] When the transcript was finally made public in 1917, several differences between Whymper's and Old Peter's versions of events became apparent. None was very germane to the issue of who was to blame, but they shared an interesting characteristic: when Taugwalder said something that differed from Whymper's statement, and was then questioned about it, he retracted his words with the admission that Whymper knew best. At the time Whymper praised Old Peter for his fortitude and his honesty. Six years later he wrote that the man was teetering on the brink of insanity – 'I am told he is now nearly incapable for work – not absolutely mad, but with intellect gone and almost crazy; which is not to be wondered at.'[26]* In the same breath he spat on Young Peter, who had vanished two days after the accident: 'Whatever may be his abilities as a guide, he is not one to whom I would ever trust my life, or afford any countenance.'[27] Whymper was revolted to learn that he returned to Zermatt the following year and, despite having been paid more than the going rate for his Matterhorn climb, was importuning tourists as a luckless beggar who had yet to receive his fee.**

Despite his smokescreens, not everyone saw Whymper as a blameless participant. T. S. Kennedy, one of Hudson's few invitees not to have turned up for the Matterhorn that season, wrote that the accident resulted from having taken too large a group and from carelessness induced by the euphoria of conquest. He also said,

---

*Old Peter Taugwalder was not quite the lunatic Whymper would have liked his readers to think. He subsequently left to make a living in America and returned to Zermatt where he died in 1888.

**Young Peter later became a capable and respected guide and was alive in 1917 to tell his story of the Matterhorn climb. He loathed Whymper but, interestingly, accused Hudson and Douglas for the disaster. Of the former he wrote that Old Peter had suggested they split into two parties, each with their own guides, but 'this did not appeal to Mr. Hudson, who modestly thought he and his companions were all better than guides'.[28] Of Douglas his comment was that 'He was not a good climber.'[29]

however, that 'A man who has spent only three or four years on the Alps is not and cannot be a first-rate mountaineer.'[30] His words were aimed at Hadow and Douglas, but Whymper, who had first seen the Alps in 1860, was barely outside the bracket. Similarly, one of the Parker brothers, who had seen the possibilities of the Zermatt route as early as 1860, was asked by Old Peter – who claimed that he had not been paid enough by Whymper – to conduct a private investigation into the matter. Parker's cautious assessment, transmitted privately to his father, was that 'Taugwalder is a very good cragsman & Whymper is said to be a bad one.'[31]

Hadow's father thought Whymper had gone too far in abrogating all responsibility. 'We have been greatly distressed at Mr. Whymper's letter in the 'Times' and the leading article which I was sure would follow,' he wrote to McCormick on 10 August. 'He might have spared those unnecessary remarks about poor Hudson, which have brought blame on him for want of prudence and caution.'[32] Emily Hudson, Charles Hudson's wife, felt the same. Lurid reports were already circulating and she was angry that Whymper should have cast her husband as the wrongdoer. 'I cannot tell you how it has distressed me,' she wrote to McCormick. 'I am very much surprised that Mr. Whymper should have been a party to it. Of course one knows the craving there is in the public mind for the *sensational*, in any form; but it really makes me sick to think of such a subject being used to gratify their tastes. Do you think it would be possible to stop it?'[33]

The one positive aspect of 1865 was that Jean-Antoine Carrel managed to climb the Matterhorn from Breuil. When Giordano heard of Whymper's success he had been downcast. 'Despite the fact that everyone did his duty, this has been a lost battle,' he reported to Sella. 'And I am upset beyond words by it. I believe, however, that revenge would still be in order.'[34] The revenge he envisaged was an immediate conquest of the Matterhorn from the Italian side. At first, nobody was willing to try it except Carrel. But an Italian priest who was also a climber and who had been given leave from his seminary to try the Alps arrived in time to stir the faint hearts. He rallied them with patriotic sentiments. How could they expect to be paid for such a job? National honour was at stake. He himself would go with them. So, on 16 July, while the search parties were leaving Zermatt, Carrel, the priest and two others went up the Matterhorn from Breuil. 'We were going of our own will, for the honour and the vengeance of our country,'[35] the priest wrote. They did not take Giordano because 'Carrel bluntly declared that he did not for the present feel like taking a tourist'.[36]

They passed all the perils on the Italian ridge before sliding around to the Swiss side where they followed Whymper's path to the summit. Whymper was impressed. He had always wanted Carrel to get to the top from Breuil simply because he was so determined to do so. 'He was *the* man,' he explained, 'of all those who attempted the ascent of the Matterhorn, who most deserved to be the first upon its summit. He was the first to doubt its inaccessibility, and he was the only man who persisted in believing that its ascent would be accomplished.'[37] It was 'the most desperate piece of mountain-scrambling upon record,'[38] Whymper wrote. It was true. The little wrinkle of rock by which they crossed from west to east is still known as Carrel's Corridor. When Whymper asked him about it five years later, Carrel replied: 'Man cannot do anything much more difficult than that!'[39]

Whymper was prone to occasional dramatisation but in this instance he was, if anything, underplaying Carrel's achievement if a future President of the Alpine Club was to be believed. 'Harder gymnastic climbs have no doubt been done,' Sir Edward Davidson wrote in 1897, 'but as a traverse over treacherous & difficult rock affording most indifferent foot and handhold & requiring perfect steadiness on the part of the whole party, I cannot recall anything worse in my experience.'[40]

And what of Tyndall? He was downcast: the mountain's forgotten supplicant, he had been beaten on all fronts. But he was not yet defeated, as he proved on 29 July 1868 when he completed the first traverse of the Matterhorn, climbing to the summit from Breuil and descending via Whymper's route to Zermatt. He did it in habitual style. 'I did not touch food preparing to reach the top . . . in a spirit of prayer and fasting,'[41] he told an old friend. He reached Zermatt after nineteen and a half hours and wrote immediately to Huxley, his pen wobbling with exhaustion. 'Many years ago you spoke to me jokingly about making a pass across the Matterhorn from Breuil to Zermatt. This I have just accomplished with great labour & some danger . . . I shall now give up this break-neck work . . . I had committed myself, and could not rest contented until I had accomplished what I had begun.'[42]

The ascent moved him deeply. Whereas Whymper had exulted in the number of peaks he could see from the summit, Tyndall was depressed. 'Hardly two things can be more different than the two aspects of the mountain from above and below,' he recorded. 'Seen from the Riffel, or Zermatt, it presents itself as a compact pyramid, smooth and steep, and defiant of the weathering air. From above, it seems torn to pieces by the frosts of ages, while its vast facettes are so foreshortened as to stretch out into the distance like plains . . . There is something chilling in the contemplation of the irresistible and remorseless character of those infinitesimal forces, whose integration through the ages pulls down even the Matterhorn. Hacked and hurt by time, the aspect of the mountain from its higher crags saddened me.'[43]

Throughout his life Tyndall had sought in the Alps a cure for the ailments which dogged him. Subconsciously, he linked physical illness to spiritual angst and hoped that by conquering the Matterhorn he would find relief from both. He was disappointed.

This notion of decay implied a reference to a period when the Matterhorn was in the full strength of mountainhood. My thoughts naturally ran back to its possible growth and origin. Nor did they halt there, but wandered on through molten worlds to that nebulous haze which philosophers have regarded, and with good reason, as the proximate source of all material things . . . Did that formless fog contain potentially the *sadness* with which I regarded the Matterhorn? Did the *thought* which now ran back to it simply return to its ancestral home? . . . When I look at the heavens and the earth, at my own body, at my strengths and weakness of mind, even at these ponderings, and ask myself, Is there no being or thing in the universe that knows more about these matters than I do? – what is my answer?[44]

There was no answer. Tyndall continued to climb mountains but did so with less and less enthusiasm. 'In 1868 I had been so much broken down on going to the Alps,' he wrote, 'that even amongst them I found it difficult to recover energy.'[45] In 1869 he scaled the Aletschhorn in order to study the colouration of the sky but by 1870, following a nasty slip that resulted in blood poisoning, he was ready to give up. The Alps agreed with him. That year, lightning ignited two forests, one of which burned for several days and nights. Tyndall watched with fascination as clumps of trees exploded into flame. A heavy bout of rain extinguished the fire and also doused Tyndall's career in the Alps. In 1877, having finally found a wife, he built a holiday home in Bel Alp, from which he led guests on gentle jaunts across the glaciers. People spoke of him with awe, the Matterhorn's lower peak was named Pic Tyndall in his honour and the Emperor of Brazil asked for two signed photographs, but never again did he climb a mountain.

Whymper was released from the inquest on 22 July 1865 and hurried down to Visp, from where he went on to Interlaken and wrote an angry note to McCormick asking how much he could claim from the Zermatt authorities for his 'detention'[46] during the trial and apologising for having borrowed his handkerchief (retrievable at 20 Canterbury Place, Lambeth Road). From Interlaken he travelled to Geneva and thence to Calais, the object of everybody's brightest interest. 'The manner in which I was persecuted by impertinent people on my way home passes all belief,'[47] he told Robertson. He came home to find himself the most talked-about person in London. A fellow Alpine Club member wrote that he was 'most truly to be pitied, for his name is so connected with the Matterhorn, and rather wild designs upon it, that people are sure to blame him for the accident'.[48]

The Matterhorn shaped the remainder of his life. Never the most sociable of people, he withdrew still further, confining himself to the family home for several years. According to his sister, 'his unfortunate habit of sleeplessness had become fixed, and he practically turned night into day'.[49] He ate supper at 10.00 p.m. when everyone else was asleep, went to bed at 3.00 a.m., breakfasted at 11.00 a.m. on his own, and lunched at 2.00 p.m. 'or later, but on no account at the same time as any family meal'.[50] Sometimes he allowed his youngest sister to run errands, occasionally he played bagatelle with his father, but his main preoccupation was writing up his journals for publication. At dusk – generally in autumn and winter – he would disappear on long tramps, returning for a late tea and toast, when he might speak a few words before spreading his papers across the table in dismissal.

Whymper did not stop exploring: he made two expeditions to Greenland, he climbed new peaks in the Andes and the Rockies with select Swiss guides – among them Carrel – and, his funds having been exhausted by these forays, wrote guidebooks to Zermatt and Chamonix. His achievements were impressive in a quiet way: in Greenland he drove across the glaciers on a dog sled (in those days a rare skill for a European) and collected an array of geological specimens unequalled outside Copenhagen; in the Andes he made important observations on the effects of altitude on the human frame when he climbed Mount Chimborazo, at 20,561 feet the highest mountain in Ecuador; his travels through the Rockies took him over scores of untrodden mountains and passes; his Alpine guidebooks were well researched and well received; he received the Royal Geographical Society's Gold Medal and was proposed for – but was not granted – membership of the Royal Society. Tellingly, however, he avoided the high Alps. He went back to them, he wrote about them, he conducted glacial experiments on them, he walked across them but hardly ever did he actually climb them. 'I have done with the Alps now,' he told a fellow climber, 'having, as you may suppose, not quite so much appetite for this sort of thing as I had.'[51] As with Tyndall, the Matterhorn had finished him.

Whymper's shunning of the Alps has been interpreted in numerous ways. The most lurid version is that he dared not face the ghosts of his lost companions. Immediate accounts tell of his being in a terrible state after the fall, weeping constantly, sitting up all night in fellow climbers' rooms fixing the details in his mind. He later wrote to McCormick begging an example of Hudson's signature as a memento. Certainly the disaster was a topic he returned to again and again in lecture halls, magazine articles and private correspondence for the forty-six years until his death. On the other hand, when he did address the subject he seemed interested only in proving that he was not to blame. In letters to a Swiss colleague – now displayed in Zermatt's Alpine Museum – he displayed, for example, only conventional regret at the deaths and dwelled far more heavily on whether or not the right decisions had been taken during the climb (he would take them again if he had to, he said defiantly). Similarly, when he reclimbed the Matterhorn to take photographs from the summit in 1874 he passed over the very spot where the disaster had occurred without even a passing mention of it in his journal. The truth is probably that he did feel some remorse, but it had nothing to do with his avoidance of the Alps. He had stalked the Matterhorn for five years, making smash-and-grab raids on lesser peaks as he did so, and in 1865 he considered his work over. At Breuil, Girdlestone had noted that Whymper 'was resolved to do the Matterhorn, and equally resolved, that when that was done, to give up mountaineering, because there were no more *new* great mountains to be conquered'.[52] In his single-minded manner, Whymper saw no reason to go back over old ground. The Alps were done, they were finished, he had conquered them. As he wrote in 1871, 'The play is over, and the curtain is about to fall.'[53] For any who wished to emulate him he had wise but depressing advice: 'Do nothing in haste; look well to each step; and from the beginning think what may be the end.'[54]

CHAPTER TWENTY-TWO

The Golden Age of Mountaineering which had begun on the Wetterhorn in 1854 ended on the Matterhorn in 1865. The Alpine Club had achieved astonishing things during these years: of forty-three first ascents in 1864 and 1865, for example, only five had been made by continental climbers. But the disaster stripped their exploits of respectability. A rebellion which had been biding its time backstage now sprang out from the wings. 'Why is the best blood of England to waste itself in scaling hitherto inacccessible peaks,' asked *The Times*, 'in staining the eternal snows and reaching the unfathomable abyss never to return? . . . Well, this is magnificent. But is it life? Is it duty? Is it common sense? Is it allowable? Is it not wrong?'[1] The *Illustrated London News* was almost hysterical at the thought of a lord falling off a cliff, an event which threatened the very fabric of society: 'When a nation is bitten with a peculiar passion, it seldom passes out of that without trouble and painful experiences, and though a dozen young men are knocked up for life each year by Alpine climbing, and this year half a dozen lives have been already sacrificed, it is by no means uncertain that a member of the Alpine Club – that pet of superfine reviewers – will not endeavour to surmount a "virgin peak" of some wondrous mountain in the year 1875 and render a family heirless and a mother unhappy for life.'[2] The *Standard* likened

climbers to a chain of convicts and *Punch* ridiculed so harshly
McCormick's efforts to raise funds for a commemorative chapel in
Zermatt that it was forced to apologise. Continental papers were sim-
ilarly incensed. 'Is it possible to believe,' ran an article in France's
Journal Illustré, 'there actually is in London an Alpine Club, the aim
of which is to suggest and glorify dangerous attempts at climbing
European mountains?'[3]

Ruskin, still alive and raving, added his bit too. 'The real ground for
reprehension of Alpine climbing,' he stated, 'is that with less cause, it
excites more vanity than any other athletic skill.'[4] This mountaineering nonsense had served only to soil the objects of his meditation
and the Alpine Club were paramountly to blame. 'You have despised
nature, that is to say, all the deep and sacred sensations of natural
scenery,' he told its members. 'You have made racecourses of the
cathedrals of the earth. The Alps, which your own poets used to love
so reverently, you look upon as soaped poles in bear gardens, which
you set yourselves to climb and slide down with shrieks of delight.'[5]
He spoke viciously of climbers returning from a conquest, 'red with
cutaneous eruption of conceit and voluble with convulsive hiccoughs
of self-satisfaction'.[6] Anthony Trollope joined the chorus, lampooning
climbers in his *Travelling Sketches*. Dickens scorned them for 'the scaling of such heights as the Schreckhorn, the Eiger, and Matterhorn
[which] contributed as much to the advancement of science as would
a club of young gentlemen who should undertake to bestride all the
weathercocks of all the cathedral spires of the United Kingdom'.[7]
The reversion of attitude had all the flavour of medievalism then so
popular thanks to the novels of Walter Scott. As in the Middle Ages,
mountains were once again appalling.

From being the most exciting association in Europe, the Alpine
Club became the most reviled. 'We are, it seems, overgrown schoolboys, who, like other schoolboys, enjoy being in dirt, and danger and
mischief,'[8] Leslie Stephen wrote sadly. New admissions dropped
abruptly, and stayed down for several years thereafter. According to
one member, 'there was a sort of palsy that fell on the good cause, particularly amongst English climbers. Few in numbers, all knowing

each other personally, shunning the public as far as possible, they went about under a sort of dark shade, looked on with a scarcely disguised contempt by the world of ordinary travellers.'[9] When Leslie Stephen visited a hotel in Berne he was distressed to find that 'they think no more of an ex-president of the Alpine Club than of a crossing sweeper'.[10]

The odium persisted in 1871. In that year Whymper published his *Scrambles amongst the Alps*, a weighty, 432-page tome containing ninety of his own illustrations and relating the long stalk that had culminated in his slaying of the Matterhorn. He took immense care over it, refusing even to divulge the title lest others steal it for their own reminiscences.* The six years it had taken to write may have caused some to doubt its accuracy: it was a tiger's skin, and Whymper had prepared it carefully before hanging it on the wall. But apart from a few flourishes – which Whymper himself admitted – it was an honest description of ten years' exploration. It was received rapturously in some quarters: 'You can almost hear the tinkle of the bells on the Alps and by the chalet,' wrote *The Times*. 'You breathe the fresh fragrance of the pine trees; and fancy listens for the sharp ring of the axe, as it makes the splinters fly.'[11] Leslie Stephen saw it as the ultimate expression of Alpinism: 'Those who have lived through the period which is just now closing – the period, that is, in which inaccessibility has been finally abolished – will probably admit, on reflection, that Mr. Whymper's book contains the most genuine utterance of the spirit in which victory has been won . . . it is the congenial record of the most determined, the most systematic, and, on the whole, the best planned series of assaults that were made upon the High Alps during the period of which he speaks.'[12] From that day to this it has been hailed as a classic of Alpine literature comparable to, but much more exciting than, Saussure's *Voyages*, Forbes's *Travels* and Wills's

---

*His caution was not misplaced. In an age when Alpine authors vied to give their works as unassuming a title as possible – 'Wanderings . . .', 'Excursions . . .', 'Hours of Exercise . . .', 'A Summer Holiday . . .', etc. – a word like 'Scrambles' was a prize. Whymper later sought and obtained an injunction against a fellow climber who tried to use it for his own book.

Wanderings. In recognition of its value, the King of Italy awarded Whymper the Order of SS. Maurice and Lazarus. Appropriately, Quintino Sella, the Finance Minister who had funded Carrel's rival ascent of the Matterhorn, was instructed to break the good news.

Nevertheless, *Scrambles* resurrected the troublesome question of whether people should explore the Alps at all. A review in the *Standard* criticised Whymper for fostering 'the depraved taste, which needs to be checked rather than cultivated, for doughty deeds in Alpine climbing'. The book was 'morally deteriorating, ministering to an unhealthy craving for excitement'.[13] Similarly, *Blackwood's Magazine* felt that Whymper showed ignobility of purpose. Mountaineering, it stated, 'is carried on at the continual risk of life – a risk undertaken with a light heart – but for no particular reason this is the weakness of all such adventures. They have no human meaning, are good for nothing, productive of nothing'.[14] Leslie Stephen offered a lopsided variant on the theme: 'There is perhaps some pleasure in being killed in trying to do what has never been done before; but there is no pleasure in being killed in simply following other people's footsteps. It is high time for sacrificing a little of our enthusiasm to common sense, and for doing our best to encourage the growth of a healthy public spirit in regard to such matters.'[15] Stephen had always been a stickler for safety and yet, when it suited him, he could poke fun at caution. 'We must admit that Mr. Whymper has provided rather strong meat for the ordinary digestion. These pictures of travellers flying through mid-air across crevasses of boundless depth, exposed to a relentless fire of stones, or camping uncomfortably on the edge of ghastly precipices, are calculated to try the nerves of placid gentlemen who lay down the canons of criticism in the quiet of a London street.'[16]

Ruskin, of course, flamed with ire. In a revised edition of *Sesame and Lilies*, in which he had made his comments about bear gardens and soaped poles, he insisted that his earlier remarks stood uncorrected – 'I . . . think it wrong to cancel what has once been thoughtfully said'[17] – and compounded them with a message to the Alpine Club: 'Believe me, gentlemen, your power of seeing

mountains cannot be developed either by your vanity, your curiosity,
or your love of muscular exercise . . . the best way to see mountains is
to take a knapsack and a walking-stick, leave alpenstocks to be flourished between one another's legs, by Cook's tourists.'[18] By this time
Ruskin was beginning to suffer from psychotic attacks (he had also,
belatedly, been elected to and had resigned from the Alpine Club).
Whymper, Stephen, Tyndall and all the others whom he singled out
for abuse were generously restrained in their rebuttals. They would
probably have agreed with Huxley's harsh advice to Tyndall: 'Men
don't make war on either women or eunuchs and I hope you will let
Ruskin have his squall all to himself.'[19]

The great sense of discovery which had pervaded the 1850s and
early 1860s had evaporated, as Leslie Stephen was honest enough to
admit. 'How very commonplace sound the adventures which then
excited so much interest!' he wrote in the 1871 edition of the *Alpine
Journal*. 'How we used to exult over scrambles which are reckoned
easy work for a beginner in his first season! And how energetically we
proclaimed to the outside world the discovery of a new pleasure which
has since become rather a threadbare topic of discussion.'[20] Climbs
which had once seemed impossible were now 'an easy day for a
lady',[21] their problems having disappeared 'like ghosts from a haunted
house'.[22] He looked back on the seminal first edition of the Alpine
Club's *Peaks, Passes and Glaciers* with amusement: 'Look at the poor
old chromolithographs which then professed to represent the
mountains!'[23] Yet the Alps still held an allure, and Stephen was quick
to point it out. Reviewing Whymper's *Scrambles*, he wrote, mischiev-
ously, that 'No advertisement of Alpine adventure is so attractive as a
clear demonstration that it is totally unjustifiable.'[24]

More than any other commentator, Stephen had his finger on the
pulse. Whymper's disaster may have aroused public disapproval but,
in private, it became a cause célèbre. It had all the elements of a
good Victorian romance: competition, betrayal, hardship, defeat at
the moment of victory and, of course, the death of a nobleman. A new
'Cut-Rope' genre of penny dreadfuls emerged, with titles such as
Greater Love Hath No Man and *The Coward: A tale of the snows*,

depending on whether the rope had been cut by the man above or the man below. Having read the story people wanted to visit the scene. Thomas Cook, who had started his first conducted tours to Switzerland in 1863, soon had his books full and by the 1870s the Alps were as busy as ever. Most visitors were pro forma types for whom Switzerland was something to be 'done', just as the Grand Tourists of yesteryear had ticked off the Alps en route to Italy. They sat in their hotels, waiting for the next leg of their trip to begin, unwitting objects of more experienced travellers' hostility. One year Leslie Stephen was immobilised by a leg wound and took the time to describe a typical Cook's man.

> His main specialities, as it seems to me from many observations, are, first and chiefly, a rooted aversion to mountain scenery; secondly, a total incapacity to live without the *Times*; and thirdly, a deeply-seated conviction that foreigners generally are members of a secret society intended to extort money on false pretences. The cause of his travelling is wrapped in mystery. Sometimes I have regarded him as a missionary intended to show by example the delights of a British Sunday. Never, at least, does he shine with such obvious complacency as when, armed with an assortment of hymn-books and bibles, he evicts all the inferior races from the dining-room of a hotel.[25]

At a slight remove from the hotel loungers were the newcomers who wanted to try a peak in search of that genuine Matterhorn experience. Too often, they found it. Until 1865 fatalities had been relatively rare, something for the exploring community to remark upon and deliberate; after that date they became commonplace. Between 1866 and 1876 there was never less than one death per annum and in 1870 an entire party of eleven got lost in a blizzard and perished on Mont Blanc. 'Alpine Accidents' became a standard feature of the *Alpine Journal*'s contents page and club members read with dismay the letters from France and Switzerland in which survivors recounted climbs that had ended in an avalanche, a crevasse, a slip of the foot or a fall without rope.

Most heart-rending of all was the fate of the 1870 party. Comprising a Scot, the Revd G. MacCorkendale, Dr J. Bean from Baltimore and his 50-year-old compatriot, a mountain enthusiast named Randall who only wanted to see Mont Blanc and had had no previous intention of climbing it, they left Chamonix on 5 September with three guides and five porters. They reached the summit on 6 September and were immediately wiped from sight by a snowstorm. When the weather cleared on 17 September, eleven days later, a rescue party found MacCorkendale and two porters sitting above the Mur de la Côte; they were unroped, their clothes were torn and they were dead. Also dead were Bean and another porter, whom they found in a disintegrated snow nest, slightly higher up and well off the usual route, surrounded by a pile of discarded equipment. They noted that the dead men were the heaviest and least fit of the group. Between 21 and 23 September the rescuers scoured the summit for Randall, the three guides and the remaining two porters. They never found them, but they picked up a trail of belongings on the steep southern face that led to the Brenva Glacier. The guides and Randall had obviously tried to save themselves but had become disorientated and gone down the wrong side. It was hard to tell whether MacCorkendale had also tried to escape or whether he had died with Bean and then tumbled down when the outer walls of the nest collapsed. Dr. Bean's diary filled in the remaining details.

Tuesday, September 6 – Temperature, 34°C below zero at 2 o'clock in the morning. I have made the ascent of Mont Blanc with ten persons . . . We arrived at the summit at half-past 2 o'clock. Immediately after leaving it I was enveloped in clouds of snow. We passed the night in a grotto excavated out of the snow, affording very uncomfortable shelter, and I was ill all night. September 7 (morning) – Intense cold; much snow, which falls uninterruptedly; guides restless. [Possibly Randall and the others left at this point.] September 7 (evening) – If

anybody finds this notebook please send it to Mrs. H. M.
Bean, Jonesborough, Tennessee, United States of America. My
dear Hessie, we have been trapped on Mont Blanc for two days
in a terrible snow-storm; we have lost our way and are in a hole
scooped out of the snow at a height of 15,000 ft. I have no hope
of descending. Perhaps this book may be found and
forwarded . . . We have no food; my feet are already frozen, and
I am exhausted; I have only strength to write a few words. I die
in the faith of Jesus Christ, with affectionate thoughts of my
family; my remembrances to all.[26]

He had two bags with him, he concluded, and the rest of his belongings could be found at the Hôtel Mont Blanc. If whoever found him
could forward his effects to the Hôtel Schweizerhof in Geneva and
pay his bill he would be most grateful, 'and heaven will reward your
kindness'.[27] On 8 September, he wrote his last entry in blurred and
indistinct handwriting: 'Morning terribly cold again and much snow.'[28]

The disaster received less publicity than it deserved, thanks to the
Franco-Prussian War: Bean's private tragedy was nothing compared to
the thousands who died at Sedan in the same year. Nevertheless, it
was one of many reminders that something had to be done. In 1882
Leslie Stephen decided that 'I am beginning to think all this mountaineering indefensible. We have paid & may expect to pay too high
a price for any advantages gained.'[29] Following a spectacularly
destructive season in which three separate parties were wiped out,
Queen Victoria's private secretary wrote on 24 August 1884 to Prime
Minister Gladstone: 'The Queen commands me to ask you if you
think she can say anything to mark her disapproval of the dangerous
Alpine excursions which this year have occasioned so much loss of
life.' Gladstone's response was negative: 'I doubt the possibility of any
interference, even by Her Majesty, with a prospect of advantage.'[30]
The casualties were so continuous that even the creaking bureau-
cracy of Austria–Hungary took notice. In August 1887 the Police
Department of the Imperial Ministry of the Interior issued a circular
to Tyrolean clubs asking what they intended to do about 'the repeated

fatal accidents to tourists making high ascents'.[31] Regulations were
needed, it said sternly. No regulations were forthcoming and so
people carried on falling off. But they fell off with some style, as continental writers grudgingly conceded.

Strolling through Zermatt one evening, the French writer and artist
Théophile Gautier saw a British party returning from the hill. It
impressed him immensely:

> A tall young man, strong and thin, dressed in brown corduroy,
> with gaiters up to the knees, a soft felt hat pulled down over
> his eyes, looking a perfect gentleman in spite of the
> unavoidable carelessness of his clothes. He was a member of
> the Alpine Club and had just successfully ascended the
> Matterhorn . . . His guides were walking behind him with their
> ropes coiled round their shoulders, holding their axes, their
> iron-spiked poles and all that was required to attack so wild a
> peak. These three resolute sunburnt faces were resplendent
> with the joy of their triumph over great difficulties . . . The
> guides entered the hotel and the Englishman remained for a
> few moments on its threshold, leaning against the wall with
> complete unconcern, looking perfectly carefree, just as if he
> were coming from his club in Pall Mall . . . While watching this
> handsome youth, probably rich and certainly used to comfort
> and refinement, who had just been risking his life with
> complete indifference in a useless and dangerous enterprise,
> we thought of the resistless passion which drives a few men to
> undertake terrific scrambles. No example can deter them.
> When going up towards the Matterhorn, this young man had
> certainly seen the graves of his three countrymen in the
> Zermatt churchyard.[32]

The young man in question was one Revd J. M. Elliott. He fell
1,000 feet to his death on the Schreckhorn the following year. Three
years later his guide, J. M. Lochmatter, was killed on the Dent
Blanche. Gautier supplied an epitaph for Elliott, Lochmatter and

every other Alpine climber. 'A peak,' he wrote, 'can exercise the same irresistible power of attraction as an abyss.'[33]

Separate from the tourists and the joy-climbers was a small band of people who genuinely wanted to explore the Alps. The Matterhorn, the grandest redoubt of all, had fallen but many other peaks and passes remained inviolate, especially in the Dauphiné. Forbes had gone through the region in the 1840s, Whymper had trampled over it twenty years later and several other climbers had picked at it. But it was still too primitive to attract the majority. Accommodation was verminous, the food was vile – if it was available – and the inhabitants were surly, dirty and backward. Guides from neighbouring areas spoke of it with revulsion. Everyone who had emerged from its depths agreed that apart from the mountains it was an awful place. It was common for British travellers to joke about living rough, the poor food they received and the fleas that infested them, but even T. G. Bonney, a sober-minded scientist, was aghast at the state of the Dauphiné. 'A good digestion and an insect-proof skin are indispensable requisites,' he wrote in 1865. 'On the great high road from Grenoble to Briançon there is fair accommodation at one or two places. Off this, everything is of the poorest kind; fresh meat can only be obtained at rare intervals, the bread and wine are equally sour, the auberges filthy, and the beds entomological vivaria. It is hardly possible to conceive the squalid misery in which the people live; their dark, dismal huts swarming with flies, fleas and other vermin; the broom, the mop, and the scrubbing-brush are unknown luxuries; the bones and refuse of a meal are flung upon the floor to be gnawed at by dogs . . . The people in many parts are stunted, cowardly, and feeble, and appear to be stupid and almost *cretins*.'[34] Even in the best 'hotels' the dining-room floorboards were invisible beneath inches of dirt and refuse. Upstairs, guests had to kick aside dogs gnawing on old bones before they could get into their rooms.

The Dauphiné did, however, contain the last great mountain in the Alps. The Meije lacked the Matterhorn's stature but, at 13,067 feet, it was far from being a molehill and the closest anyone had come to conquering it was when Whymper had crossed its shoulder, the Brèche, in 1864. In twos and threes, mountaineers began to explore the region and very soon the Meije became the object of fierce competition. Leading the field was an American team comprising William Coolidge, his aunt Miss Meta Brevoort and their dog Tschingel.

CHAPTER
TWENTY-THREE

The Matterhorn, that monolithic pyramid which for so long had been the grail of Alpine exploration and whose conquest had caused such heartache, was, ironically, the agent of the Meije's downfall. Among the scores of tourists who came to Zermatt in the wake of the 1865 disaster were two Americans: Meta Brevoort and William Coolidge. The former was a spinster in her late thirties, conservative and rather stern-looking but determined and adventurous. The latter was her nephew, a podgy, short-sighted, intelligent teenager whose head bulged peculiarly above his collar and who was interested in history. They had no intrinsic yearning for the Alps and had only come to Europe the previous year because Coolidge suffered from typhoid fever: his doctor had ordered him abroad and his aunt had been sent to look after him. With them came Mrs Coolidge, William's mother, and her daughter Lil, both of whom were also unwell. What started as a simple change of air developed into lifelong European residence. All thanks to the Matterhorn.

On arrival the Coolidges drifted across Europe, staring at the usual sights, admiring the usual museums and doing what sightseers usually did. When news came in of the Matterhorn disaster, Coolidge and his aunt followed the herd to Zermatt. Meta Brevoort was immediately hooked by the tragedy. She interviewed Whymper's chambermaid and added a few more details to the story:

> Said it was dreadful to have to go into the dead men's rooms full of their scattered clothes etc. Described the excitement in Zermatt the day they reached the top . . . Then the horror the next day when they went to seek for the bodies & then the arrival of the relatives & especially of poor Douglas' brother. She says he would stay in the same room & bed his brother had occupied & that one morg. he started off leaving a letter on the table saying he was going to look for his brother. He was alone & without any provisions. They followed & found him near the foot of the mtn. half crazy. As to Whymper she says he neither eat nor slept but went abt. crying all the time afterwards whilst he was here.[1]

Young Coolidge was overwhelmed by proximity to fame. He wrote to his mother on a sheet of notepaper headed by a view of Zermatt and the Matterhorn. His letter contained details of everything he and 'aunty' had been doing and could have been sent from the seaside were it not for a few schoolboyish sentences: 'The two dots you see on the picture represent where they fell from, and where they fell. A horrible distance. The house with the dot is our hotel, du Mont Rosa.'[2] Just as Whymper, when young, had been awed by the Franklin disaster, so were the Coolidges, in turn, awed by Whymper's own tragedy. Franklin's had been a distant, untouchable, romantic doom. The deaths of Croz, Douglas, Hadow and Hudson, on the other hand, while equally romantic – or perceived as such – were present and all too tangible. 'I can say for certain,' Coolidge later wrote, 'that it was this accident which drew me first to Zermatt.'[3]

The Matterhorn led Meta Brevoort and her nephew to other parts of the Alps. Later that year she climbed Mont Blanc, danced on the top and sang the Marseillaise, while Coolidge went up La Flégère opposite and watched her progress. Meta Brevoort climbed several more mountains and acquired a taste for it. Coolidge, though too young to go up anything serious, became fascinated by Alpine history. Like so many *étrangers* before them, they became entranced. The Alps offered Meta Brevoort all the climbing she wanted and William Coolidge was very content to record first her ascents, then, as he grew older, their joint ascents and finally the ascents of anybody who had set foot in the region in the last four hundred years. The Rockies, the Andes, the White Mountains and other New World ranges seemed crude in comparison. That Christmas, Meta Brevoort gave Coolidge the complete set of the Alpine Club's *Peaks, Passes and Glaciers*. It was as much a gift to herself. 'We pored over those volumes with an almost unbelievable intensity,' Coolidge recorded. 'We wished to become complete mountaineers.'[4] He was then 15 years old.

Newcomers to the Alpine scene, they found nothing boring in the chromolithographs of yore, nor were they put off by the fact that everything seemed to have been climbed already. For the next five years Coolidge and his aunt stomped across the Alps, following the routes described by members of the Alpine Club. Basing themselves in Grindelwald, they adopted Christian Almer as their personal guide, and while climbing few new peaks made numerous second ascents. With Almer's assistance they started the (never very popular) trend for winter mountaineering, becoming the first people to make winter ascents of the Wetterhorn, the Jungfrau and other Oberland peaks. They also instigated the concept of the high bivouac, in which a single tent pitched at a high level enabled them to climb peak after peak in succession, thereby cutting out the tiresome and time-consuming slog from the valley. Meta Brevoort was the more adventurous of the two; Coolidge was tough but technically insecure. He was insecure in other ways too: lacking a mother he clung to his aunt; and when, after a retreat from the Eiger in 1868, Christian Almer gave him a consolation gift of a tan mongrel named Tschingel, he clung to the dog too. Tschingel became famous as the dog that climbed Alps, following his master up peak after peak. During his lifetime Tschingel made eleven first ascents, and accompanied Coolidge up more than 150 other mountains. After several litters of puppies Coolidge began to refer to him as 'her', but Meta

Brevoort was made of sterner stuff: for her, Tschingel was always a 'him'.

In 1870 the unique combination of aunt, dog and nephew – who was by now a bulbous-headed 20-year-old – reached the Dauphiné. 'I am not quite sure what it was that made us choose Dauphiné as our battleground,' Coolidge later wrote, 'but I believe it was ambition. There was a whole world out there and that was enough for us.'[5] It was an unsavoury world but it was one that contained the highest unclimbed mountain in the Alps and so, that June, he, his aunt and their dog, escorted by Christian Almer and his son, Ulrich, set out to conquer the Meije.

Coolidge and his aunt had studied the available literature and in doing so must have come across A. W. Moore's report to the Alpine Club on the Meije's accessibility. Peering at it in the winter of 1869 Moore wrote that 'the more I looked at the mountain, the less hopeful did I become; and in the end I signally failed to discover any line of approach at all promising. The final peak resembles the Aiguille du Dru, and even to reach its base would be no easy task.'[6] He hoped, however, 'that some enterprising person will, at any rate, go and give the mountain a fair trial; if successful, he will have the satisfaction of vanquishing one of the noblest and most formidable of Alpine peaks'.[7]

Coolidge wanted to be that enterprising person. He and his aunt walked over the passes to La Grave where Meta Brevoort found everything that had been said about the Dauphiné to be true. 'Such an inn!' she wrote to Coolidge's mother. 'The floor of our room black as the ace of spades, a bag of flour and a sieve in one corner. No means of washing apparent, flowers spread out to dry on the floor, no pillows, sheets like dishcloths! Will went to bed while his clothes were drying and, concluding it was the best place for him, stayed there.'[8] Outside the Meije looked 'so unpromising that we entertained but slight hope of succeeding in attaining its summit'.[9]

The Meije – whose name they discovered was patois for *femme* – comprised three peaks skirted by glaciers. One peak, the easternmost, was lower than the other two and linked to them so casually

that it might almost have been a separate entity. It was to the central
and western peaks, therefore, that they turned their attention. From
where they stood the central peak looked the highest. It also looked
the most difficult, a triangle of sheer rock that leaned outward
towards La Grave. On 25 June they sent the Almers to reconnoitre
while they dawdled away an afternoon in the woods, Meta Brevoort
knitting while Coolidge recited Macaulay on the banks of a stream.
The Almers returned with the information that the central peak
looked difficult but not impossible; the overhang could be circum-
vented and they had found a place where they could bivouac on the
first night.

The party left at 11.00 a.m. on 27 June 1870, and crossed the glacier
to the Almers' chosen campsite. The wind blew and none of them
slept very well. At 4.20 a.m. on Tuesday, 28 June, they left Tschingel
in the tent and moved on. They had a nasty moment when they
climbed a set of rocks so steep and smooth that, in Christian Almer's
view they were as bad as 'the rocks on the Italian side of the
Matterhorn without the ropes'.[10] But they managed to wriggle over
them – Meta Brevoort having discarded her dress in favour of
trousers – and at 12.10 p.m. they reached the top where, to Coolidge's
dismay, they saw that they had climbed the wrong peak: 'what was our
horror to find that the west peak overtopped us'.[11] The difference in
height was minimal – some 40 feet, by Coolidge's estimate – and he
had wild hopes of crossing the ridge that linked them but was stopped
by Almer, who 'pronounced it utterly impossible for any human being
to reach the summit as it was sheer on all sides'.[12] With that admoni-
tion they retreated to their tent, where Tschingel greeted them
delightedly. They spent the night there and reached La Grave at
10.45 the next morning.

Meta Brevoort's heel was hurting from a pair of boots that had not
been worn in, Christian Almer was snow-blind, they were all 'in a very
much burnt condition',[13] and they had not reached the summit. They
had, however, done what none of the best mountaineers dared do.
The central peak – any peak – of the Meije had escaped Whymper,
Moore, Walker and other big names from the Golden Age. The

American parvenus had climbed it at first go, so they had cause for congratulation. They clambered into a carriage with the Almers and rode exultantly through the mountains to Monastier, a village that was a good base for future conquests and in which they were mistaken for wizards accompanied by a witch. Here they settled into another Dauphiné hotel. 'We are lodged in a most peculiar room with a vaulted roof,' wrote Meta Brevoort. 'Almost everything is kept in it. Flour, bed clothes, saws, shovels, bird cages, wine skins, hub, clothes, sieves, an old clock, water pipes, brooms, old chest of trunks; and Will's bed is made of a table which is also a large chest with a sliding top to it.'[14]

Meta Brevoort was crippled by her boots and remained at Monastier while Coolidge and the Almers rushed over the Écrins, Mont Pelvoux and – a first – the 12,874-foot Ailéfroide. As she waited she barricaded her room against a drunken debauch that lasted until 2.00 in the morning and thereafter came out only to collect her meals. 'The eggs became exhausted, which were my principal food,' she told her sister, 'so I have lived on nuts and bread and honey and a small allowance of water. Soup (which is water, butter, salt, potatoes and herbs) I have eaten on days I did not happen to see it made.'[15] They walked back to civilisation having spent a fortnight in the Dauphiné and caught carriages and coaches back to Britain. The Meije was unbroken but, as Coolidge said, 'for me it will ever be surrounded by a halo of romance'.[16] Others thought so too.

In 1873 a team of six Britons surveyed the western peak from La Grave and were disheartened. Their two guides, both named Baumann, thought the task impossible. 'When Hans Baumann was questioned about it he gave it as his opinion that one Herr and two guides might get up, if they never wished to come down again,' wrote their leader. 'Peter Baumann, doubling the amount at which he usually declined anything, declared two thousand francs an insufficient sum to induce him to make the attempt.'[17] Nevertheless, they went up the central peak, following in Coolidge's steps, and tried the arête to the western peak only to find it 'unspeakably formidable'.[18] They returned to London with the news that the Dauphiné was as

squalid as ever, that their landlord had added the day of the month to
their bill and that 'the maps of the neighbourhood of the Meije
are . . . without a single exception . . . grossly and grotesquely
inaccurate'.[19]

Clouds of mountaineers swirled round the Meije over the next
four years. French, Swiss, British and Italian, they came, failed and
went home again. They tried to climb the western peak from all
points of the compass; they went singly, in large groups and in small;
they attacked it year after year and day after day. In 1875 ten parties –
two of which were composed of guides alone – poked and prodded at
the Meije. That August one group climbed the central peak twice and
made a determined assault from a different direction within the space
of three days. The mountain was only slightly less busy in 1876. A
Frenchman named Cordier claimed to have conquered the western
peak but was forced to retract when it became obvious that he had
not. Another Frenchman, Henri Duhamel, wrestled with the southern
face for three successive days, trying three new and fruitless routes
before departing in search of easier prey – and at the end of his journey reporting that, whatever the English might think, French
surveyors had triangulated the Meije impeccably.

'I have no hesitation in saying that every one of these [routes]
ought to be tried again,' wrote a British climber, Henry Gotch, who in
June 1876 had joined the list of failures. 'A little more or less snow
might make all the difference wanted. But the assailant of the Meije
should be no ordinary man; he should be able to subsist on anything
or nothing, he should be flea-proof and fly-proof, he should be able to
sleep in any posture or go without sleep altogether, his senses of smell
and hearing should be removable at will, he should have no prejudices
as to his personal cleanliness or health, and above all he should have
the power of waiting.'[20]

Coolidge also returned for a second attempt in that year but
decided the weather was too bad. Meta Brevoort, who was unable to
accompany him, was despondent when Coolidge sent a letter detailing the depth of competition. 'Alas! Alas!' she replied, 'And to think
of all the others who will be coming and of the *one* who may succeed.

Dear Will, give my love . . . to that glorious Meije and ask her to keep herself for me.'[21] In a burst of adopted patriotism she feared not only that someone other than herself might climb the Meije but that that someone might be a foreigner. 'Have you found out whether, as we thought there must be, there is any English blood in Cordier?'[22] she enquired.

Brevoort was then staying at the Hôtel Bel Alp above the Aletsch glacier, looking after Coolidge's sick sister Lil. While she was there she had the opportunity of meeting one of the giants of the Matterhorn, John Tyndall, who had come to Bel Alp for his honeymoon. The struggle which had first inspired Meta now seemed a distant and uninteresting thing compared to her own. She did not engage with the Tyndalls, but sneered at them from a distance. 'She is very plain and thirty if a day old. He looks old and ghastly,' she wrote, disapprovingly. 'Professor T and his wife are very tender in their behaviour to one another, even in public. They walk off with their arms around one another and were seen kissing on one of the spurs of the Sparrenhorn the other day. They only join the vulgar herd at dinners, when he lectures away as usual.'[23] It was a strange judgement for, by all accounts, the Tyndalls were a charming couple and the combative scientist had been mellowed by age and ill health. But Tyndall had lost the battle for the Matterhorn and it was perhaps this that soured Meta Brevoort against him; at such a crucial juncture she did not want to be associated with failure, particularly when it seemed so likely that she would, indeed, be beaten to the top of the Meije. Neither, perhaps, did she want to be reminded that Tyndall was a defeated man of 56 years and looked it; she herself was pushing 50 and might soon look similarly time-worn. Distraction came with the prospect of climbing Mount Everest. Among her fellow guests were a British couple named Walker from India. 'He has told me lots about Mt. Everest,' she wrote to Coolidge. 'No fear of wild beasts, nor rains at the proper season, nor hostile natives if one could get properly accredited, but the height he thinks would be an insuperable objection.'[24] She and the Walkers went outside where, by pointing at a cloud, Mrs Walker tried to explain how high Everest appeared on the horizon. Height was a mere technicality, Meta Brevoort decided. Within days she was firing off letters to friends enquiring about the practicalities of such an expedition. The power of waiting, which Gotsch had recommended, was not one of her fortes.

That August, while Brevoort fretted in Bel Alp, Coolidge went with Christian Almer on a tour of the Dolomites, the precipitous towers of orange rock that lay to the east of Switzerland. 'A veil of mystery still shrouded the Dolomites,' he wrote, 'even in the case of those who do not count themselves to belong to the vulgar crowd.'[25]* He had 'some vague idea of undertaking their minute exploration, if they and I happened to agree'.[26] They did not agree: they lacked snow; the sight of so many vertical pinnacles made him uneasy; to climb them required mountaineering methods that had yet to be introduced; and the Meije still waited. 'I still have longings after this marvellous region,' he later wrote. 'But my attention became gradually fixed on the more westerly portion of the Alps. Yet in the Autumn of 1876 it for a while hung in the balance . . . The South Western Alps won the day.'[27]

Christmas approached. Coolidge and his aunt were by this time living in Oxford, where his intellectual precocity had gained him a Fellowship at Magdalen College – of which, as a displaced foreigner, he was rightly proud. He was planning their campaigns for 1877 and she was compiling material for a sensational book to be called 'Perils of the Alps'. Everything seemed hopeful and positive. Then Meta caught rheumatic fever. It was bad but not that bad, and recovery seemed certain. She was in good health on the morning of 19 December when she received a request for her signed photograph from one of her Meije rivals, Duhamel. Quite suddenly, that afternoon, she died.

Coolidge was bereft. He had been exceptionally close to his aunt – so much so that some thought he was her son. He had spent a

---

*The Dolomites were named after a geologist called Dolomieu who visited the region at the turn of the eighteenth century. He had wanted to call them after Saussure, in homage to the father of Alpine exploration, but Saussure had modestly declined the honour.

formative part of his life with her. She had been his closest companion during the unsettling process of moving from one continent to
another. She had been his 'dear Ducky' and he her 'darling Will'.
When she died, his life changed irrevocably – or, more exactly, it
ceased to change. After 19 December 1876, he sought nothing new,
made no close relationships, looked only to the past and travelled
only to places with which he was acquainted. From the safety of his
cloisters (where he taught history) he now peered at the world, suspiciously and antagonistically, through the shade of Meta Brevoort.

His aunt's memorial was to be the conquest of the Meije. In 1877
Coolidge went back to the Dauphiné to complete the task on her
behalf. The Meije was as frantic as ever. Duhamel was there, so was
Cordier and their compatriot Paul Guillemin. A fourth Frenchman
was also in evidence, a pop-eyed youngster named Emmanuel
Boileau de Castelnau. Britain's Lord Wentworth sprang fruitlessly at
the mountain twice in two late June days. Meanwhile, hovering fitfully in the background was a Briton called Maund, 'whose fitness is
a chronic marvel'.[28] By now they were hammering at the mountain
from all directions. La Bérarde, a village which lay to the south of the
Meije, was almost as thronged as La Grave to the north. Coolidge
eschewed both north and south faces, choosing instead an approach
via the Brèche on 22 July. He failed, like everybody else. Guillemin
attacked it from two different angles on 30 July; Boileau de Castelnau
also returned disappointed on 30 July, despite having the assistance of
the Dauphiné's best guides, Pierre Gaspard and his son. Cordier did
not even bother to try, but went up a nearby peak and was killed
when, short-sightedly, he glissaded into a glacial stream – tragically,
the drop was only twelve feet. Coolidge decided there was nothing
more to be done that season and went back to Oxford. He was slightly
disturbed by Boileau de Castelnau, who was plotting a fresh attempt
even as he left. But he was sure that the Frenchman would never
make it.

CHAPTER
TWENTY-FOUR

'Goblins and devils have long vanished from the Alps,' Henry Gotch told the Alpine Club in May 1877, 'and so many years have passed without any well-authenticated account of the discovery of a dragon that dragons too may be considered to have migrated.'[1] A new creature, however, had arrived to take the dragons' place. *The Hunting of the Snark*, published in 1876 by the Revd Charles Dodgson under the pseudonym Lewis Carroll, described the surreal adventures of a band of misfits seeking an elusive beast known as the Snark. They dreamed of the Snark, it occupied their waking moments, they threw all their ingenuity into its discovery. They hunted it, clad in seven coats, through deep valleys surrounded by dangerous peaks and chasms. And then, when one of their number found it, both he and the Snark vanished. *The Hunting of the Snark* was possibly an allegory for the pursuit of happiness. It was possibly, too, an allegory for the wild objectives Victorian explorers set themselves. Whatever interpretation Dodgson favoured, the Meije was a very obvious Snark. And it was captured in much the same way as the poem described.

Emmanuel Boileau de Castelnau was a latecomer to the hunt. Born in 1857, the same year in which the Alpine Club had been inaugurated, he was the youngest scion of a noble French family fallen on hard times. Like so many other climbers he had been a sickly child and had encouraged himself with dreams of the unknown: 'The one thing which interested me was reading accounts of distant exploration. I knew everything about recent discoveries in Africa and Asia and about Polar expeditions.'[2] Like others with similar dreams, he went to the Alps instead. Between 1872 and 1874 he went up Mont Blanc four times, climbed the Matterhorn, the Jungfrau, the Finsteraarhorn, the Dent Blanche, the Écrins, the Col du Géant and a host of other mountains. He was one of the founding members of the French Alpine Club. Little else is known about him but, from surviving diaries, he was obviously tough. He trained for months before embarking on a campaign and was harder even than Whymper. On one ascent he and his guide climbed barefoot in order to get a finer grip of the rock – though he did not, as chamois hunters were reputed to do, cut his feet so that the congealing blood gave that extra bit of purchase. He tried the Meije first in 1874, again three years later, and then, on 16 August 1877 he stood on its summit.

He described the climb in nonchalant terms. Starting from La Bérarde, in conditions that were 'splendid, cold and piercing',[3] he and his guides simply went up, skirted to one side and after a bit of hard ice work and a nasty moment with an overhang that forced them to traverse onto the north face, they reached the top at 3.30 p.m. They were cold, there was no view, they felt hungry and they came down, whereupon Boileau de Castelnau slept for sixteen hours. He subsequently joined the army and rarely climbed in the Alps again. Like the man who found the Snark, he vanished, along with the last great unclimbed peak in the Alps. No greater anti-climax could be imagined.

'One bright summer morning in August 1877,' wrote Coolidge, 'soon after my return from an unusually short holiday among the mountains, a foreign postcard was placed in my hand which proved to contain the startling news of the conquest of the Meije.'[4] It informed him that Boileau de Castelnau had climbed up the south face of what was now called the 'Grand Pic'. Coolidge was appalled. He had met Boileau de Castelnau three weeks earlier at the foot of the Meije and had left him to his own devices, confident that the Meije could only be surmounted via the arête leading from the central peak, or the 'Pic Central'. Who was this man? Enquiring of the Alpine Club he learned that Boileau de Castelnau was an excellent mountaineer who was on the list for next year's admissions. Still, why was he not more famous? How had he beaten all the older, more experienced continental climbers who had shown an interest in the Meije, such as Cordier, Duhamel and Guillemin? He did not believe it. It was a false report, just like the one Cordier had put about in 1876. But as more letters came in from unimpeachable sources, Coolidge was forced to acknowledge the truth.

The truth made him no happier. He could not see how the Meije could have been conquered. Had it *really* been conquered by the south face? In Coolidge's mind no conquest was complete until every footstep had been set down on paper. The meagre details which appeared in French journals did not satisfy him, nor did Boileau de Castelnau's brief narrative, the proofs of which Coolidge acquired from the printers in Paris. In fact, the more he looked at it, the more unlikely it seemed that Boileau de Castelnau had climbed the Meije. There was only one way to make sure. In July 1878, Coolidge hired Christian Almer and his son 'young Christian' to take him up Boileau de Castelnau's route.

They arrived on 3 July to find La Bérarde in turmoil. Several amateurs had already settled in the surrounding villages and the more serious mountaineers – 'whom I looked on as dangerous rivals,'[5] – were plodding over the passes that led to the Meije. Coolidge and the Almers moved fast. By 9 July they were in a position to start the climb. 'Never have I been in a greater state of nervous excitement on starting for any ascent than on this occasion,'[6] Coolidge wrote. 'The Meije had exercised, and indeed still exercises, the same strange influence over me which the Matterhorn had on its early explorers; and though I knew I could trust my two faithful guides, yet I scarcely dared hope that it would be given to me to attain the much-desired summit.'[7]

He spoke as if he was the first man to climb the Grand Pic. In his mind, he probably was. He and the Almers followed Boileau de

Castelnau's track, and at each stage Coolidge wondered whether the Frenchman's report was accurate, whether they might be crossing new ground. But they weren't. Every move was exactly as Boileau de Castelnau had described it. Only when they reached the arête linking the Pic Central and the Grand Pic did Coolidge have a moment of satisfaction. Boileau de Castelnau had described climbing a ten-metre-high rock face to reach the arête and then leaving a rope behind for other climbers. Coolidge saw the face but he saw no rope, nor did he see any way in which Boileau de Castelnau could have climbed the face other than 'a narrow gully of most uninviting appearance, filled with just enough snow to make it dangerously slippery'.[8] Discomfited at the prospect of failure but heartened at the thought of proving Boileau de Castelnau a fraud, he paced along the face searching for the rope. It was not there. Then he looked down and saw it lying in the snow beneath the gully; flayed by ice and wind over the course of a year, it had fallen to the ground. The way having been pointed out to them, Coolidge and the Almers crawled up the gully and reached the arête from where they walked to the summit, a disappointing sight, being sheer on one side but gently rounded on the other, and far from the precipitous peak Almer had described in 1870.

Coolidge was solemn: 'I am ashamed to say that I paid but little attention to the view. The Meije had been in my eyes a mountain to be climbed for its own sake, and not for the sake of the view – a fault or merit which I cannot attribute to many other mountains.'[9] On his return he snipped off a bit of the rope to prove he had been there, and then retreated to La Bérarde. What Boileau de Castelnau had neglected to record was supplied by Coolidge to the Alpine Club in 1879: 'the whole climb ranks with, and even surpasses in point of length and of *continuous* difficulty, the most difficult mountains with which I am acquainted'.[10] Of an exceptionally awkward face he said: 'The descent of this wall will always remain in my mind as the most arduous and terrible piece of climbing it has ever fallen to my lot to perform. When I say this, I am speaking deliberately, and in the conviction that I am not exaggerating the impression it made upon me.'[11]

Coolidge could not but admire Boileau de Castelnau's achievement. Yet it was a forestalment he never forgave. He had climbed the
Pic Central with his aunt and had hoped to accompany her up the
Grand Pic, which stood such a minuscule distance higher. When he
did reach the top, he dedicated it to her. When he returned, he dedicated his failure to Boileau de Castelnau. All the best peaks in the
Dauphiné had been climbed by Britons, he said, and it was an unfortunate mistake that the Meije wasn't among them. With petulant
hauteur he announced (inaccurately) that it had fallen 'by a kind of
accident to a young Frenchman who was a chamois hunter'.[12]

The Grand Pic of the Meije was Coolidge's last big climb. He did not
renounce the Alps – during his lifetime he made more than 1,200
ascents, adding a silver medallion to Tschingel's collar for every first –
but he treated them thereafter as specimens, objects to be categorised
and slotted into order. Having helped bring the age of Alpine exploration to a close he set himself up as its chronicler, creating an oeuvre
of historical studies that was as painstakingly accurate as it was massive and dull. Over the years he contributed more than 230 pieces to
the *Alpine Journal* and wrote for some thirty other Alpine periodicals.
He was the author, co-author or consultant of sixty-one separate titles.
His encyclopedia articles were as flies in a stable. After several
decades his outpourings became so voluminous that he made them a
subject of a book itself. *A List of Writings (not being Reviews of Books)
dating from 1868 to 1912 and Relating to the Alps or Switzerland of
W. A. B. Coolidge* was published in 1913. Such a list may have been
needed but its public appeal was limited. For apart from one or two
major works Coolidge's writing comprised a maze of footnotes, references and pettifogging detail impenetrable to most. He was no
Whymper; he was not even a Tyndall, Wills or Forbes. Pedantry took
precedence over passion, prose and linear progression. 'I personally
cannot forgive him,' wrote a later President of the Alpine Club, 'for
the fact that he never tried seriously to communicate to the world the
knowledge which he possessed, but was content to fling it out in a
disorderly mess.'[13]

Coolidge was stunted by his aunt's death. From 1876 he wanted nothing more than to recreate his early life. He professed pleasure in mountains but he never went to the English hills of Cumbria, nor did he climb Wales's Mount Snowdon; he never crossed the border to Scotland, whose Highlands were as magical and whose rock-climbing as taxing as anything to be found in Europe. He did not go to the Pyrenees, nor to the Andes or the Rockies or the Himalayas. He just went to the Alps, again and again, employing no guide other than Almer. Whenever possible he took Tschingel on his trips, but Tschingel was growing old. She gradually turned white – not just the muzzle but the whole coat – her teeth dropped out, she went blind and on 16 June 1879, the day before she was due to be put down, she died in front of the kitchen fire. 'I am at present in great affliction at the death of my dear old dog,'[14] Coolidge wrote a few days later. Yet another link to the past had been lost. In 1880 he investigated the possibility of Holy Orders and two years later he was ordained; this, combined with archaic regulations stipulating that Oxford dons be bachelors, created a monastic cocoon in which he wrapped himself ever closer as the years passed, emerging only to investigate the finer points of Alpine history.

From 1880 to 1889 Coolidge was editor of the *Alpine Journal*, a post which gave him ample opportunity to indulge his mania. He plagued himself – and others – with picayune queries regarding precedence and accuracy. Seasoned climbers, who had gone to the Alps just for the fun of it, received bewildering enquiries on details they had forgotten years ago. 'Such questions seemed to him of the highest importance,' recalled an acquaintance, 'and he insisted on his own view as though it was a matter of principle. In the upshot he maintained with vigour, and, I believe, with real enjoyment, a number of quarrels which lasted for years. When his opponent became tired, and ready to let the question drop, he was fresh as paint, and as eager to reply and counter-reply.'[15] Nothing was too unimportant for Coolidge: he could turn a misplaced comma into a lifelong feud.

Frequently his quibbles concerned mistaken reports of his own ascents. Having conquered in 1878 the double-peaked Aiguille de

Péclet, for example, he was concerned when a French journal suggested seven years later that its lower peak – which had first been
climbed in 1877 by two Frenchmen – might be the higher of the two.
Coolidge protested vehemently, and when the allegation was
repeated in 1905 he threatened to resign from the French Alpine
Club (of which he was an Honorary Member). An amendment was
duly published. But Coolidge did not forget the incident. Nor did the
French, apparently, for thirteen years later Coolidge was able to write:
'One of my English friends, Colonel Strutt, climbed the Péclet and
assures me that the *Southern* summit (mine) is a metre higher than the
north summit, but that the latter is now crowned by a huge cairn so
that it is, in fact, the higher.'[16]

His conservatism was reflected in his mountaineering. He was willing to make new ascents for historical purposes – always led by
Almer – but when offered an Alp he generally insisted on going up
well-known routes so that he could trace the steps of those who had
preceded him. One companion, who wanted to go up an old hill a new
way, was slightly infuriated when Coolidge insisted they pass such-
and-such a rock by the right rather than the left, merely to satisfy
himself that the man who had first described the ascent had done so
correctly. On one occasion, when climbing with a friend and fellow
Alpine Club member, Frederick Gardiner, he refused to continue
unless Gardiner placed his hands and feet in exactly the same spots as
did Almer. The same lack of adventure typified his university career.
He was 'one of a block . . . of stubborn dons who resisted every
reform', wrote a colleague, 'and could always be relied upon to turn up
when it came to voting. They systematically non-placetted every
reform.'[17] When beards were becoming unfashionable Coolidge wore
one all the same, posing for photographic portraits as if he were a scientist of old – or as if he were a guide. Coolidge's biographer called
him 'The Magdalen Hedgehog'. It was a perfect description. He was
spiky, defensive and unapproachable. He made few friends, preferring to curl up in the dry leaves of correspondence with which he
documented a dying age.

CHAPTER TWENTY-FIVE

The geographical conquest of the Alps ended effectively with the Meije. There were other places yet to be discovered, but though they were beautiful and interesting they were straws at which the Alpine Club grasped with increasing desperation. By 1885 the Alps were deemed to have been done. The last dragons had been slain and there was little more to be found. What else was there to do? as more than one President asked his members in the dog years of the nineteenth century.

There was quite a lot more to do. The Alpine Club encouraged members to climb mountains in different, more difficult ways. A. F. Mummery exemplified the new approach. Outwardly the feeblest of specimens, he was so stringy that his feet touched the ground when he rode on a donkey; when found in anything but an erect posture he looked like a pile of sticks on which a passer-by had thrown some old tweed. Yet he was possessed of enormous power and his spidery limbs allowed him to crawl up sheer faces, his whole body expanding and contracting like a hand measuring the length of a table. He wedged himself into tiny fissures, he hung from crags and he eased himself round perilous boulders. His published journals contained photograph after photograph of unthinkably nasty pinnacles and of precipices that had once been thought unclimbable. His writing, couched in the jocular 'oh-it-was-nothing' tone that had become fashionable, described scenes of casual terror – as, for example, when contemplating his next move, he looked to one side and found that the ice outcrop to which he clung was so thin that he could see every feature of the valley below. For a long time he was blackballed by the Alpine Club – he was a tanner, which upset some of the stuffier members – but when finally he was admitted he instigated a new trend in mountaineering.

Another new trend came with the advent of women climbers. Women were perfectly capable of climbing mountains, as Marie Paradis and Henriette D'Angeville had shown in the first half of the century; in the 1860s and 1870s other women had come forward, such as Lucy Walker, Meta Brevoort and the redoubtable Katherine Richardson who became the first woman to climb the Meije. Until the 1880s, however, women featured mostly as observers, whose honeymoons were spent waiting for their husbands to return from the hill, and whose subsequent summers were passed in similar fashion. Women were not allowed to join the Alpine Club – although it was agreed they had the necessary qualifications – and if they submitted an article to the *Alpine Journal* they had to persuade a man to put his name to it. Continental clubs were less exclusive – France prided itself on including women from the start – but it was still unusual for females to stray from the lower slopes. They were treated with dangerous condescension. In 1870, a Mrs Marke had sought assistance from her guide while crossing a glacier at Chamonix. The guide, quite understanding her fears, had taken her by the elbow and offered to lead her home. Unroped, they both fell into a crevasse and died.

Mrs Mummery was one of the first to scoff at the Alpine Club's exclusivity. 'The masculine mind is, with rare exceptions, imbued with the idea that a woman is not a fit comrade for steep ice or precipitous rock, and, in consequence,' she wrote, 'should be satisfied with watching through a telescope some weedy and invertebrate masher being hauled up a steep peak by a couple of burly guides, or by listening to this same masher when, on his return, he lisps out with a sickening drawl the many perils he has encountered.'[1] She forced her husband to take her up mountains with him. Her example was followed by scores of others, notably Miss Elizabeth Hawkins-Whitshed from Killancrick, a feisty person who became first Mrs Burnaby, then Mrs Main and then Mrs Aubrey Le Blond. She was so energetic that her mother received the following telegram: 'Stop her climbing mountains! She is scandalising all London and looks like a Red Indian.'[2] Miss Elizabeth took no notice. Her only concession to femininity was to cover her climbing trousers with a skirt that she removed once out of sight of civilisation, and to have her maid accompany as high as possible to help her with her boots. Her example was followed by others. One woman climber became so enamoured of the Alps that she married her guide, a move that took everyone by surprise.

Explorers who could not find satisfaction in the Alps went elsewhere. They went to the Caucasus, they went to Greenland, Spitsbergen and the Himalayas, taking their expertise and their guides with them. Sometimes they did not return: Mummery vanished in 1895 on the face of Nanga Parbat. But sometimes they did: Sir Martin Conway climbed the Alps from west to east in a three-month, 1,000-mile hike accompanied by two Ghurkas whom he wanted to train as instructors for Indian mountain regiments. When he went back to the Himalayas the Alps followed him. On one mountain he wrote:

I was sitting alone in the tent door, with a marvellous view stretching before me from the great featureless snow-field down the long valley – fifty or sixty miles long – up which we had come. All was perfectly still about me and there was not a soul in sight. I was awaiting the arrival of the rest of the men, and my mind was a blank. It surprised me then to see a queer white thing like some sort of animal dancing toward me over the snow-field as intermittent puffs of wind carried it. It danced a few yards and stopped; then it danced again, and so on. I could not make out what it was till at last, with a final jump, it landed in my lap. It was a torn fragment of newspaper.[3]

It had been part of his expedition's packaging and had inexplicably been blown miles over the Himalayas in his wake. When he read it, he found it contained a lecture given by a member of the Alpine Club.

Conway was an art critic and mystic who managed to rescue the Alps from the spiritual battering they had received at the hands of Whymper and other peak-bagging toughs. He was like Ruskin in many respects, proselytising for both the beauty of the mountains and the benefits that beauty could confer on mankind. Unlike Ruskin, however, he did not stand back waving his hands in horror, but marched forward to find what beauty meant at close quarters. Every inch the late Victorian explorer, from his turban and moustache to his tweeds and sturdy boots, he asked people not to understand the mountains but to understand themselves by means of the mountains. He saw his transalpine tramp as a process of spiritual initiation, an engagement of mind, body and nature that led to a higher state of being. As he wrote, 'It is not Nature that illuminates the mind, but the mind that glorifies Nature. The beauty that we behold must first arise in ourselves. It is born for the most part in suffering.'[4] Others felt the same way, and by the beginning of the twentieth century Alpine exploration had taken a new twist. One could climb any cliff, forge any glacier, stand on any peak and no matter how well-trodden they were, one could claim a discovery not of topography but of self. Similar sentiments had been expressed before; but now, with everything having been 'done', they became more pertinent. Poetical climbers like Geoffrey Winthrop Young revelled in the Alps for no reason other than personal inspiration; so did George Mallory who started climbing in the 1900s and when asked why he went to the mountains replied 'because they are there' – to which was added the unspoken words 'and so am I'.

Conway and his followers succeeded in recapturing the spiritual impetus of the early days. Science, however, which had been such a distinguishing feature of early Alpine exploration, became increasingly irrelevant. Scientists who now trod the hills did so in a state of resignation. Typical of the period was a French astronomer, Dr Janssen, who erected a wooden observatory with great difficulty on the top of Mont Blanc where, according to Whymper, there was a complete absence of building materials – 'nothing even as big as the stone of a prune'.[5] The cold froze the instruments; lightning struck the shed, killing one observer; then it sank into the ice, hastened in 1907 by an earthquake. The instruments were dug out and the remaining planks were used as fuel. Janssen, old and crippled, visited his creation only three times, on each occasion being hauled up on a sledge. Nothing illustrated the gap between science and mountaineering better than the behaviour of Janssen and Whymper, who once found themselves marooned in a hotel by bad weather. For three whole days they scowled across the fire without speaking, each considering it the other's duty to pay the first respects. When the weather cleared they went their separate ways, not having exchanged a word.

Not everybody shared Conway's vision of the mountains. In 1894 the English writer Samuel Butler went up the Rigi accompanied by Alfred, his manservant. Surrounded by stupendous scenery, Alfred had only this to say: 'now if you please Sir, I should like to lie down on the grass here and have a read of *Tit-Bits*'.[6] On a deeper and more disturbing level was the reaction of the guide Melchior Anderegg whom Leslie Stephen invited to London one year to see the industrial horrors that drove himself and fellow Britons to the Alps every summer. Stephen took him to a point where they could see 'the dreary expanse of chimney-pots through which the South-Western railway escapes from this dingy metropolis'.[7] 'That is not so fine a view as we have seen together from the top of Mont Blanc,' he said in comradely fashion. 'Ah, Sir!' replied Anderegg. 'It is far finer!'[8] Anderegg's statement pained Stephen. He later redeemed himself by preferring Madame Tussaud's waxworks to the splendours of Westminster Abbey, but his words hung in Stephen's memory as the point at which Romanticism finally broke. Whether it be a manservant hankering after home comforts, or a guide yearning for material progress, opinion now favoured the speediest possible access of modernity to the Alps.

Many of the old Alpine stalwarts built themselves houses near their favourite peaks. Wills, for example, presided over The Eagle's Nest at Sixt; Tyndall could be found every summer in a hideous structure at Bel Alp; Coolidge would eventually retire to a chalet in Grindelwald; even Ruskin tried to purchase a plot but was thwarted by local regulations. As these semi-retired explorers gazed over the Alps they must have been conscious of the extent to which the mountains had changed since they first visited them. Witches, goblins and dragons had vanished, along with a whole world. The last lammergeier was shot in the 1860s. The Bouquetin ibex, plentiful at the start of the century, was by the 1870s reduced to a rump of some 400. The chamois, which once could be encountered on the Mer de Glace, now hid nervously on the peaks. Even the cretins and goitre sufferers were disappearing, with the discovery that iodine could alleviate their conditions.* Just as Ruskin had feared, industry was on the up and nature on the down. In 1860, the burghers of Grindelwald had begun to hack away at their glaciers. In 1866, 100,000 francs' worth of ice were packed in straw and sent, dripping, to restaurants in Paris and beyond. By the turn of the century a stone chute, several hundred yards long, had been constructed to facilitate the flow – workers were warned on pain of dismissal not to hitch a ride down it – and ice had become a major export. Similarly, in the 1890s, work started on a funicular railway that wound its way from Grindelwald to the Jungfraujoch, burrowing en route through the Eiger. The line,

---

*Goitre still secured exemption from military service and many people refused the iodine lozenges dispensed by hopeful medical officers. Whymper thought they should be drafted immediately: 'Let them be formed into regiments by themselves, brigaded together, and commanded by cretins. Think what *esprit de corps* they would have! Who could stand against them? Who would understand their tactics?'[9] In 1870 the canton of Valais contained one cretin for every twenty-five healthy people.

completed in the early 1900s, ended at the highest station in Europe and was linked to Switzerland's main railway system so that, if anyone was so inclined, they could catch a train from Geneva and in a matter of hours be almost within touching distance of a cumulus cloud drifting past the Mönch. Similar projects were planned for the Matterhorn and other mountains but they were halted by over-whelming protest. When the British Minister to Switzerland made a speech at the opening of the Jungfraujoch railway, he did so in diplo-matic terms, but his real feelings on mountain-top railways were this: 'I sincerely hope that this insensate scheme has since been aban-doned, and the process of vulgarising the "playground of Europe" has been abandoned.'[10]

Railways were the emissaries of industry. They were also conduits for a new breed of tourist: the living dead. For decades tuberculosis had been the scourge of industrial societies. It was a hideous disease, which involved the steady and irreversible collapse by haemorrhage and ulceration of whatever part of the body it affected. It could strike anywhere – tuberculosis of the leg, arm and neck were common – but most dramatically it hit the lungs, creating little pockets of infection that incubated without symptom until they burst, releasing a flood of tubercules. The first sign would be a cough, which produced pus. Later, as the tubercules spread and began to eat away at neighbouring sections of lung, the cough worsened. Blood appeared in the pus and the patient became anaemic, displaying characteristic pink cheeks on a pale face. The course of the disease was uncertain, unpredictable and unstoppable. For most, the end came without warning in a sudden, drowning haemorrhage. Tuberculosis was not the major killer in nineteenth-century Europe – it was outstripped by diphtheria, cholera, smallpox and typhoid – but it possessed a horrid fascination. It lingered like no other ailment. Once it took hold there was no telling when it might end – tomorrow, in a month's time or ten years' hence. Sufferers were recognisable physically and mentally: they were certain they would get better; they had a clearer insight into the world's workings; and their imaginations became as flushed as their cheeks. It was an industrial disease that spread in the cities and especially – but not exclusively – in the poorer quarters inhabited by artists and writers. Keats died of tuberculosis, so did Robert Louis Stevenson, Katherine Mansfield, Aubrey Beardsley, two of the Brontë sisters and many others. If any disease could be described as à la mode, tuberculosis was it. In the 1860s, however, a refugee German doctor living in Davos, a high-altitude Swiss village, announced that he had found a cure.

Dr Spengler discovered his cure by political chance. Outlawed from Germany following the 1848 revolutions, he had settled in Davos. During his stay he had noticed that tuberculosis was rare in Swiss villages and that those who contracted it when they left were soon cured on their return. He put it down to low atmospheric pressure. The prevailing wisdom was that tuberculosis of the lung could be alleviated only by dry air and rest. Most tubercular patients therefore went to Egypt, if they could afford it, and lounged alongside the Nile. The Alps, however, also had dry air and their rarefied atmosphere offered weary lungs more chance of rest and recovery. It was cheaper for Europeans to go to the Alps than to Egypt and altitude did seem to have amazing results. Several famous people, including doctors, were supposedly cured by a summer in Davos. Davos sprouted hotels and so too did other villages. Soon the Alps were dotted with sanatoriums, large wedding-cake structures that differed from other hotels only in their medical facilities. They offered fine cuisine, concerts, parties, amateur theatricals, outdoor entertainments and expensive shopping. By the turn of the century they also offered a range of surgical delights: very popular was artificial pneumothorax, a procedure in which the lung was collapsed, and therefore rested, by injecting gas, wax or oil into the pleural sac; an uncomfortable variant, pneumoperitoneum, achieved the same result by pumping air into the abdomen; then there was so-called phrenic crush, in which the diaphragm was paralysed by smashing certain nerves in the neck; and finally, thoracoplasty, which collapsed the lung by removing the entire chest wall, ribs, muscles and all. None of these treatments was particularly successful and more people died from the shock of thoracoplasty than benefited from it.

The surgeons who performed these monstrosities were themselves often tubercular.*

To begin with, Davos and its successors had a positive attitude. 'Davos demands qualities the very opposite of resigned sentimentalism,' ran an 1880 guidebook. 'Here is no place for weak and despairing resignation . . . here you are not pusillanimously helped to die.'[11] Inevitably, though, many guests did die. Altitude was not the great cure-all that Spengler had envisaged. It was most effective when the disease was in its early stages (doctors, mindful of their reputations, were initially reluctant to admit any other case) and did little but retard the deterioration of those who rushed to the Alps in a last-minute grasp at life. Isolated amid the snows for much of the year, the resorts developed a death-fuelled licentiousness. 'Some patients, especially hopeless cases, were tempted to plunge into a round of parties, drinking, gambling and worse,' wrote a British doctor in 1888. 'I had witnessed some terrible scenes in the winter.'[12] The atmosphere was like that which prevailed at the fashionable Swiss spas in Saussure's time but with an added frenzy. There was something typically fin-de-siècle in the knowledge that while the music played, the snow fell and the chocolates were passed only a few discreetly placed doors separated them from the crawling rubber hoses of pneumothorax, the mallets of phrenic crush, and the saws and scalpels of thoracoplasty. Being in a Swiss resort was akin to spending a luxurious stretch on death row.

Guests were able to leave any time they wished, but they did so at their own peril. Their consultants, who usually owned the sanatorium and profited from all those expensive meals – with tuberculosis it was necessary to build oneself up – were reluctant to discharge fee-payers. Additionally, many people became acclimatised to life at high

---

*The idea that ailments could be cured at high altitude was not new. In the 1840s a Dr Guggenbuhl had created a mountain sanatorium for cretins. He hoped that his patients would be transformed by fresh air, exercise and equal opportunity. When his experiment fizzled out the sad community dispersed to the valleys having learned how to fetch water from a well, get married, go for a walk and little else.

altitude and dared not descend to the plains where remission might revert to a familiar cough. When their condition stabilised and their money began to run out, they moved to cheaper accommodation nearby. Soon, the hotels were surrounded by a melancholy *banlieue* of boarding houses.

During the long Alpine winter it was important for sanatoriums to keep their inmates occupied. The answer was winter sports. The origin of winter sports has been argued over endlessly. Persistently it has been ascribed to one Johannes Badrutt, a hotelier in St Moritz, a rival resort to Davos. In 1864 Badrutt told his summer guests that if they came back in winter and didn't like it they could stay for free. The sun shone, he said, and they would be able to walk about in their shirtsleeves. Four people were reckless enough to accept his invitation. To their amazement everything Badrutt said was true. The sun did shine, they could walk around in their shirtsleeves. (Badrutt greeted them in summer clothes, despite grumblings from neighbours who said he would have worn summer clothes had the temperature been sub-zero, which it often was.) The four were deeply impressed. 'On an average we were out 4 hours daily, walking, skating on the lakes, sleighing or sitting on the terrace reading,' ran one entry in Badrutt's guest book. 'Twice in January we dined on the terrace, and on other days had picnics in our sledges. Whilst at St Moritz I was far stronger at the end of winter than at its commencement.'[13] Badrutt quickly started buying land. Ten years later, St Moritz had more than three hundred winter visitors and he was a very wealthy man.

Badrutt's may have been the first mention of winter sports in a touristic context but undoubtedly they already existed as a pastime for locals. In the winter of 1866, Alpine Club member A. W. Moore described the thrill of sledging down an icy road in Grindelwald in a twelve-man bobsleigh that travelled – as he calculated – at the terrifying speed of 20 m.p.h. 'I believe that the Alps in winter offer as great attractions to the dilettante tourist who, in all sincerity, considers that going to the top of a mountain is a mistake, as to the enthusiast who cares more for the climbing, pure and simple, than for the picturesque,' he wrote. 'Given fine weather, I am satisfied that anyone who may try the experiment will return, as I did, anxious to repeat it at the earliest opportunity.'[14]

Bobsleighs were considered too hectic for invalids and for most tourists, for whom winter sports consisted initially of skating and sledging, the latter comprising a sedate, upright trundle down a gentle slope with much falling off. Not until 1884 did matters change when St Moritz unveiled the Cresta Run, with its head-first racing toboggans. Skiing was introduced from Norway in 1892 by the British travel agent Henry Lunn and rapidly gathered its own group of enthusiasts. Lunn was a major promoter of Alpine tourism – a cold weather Cook – and soon he was bringing 5,000 clients to the Alps every winter. Few of his people went skiing, however. In England it was a minority sport reserved for the elite – some clubs refused members who had not attended public school or been to university. Matters were little different on the continent: in 1904 Switzerland's sixteen ski clubs mustered just 731 members between them. For a long while, up to the 1920s at least, winter sports retained the passivity of their tubercular origins. Skiing lagged in popularity behind sledging and above all ice sports, which by then included not only figure skating but curling (introduced by Scottish visitors who brought their own stones with them), ice hockey and the novel recreation of ice tennis.

Whether prompted by illness or health, tourism became a major part of the Alpine economy. A 1912 survey revealed that Switzerland contained 12,640 hotels, pensions and inns with a total of 384,744 beds – a 25 per cent increase over the previous seven years. Hotels were at saturation point all year round and earned 61.7 million francs net per annum as opposed to 16 million in 1880. They employed 43,136 staff, which made them Switzerland's most labour-intensive business other than manufacturing. Capital invested since 1894 had risen by 119 per cent. The year 1912 was so busy that its intake of guests would not be equalled until the mid-1960s.

There were many who saw tourism as a damaging influence. Britons bemoaned the despoliation of their handy wilderness. The Swiss, meanwhile, feared the destruction of traditional values.

Cautionary novels warned in French and German of the dangers presented by tourism. Foreigners who wished to purchase land were depicted as thieves – Jewish thieves at that. Easy money was frowned upon and villagers were advised not to sell their souls for lucre. Love was also condemned: several books expanded on the dangers presented to young men by glamorous foreign females. Skiing was considered exceptionally hazardous in this respect: instructors were advised to remain vigilant at all times. Unfortunately, the peasants at whom these books were aimed were mostly illiterate; and even if they weren't they had an uncanny knack of being able to distinguish between a moralising tract and a pocketful of francs. The moralisers continued to preach, the villagers continued to ignore them and the tourists continued to come. The Alps were at last making money – Ruskin would have been pleased – and they were making it at a tremendous rate.

CHAPTER TWENTY-SIX

By the turn of the century, memories of the old Alps were disappearing fast. Forbes had died in 1868 and his adversary Agassiz in 1873.* Tyndall died on 4 December 1893, his wife having accidentally given him an overdose of chloroform. Ruskin went in 1900 and Stephen four years later. The new generation who came in their place were of a different breed. Following Mummery's example they plastered themselves to seamless faces, often taking no guides but relying on their own efforts to see them to the top. The decade from 1900 was a Silver Age of mountaineering that saw the conquest of areas beyond the reach of the Golden. For the old-timers it was a regrettable turn, involving too hectic an approach and too little appreciation. Conway, for example, quit his climbing career at the early age of 47, explaining that 'For all of us there are many kinds of joy as yet unexperienced, many activities untried, many fields of knowledge unexplored. We must not spend too large a fraction of life over one or the next will escape us. It is life, after all, that is the greatest field of exploration.'[1]

---

*A block of granite from the Unteraar glacier was placed on his grave. In 1923, the remains of his Hôtel spilled from the glacier's snout. Two chunks of stone, on which were engraved the signatures of Agassiz and Vogt, were sent to Bern's Alpine Museum.

But there were some who preserved the flame. Whymper was one of them. Although he had effectively cut himself off from the high peaks, he visited the Alps every summer to revise his guidebooks, collect royalties from recalcitrant bookstores, put up advertising placards, take photographs and, now and then, walk across the odd pass. At home and in America he was renowned for his lectures, Winston Churchill being one of the many people who listened to, and was influenced by, his tale of the Matterhorn disaster. Like Sir John Franklin, whose death in the Arctic had won the admiration of thousands – among them Whymper himself – he had become one of the century's icons. When the name Whymper appeared on a lecture bill, organisers could expect a full house. In 1894 he gave the same talk forty-eight times, addressing 50,000 people in England alone.

Grim and sonorous, Whymper cut an impressive figure at the podium, even when he dropped his aitches – something that worried him; he hired his nephew to snap his fingers every time it happened. Privately, he remained the same, tight-lipped person as always. His face now wore a permanent scowl, he smoked ceaselessly, grinding his pipe tobacco into a powder that left pinhole burns on his chairs, sofas, carpets and tablecloths. He smoked in bed, and his chest was covered in scars as a result. He feared fatness and became faddish about his food, sifting sugar so that only the finest grains found their way into his system. One relation was astounded by his way with meat pies; he would lift the pastry lid, spoon out the meat, replace the lid and move onto the next. He eschewed convention, appearing in the grandest restaurants without a tie or cravat, or even a shirt, only a singed sweater. He worried about his finances, technology having made the wood-engraving business moribund – 'There is practically no engraving being done here,' he told his father in March 1894. 'The amount which has been done so far this year, and the little which is in hand, will not pay for coal and gas.'[2] He also worried about Coolidge, whose chippy, ivory-tower intellect had fastened on the bible of Alpinism, Whymper's *Scrambles*.

Conway wrote of Coolidge: 'Some people called him cantankerous . . .'[3] This did not even touch the surface. Rude, pedantic and touchy, Coolidge made enemies as simply and as naturally as he tied his shoelaces. Far from trying to reconcile differences he nourished them, 'putting them down as other men put down bottles of wine, with the prospect that they would mature for use at some future date'.[4] One of his longest-standing enmities was with Sir Edward Davidson, who became Secretary of the Alpine Club the year after Coolidge became editor of its *Journal*. There was something about Davidson that Coolidge could not stomach – probably his lofty, aristocratic manner, his climbing success and his disdain for words as opposed to action. When Mummery was blackballed from the Alpine Club, Coolidge suspected without a shred of proof that Davidson had been responsible. When Mummery informed him that 'a well-known member of your club'[5] had tried to bribe his guide to make his latest expedition a failure, Coolidge suspected, again without any proof, that it had been Davidson. In return he altered the minutes of the *Alpine Journal* and at the next election shifted the balls in the ballot box so that Mummery gained his membership. 'Yes, I *cheated* Mummery into the Club,'[6] he gloated. Davidson replied by drawing an illustration for a book on mountaineering, in which several porters were shown hauling luggage onto a lake steamer. Every trunk had the initials of a famous climber, and bringing up the rear was a parrot in a cage with the label W.A.B.C. On publication the W. was removed for fear of a lawsuit, but Coolidge noticed it all the same. In 1896, Davidson struck again. That year, two Alpine Club members published Christian Almer's führerbuch, or service record, and in it was a photograph of a page in which Coolidge had spelt Schreckhorn without its first 'c'. To make the insult worse, an anonymous climber had pointed out the error, writing underneath that 'The usual spelling among Germans is S*c*hreckhorn.'[7] The anonymous climber was none other than Davidson, to whom the book had also been dedicated. It was a typical establishment put-down and Coolidge recognised it as such. Unfortunately, Coolidge did not realise that the point of the insult lay in the predictability of his response. 'I hunted and hunted,' he wrote. 'At last I found that Davidson had put his name to Jungfrau without a *g*.'[8] He revealed this abominable error in the *Alpine Journal* and Davidson was duly censured amidst peals of muffled laughter. That year Coolidge left Britain and went to live in Grindelwald.

Coolidge took with him an Alpine library that numbered 15,000 volumes plus several crates of correspondence from which he picked as his irritability took him. Almost immediately, he struck up an argument with Whymper. In 1899 he was asked by the Swiss Alpine Club to write an obituary of Christian Almer who had died the previous year. In doing so, he stated that Almer's famous leap on the Écrins was pure fiction. The gap did not exist, he said, and when in 1871 he had shown Almer the picture Whymper had drawn of it, Almer had disavowed it: '[he] assured me, in all earnest, that he had never done such a thing and could never be able to do it'.[9] Coolidge had climbed the Écrins in 1870 – of which he was very proud – and had seen no sign of the gap; nor had any other climber since. This did not mean that Whymper was wrong: the Alps eroded so rapidly that nobody could be sure that the obstacles they had encountered one year would be there five years hence. All the same, Coolidge was calling Whymper a liar.

The two bachelors had already exchanged words in the 1880s. The exact cause of their dispute is unknown. Possibly it was an unintentional slip on Whymper's behalf, when he stated in *Scrambles* that Coolidge had climbed one of the highest peaks of the Ailéfroide instead of *the* highest peak. This was just the kind of petty error around which Coolidge's life revolved and it upset him. At any rate, he seems to have complained about something, and Whymper had replied with an uncharacteristic apology. 'My dear Coolidge,' he wrote on 22 December 1883:

> Many thanks for your frank and manly letter. It has grieved me
> much to think how greatly I must have been misunderstood by
> you whom I have always respected, and have since grown to
> look upon with a warm feeling of regard . . . I heartily rejoice
> that this mistake has been rectified and earnestly hope that
> ours may be a life of friendship. Now, my dear Coolidge, grant
> me two favours. 1) Will you tell those of your friends in

College . . . that you think better of me than you did.
2) Sometime when we are alone tell me how I contrived to
give you an impression of myself which we know was
incorrect. I fear there must be something queer about me or
some fault which sorely needs correction and which I will
correct if you as a true and kind friend will point it out. I thank
God that you were not the innocent means of depriving me of
what has been the joy of my life . . . Excuse faults of style in
this letter, not an easy one to write. When I give my hand I
give my heart.[10]

This frank – and almost frantic – attempt at conciliation is mystifying.
If it really did concern the perceived slight regarding the Ailéfroide, it
would suggest that Whymper was trying to save a friendship of long
standing. But although they had corresponded on occasions, Coolidge
maintained they had only met once before this date. A more sinister
interpretation is that Coolidge's files contained information damaging
to Whymper's reputation and that Whymper was desperate for it not
to come out. Coolidge did have something on Whymper and in later
years he would release it. In 1883, however, he was sufficiently mol-
lified to bide his time. As his biographer stated, the only certain
implication to be drawn from Whymper's letter was that 'the men
were on far more self-revelatory terms than either was willing publicly
to admit'.[11]

Regardless of what lay in Coolidge's files, Whymper could not
ignore the charge of lying. He gathered affidavits from all those
involved in Almer's leap and presented them to the Alpine Club, at
the same time threatening legal action. The veteran climber Horace
Walker took Whymper's side and wrote to Coolidge in an attempt to
defuse the situation. Coolidge replied angrily, fuelling his arguments
with the tedious subject of the Ailéfroide. 'You mention Whymper's
"veracity." May I therefore direct your attention to a falsehood relating to myself told by Mr. W. in the first edition of his book (1871) and
repeated in the fourth edition, note on page 192? . . . Despite this mis-
statement of nearly 30 years standing I have never yet taken the

trouble to notice it publicly. There are a great many other mis-statements in his book and Mr. W. would do better to raise no public discussion as to his "veracity" or he will meet with some unpleasant surprises. His list of ascents of the Matterhorn is laughably wrong.'[12] Coolidge then proceeded to accuse Whymper of having plagiarised, in one of his guidebooks to Zermatt, a similar book written several years earlier by himself and Conway. 'I could write much more,' he concluded, 'but what I have said may show you that Mr. W. had better not try to raise any public controversy with me.'[13]

Tuckett, who was next to intervene, received a similar response. 'I decline in the most absolute manner to "rectify" a statement made to me *repeatedly* by old Almer,'[14] Coolidge told him. Tuckett tried hard to put the affair in perspective. 'Do leave historial accuracy to take care of itself for a bit,' he advised, 'and remember that none of us are such encyclopedias of Alpine knowledge as yourself, rarely have as complete a knowledge of what others have written or perhaps, may I venture to say, even care to know?'[15] Coolidge had no intention of letting matters be. The very suggestion that accuracy was unimportant and that some people might not care about it made him more determined than ever to hold out. In this he was supported by Douglas Freshfield, another Alpine Club member, who met Whymper and, as reported by Coolidge, told him 'to his face that he was an ass to take serious offence, and that Wh. submitted quite meekly to being told that every one knows that his illustrations are "subjective."'[16] Reviewing his files, Coolidge told a colleague at Magdalen College: 'I am "unmuzzled" and if necessary shall speak out very plainly.'[17]

Coolidge was, however, very worried about the prospect of a libel case. 'He hasn't any money (wood engraving being dead) save from his books,'[18] he encouraged himself. 'It is very unlikely too that he can touch me in England for I am legally an American citizen and the thing appeared in Switzerland.'[19] But he himself was afflicted by a poor income. 'If he were to do as he says I have no money for defence and must be "sold up", books and all,' he admitted to Tuckett. 'Don't tell Whymper all this, of course.'[20] Neither of them could afford a law suit and in the end they settled it as inexpensively as honour allowed.

Whymper issued a sixteen-page pamphlet – 'the Anti-Coolidge Manifesto',[21] Davidson called it – containing a copy of the illustration, plus letters of support, to every member of the Alpine Club. He demanded an immediate sitting of the Alpine Club committee, pledging at the same time to have Coolidge drummed out of the club. Coolidge resigned before his hearing came up and the ridiculous controversy came to an end. Both parties later recanted. In 1900 Coolidge wrote to Freshfield that 'perhaps it was not judicious to print the note'.[22] And in 1907 Whymper recalled as many copies of his pamphlet as he could find and burned them, stating that he had taken things far too seriously. 'I have no doubt,' he wrote to the American alpinist H. F. Montagnier, 'that it would have been better to have allowed the matter to pass unnoticed, or to have arranged it otherwise.'[23]

Coolidge was the eventual winner. He had plenty of anti-Whymper material in his files. 'Of course, I know far more about Moore's views than I have yet revealed [Moore having been Whymper's companion during the supposed leap],' he told Freshfield, 'while if I was to repeat Almer's stories of Wh. during that 1864 Dauphiné round, Wh. would become a raving lunatic.'[24] In 1905, when his friend Conway became President of the Alpine Club, Coolidge was re-elected as an Honorary Member. To a friend, he wrote complacently that he had received an 'apology, which grovels, though a little defiantly, too much to prevent me from accepting it'.[25] Davidson was furious: 'the present Committee of the A. C. are such asses,' he complained to Whymper. 'In its present state the Alpine Club is not a creditable body to which to belong.'[26] Surprisingly, Whymper made no objection to Coolidge's reinstatement. Maybe he had a suspicion of what lay in the files. In that year, however, he had more immediate things to worry about.

Whymper's health was deteriorating. Since 1903 he had been prone to unexpected collapses that left him in a state of semi-consciousness; in 1905 a fall on a mountain path damaged several of his ribs; and then he received a severe blow to the head in a railway accident. 'My present condition is deplorable,' he wrote on 29 October 1905. '*My memory has gone*! . . . [I am] a Wreck without Brains.'[27] He tried to make light of it: 'I shall devote what time as remains to me to Love and Luxury and to digging (or supervising the digging) of Potatoes, and to such other pursuits as are suitable to a male animal who is entering his second childhood.'[28] His memory returned but he was obviously concerned about his condition. He was losing the physical fitness on which he had always prided himself and, when he visited Zermatt a few weeks after the crash, it appeared that he was losing his fame as well. It was freezing, nobody was there to greet him, the hotels were full; he drew together two station benches and slept on them under a rug. When he found space in a *pension* the next day his circumstances improved marginally. 'The meat was horrid,' he wrote in his diary. 'I could hardly stomach it, and the place was very cold. Walked from one end of Zermatt to the other and noted a few changes. The place does not increase in beauty, and the street, as usual, was dirty.'[29]

In 1906 Whymper married. His relations with women had not always been successful. In 1899, however, he had fallen in love with Charlotte Hanbury, one of the few women climbers who were active in the Alps. She was ten years his senior and died unexpectedly on 23 October 1900. The news reached him just as he was starting a lecture in America. 'My beloved friend gone!' he wrote to his sister. 'I hardly know how to carry on!'[30] But he did carry on and on 25 April 1906 he married Miss Edith Mary Lewin of Forest Gate, London. She was forty-five years younger than him. His nephew Robert – whom he had previously tried to buy from his parents – was the only member of his family invited to the ceremony. It was a grisly occasion, conducted in great secrecy. At the wedding breakfast it took half an hour's persuasion before Whymper could be dragged out of his bedroom. McCormick, the presiding vicar, gave a leery address about the difference in their ages which went down badly with Whymper's nephew: '[It] rather revolted me. On meeting the Reverend Canon in later years, I found myself still repelled.'[31] When it was over, Whymper told him to search the guests in case they had stolen the silver.

The union did not last. They had a daughter and then divorced in

1910. The separation was bitter and although Whymper wrote at the time that he was 'only too glad to get rid of her',[32] he was feeling the loss only months later: 'I am distracted by the desertion of my wife,' he told Montagnier. 'All day long I am annoyed, bored and made miserable.'[33] Any feelings of remorse were quashed when the alimony demands came in. 'Her sole aim is money,' he wrote to his youngest sister Annette. 'I have already lost £2000 over her, and if I am forced to leave the country to escape her I shall lose as much more . . . It will go very much against the grain to do it, but I am contemplating being forced into it.'[34] In the end he stayed at home, selling his house, his books and even his climbing equipment in order to stay financially afloat. To make life worse, his eyes began to fail – occasioned, he diagnosed, by his railway accident – and he conducted his correspondence with the aid of spectacles and a large magnifiying glass. 'I am now unable to read anything, and can only guess at what I am writing,' he told Montagnier. 'I write seriously in saying that . . . I frequently think of suicide.'[35]

He tried, repeatedly, to heal the breach between himself and Coolidge. In 1908, a year after he had recalled his pamphlets, Coolidge had a heart attack. Whymper 'took the opportunity of his illness to send a few sympathetic words, and they seem to have been appreciated'.[36] With them he enclosed a drawing of a hatchet and a tombstone on which was written 'Buried 1908.' It did no good. Three years later when Coolidge was again seriously ill Whymper tried once more. 'From what the *alphabetical gentleman* says of himself he appears to be in a bad way. I am going out of my usual beat to pay him a visit, to attempt to show that friction is over.'[37] He warned Coolidge of his intentions: 'When I come, I shall come in the old style, shall walk up, not order rooms in advance, and take my chance as to finding a room. If none can be had I shall camp out.'[38]

On 11 August 1911 they spent a whole day closeted in Coolidge's Chalet Montana in Grindelwald and although neither party divulged what passed between them – Whymper did gave a vague hint that he thought Coolidge was mad – the meeting was less stormy than it might have been. That evening Whymper walked over to Zermatt, from where he went to Geneva and then up to Chamonix. It was to be his last Alpine scramble, and perhaps he knew it. At Chamonix he checked into a hotel where the staff were accustomed to his preference for being left alone. He visited a few bookshops, made arrangements to find the corpses from the 1870 Mont Blanc disaster which were expected soon to emerge from the glacier and then, suddenly, went back to his hotel and locked himself in his room. For the next two days, while chambermaids busied themselves in the corridor, Whymper died. On 20 September, two guides went round Chamonix, knocking on every door with the message, 'Edward Whymper will be buried here today, and you are asked to attend his funeral at 2.30 this afternoon.'[39] The whole village turned out to watch him being lowered into the silt.

Whymper's death deprived Coolidge of one of his few remaining links to the Alps of his youth. Old, lonely and sick, he retired into obscurity sustained only by his researches and by what embers of enmity he could blow into a flame – as, for example, when his old foe Davidson was elected President of the Alpine Club. Coolidge immediately resigned his Honorary Membership and, to further express his outrage, demanded that his name never again be mentioned in the *Alpine Journal*. His resignation was accepted but his latter request was declined politely. Meaning well, the assistant editor added a barbed postscript: 'Not 10% of the A.C. Members have realised that you are no longer a member or an Hon. Member of the A.C.'[40]

The 'Nestor of the Alps', as the *Daily Mail* called him, became ever more reclusive. He was rarely seen in the village of Grindelwald and, indeed, only now and then went into his own garden. For company he relied on a male nurse called Albert Hurzeler and a succession of dogs which were chosen deliberately to be as unlike Tschingel as possible. '*Quite incapable* of making climbs,'[41] he wrote of Nero, his black Newfoundland. If questioned about the company he kept he would point, wordlessly, to Tschingel's collar which hung near the front door.

When war broke out in 1914, Coolidge became more isolated. His health deteriorated, his steadily diminishing income could not cope with wartime inflation and he began to dislike 'these rascally Swiss'.[42] He could not have failed to be depressed by the destruction occurring in the eastern Alps as the Italian and Austro-Hungarian armies fought themselves into a Flanders-like stalemate, squabbling with high explosive over each crag and, when their patience ran out, eradicating whole peaks with tons of carefully sapped dynamite. 'I live rather a lonely life nowadays,'[43] he wrote during a low point in 1916. Two years later he was in despair: 'I do wish I had never come out to live. *Very* few compensations . . . *how old* I am getting!'[44] The death in 1919 of Frederick Gardiner, the last of his contemporaries, added to his depression. As Coolidge noted, Gardiner had been only six days older than him. But he received an unexpected fillip when the Alpine Club asked him to write Gardiner's obituary for their journal. 'I am, of course, well qualified to do this,' he told a colleague. 'But as the ruling authorities of the A.C. drove me out of that society in 1910, and have since been attacking me violently and personally in each no. of that periodical, I am steadily resisting.'[45]

Gardiner's obituary was too meagre a controversy to revive Coolidge fully.* What he needed was something big, and in 1921 he delivered it. Writing to a friend, Charles Gos, regarding some minutiae on an eighteenth-century map, he threw in a casual aside: 'Strictly in confidence, I learned yesterday from a very reliable source that the rope on the Matterhorn in 1865 had been effectively cut. But it is better not to insist on this certain fact!!!'[46] The news came from Conway who had it in turn from one Dr G. F. Browne, late Bishop of Bristol, to whom Whymper had reportedly gone for advice after the disaster. Browne told Conway that 'he was the only living man who knew the truth about the accident and that that knowledge would perish with him'.[47] It did perish with him, but maybe he divulged some of it because Conway later suggested that 'two or three strands of the rope might have been severed beforehand without anyone

---

*Unable to resist the temptation he did, eventually, publish a very tedious book detailing Gardiner's climbs.

knowing. The end of the rope would have retained some sign of the cutting. The end engraved in "Scrambles" is not the one where the breakage occurred. It is the right rope but not the broken end.'[48] Was this what Coolidge had been threatening Whymper with as far back as 1883? Had he by that time got a whiff of the scandal that Conway elaborated upon in 1921? No more was said on the subject and the truth – if there was any truth to it – died with both men.

By the 1920s Coolidge was in poor shape. He suffered from palpitations and dropsy, and hated the injections which were necessary to keep him alive. Nero had died and his one comfort was now a terrier named Max. 'I dread to think of losing him!' he wrote. 'How old do such *small* dogs live on average?'[49] Max was then seven and a half. He outlived his master. Coolidge died of a heart attack on Saturday, 8 May 1926 and, as his headstone recorded, 'at his own request he was buried among the mountains he loved so well'. An imp of perversity was loose in Grindelwald that season – either that or the Swiss possessed a keener sense of humour than they were normally credited with – for the great pedant was given an exquisitely apt send-off. The *Echo von Grindelwald* misspelled his name in its official notice, the authorities put the wrong age on his headstone and the carver missed out the 'u' in 'mountains'.

CHAPTER
TWENTY-SEVEN

Coolidge had been the last man who could speak of heroes. While alive he had been regarded as an institution and had become an object of pilgrimage for younger mountaineers willing to brave his irritability. With his death it became suddenly apparent how much the Alps had changed since the Golden Age. Sanatoriums and winter sports were in the ascendant and the old, casual attitude to exploration had been replaced by a more technical approach. New mountaineering techniques had evolved, their adherents claiming Mummery as a spiritual father, and new mechanical aids had been introduced such as the piton and the karabiner clip which allowed climbers to attack previously impossible faces. The British and, to a degree, the French and Swiss, rejected pitons and the like as unsporting. They preferred to don tweeds and hire a guide to take them on a Whymper-style scramble. The British refused even to coin a word for the karabiner, 'because the thing is un-English in name and nature'.[1] The Germans and Italians, however, adopted the new methods eagerly. A young Munich mountaineer named Willy Welzenbach introduced a system of grading the rock climbs that mechanical devices had brought within reach. Ranging from an easy 1 to a 6 that strained 'the limit of human capability',[2] the grades were slapped heroically across the Alpine map.

It was a slightly meaningless exercise: the grades were not always consistent; they did not include ice slopes, thereby excluding some of the most difficult ascents; and they took no account of weather conditions which could turn a Grade 3 into a Grade 6 in a matter of hours – as Leslie Stephen had once said, 'nothing can be less like a mountain at one time than the same mountain at another'.[3] Nevertheless, Welzenbach's grades did provide a framework that satisfied the urgency of the time.

Since the 1880s the Alps had been either a playground or a battlefield. Nobody had thought of them much in terms of exploration for, with the conquest of the Meije and lesser Dauphiné peaks, there were few summits left to explore. What Welzenbach and his ilk recognised, however, was that the new methods opened new avenues of exploration. It was not primary exploration – no dragons, no surprises, here – but on a secondary level it provided the same excitement: once again it was possible to go where none had previously gone; once again it was possible to recapture the thrill of treading untrodden ground; and with the grading system it was possible to measure one's conquests against those of others.

Alpine exploration had always involved a degree of rivalry but now, with Welzenbach's grades, it became a competitive sport. During the 1920s and 1930s Italian, German and Austrian mountaineers vied to conquer the most difficult faces by the most dangerous routes. Typically they were north faces, the nastiest possible; and, by the dogma of the period, they had to be climbed by an ascent *direttissima*, whose purity could be measured by drawing a straight line from top to bottom. This approach resulted in an unusually high death rate. Mountaineers dropped like flies – by the late 1930s the annual toll was pushing 100 – but for every man who died there were plenty to take his place. The patriotic drive which Whymper had faced on the Matterhorn so long ago was now rampant. According to one Italian newspaper: 'A climber has fallen. Let a hundred others arise for the morrow. Let other youths strew edelweiss and alpenrose upon the body of the fallen comrade, and lay it with trembling devotion face upturned under the soft turf. Then up, once more to the assault of the rocks and of the summit, to commemorate the fallen one in the highest and most difficult of victories.'[4]

Britain, which had hitherto considered the Alps its private territory, raised its hands in horror. There was something abhorrent about other nations trespassing so rudely on the hallowed heights. Members of the Alpine Club fumed with a vague and indefinable resentment. One man, R. Irving, tried to rationalise their antipathy:

> A Munich expert estimated that after seven years of very difficult climbing a man was fit for nothing more, if he was still alive. My own experience has been that the thrill of climbing a step near the limit of my powers has settled down into what I can best describe as discomfort. If a man depends on difficulty and the thrill of danger or of high achievements, he must keep pushing his standard of difficulty up till it can go no higher. If he has got so far without falling off himself, then his enthusiasm must begin to fall from him unless he has advanced in appreciation of what I may call more absolute values of mountaineering.[5]

It was not a new argument. The disapproval of professionalism had been voiced intermittently ever since Ruskin's time, rising to a clamour each time someone overstepped the mark. Whymper had caused an outcry; so had his contemporary, A. C. Girdlestone, who had been officially censured for the suggestion that climbers could dispense with guides. Mummery had likewise infuriated people with the notion that it was acceptable to climb for the love of difficulty and danger alone. But, as he replied, in answer to Ruskin's soaped-pole argument, if one liked sliding down soaped poles what was the harm in doing so? In Leslie Stephen's words: 'If I were to say that I liked eating olives, and someone asserted that I really ate them only out of affectation, my reply would be simply to go on eating olives.'[6] The hypocrisy of Britain's attitude was demonstrated by the numbers who went annually to the Himalayas to do exactly what Irving considered bad form: to push themselves to the limit as they struggled up the world's highest and most hazardous mountains. Irving himself was a culprit. What it amounted to was Britain's dislike of other countries doing better than itself.

In 1931 the Schmid brothers climbed the north face of the Matterhorn and Germany exploded with excitement. Newspapers eulogised them in mythological terms and when Franz, the older brother, published his dry, factual account of the climb, they turned it into a tale of fantastical triumph. The press wavered only slightly when Toni Schmid, the younger brother, fell to his death off the Weissbachhorn some years later. The Alps were a propaganda gift to Europe's fascist states. Mussolini struck a *Pro Valore* medal for those who completed a new Grade 6 *direttissima* ascent. Hitler, more reserved, offered a handshake. In the run-up to the 1936 Berlin Olympics it was suggested that mountaineering become an eligible event, a notion that was only dropped when both Switzerland and Britain condemned it as 'something to be deprecated at all costs'.[7]

German newspapers and broadcasters praised the *Bergkameraden*, or 'mountain warriors', who cycled and walked to Switzerland each year to attack a new face. They were portrayed as clean-cut, bronzed Aryans who came to conquer, to do battle with nature at its wildest and most romantic, unafraid of death. These youngsters, who were rarely older than 30 and often still in their teens, made an impressive sight. Camping at the base of a mountain, they bided their time until conditions were right and then made their attack, clanking with pitons and carrying hundreds of feet of rope. For a while Alpine motion pictures became the rage, and audiences across the continent flocked to see re-enactments of dramas such as the conquest of the Matterhorn which were produced by Europe's interwar film industry. Leni Riefenstahl, the famous German film director of the 1930s, began her career as an actress in the snow. More often than not, however, the actors who flickered on the screens were genuine climbers. The mountaineering nationalism that had raised its head in Italy during the 1860s was manifest in the Germany of the 1930s. By 1934 the German and Austrian Alpine Club (now merged) felt able to declare that 'Our mountaineers have in recent times been successful beyond compare . . . their exploits, contrasted with those of other nations, stand without question on an overwhelming pinnacle.'[8]

As with so much Nazi propaganda the glorious image hid a gim-crack reality. The Nordic gods of repute were as snaggle-toothed, narrow-shouldered and unexceptional as anyone else. Close analysis – provided by the Alpine Club – showed that Germany lagged far behind other nations in new ascents. Apart from the north face of the Matterhorn German climbers had achieved very little: the men who climbed the Dolomites, the Grandes Jorasses and other rock faces were almost exclusively French, Swiss, Italian or Austrian. Still, Germany persisted in the fabrication that its climbers were better than any others: 'It is an ancient English custom to climb in the Alps with professional guides,' said the Austro-German *Alpine Journal*. 'The German mountaineer finds as a rule his own way, he cuts his own steps and trudges through deep snow relying on his own steam.' It sneered at Britain's ambitions in the Himalayas. 'Owing to these traditions we are still more prepared than the English for the struggle with the eight-thousanders.'[9] Britain retorted that the self-sufficient Teutons could not move an inch in the Himalayas without local porters and that Germany should remember that those porters were subjects of the British Empire.

Amidst the wrangling, the Alps sat patiently as the *Bergkameraden* addressed what they called 'the problems'. These were rock faces graded 6 or above and there were plenty of them. But no sooner had one problem been solved than another arose, until the climbing fraternity were finally faced with the 'last problem'. The north face of the Matterhorn had been a last problem. When it ceased to be so, the north face of the Eiger took its place – though not for very long: in 1932 it was conquered by a pair of Swiss climbers accompanied by two guides. In the eyes of the *Bergkameraden*, however, there was something unsatisfactory about the Swiss triumph. It had been conducted smoothly, professionally, in traditional style and with the minimum of publicity – admirable qualities no doubt, but failing utterly to conform with German notions of endeavour. What was needed was something with a bit more punch. After some deliberation it was decided that if the last problem had been solved so easily it must not have been the last problem.

The north face of the Eiger could be subdivided into two sections: the 'easy' face which the Swiss had climbed and a far more difficult face to the west known as the Eigerwand, or 'Eiger Wall'. Here, obviously, was the true last problem. The Eigerwand was unclimbable in orthodox terms. It was steep, it was icy, it was rotten; in places the rocks formed an overhang; boulders bounced down it without cease; it had its own microclimate, trapping clouds and cold air in its concave basin so that while the surrounding valley basked in sunshine, the north face was whipped with rain and hail. In short, it was very horrible. But, as one German climber queried, 'was its horror stronger than Man's will-power, than his capacity? Who could answer that question?'[10]

In August 1935 two Bavarians, Max Sedlemayer and Karl Mehringer, became the first to do so. Peering through their field glasses they scanned the Eigerwand for a route to the summit. The first 800 feet seemed easy enough, if steep and prone to avalanches and rockfalls. Above this a large hole had been blasted out of the mountain to create a viewing gallery – officially the Eigerwand Station – for passengers on the Jungfraujoch line. Four hundred yards to the east was another hole, Kilometre 3.8, so called because it marked the point, 3.8 kilometres from the start of the track, where the tunnel engineers had drilled an opening through which they could jettison rubble. From the Eigerwand Station for a distance of perhaps 600 feet rose what appeared to be a vertical stretch of rock, ending in an ice field. A 300-foot rock face separated this ice field from a second one which, in turn, led diagonally to a third. From the third ice field a steep arête climbed up to a blodge of snow and ice whose white runnels spread out like spider's legs – the 'White Spider'. The topmost legs joined with a section of splintered rock; and above the rock was a final ice field that swept steeply to the 13,042-foot summit. It was impossible from a distance to tell what any of these obstacles would be like close to, but they appeared to be the only way up the Eigerwand.

At 2.00 a.m. on Wednesday, 21 August, Sedlemayer and Mehringer started their climb. News had spread and, when daylight came, people queued up at the Grindelwald telescopes to see how the pair were doing. By dusk they were well above the Eigerwand Station. On Thursday they crossed the first ice field and bivouacked at its upper rim. It took them all of Friday to pick their way up the next rock face to the second ice field. That night the Eiger was swept by a tremendous thunderstorm that continued throughout Saturday. Avalanches of stone, ice and snow poured down the north face; by all rights the two Bavarians should have been swept away. But, to the observers' disbelief, when the clouds cleared on Sunday, Sedlemayer and Mehringer could be seen moving slowly up the second ice field. The crowd interpreted this as a good sign: if, having spent five days on the face, having endured murderously cold nights, having escaped death by avalanche and rockfall, Sedlemayer and Mehringer had not turned back, it could only mean that they were confident of reaching the top. Their optimism was misplaced: the two climbers had carried on only because they could not turn back. The rocks up which they had struggled were now glazed with ice and streaming with waterfalls; moreover, the fresh snow had increased the risk of avalanches. It had been hard enough getting up; in such conditions it would have been death to retreat; their only option was to continue in the hope that they could climb themselves out of the trap. That evening the mists closed over the Eigerwand, heralding yet another bout of ferocious weather. This time the Bavarians were lost.

Local guides were put on alert. By Tuesday German climbers had arrived in Grindelwald to assist in any rescue operation, but there was nothing that they or anybody else could do. The rocks were too treacherous to permit an attempt from below, and a descent from above was equally out of the question. Swiss army planes scoured the mountain but could see little through the mist. When the weather cleared on 19 September, the German air ace Ernst Udet and the Grindelwald guide Fritz Steuri went up for a final search. Flying 60 feet from the face, they spied a body: it was frozen upright, knee-deep in the snow at the top of the third ice field. Despite repeated passes they could not tell who it was, nor could they see any sign of a second corpse. Recovery was impossible, so the unidentified climber was left where he stood, on a spot which became known as Death Bivouac, a gruesome testimonial to the Eigerwand's hazards. That season Grindelwald hoteliers charged double for the use of their telescopes.

Alpine purists were swift to condemn. If the two men had succeeded, said the Berne-based *Sport*, 'according to our opinion even then no mountaineering deed had been achieved, merely a degradation inflicted on one of our great peaks, with the honoured traditions of mountaineering perverted into monkey tricks . . . It cannot sufficiently be stressed that such juggling with human life has no connection whatever with mountaineering. It is a German's affair if he be compelled to exercise his modern psychology in "direct" ascents.'[11] The *Alpine Journal* offered its condolences but pointed out that some thirty people had died in the Alps that year, largely through carelessness, and that Sedlemayer and Mehringer (misspelled as Nihringer) offered one of the most 'flagrant examples of the neglect of every sane principle in an attempt to gain cheap notoriety'.[12]

One winter sufficed to cleanse the Eigerwand of its corpses and the memories of those who sought to conquer it. By the end of May 1936 – extraordinarily early – another two Bavarians, Albert Herbst and Hans Teufel, were in Grindelwald. 'They were splendid climbers, to be sure,' wrote a contemporary, 'but perhaps lacking in that calm and relaxation which is the hall-mark of the accomplished master-climber.'[13] On 1 July, to get in training for the Eiger, they went up the unclimbed north face of the Schneehorn. They reached the summit without difficulty; on the descent, however, they were swept 600 feet downhill by an avalanche. Herbst survived; Teufel hit the lip of a crevasse and broke his neck. The incident was reported under 'Accidents and Crimes'.

The Herbst–Teufel disaster was still fresh when another duo, this time from Austria, threw themselves at the Eigerwand. Willy Angerer and Edi Rainer had studied the north face and come to the conclusion that there must be an easier way of reaching the first ice field than by the perilous rock face which rose above the Eigerwand Station and which had trapped Sedlemayer and Mehringer. To the right were a series of rock pillars from which it might be possible to traverse sideways onto the ice. On 6 July they climbed up the rock pillars, saw that a crossing might be feasible and came down the next day, nearly killing themselves in a 120-feet fall as they did so. 'Grim?' they told reporters, 'No, only a trifle wet!' They said other things too: 'We have to climb your Wall for you if you won't do it yourselves' and 'We must have the Wall or it will have us.' Most importantly, 'We shall go up again as soon as conditions improve.'[14] The press loved it and blazed headlines like 'The Battle with the Eiger Wall', 'New Life on the Face' and 'The All-Out Investment'. They also introduced a new word for the north face. It was no longer the *Nordwand*, or north wall, but the *Mordwand*, the murder wall.

On Saturday, 18 July 1936 Angerer and Rainer returned to the rock pillars – 'in the teeth of every conceivable warning from local guides and experts'[15] – pursued by a German team comprising Andreas Hinterstoisser and Toni Kurz. The two parties climbed independently for a while; then, as the Germans drew level with the Austrians, they decided to join forces. It was a good decision. Intrepid as Angerer and Rainer were, they lacked the climbing skills of the Germans. Hinterstoisser, in particular, was an adept at rock faces, having mastered the craft of manoeuvring by pitons and belays over seemingly impossible obstacles. With Hinterstoisser in the lead, they embarked on the traverse towards the first ice field. By train and bus, hordes of spectators came to Grindelwald to enjoy the spectacle.

Hinterstoisser performed magnificently, hammering his pitons across the near-vertical face, steadily paying out rope for the others. In Grindelwald and on the Kleine Scheidegg pass, the telescope tourists watched every move. When the last man had crossed the face, Hinterstoisser drew up the rope. The watchers were bemused: surely the point of finding a new approach was that it would provide a new retreat. Without a rope there could be no going back. But this was a strong team, they told themselves. Hinterstoisser knew what he was doing. He must have taken the rope because it was needed for the next part of the climb. On 20 July they rejoiced as Hinterstoisser and

Kurz led the way in clear weather towards Death Bivouac, the two
Austrians lagging slightly behind. Then something happened. The
Austrians had stopped. The Germans came back down and, after
some time, the whole team retraced its steps. Angerer, it transpired,
had been hit on the head by a rock. On 21 July, having helped Angerer
over more than 1,000 feet of rock and ice, they were once more at the
head of the traverse. Without a fixed rope, however, it was impossible
to retrace their steps. The only way down was via the rock face which
Sedlemayer and Mehringer had rejected as being too dangerous in
1936 and which was no safer now. Hinterstoisser led the way and, to
his great credit, brought the team safely down the first few hundred
feet.

Albert von Allmen, an elderly employee on the Jungfrau Railway,
had heard of the attempt and wondered how things were going. At
noon on 21 July, he opened the wooden door that linked Kilometre
3.8 to the bleak cliffs outside and shouted to see if anyone was there.
To his surprise there came a call from almost directly above. Instead
of braving the whole descent Hinterstoisser had decided to take his
men to one of the railway galleries. They would soon be with him,
they told Allmen; everything was fine. Mistaking their relief for confidence, Allmen said he'd put the kettle on and shuffled back to his
office. He waited for two hours, shifting the kettle on and off the
hob, before he went back to the door. This time when he shouted
only Kurz replied. The others were all dead and he himself was stuck.
Allmen ran to the telephone.

A train was sent up the line, carrying four guides. On arriving at
Allmen's gallery the rescuers climbed onto the face and learned what
had happened from a shouted conversation with Kurz. Hinterstoisser,
in the lead, had detached himself from the rope to give Angerer
behind him greater freedom of movement. In doing so he had fallen
off the mountain. Angerer in turn had also slipped and, by evil mis-
chance, the rope had wrapped itself around his neck. The jerk pulled
Rainer off his feet jamming him tight against the piton to which the
rope was attached. Unable to move, Rainer froze to death. Kurz, the
last man on the rope, was left dangling against the face, one corpse

pinned to the cliff above, another hanging by the neck below. The rescuers did their best to reach him but were driven back by icy rocks and fading daylight. Reluctantly they retreated to the gallery, pursued by Kurz's shouts of anger and despair.

When they returned the next morning Kurz was still alive but his condition had worsened. That night, his fourth on the face, had been cold: icicles eight inches long hung from his crampons; he had lost a mitten and his left arm was frozen into near immobility. The rope, meanwhile, had swollen and stiffened into a thick, unwieldy cable. The four guides reached a point 130 feet below him, but were prevented from going higher by an overhang. Using rockets, they tried to get Kurz a line which he could then use to haul up a rope. But they were too close to the overhang: the rockets flew out from the face, within Kurz's view but tantalisingly out of reach. Calling up to their invisible quarry they instructed him to climb down, cut Angerer from the rope, then climb back up and cut the rope beneath Rainer. Once he had done that he could unravel the rope, join the strands together and let down a line. In normal circumstances this would have been a difficult task. For Kurz, it was well nigh impossible. Incredibly, however, he began to hack his way across the face, first to Angerer – whose body had frozen to the face overnight – and then to Rainer, clutching the rope in his disabled hand and swinging the axe with his other.

The rope having been salvaged, Kurz faced the task of unravelling it. For five hours he picked at the strands, using his one good hand and his teeth. As he did so an avalanche swept past the rescuers, followed by a block of ice that narrowly missed one guide's head. In its wake came Angerer's body, which had unglued itself from the rocks. Then, unbelievably, a narrow line slithered down the overhang. Kurz was alive. The rescuers fastened a rope and pitons to the line, shouted an OK, and watched it creep slowly upwards. The rope, however, was too short, so they spliced a second rope to the end of the first and, once that had been accomplished, Toni Kurz began his abseil to safety. An hour later he slithered over the lip of the overhang. At that point, within ten feet of safety, the splice snagged on a piton. Kurz could go no further. He hauled on the rope but the knot was firmly stuck. The rescuers, who could touch his crampons with their ice axes, told him to pull harder. Kurz replied slowly and very clearly: 'I am finished.' He swung out into space, dead.

Three days later the European press gave its judgement. For once, notions of Wagnerian glory were cast aside. 'When the search for notoriety and obstinate will-power conspire to bring a man to grief, one cannot really register regret,'[16] said one newspaper. Ugly rumours spread that the ascent had been deliberately planned to coincide with the Berlin Olympics. It escaped nobody's attention that Hinterstoisser and Kurz were both members of Germany's 100 Jager Regiment and, under the headline 'Climbing to Orders', a correspondent wrote from Grindelwald that 'A report is current here that the four climbers had been ordered to make the ascent. It has been said that they were very excited on Friday evening; that they would never have taken such a grave risk as free agents.'[17] Without naming names the Alpine Club also put the blame on Hitler.

Others took a less partial view. According to one paper,

Perhaps these young men have nothing more to lose . . . what is to become of a generation to which Society offers no social existence and which has only one thing left to look to, a single day's glory, the swiftly tarnishing highlight of a single hour? To be a bit of a hero, a bit of a soldier, sportsman or record-breaker, a gladiator, victorious one day, defeated the next . . . The four recent victims of the Eiger's North Face were poor creatures. When some kindly folk in Grindelwald invited them to dinner, they tucked in to the proffered meal like true warriors; afterwards, they said they hadn't had such a good meal for three years. When asked what was the purpose of their risky venture, they replied that its main object was to improve their positions. They believed that such an exceptional feat would bring them honour and glory, and make people take notice of them.[18]

Had the dead men been victims of a propaganda drive that went

wrong? Probably not. They may have been suffused by the nationalism of the decade and they may well have been supporters of Hitler.
Every German newspaper lauded them, and the frenzy for conquest
was exactly the same as that which drove Whymper's Italian oppo-
nents – and Whymper himself – up the Matterhorn. On the other
hand Hinterstoisser's commanding officer had sent a cable instructing
him to desist – it arrived too late – and if the team had been climbing
under orders it would surely have been better provisioned. Compared
to Sedlemayer and Mehringer who, prior to departure, had climbed
the Eiger by the standard route to deposit a cache of food on the
summit, Hinterstoisser's men were dismally ill-prepared. Rope, tent
and pitons aside, their supplies – for what they knew could not be a
climb of less than five days – had comprised per person, one pound of
bread, half a pound of bacon and a tin of sardines. They may have
been afflicted by the mood of the time, but the image of 'poor creatures' hoping for a bit of fame, rings truer than that of four daredevils
risking all for the Reich. Perceptively, one Swiss academic likened the
rush for the Eigerwand to the Children's Crusade.

Later that year rescue parties picked up the remains. Angerer and
Rainer were easily identifiable. Less so were the two heaps of bones
which had once been Sedlemayer and Mehringer. A German team
took precedence in Kurz's retrieval and cut his body free with a knife
attached to a pole. German radio promptly stated that they had been
responsible for the whole rescue operation, a claim that was greeted
by widespread jeers. One commentator remarked tartly that in the
worst conditions it had taken the slowest Swiss guide forty-five
minutes to reach Kurz from the gallery window; the Germans had
struggled to complete the distance in four hours.

The 'suicidal follies of the Eigerwand',[19] as the *Alpine Journal* put
it, continued into 1937. On 15 July two Austrians, Franz Primas and
Albert Gollacher, braved the Eiger in a display of monstrous incompetence. Gollacher, merely 18, was quite inexperienced, forgot to
take any food with him and after five days on the mountain went
mad and tried to throw Primas over the edge before freezing to death.
Primas, who had neglected to bring a tent, was rescued from a snow

cave on 20 July, suffering from severe frostbite. In a separate attempt
two Italians also had to be rescued. Another Austrian team made it to
Death Bivouac and returned safely – collecting Hinterstoisser's body
en route – therefore earning the dubious accolade of being the first to
return intact from such a height. A Swiss woman accompanied by a
guide climbed a few thousand feet before retreating unscathed. And
two Germans who had tried to extort free drinks and food under the
pretence of being Eiger men were expelled from the country.
Meanwhile, telescopes swivelled to and fro, as 'the proletariat, herd-
ing around the base, awaited events with the same deplorable
expectancy as in 1935–6'.[20]

The Alpine Club spluttered with rage. 'The Eigerwand . . . con-
tinues to be an obsession for the mentally deranged of almost every
nation,' the President said on 6 December 1937. 'He who first suc-
ceeds may rest assured that he has accomplished the most imbecile
variant since mountaineering first began.'[21] In Grindelwald the
authorities forbade any further attempts on the Eigerwand, with the
rather feeble sanction of a fine. Later, realising that dead men could
not pay, they withdrew the notice and substituted a threat that no
rescue operations would be mounted if climbers became stranded. It
had not the slightest impact. At the next Nuremberg Rally, Hitler
invited the Reich's foremost climber, Anderl Heckmair, to stand with
him on the balcony. The spotlights swirled, the stadium cheered and
the Eigerwand became a tacit part of the Nazi dream. Meanwhile,
scraps of the banning notice drifted forlornly over the Eiger's lower
slopes.

In 1938 the usual collection of hopefuls arrived in Grindelwald,
erecting their tents in the meadows, sleeping in hayricks or lurking in
the forest. Fearing public condemnation, they were more secretive
than before, and avoided the press. But nothing could hide their
voracity for the Eigerwand. The season started on 21 June with the
deaths of two Italians. Bartolo Sandri and Mario Menti were youngsters of 23 who worked in a wool factory and had no experience of ice.
Sandri was discovered in a patch of snow at the foot of the face; Menti
was recovered a few days later from the bottom of a 150-foot crevasse.

Then, on 21 July, four Austrians emerged from the trees and started up the Eigerwand. Two of them later dropped out, but the other two, Heinrich Harrer and Fritz Kasparek, carried on. They were at the rock pillars when they realised they were not alone. Heckmair, of Nuremberg fame, had also been hiding in the trees and had sprung up the face with incredible rapidity. He and his partner Ludwig Vörg were waiting when Harrer and Kasparek arrived. Harrer had no choice but to continue the ascent with them. It was as well he did, because Heckmair was a phenomenal mountaineer. Taking the lead, he vaulted up the face, at times seeming to levitate himself over insurmountable cliffs.

'He treated us to an acrobatic *tour de force*,' wrote Harrer, 'an exhibition exercise, such as we had rarely witnessed before. It was half superb rock-technique, half a toe-dance on the ice – a toe-dance above a perpendicular drop. He got a hold on the rock, a hold on the ice, bent himself double, uncoiled himself, the front points of his crampons moving ever upwards, boring into the ice. They only got a few millimetres purchase but that was enough.'[22] The weather worsened but Heckmair forged on. They climbed by day and during the shadowy pre-dawn light – 'Fear's friendly sister,'[23] Harrer called it. They slept upright on the narrowest of ledges, buffeted by winds, held in place only by their ropes. Gales shrieked around them, snow fell, water poured down their necks and came out at their ankles. After one meal Heckmair was poisoned by a bad sardine, but still he continued. He led them higher and higher, beyond Death Bivouac, beyond the third ice field, beyond the White Spider and onto the final stretch. They slipped and cut each other with their crampons. Vörg almost lost his hand when the man above trod on it. At one point Heckmair fell, ripping a string of pitons from the cliff before the rope stopped him. Undeterred, he climbed up and hammered every piton back in place. They watched avalanches and timed them to take advantage of the intervals between falls. And then, at 3.30 p.m. on 24 July 1938, they chopped through the final cornice. It had taken them eighty-five hours, but at last they had beaten the Eigerwand.

Victory brought only numbed acceptance:

Joy, relief, tumultuous triumph? Not a bit of it,' wrote Harrer.
'Our release had come too suddenly, our minds and nerves
were too dulled, our bodies too utterly weary to permit of any
violent emotion . . . The storm was raging so fiercely on the
summit that we had to bend double. Thick crusts of ice had
formed around our eyes, noses and mouths; we had to scratch
them away before we could see each other, speak or even
breathe. We probably looked like legendary monsters of the
Arctic . . . This was no place in which to turn handsprings or
shriek with joy and happiness. We just shook hands without a
word. Then we started down at once.[24]

The descent was nothing compared to what they had already endured
but it was nevertheless 'full of spite and malice'.[25] The blizzard closed
visibility to a small circle; the ice was treacherous and overlaid by
three feet of snow. As they slipped and staggered through the murk
they lost their way and, heartbreakingly, had to climb back hundreds
of feet. Heckmair, who had been sustained by nervous energy during
the ascent, now collapsed; unable to take the lead, he trudged
mechanically behind the others.

When snow gave way to rain they realised they had climbed below
the storm. But by this time they were all more or less dazed. They saw
black dots coming to greet them and wondered what so many people
could be doing out on the glacier. They saw the Kleine Scheidegg
hotel and thought how nice it would be to have a bed there – if only
they had remembered to bring money. A boy swam into view, stared
at them as if they were ghosts, then ran away shouting, 'Here they are!
They are coming!'[26] Down they trudged, still not quite connecting
what was happening with what they had done, until they were surrounded by well-wishers. There were friends from Vienna and
Munich, guides from the Rescue Service, reporters, tourists and
Grindelwald locals. They offered to carry their rucksacks, lit cigarettes
for them, gave them flasks of brandy and promised free accommodation in any hotel of their choice. They would have carried them on
their shoulders had they been allowed. Harrer was overcome: 'For the

first time, we felt the intense satisfaction, the relaxation, the relief from every care, and the indescribable delight at having climbed the North Face . . . In the rush and whirl of everyday things, we so often live alongside one another without making any mutual contact. We had learned on the North Face of the Eiger that men are good and the earth on which we were born is good. And now that earth was welcoming us home.'[27]

Back in Berlin, Harrer, Heckmair, Kasparek and Vörg became heroes. Medals were awarded, and Heckmair was once more paraded before the party faithful. Hitler shook his hand and, to the popping of flashbulbs, gave him tickets for a free cruise of the Scandinavian fjords. Harrer was rewarded by a place on Germany's 1939 Himalaya expedition, the results of which were his wartime internment in India and, following his escape, seven years' seclusion in Tibet. Kasparek received nothing and fell off a Peruvian cornice in 1954. Vörg was promoted to an elite mountaineering regiment and died on the Eastern Front in a wasteful attack on a Russian position.

Inevitably, there was resentment. The *Alpine Journal* offered little in the way of congratulation and gave the most grudgingly bland account of their triumph. A Frenchman famously remarked that '*C'est pas de l'Alpinisme, ça, c'est la guerre.*'[28] And then, of course, there were accusations that they had been climbing for the benefit of the Third Reich. Harrer rejected the charge angrily. 'To ascribe material motives and similar external rewards of success to our climb would be a lie and a slander. Not one of us improved his social position one whit thanks to a mountaineering feat which excited such general admiration. Nobody dangled Olympic or other medals before our eyes . . . As to the report that we climbed on the orders, or even at the wish, of some personage or other, it is absolutely off the mark. We followed the dictates of our own will solely.'[29] (But from where had those dictates sprung?) Heckmair spoke more bluntly. Of his official reception he said, 'It could have happened to a dancing bear.'[30]

In a way, it did not really matter whether they had been sponsored by Hitler or not. They had climbed the Eigerwand and, whatever their motives, nothing could diminish this extraordinary feat. Indeed,

it would have been beautifully apt if they had been offered induce-
ments; for their triumph was part of a process that had started some
175 years before when Horace Bénédict de Saussure first put a price
on Mont Blanc's head.

The Eigerwand did not mark the end of Alpine exploration. In
years to come there would be other last problems as climbers sought
new approaches to old hills and tackled them from different angles.
Its conquest, however, was definitive when the Alps still wore a cloak
of mystery – albeit a tattered and increasingly threadbare one.
Tourism was growing during the 1930s but it was restricted to a few
major resorts, such as Zermatt, Grindelwald, Chamonix, and St
Moritz; away from the major destinations individuals could still
wander across barren glaciers and through untouched valleys whose
villagers and chalet-dwellers were not much different from those of
the previous century.

After World War II the Alps changed irrevocably. Ski resorts prolif-
erated as entrepreneurs devoured the empty spaces. The discovery of
antibiotics killed the sanatoriums almost overnight; those few that
survived did so only because they were well placed to exploit the
winter influx, their expensive medical facilities catering to injury
rather than illness. Pylons for ski lifts, gondolas and cable cars
marched across every slope. Gradients were bulldozed and forests
were cut down to create pistes. Ropes were pinned to the Matterhorn
to make life easier for those wishing to conquer the Big Rock. Tunnels
were blasted through obstructive mountains to facilitate the flow of
traffic between Italy and the rest of Europe. In the postwar years
more people travelled through the Alps, more people came to stay in
them and more business was conducted there than at any time in the
area's long history.

This well-groomed wilderness was no place for dragons. Yet its
upper levels retained a strange fascination. Climbers still strode across
passes, clambered over glaciers and struggled with dangerous new
routes. Far fewer in number than the thousands who rushed to the
Alps every winter, they preserved a glimmer of the old romance. They

could not enjoy the freshness which had been the trademark of the Golden Age – up to a hundred a day were known to climb the Matterhorn – but they could experience the same sense of accomplishment. Like their predecessors, they were trespassers in a hostile environment; they were adventurers in an old tradition.

The pioneers were driven to climb the Alps for varied and complex reasons. Scientific inquiry played a part; sheer egotism was an even stronger motive. Some of them were escaping modern life; others saw Alpine achievement as the culmination of modernity; others, still, considered climbing a spiritual necessity. And, of course, some went just for the hell of it. Swirling in their wake came painters, poets and pedants, each of whom imagined the Alps in their own particular way. But if one had to choose a single sentence to encapsulate the essence of Alpine exploration, the magic which drove men and women to the peaks again and again; if one sifted through the archives, from Master John de Bremble, Leonardo da Vinci, Conrad Gesner, Bourrit, Saussure and Forbes, to Wills, Whymper, Tyndall, Conway, Coolidge and beyond, no words are better than those of Harrer on returning from the Eigerwand. Echoing a sentiment that was shared by hundreds of climbers across two centuries, Harrer said, simply: 'We had made an excursion into another world and we had come back.'[31]

SELECT BIBLIOGRAPHY

The following is a list of the main sources consulted during the preparation of this work. It is not exhaustive and does not do true justice to the *Alpine Journal*, which figures rather ignominiously in the section 'Periodicals, Newspapers, etc.' First issued in the early 1860s, the *AJ* is not so much a journal as a small book. It is still in publication and its many volumes are invaluable to anyone interested in the history of the Alps or mountain/glacier exploration.

Books

Agassiz, C. (ed.) – *Louis Agassiz: His Life and Correspondence* (2 vols.). Macmillan, London, 1885.

Agassiz, L. – *Etudes sur les Glaciers*. Nicolet, Neuchatel, 1840.

Annan, N. – *Leslie Stephen: the Godless Victorian*. Weidenfeld and Nicolson, London, 1984.

Auldjo, J. – *Narrative of an Ascent to the Summit of Mont Blanc*. Longman, London, 1828.

Bailey, R. – *Glacier*. Time-Life Books, Alexandria Va., 1982.

Ball, J.(ed.) – *Peaks, Passes and Glaciers*. Longman, London, 1859.

Baxter, G. and MacGregor, J. – *The Ascent of Mont Blanc*. Privately published, 1855.

Bennett, G. – *Beyond Endurance*. Secker & Warburg, London, 1983.

Bernard, P. – *Rush To The Alps*. East European Quarterly, Boulder, 1978.

Bicknell, J. (ed.) – *Selected Letters of Leslie Stephen* (2 vols.). Macmillan, London, 1996.

Bonney, T. – *The High Alps of Dauphin*. Longman, London, 1865.

—— *Memories of a Long Life*. Metcalfe, Cambridge, 1921.

Bourrit, M-T. (trans. Cha. and Fred. Davy) – *A Relation of a Journey in the Glaciers in the Duchy of Savoy*. Beatniffe, Norwich, 1777.

—— *Nouvelle Description des Glacieres et Glaciers de Savoy*. Paul Barde, Geneva, 1785.

—— *Nouvelle Description des Alpes* (2 vols.). Paule Barde. Geneva, 1783.

—— *Description des Cols ou Passages des Alpes* (2 vols.). Manget, Geneva, 1803.

Brockedon, W. – *Illustrations of the Passes of the Alps* (2 vols.). London, 1828.

—— *Journals of Excursions in the Alps*. James Duncan, London, 1833.

Browne, G. – *Recollections of a Bishop*. Smith, Elder, London, 1915.

Clark, J. and Hughes, T. – *The Life and Letters of Adam Sedgwick*. (2 vols.). Cambridge University Press, Cambridge, 1890.

Clark, R. – *An Eccentric in the Alps*. Museum Press, London, 1959.

—— *The Early Alpine Guides*. Phoenix, London, 1949.

—— *The Victorian Mountaineers*. Batsford, London, 1953.

—— *The Alps*. Weidenfeld & Nicolson, London, 1973.

Conway, W. – *The Alps from End to End*. Constable, London, 1895.

—— *The Alps*. Adam and Charles Black, London, 1904.

—— *Mountain Memories*. Cassell, London, 1920.

—— *Episodes in a Varied Life*. Country Life, London, 1932.

Coolidge, W. – *Swiss Travel and Swiss Guide Books*. Longman, Green & co., London, 1889.

—— *A Run Through the Dolomites in 1876*. Ben Johnson, York, 1902.

—— *Josias Simler et les Origines de l'Alpinisme*. Imprimerie Allier Freres, Grenoble, 1904.

—— *The Central Alps of the Dauphiny*. Fisher Unwin, London, 1905.

—— *The Alpine Career (1868–1914) of Frederick Gardiner*. Privately printed, 1920.

—— *Alpine Studies*. Longmans, Green & co. London, 1912.

Coxe, W. – *Travels in Switzerland* (2 vols.). Cadell London, 1794.

D'Arve, S. – *Histoire Du Mont Blanc et de la valle de Chamonix*. Delagrave, Paris, 1878. (Reprinted La Fontaine de Silo, 1993)

De Beer, G. – *Early Travellers in the Alps*. Sidgwick & Jackson, London. 1930.

—— *Alps and Men*. Edward Arnold, London, 1932.

—— *Travellers in Switzerland*. Oxford University Press, London, 1949.

De Luc, J-A. – *Lettres Physique et Morales sur l'Histoire de la Terre et de l'Homme* (5 vols.). Duchesne, Paris, 1779.

—— *Trait, Elémentaire de Géologie*. Courcier, Paris, 1809.

Dormandy, T. – *The White Death*. Hambledon, London, 1999.

Engel, C. – *A History of Mountaineering in the Alps*. Allen & Unwin, London, 1950.

—— *They Came to the Hills*. Allen & Unwin, London, 1952.

—— *Mont Blanc: an Anthology*. Allen & Unwin, London, 1965.

Eve, A. & Creasey, C. – *Life and Work of John Tyndall*. Macmillan, London, 1945.

Fellows, C. – *Narrative of the Ascent to the Summit of Mont Blanc*. Privately published, 1827.

Figuier, L. (trans. Davenport Adams, W.) – *Earth and Sea*. Nelson, Edinburgh, 1870.

Fitzsimons, R. – *The Baron of Piccadilly: the travels and entertainments of Albert Smith 1816–1860*. Geoffrey Bles, London, 1967.

Forbes, James – *Travels through the Alps of Savoy*. Adam & Charles Black, Edinburgh, 1843.

—— *Norway and its Glaciers*. Adam & Charles Black, Edinburgh, 1853.

—— *Occasional Papers on the Theory of Glaciers*. Adam & Charles Black, Edinburgh, 1859.

Forbes, John – *A Physician's Holiday*. Murray, London, 1850.

Fraser, C. – *The Avalanche Enigma*. Murray, London, 1966.

Freshfield, D. – *The Life of Horace Benedict De Saussure*. Edward Arnold, London, 1920.

Gesner, C. (trans. Dock, W.) – *On the Admiration of Mountains*. The Grabhorn Press, San Francisco, 1937.

Gribble. F. – *The Early Mountaineers*. Fisher Unwin, London, 1899.

Harrer, H. (trans. Merrick, C.) – *The White Spider*. Flamingo, London, 1995.

Hawes, B. – *A Narrative of an Ascent to the Summit of Mont Blanc . . . by Mr. William Hawes and Mr. Charles Fellows*. Privately published, 1828.

Heckmair, A. (trans. Sutton, G.) – *My Life as a Mountaineer*. Victor Gollancz, London, 1975.

Herbert, R. – *The Art Criticism of John Ruskin*. Da Capo Press, New York,1964.

Hinchliff, T. – *Summer Months Among the Alps*. Longman, London, 1857.

Hort, A. – *Life and Letters of Fenton John Anthony Hort* (2 vols.). Macmillan, London, 1896.

Hudson, C. & Kennedy, E. – *Where There's A Will There's A Way*. Longman, London, 1856.

Huxley, L. – *Life and Letters of Thomas Henry Huxley* (3 vols.). Macmillan, London, 1913.

Irving, R. – *The Alps*. Batsford, London, 1947.

Keenlyside, F. – *Peaks and Pioneers*. Elek, London, 1975.

Kemp, W. (trans J. van Heurk) – *The Desire of My Eyes: The life and work of John Ruskin*. HarperCollins, London, 1991.

Kennedy, E. (ed.) – *Peaks, Passes and Glaciers*. Second Series. (2 vols.). Longman, London, 1862.

Lunn, A. – *The Alps*. Thornton Butterworth, London, 1914.

—— *Come What May*. Eyre & Spottiswoode, London, 1940.

Mathews, C.A. – *The Annals of Mont Blanc*. Fisher Unwin, London, 1898.

Moore, A. (ed. Kennedy, A.) – *The Alps In 1864; A private journal*. David Douglas, Edinburgh, 1902.

Mumm, A. – *The Alpine Club Register* (3 vols.). Edward Arnold, London, 1923.

Mummery, A. – *My Climbs in the Alps and Caucasus*. Fisher Unwin, London, 1895.

Payot, P. – *Au Royaume Du Mont-Blanc*. La Fontaine de Siloé, Montmélian, 1996.

Pinkerton, J. – *Voyages and Travels* (Vol. IV). Longman, London, 1809.

Rébuffat, G. (trans. Brockett, E.) – *Men and the Matterhorn*. Nicholas Vane, London, 1967.

Roth, A. – *Eiger: Wall of Death*. Victor Gollancz, London, 1982.

Ruskin, E. – *Effie in Venice* (ed. Mary Lutyens). Murray, London, 1965.

Ruskin, J. – *Letters to M.G. and H.G. Harper*. London, 1903.

—— *Modern Painters*. (ed. David Barrie). Andre Deutsch, London, 1987.

—— *Sesame and Lilies*. George Allen, London, 1893.

Saussure, H-B. – *Voyages Dans Les Alpes. précédés d'un essai sur L'Histoire Naturelle des environs De Genéve.* Barde Manget, Geneva, 1786 (vols 1&2) and 1796 (vols 3&4).

Scheuchzer, J. – *Itinera per Helvetiae Alpinas Regiones.* Vander, London, 1723.

Seth-Smith, M. – *The Cresta Run.* Foulsham, London, 1976.

Shairp, J., Tait, P. & Adams-Reilly, A. – *Life and Letters of James David Forbes.* Macmillan, London, 1873.

Skelton, J. – *The Table-Talk of Shirley.* Blackwood, Edinburgh, 1896.

Smith, A. – *A Month at Constantinople.* David Bogue, London, 1850.

—— *Mont Blanc.* Ward and Lock, London, 1860.

Smythe, F.S. – *Edward Whymper.* Hodder & Stoughton, London, 1940.

Stephen, L. – *The Playground of Europe.* Longman, London, 1871.

—— *Some Early Impressions.* Hogarth Press, London, 1924.

Thorington, J. – *Mont Blanc Sideshow: The Life and Times of Albert Smith.* The John C. Winston Company, Philadelphia, 1934.

T'pffer, R. – *Nouveaux Voyages en Zig Zag.* Victor Lecon, Paris, 1854.

Tuckett, F. – *A Pioneer in the High Alps; Alpine diaries and letters 1856–1874.* Edward Arnold, London, 1920.

Tyndall, J. – *The Glaciers of the Alps.* Murray, London, 1860.

—— *Mountaineering in 1861.* Longman, London, 1862.

—— *Hours of Exercise in the Alps.* Longman, London. 1871.

—— *New Fragments.* Longman, London 1892.

Unsworth, W. – *Savage Snows: the story of Mont Blanc.* Hodder & Stoughton, London, 1986.

Whymper, E. – *Scrambles Amongst the Alps in the years 1860–69.* Murray, London, 1871.

—— *Scrambles . . .* (6th edition). Murray, London, 1936.

—— *The Valley of Zermatt and the Matterhorn.* Murray, London,1897.

Wills, A. – *Wanderings Among the High Alps.* Bentley, London, 1858.

Young, G. – *On High Hills.* Methuen, London, 1933.

Periodicals, Newspapers etc.

Alpes
Alpine Journal
Blackwood's Magazine
Daily News
Fraser's Magazine
Illustrated London News
Journal of the Royal Geographical Society
Times

SOURCES

The following abbreviations have been used:

AC	–	Alpine Club
AJ	–	Alpine Journal
BL	–	British Library
IC	–	Imperial College, London
MC	–	Magdalen College, Oxford
RI	–	Royal Institution of Great Britain
SPRI	–	Scott Polar Research Institute

Chapter One

1 Coolidge, W. – *Josias Simler et les Origines de l'Alpinisme*. Imprimerie Allier Freres, Grenoble, 1904. p. iii.

2 Bernard, P. – *Rush to the Alps. East European Quarterly*, Columbia Press, New York, 1978. p. 2.

3 Lunn, A. – *The Alps*. Williams & Norgate, London, 1914. p. 22–23.

4 Coolidge, W. – *Swiss Travel and Swiss Guide Books*. Longman, Green & Co., London, 1899. p. 9.

5 Gribble, F. – *The Early Mountaineers*. Fisher Unwin, London, 1899. p. 24.

6 Coolidge – *Josias Simler . . .* op cit. p. iii–iv.

7 Gesner, C. (trans. Dock, W.) – *On the Admiration of Mountains*. The Grabhorn Press, San Francisco, 1937. p. 31.

8 De Beer, G. – *Early Travellers in the Alps*. Sidgwick & Jackson, London, 1930. p. 83.

9 Ibid. p. 88.

10 Gribble, op cit, p. 75.

11 Mathews, C. – *The Annals of Mont Blanc*. Fisher Unwin, London, 1898. p. 6.

12 De Beer, op cit. p. 90.

13 Ibid.
14 Mathews, op cit. p. 336
15 Ibid.
16 Ibid. p. 338.
17 Ibid. p. 339.
18 Ibid. p. 340.
19 Ibid.
20 Engel, C. *A History of Mountaineering in the Alps*. Allen and Unwin, London, 1950. p. 39.
21 Stephen, L. – *Playground of Europe*. Longmans, London, 1871. p. 2.

Chapter Two

1 Freshfield, D. – *The Life of Horace Benedict De Saussure*. Edward Arnold, London, 1920.
2 Saussure, H. – *Voyages Dans Les Alpes*. Barde, Manget, Geneva, 1786. Vol I, p. x.
3 Ibid.
4 Freshfield, op cit. p. 66.
5 Saussure, op cit. p. 429.
6 Ibid.
7 Freshfield, op cit. p. 71.
8. Ibid. p. 182.
9 Engel, C. – *A History of Mountaineering in the Alps*. Allen and Unwin, London, 1950. p. 34.
10 Bourrit, M. (trans. Davy C. & F.) – *A Relation of a Journey to the Glaciers in the Dutchy of Savoy*. Richard Beatniffe, Norwich, 1776. Editor's Preface.
11 Engel, op cit. p. 37.
12 Freshfield, op cit. p. 185.
13 Ibid. p. 79.
14 Saussure, op cit. p. xi.
15 Freshfield, op cit. p. 182.
16 Engel, op cit. p. 35.
17 De Beer – *Travellers in Switzerland*. Oxford University Press, London, 1949. p. 79.
18 Freshfield, op cit. p. 178.
19 Ibid. p. 179.
20 Gribble, F. – *The Early Mountaineers*. Fisher Unwin, London, 1899. p. 130.
21 Engel, op cit. p. 30.
22 Ibid. p. 29.
23 Ibid. p. 32.
24 Ibid.
25 Ibid.
26 Ibid.
27 Ibid. p. 31.

Chapter Three

1 Freshfield, op cit. p. 78.
2 Ibid. p. 83.
3 Ibid. p. 149.
4 Ibid. p. 162.
5 Ibid. p. 55.
6 Bourrit, M. – *Description des Cols ou Passages des Alpes*. Manget, Geneva, 1803. Vol I, p. 266.
7 Saussure, H. – *Voyages . . .* op cit. Vol IV, p. 219.
8 Saussure, op cit. Vol II, p. 554.
9 Bourrit M. (trans. Davy C. & F.) – *A Relation of a Journey to the Glaciers in the Dutchy of Savoy*. Richard Beatniffe, Norwich, 1776. p. 64.

10 Ibid. p. 72.
11 Ibid. p. 94.
12 Freshfield, op cit. p. 182.
13 Ibid. p. 201.
14 Mathews, C. – *The Annals of Mont Blanc*. Fisher Unwin, London, 1898. p. 35.
15 AC – Paccard's Journal.
16 Ibid.
17 Bourrit, M. – *Nouvelle Description des Glacieres et Glaciers de Savoy*. Paul Barde, Geneva, 1785. p. 305.
18 AC – Paccard's Journal.
19 Ibid.
20 Engel, C. – *A History of Mountaineering in the Alps*. Allen and Unwin, London, 1950. p. 49.
21 Saussure, op cit. Vol. II, p. 554.
22 Ibid. p. 562.
23 Freshfield, op cit. p. 206.
24 Ibid. p. 203.
25 Ibid. p. 204.
26 Ibid.
27 Ibid.
28 AC – Paccard's Journal.
29 Freshfield, op cit. p. 208.

Chapter Four

1 AC – Paccard's Journal.
2 Mathews, C. – *The Annals of Mont Blanc*. Fisher Unwin, London, 1898. This quote and the following can be found between pages 54 and 71.
3 Ibid. p. 98.
4 Ibid. p. 99.
5 Ibid. p. 100.
6 Ibid.
7 Engel, C. – *A History of Mountaineering in the Alps*. Allen and Unwin, London, 1950. p. 53.
8 Freshfield, op cit. p. 216.
9 Payot, P. – *Au Royaume du Mont Blanc*. La Fontaine de Siloé, Montmélian, 1996. p. 228.

Chapter Five

1 Freshfield, op cit. p. 222.
2 Ibid. p. 223.
3 Ibid.
4 Saussure, H. – Voyages . . . Vol. IV, p. 144.
5 Ibid.
6 Ibid.
7 Freshfield, op cit. p. 225.
8 Saussure, op cit. p. 156.
9 Ibid. p. 157.
10 Ibid. p. 161.
11 Ibid. p. 157.
12 Ibid. p. 144.
13 Ibid. p. 145.
14 Freshfield, op cit. p. 231.
15 Ibid, p. 230.
16 Ibid.

17 Saussure, op cit. p. 145.
18 Freshfield, op cit. p. 231.
19 Saussure, op cit. p.175
20 Ibid.
21 Ibid. p. 147.
22 Freshfield, op cit. p. 233.
23 Ibid.
24 Ibid. p. 234.
25 Ibid. p. 235.
26 Ibid.
27 Ibid. p. 238.
28 Ibid. p. 240.
29 Ibid. p. 236.
30 Bourrit, M. – *Description des Cols ou Passages des Alpes*. Manget Geneva, 1803. Vol.I, p. 101.

Chapter Six

1 Freshfield, op cit. p. 249.
2 Freshfield, op cit. p. 248.
3 Ibid. p. 250.
4 Engel C. – *A History* . . . op cit. p. 62.
5 Freshfield, op cit. p. 251.
6 Engel, op cit. p. 62.
7 Saussure, H. – Voyages . . . op cit. Vol IV, p. 224.
8 Freshfield, op cit. p. 257–8.
9 Saussure, op cit. p. 222.
10 Ibid. p. 223.
11 Ibid. p. 222.
12 Freshfield, op cit. p. 257.
13 Ibid. p. 258.
14 Ibid. p. 256.
15 Saussure, op cit. p. 224.
16 Freshfield, op cit. p. 254.
17 Bourrit, M. – *Nouvelle Description des Alpes*. Paul Barde, Geneva, 1783. Vol II, p. 263.
18 Freshfield, op cit. p. 371.
19 Ibid. p. 375.
20 Ibid. p. 383.
21 Ibid. p. 389.
22 Ibid. p. 276.

Chapter Seven

1 De Beer, G. – *Travellers in Switzerland*. Oxford University Press, London, 1949. p. 94.
2 Ibid. p. 100.
3 Ibid. p. 101.
4 Saussure, H. – Voyages . . . op cit. Vol IV, p. 154.
5 De Beer, op cit. p. 90.
6 Engel, C. – *Mont Blanc*. Allen and Unwin, London, 1965. p. 55.
7 Bourrit, M. – *Description des Cols ou Passages des Alpes*. Manget, eva, 1803. Vol I, p. 105.
8 De Beer, op cit. p. 96.
9 Bourrit, op cit. p. 105.
10 De Beer, op cit. p. 113.
11 Ibid. p. 115.

12 Mathews, C. – *The Annals of Mont Blanc.* op cit. p. 118.
13 Ibid.
14 Payot, P. – *Au Royaume du Mont-Blanc.* La Fontaine de Siloé, Montmélian, 1996. p. 241.
15 Ibid.
16 Ibid.
17 De Beer, G. – *Alps and Men.* Edward Arnold, London, 1932. p. 28.
18 Bourrit, op cit. p. 79.
19 Payot, op cit. p. 232.
20 Ibid.
21 Clark, R. – *The Early Alpine Guides.* Phoenix House, London, 1949. p. 25.
22 Payot, op cit. p. 232.

Chapter Eight

 1 Bourrit, M. – Description des Cols ou Passages des Alpes. Manget, Geneva, 1803. Vol I, p. 43.
 2 Ibid. p. 133.
 3 Coolidge, W. – *Swiss Travel and Swiss Guide Books.* Longman, Green & Co., London, 1889. p. 60.
 4 Ibid. p. 61.
 5 De Beer, G. – *Travellers in Switzerland.* Oxford University Press, London, 1949. p. 139.
 6 Lutvens M. (ed.) – *Effie in Venice.* Murray, London, 1965. p. 47.
 7 De Beer, op cit. p. 138.
 8 Coolidge, op cit. p. 69.
 9 Ibid. p. 76.
10 Ibid. p. 59.
11 Ibid. p. 61.
12 Ibid. p. 62.
13 *Blackwood's Magazine,* Nov. 1818, No. XX.
14 Ibid.
15 Mathews, C. – *The Annals of Mont Blanc.* Fisher Unwin, London, 1898. p. 123.
16 Ibid.
17 Bourrit, op cit. Vol I, p. 112.
18 Brockedon, W. – *Journals of Excursions in the Alps.* James Duncan, London, 1833. p. 153.
19 Ibid. p. 155.
20 Stephen, L. – *Playground of Europe.* Longmans, London, 1871. p. 85.
21 Mathews, op cit. p. 225.
22 Ibid. p. 227.
23 Auldjo, J. – *Narrative of an ascent to the Summit of Mont Blanc.* Longman, London, 1828. pp. 63–4.
24 D'Arve, S. – *Histoire du Mont Blanc.* La Fontaine de Siloé, Montmélian, 1993. p. 69.
25 Mathews, op cit. p. 226.
26 D'Arve, op cit. p. 70.
27 Mathews, op cit. p. 128.
28 Ibid. p. 129.
29 Ibid. p. 130.
30 Payot, P. – *Au Royaume du Mont-Blanc.* La Fontaine de Siloé, Montmélian, 1996. p. 270.
31 Mathews, op cit. p. 135.
32 Payot, op cit. p. 42.
33 De Beer, op cit. p. 149.
34 De Beer, op cit. p. 167.
35 Ibid. p. 169.
36 Brockedon, op cit. p. 36.

37 De Beer, G. – *Alps and Men*. Edward Arnold, London, 1932. p. 192.
38 Ibid. p. 183.
39 Fellows, C. – *Narrative of the Ascent to the Summit of Mont Blanc of the 25 July 1827*. Privately printed, London, 1827. p. 4.
40 Ibid.
41 Ibid. p. 7.
42 Ibid. p. 14.
43 Ibid. p. 16.
44 Ibid. p. 18.
45 Ibid. p. 16.
46 Ibid. p. 21.
47 Hawes, W. – *A Narrative of an ascent to the summit of Mont Blanc*. Privately printed, 1828. p. 21.
48 Fellows, op cit. p. 23.
49 Ibid. p. 26.
50 Ibid. p. 27.
51 Ibid. p. 30.
52 Ibid. p. 31.
53 Ibid. p. 32.
54 Ibid.

Chapter Nine

1 Auldjo, J. – *Narrative of an ascent to the Summit of Mont Blanc*. Longman, London, 1828. p. 25.
2 Auldjo, J. – *Narrative . . .* (2nd edition, 1856) p. vii.
3 AC – Paccard's Journal.
4 Auldjo, op cit. p. 4.
5 Coolidge, W. – *Swiss Travel and Swiss Guide Books*. Lonqman, Green & Co., London, 1889. p. 76.
6 Forbes, John – *A Physician's Holiday*. Murray, London, 1850. p. 2.
7 Ibid. p. 8.
8 Ibid.
9 Ibid. p. 242.
10 De Beer, G. – *Alps and Men*. Edward Arnold, London, 1932. p. 109.
11 Ibid.
12 Topffer, R. – *Nouveaux Voyages en Zigzag*. Victor Lecon, Paris, 1854. p. 139.
13 Agassiz, E. (ed.) – *Louis Agassiz; his Life and Correspondence*. Macmillan, London, 1885. Vol. I, p. 380.
14 Clark, J. and Hughes, T. (eds) – *The Life and Letters of Adam Sedgwick*. Cambridge University Press, Cambridge, 1890. Vol. I, p. 432.
15 De Beer, op cit. p. 153.
16 Ibid. p. 157.
17 Clark and Hughes, op cit. Vol. I, p. 447.
18 Agassiz, op cit. Vol. I, p. 340.
19 Ibid. Vol I, p. 323.
20 De Beer, op cit. p. 208.
21 Forbes, James – *Norway and its Glaciers*. Black, Edinburgh, 1853. p. 297.
22 Ibid.
23 Shairp, J., Tait, P. and Adams-Reilly, A. – *The Life and Letters of James David Forbes*. Macmillan, London, 1873. p. 266.
24 Ibid.
25 Forbes, James op cit. p. 304.
26 Ibid. p 307.

27 Ibid. p. 320.
28 Ibid.
29 Ibid. p. 322.
30 Engel, C. – *A History of Mountaineering in the Alps*. Allen and Unwin, London, 1950. p. 94.
31 Forbes, James op cit. p. 324.
32 Ibid.
33 Ibid. p. 298.
34 Agassiz, op cit. Vol I, p. 338.
35 Ibid. p. 343.
36 Ibid. p. 353.
37 Ibid. p. 358.

Chapter Ten

1 Shairp, J., Tait, P. and Adams-Reilly, A. – *The Life and Letters of James David Forbes*. Macmillan, London, 1873. p. 147.
2 Ibid. p. 453.
3 Forbes, James – *Travels through the Alps of Savoy*. Black, Edinburgh, 1843. p. 16.
4 Forbes, James – *Norway and its Glaciers*. Black, E£dinburgh, 1853. p. 256.
5 Forbes – *Travels* . . . op cit. p. 5.
6 Ibid. p. 14.
7 Ibid. p. 6.
8 Ibid. p. 37.
9 Ibid. p. 15.
10 Shairp etc. op cit. p. 557.
11 Forbes – *Travels* . . . op cit. p. 103.
12 Ibid. p. 83.
13 Ibid.
14 Ibid. p. 84.
15 *Journal of the Royal Geographical Society*. Vol 14. Murray, London, 1844. p. 322.
16 Shairp etc. op cit. p. 533.
17 Bailey, R. (ed.) – Glacier. Time-Life Books, Alexandria, Virginia, 1982. p. 24.
18 Forbes – *Travels* . . . op cit. p. 265.
19 Ibid. p. 267.
20 Ibid. p. 323.
21 Ibid. p. 199.
22 Ibid. p. 239.
23 Ibid. pp. 280–1.
24 Ibid. p. 281.
25 *Journal of the Royal Geographical Society*. Vol. 14. Murray, London, 1844. p. 322.
26 Journal of the Royal Geographical Society. Vol. 13. Murray, London, 1843. p. 134.
27 Ibid. p. 135.
28 Ibid. p. 148.

Chapter Eleven

1 Kemp, W. (trans. Van Heurk, J.) – *The Desire of my Eyes*. HarperCollins, London. 1991. p. 231.
2 Clark, R. – *Victorian Mountaineers*. Batsford, London, 1953. p. 35.
3 Engel, C. – *A History of Mountaineering in the Alps*. Allen and Unwin, London, 1950. p. 111.
4 Ruskin, J. – *Deucalion and other studies in Rocks and Snow*. (Library Edition Vol. XXVI). George Allen, London, 1909. p. 220.
5 Clark, op cit. p. 35.

6 Ibid.
7 Ibid. p. 36.
8 Ibid. p. 35.
9 Ibid. p. 36.
10 Hayman, J. (ed.) – John Ruskin: *Letters from the Continent*. University of Toronto Press. Toronto, 1982. p. 192.
11 Kemp, op cit. p. 172.
12 Ruskin, J. – *Letters 1870–1889*. (Library Edition Vol. XXXVII). George Allen, London, 1909. p. 142.
13 Clark, op cit. p. 39.
14 Kemp, op cit. p. 258.
15 Quarterly Review CXCVI, Art. IV.
16 De Beer, G. – *Alps and Men*. Edward Arnold, London, 1932. p. 233.
17 Clark, op cit. p. 37.
18 Forbes, John – *A Physician's Holiday*. Murray, London, 1850. p. 158.

Chapter Twelve

1 Smith, A. – *Mont Blanc*. Ward and Lock, London, 1862. p. 2.
2 Ibid. p. xii.
3 Ibid. p. 3.
4 Ibid. p. 18.
5 Ibid. p. 19.
6 Ibid. p. 20.
7 Fitzsimons, R. – *The Baron of Piccadilly: the travels and entertainments of Albert Smith 1816–1860*. Geoffrey Bles, London, 1967. p. 31.
8 Thorington, J. – *Mont Blanc Sideshow. The Life and Times of Albert Smith*. The John C. Winston Company, Philadelphia, 1934. p. 30.
9 Smith, op cit. p. 43.
10 Smith, op cit. p. xii.
11 Smith, A. – *A Month at Constantinople*. David Bogue, London, 1850. p. 80.
12 Thorington, op cit. p. 55.
13 Fitzsimons, op cit. p. 152.
14 Smith – Mont Blanc. op cit. p. xxiv.
15 Mathews, C. – *The Annals of Mont Blanc*. Fisher Unwin, London, 1898. p. 181.
16 Ibid. p. 182.
17 Fitzsimons, op cit. p. 64.
18 Thorington, op cit. p. 65.
19 Ibid.
20 Ibid. p. 132.
21 Smith – Mont Blanc. op cit. p. 202.
22 Mathews, op cit. p. 184.
23 Fitzsimons, op cit. p. 117.
24 Ibid. p. 114.
25 Smith – Mont Blanc. op cit. p. 240.
26 Ibid. p. 238.
27 Fraser's Magazine. Vol. LII. John Parker, London, 1855. p. 10.
28 Smith – Mont Blanc. op cit. p. 252.
29 Ibid. p. 260–1.
30 Fraser's Magazine. op cit. p. 13.
31 Smith – Mont Blanc. op cit. p. 262.
32 Ibid. p. 270.
33 Daily News, 21 Aug. 1851.

34 Smith – *Mont Blanc.* op cit. p. 47.
35 Daily News, 21 Aug. 1851.
36 Daily News, 30 Aug. 1851.
37 Smith – *Mont Blanc.* op cit. p. 47.
38 Fitzsimons, op cit. p. 141.
39 Ibid. p. 142.
40 Fitzsimons, op cit. p. 140.
41 Clark, R. – *Victorian Mountaineers.* Batsford, London, 1953. p. 54.
42 Thorington, op cit. p. 153.
43 MacGregor, J. and Baxter, G. – *The Ascent of Mont Blanc.* Privately printed. 1855. p. 2.
44 Smith – Mont Blanc. op cit. p. xvii.

Chapter Thirteen

1 Fleming, F. (ed.) – *The Pulse of Enterprise.* Time-Life Books, Amsterdam, 1990. p. 73.
 2 Kennedy, E. (ed.) – *Peaks, Passes and Glaciers.* (Second Series.) Longman, London, 1862. Vol. II, p. 58.
 3 Ibid.
 4 Wills, A. – *Wanderings Among The High Alps.* Richard Bentley, London, 1858. p. 262.
 5 Ibid. p. 263.
 6 Ibid. p. 276.
 7 Ibid. p. 275.
 8 Ibid. p. 277.
 9 Ibid.
10 Ibid. p. 284.
11 Ibid. p. 285.
12 Ibid. p. 286.
13 Ibid.
14 Ibid. p. 287.
15 Ibid.
16 Ibid.
17 Ibid. p. 291.
18 Ibid. p. 292.
19 Ibid. p. 293.
20 Ibid. p. 294.
21 Ibid. p. 300.
22 Ibid. p. 305.
23 AJ Vol. IX, p. 50.
24 Hort, A. – Life and Letters of Fenton John Anthony Hort. Macmillan, London, 1896. Vol I, p. 391.
25 Ibid.
26 Ibid.
27 Clark, R. – *Victorian Mountaineers.* Batsford, London, 1953. p. 81.
28 AJ Vol. VIII, p. 87.
29 Mumm, A. – *The Alpine Club Register.* 1857–1863. Edward Arnold, London, 1923. p. 5.
30 Blackwood's Magazine. Vol. LXXXVI, July–December 1859. Blackwood, Edinburgh, 1859. p. 456.
31 Peaks, Passes, and Glaciers. Vol. I. p. 366.
32 Ibid. p. 368.
33 Blackwood's Magazine. op cit. p. 456.
34 Ibid.
35 Ibid.
36 Ibid. p. 457.

37 Ibid. p. 470.
38 Ibid. p. 469.

Chapter Fourteen

1 Eve, A. and Creasey, C. – *Life and Work of John Tyndall*. Macmillan, London, 1945. p. 53.
2 Ibid. p. 341.
3 Ibid.
4 Ibid.
5 RI – Tyndall's Journal. p. 1161.
6 RI – W. Hopkins to J. Tyndall, 3 Nov. 1860.
7 RI – Ibid.
8 Eve & Creasey, op cit. p. 71.
9 Ibid. p. 59.
10 Ibid. p. 70.
11 Tyndall, J. – *Glaciers of the Alps*. Murray, London, 1860. p. 86.
12 RI – J. Tyndall to M. Faraday, 27 Aug. 1856.
13 RI – Tyndall's Journal. p. 1197.
14 RI – Ibid. p. 1222.
15 RI – Ibid.
16 Tyndall, op cit. p. 190.
17 Tyndall, J. – *Hours of Exercise in the Alps*. Longman, Green & Co., London, 1871. p. 56.
18 Ibid. p. x.
19 Enqel, C. – *They Came To The Hills*. Allen & Unwin, London, 1952. p. 54.
20 Ibid. p. 55.
21 Tyndall – Hours of Exercise. op cit. p. 20.
22 Ibid. p. 23.
23 Ibid
24 Ibid.
25 Ibid.
26 Ibid. p. 25.
27 Ibid.
28 *The Times*. 8 Sept. 1860.
29 *The Times*. 12 Sept. 1860
30 Tyndall – *Hours of Exercise*. op cit. p. viii.
31 Hinchliff, T. – *Summer Months Among the Alps*. Longman, London, 1857. p. x.
32 Hudson, C. and Kennedy, E. – Where there's a Will there's a Way. Longman, London, 1856. p. xi.
33 Smith, A. – *Mont Blanc*. Ward and Lock, London, 1862. p. 210.
34 D'Arve, S. – *Histoire de Mont-Blanc*. Delagrave, Paris, 1878. p. 78.
35 Ibid. pp. 72–3.
36 Ibid. p. 74.
37 AJ Vol. I, p. 141.

Chapter Fifteen

1 Hudson, C. and Kennedy, E. – Where there's a Will there's a Way. Longman, London, 1856. p. xii.
2 Ibid. p. xiii.
3 Tyndall, J. – *Glaciers of the Alps*. Murray, London, 1860. p. 146.
4 RI – Tyndall's Journal 11 Aug. 1857.
5 RI – Tyndall's Journal 12 & 19 Aug. 1857.
6 RI – Tyndall's Journal 21 Aug. 1857.

7   RI – Tyndall's Journal 10 Aug. 1858.
8   RI – Tyndall's Journal 2 Aug. 1858.
9   Tyndall, J. – *Hours of Exercise in the Alps.* Longman, Green & Co., London, 1871. pp. 31–33
10 Ibid. p. 32.
11 Ibid.
12 Ibid. p. 30.
13 Ibid. p. 35.
14 Ibid. p. 36.
15 Ibid. p. 37.
16 Ibid. p. 41.
17 Ibid.
18 Ibid. p. 42.
19 Ibid. p. 43.
20 Ibid.
21 Ibid. pp. 44–45
22 Ibid. p. 47.
23 Ibid. p. 48.
24 Ibid. p. 49.
25 Ibid.
26 Ibid. p. 153.
27 Ibid. p. 123.
28 Ibid.
29 Ibid. p. 89.
30 Ibid. p.134.
31 Ibid.
32 Ibid. p. 135.
33 Ibid.
34 Ibid. p.138.
35 RI – J. Tyndall to M. Faraday, 21 Aug. 1861.
36 Tyndall, op cit. p. 91.
37 Ibid. p. 92.
38 Ibid. p. 95.
39 Ibid. p. 96.
40 Ibid. p. 97.
41 Ibid. p. 102.
42 RI – J. Tyndall to M. Faraday, 21 Aug. 1861.
43 Tyndall, op cit. p. 99.
44 Ibid. p. 100.
45 Ibid. p. 101.
46 RI – J. Tyndall to M. Faraday, 21 Aug. 1861.
47 Tyndall, op cit. p. 103.
48 Ibid. p. 104
49 Ibid.
50 Ibid. p. 105.
51 Ibid. p. 106.
52 Ibid. p. 111.
53 Ibid. p. 110.
54 Ibid.

Chapter Sixteen

1   AJ Vol. I, p. 3.
2   Ibid. p. 20.

3   Ibid. p. 19.
4   Ibid. p. 20.
5   Ibid. p. 3.
6   Engel, C. – *They Came to the Hills*. Allen and Unwin, London, 1952. p. 65.
7   Ibid.
8   Ibid.
9   Stephen, L. – *Some Early Impressions*. Hogarth Press, London, 1924. p. 47.
10 Stephen, L. – *Playground of Europe*. Longman, London, 1871. p. 82.
11 Bicknell, J. (ed.) – *Selected Letters of Leslie Stephen*. Macmillan, London, 1996. Vol. I, p. 105.
12 Ibid. Vol. I, p. 48.
13 Stephen – *Playground . . .* op cit. p. 285.
14 Ibid. p. 274.
15 Ibid. p. 193.
16 Stephen – *Some Early Impressions*. op cit. p. 189.
17 Ibid.
18 Eve, A. and Creasey, C. – *Life and Work of John Tyndall*. Macmillan, London, 1945. p. 387.
19 Ibid.
20 Ibid.
21 RI – Tyndall's Journal 1 Jan. 1861.
22 Eve & Creasey, op cit. pp. 387–8
23 Stephen, L. – *Playground of Europe*. Longman, London, 1871. pp. 107–8.
24 Eve & Creasey, op cit. p. 389.
25 RI – Tyndall's Journal 24 Nov. 1859.
26 RI – Tyndall's Journal 17 Nov. 1860.
27 Smythe, F. – Edward Whymper. Hodder and Stoughton, London, 1948.
28 This and above, Ibid. pp. 86–103.
29 Ibid. p. 101.
30 Ibid. p. 93.
31 Ibid. p. 87.
32 Ibid. p. 85.
33 Ibid. p. 86.
34 Ibid. pp. 87–88.
35 AJ Vol.V, p. 237.
36 Smythe, op cit. p. 118.
37 Whymper, E. – *Scrambles Amongst the Alps*. Murray, London, 1871. p. 82.

Chapter Seventeen

1   Smythe, F. – *Edward Whymper*. Hodder and Stoughton, London, 1940. p. 114.
2   Ibid.
3   Whymper, E. – *Scrambles Amongst the Alps*. Murray, London, 1871. p. 103.
4   Ibid.
5   Ibid. p. 104.
6   Ibid. p. 105.
7   Ibid. p. 109.
8   Ibid.
9   AJ Vol. II, p. 9.
10 Ibid.
11 Ibid.
12 Whymper, op cit. p. 119.
13 Ibid. p. 122.
14 Ibid. p.121.
15 Ibid. pp. 122–3.

16 Ibid. p.121.
17 Ibid.
18 Ibid. p.123.
19 Ibid. p.124.
20 Ibid.v p.125.
21 Ibid.
22 Ibld. p.126.
23 Ibid.
24 Ibid.
25 Ibid.
26 IC – J. Tyndall to T. Huxley 29 Aug. 1862.
27 Tyndall, J. – *Hours of Exercise in the Alps*. Longmans, Green & Co., London, 1871. pp. 166–7.
28 Whymper, op cit. pp. 126–7.
29 Tyndall, op cit. p. 155.
30 Ibid. p. 156.
31 Ibid. p. 158.
32 Ibid. p. 159.
33 Whymper, op cit. p. 127.
34 Tyndall, op cit. p. 160.
35 Ibid. p. 161.
36 IC – J. Tyndall to T. Huxley 29 Aug. 1862.
37 Tyndall, op cit. p. 162.
38 Ibid.
39 Ibid.
40 Ibid. p. 163.
41 Ibid. p. 162.
42 Ibid.
43 IC – J. Tyndall to T. Huxley 29 Aug. 1862.
44 Tyndall, op cit. pp. 163–4.
45 Whymper, op cit. p. 134.
46 Tyndall, op cit, p. 164.
47 Ibid.
48 Ibid. p. 165.
49 Whymper, op cit. p. 129.
50 AJ Vol. V, p. 331.
51 BL Add. MS 63092 – J. Tyndall to Mrs. Pollock 1 Aug. 1862.
52 Whymper, op cit. p. 129.
53 Tyndall, op cit. p. 167.
54 AJ Vol. V, p. 332.
55 Ibid. pp. 330–1.1
56 Ibid. p. 133.
57 IC – J. Tyndall to T. Huxley 29 Aug. 1862.

Chapter Eighteen.

1 AJ Vol. LIII, p. 127.
2 Browne, G. – *Recollections of a Bishop*. Smith Elder, London, 1915. p. 105.
3 Whymper, E. – *Scrambles Amongst the Alps*. Murray, London, 1871. p. 132.
4 Ibid.
5 SPRI – MS 822/2 Whymper's Journal 1863–1865.
6 Whymper, op cit. p. 159.
7 Ibid. pp. 159–60.

 8 Ibid. pp. 154–5.
 9 Ibid.
10 Ibid.
11 Ibid. p.169.
12 Ibid.
13 Ibid. p. 171.
14 Ibid.
15 Ibid.
16 Ibid.
17 Ibid. pp. 171–2.
18 Ibid. p. 175.
19 Ibid. p. 176.
20 Ibid. p. 178.
21 Ibid. p. 179.
22 Ibid. pp. 180–1.
23 Ibid. p. 195.
24 Ibid. pp. 190–1.
25 Ibid. p. 192.
26 Ibid.
27 Ibid. pp. 198–9.
28 Ibid. p. 202.
29 Ibid. p. 209.
30 Ibid. p. 203.
31 Ibid. pp. 212–3.
32 §Ibid. p. 214.
33 Ibid.
34 Ibid. p. 216.
35 Ibid.
36 Moore, A. – *The Alps in 1864*. David Douglas, Edinburgh, 1902. p. 73.
37 Whymper, op cit. p. 221.
38 Ibid. p. 227.
39 Ibid. p. 229.
40 Ibid. p. 230.
41 Ibid. p. 234.
42 AJ Vol. II, p .97.
43 Whymper, op cit. p. 234.
44 Ibid. p. 235.
45 Ibid. pp. 251–2.

Chapter Nineteen

 1 Whymper, E. – *Scrambles Amongst the Alps*. Murray, London, 1871. p. 253.
 2 Ibid.
 3 Ibid. p. 254.
 4 Ibid. p. 255.
 5 Ibid. p. 257.
 6 Moore, A. – *The Alps in 1864*. David Douglas, Edinburgh, 1902. p. 29.
 7 Ibid. p. 295.
 8 Whymper, op cit. p. 260.
 9 Moore, op cit. p. 299.
10 Whymper, op cit. pp. 261–2.
11 Ibid. p. 263.
12 Tyndall, J. – Hours of Exercise in the Alps. Longman, Green & Co., London, 1871. p. 199.

13 Ibid. p. 200.
14 Ibid. p. 201.
15 Ibid. pp. 201–2.
16 Ibid. p. 203.
17 Ibid. p. 206.
18 Ibid. pp. 211–2.
19 Ibid. p. 212.
20 Ibid. p. 208.
21 Ibid. p. 210.
22 Ibid. p. 212.
23 Ibid. p. 213.
24 Ibid. p. 214.
25 Ibid.
26 Ibid. p. 216.
27 Ibid.
28 Ibid. p. 217.
29 BL Add. MS 63092 – J. Tyndall to Mrs. Pollock 18 Aug. 1864.
30 De Beer, G. – *Travellers in Switzerland*. Oxford University Press, London, 1949. p. 301.

Chapter Twenty

1 AJ Vol. V, p. 237.
 2 SPRI – MS 822/2 Whymper's Journal 1863–1865.
 3 Whymper, E. – *Scrambles Amongst the Alps*. Murray, London, 1871. p. 293.
 4 Ibid.
 5 SPRI – MS 822/2 Whymper's Journal 1863–1865.
 6 Illustrated London News 25 Dec. 1858.
 7 Whymper, op cit. p. 345.
 8 SPRI – MS 822/2 Whymper's Journal 1863–1865.
 9 Smythe, op cit. p. 166.
10 Whymper, op cit. p. 364.
11 Smythe, F. – *Edward Whymper*. Hodder and Stoughton, London, 1940. p. 170.
12 Whymper, op cit. p. 365.
13 SPRI – MS 822/2 Whymper's Journal 1863–1865.
14 Whymper, op cit. p. 377.
15 Ibid. p. 378.
16 Smythe, op cit. p. 173.
17 Whymper, op cit. (6th ed. 1936) p. 339.
18 Whymper, op cit. p. 379.
19 Ibid.
20 Whymper, op cit. (6th ed. 1936) p. 340.
21 Whymper, op cit. p. 380.
22 The Times, 17 Aug. 1861.
23 AJ Vol. LXX (1), p. 33.
24 Whymper, op cit. p. 382.
25 Ibid. p. 385.
26 Smythe, op cit. p. 178.
27 Whymper, op cit. p. 385.
28 Ibid. p. 383.1
29 Ibid.
30 AJ Vol. LXX (1), p. 18.
31 Smythe, op cit. p. 180.
32 Whymper, op cit. p. 386.

33 Ibid. p. 387.
34 Rébuffat, G. (trans. Brockett, E.) – *Men and the Matterhorn*. Nicholas Vane, London, 1967. p. 136.
35 Whymper, op cit. p. 388.
36 Ibid. p. 389.
37 Ibid.
38 Ibid.
39 Ibid. p. 391.
40 Ibid.
41 Ibid. pp. 393–4.
42 Ibid. p. 392.

Chapter Twenty-One

1   Whymper, E. – *Scrambles Amongst the Alps*. Murray, London, 1871. pp. 397–8.
2   Ibid. p. 398.
3   Ibid. p. 399.
4   Ibid. p. 400.
5   Ibid. p. 399.
6   BL – Add. MS 63112 E. Whymper to Mr. Brock 5 Aug. 1865.
7   Whymper, op cit. p. 401.
8   Ibid.
9   Smythe, F. – *Edward Whymper*. Hodder and Stoughton, London, 1940. p. 195.
10 Whymper, op cit. p. 401.
11 Smythe, op cit. p. 198.
12 Whymper, op cit. p. 402.
13 Smythe, op cit. p. 199.
14 Smythe, op cit. p. 200.
15 AJ Vol. LXI, p. 498.
16 AJ Vol. LXII, p. 49.
17 AJ Vol. LXX (1), p. 16.
18 Eve, A. and Creasey, C. – *Life and Work of John Tyndall*. Macmillan, London, 1945. p. 381.
19 Browne, G. – *Recollections of a Bishop*. Smith Elder, London, 1915. p. 105.
20 Tyndall, J. – *New Fragments*. Longman, London, 1892. p. 458.
21 Bennett, G. – *Beyond Endurance*. Secker & Warburg, London, 1983. p.50.
22 BL – Add. MS 63112 E. Whymper to W. Wigram 9 Aug. 1865.
23 BL – Add. MS 63112 W.Wigram to E. Whymper 10 Aug. 1865
24 Whymper, op cit. pp. 403–4.
25 Ibid.
26 Ibid.
27 Ibid.
28 AJ Vol. LXI, p. 489.
29 Ibid.
30 AJ Vol. LXX (1), p. 22.
31 Ibid. p. 33.
32 Ibid. p. 17.
33 BL – Add. MS 63162 E. Hudson to J. McCormick Aug. 1865.
34 Rébuffat, G. (trans. Brockett, E.) – *Men and the Matterhorn*. Nicholas Vane, London, 1967.p. 136.
35 Ibid. p. 137.
36 Ibid.
37 Whymper – *Scrambles* (4th ed.) p. 379.
38 Whymper, op cit. p. 393.

39 Ibid.
40 BL – Add. MS 63112 J. Davidson to E. Whymper 21 July 1897.
41 BL – Add. MS 63092 J. Tyndall to T. Hirst 1868.
42 IC – J. Tyndall to T. Huxley 29 July 1868.
43 Tyndall, J. – *Hours of Exercise in the Alps*. Longman, Green & Co., London, 1871. pp. 292–3.
44 Ibid. pp. 293–4.
45 Ibid. p. 316.
46 BL – Add. MS 63090 E. Whymper to J. McCormick 25 July 1865.
47 Whymper, op cit. (6th ed. 1936) p. 381.
48 Hort, A. – *Life and Letters of Fenton John Hort*, Macmillan, London, 1896. Vol. II, p. 39.
49 BL – Add. MS 63112 Memories of Annette Whymper transmitted to F. Smythe.
50 Ibid.
51 Whymper, op cit. (6th ed. 1936) p. 382.
52 Hort, op cit. Vol II, pp. 39–40.
53 Whymper, op cit. p. 406.
54 Ibid. p. 408.

Chapter Twenty-Two

1 The Times 27 July 1865.
2 London Illustrated News July 29, 1865.
3 Engel C. – A History of Mountaineering in the Alps. Allen & Unwin, London; 1950. p. 144.
4 Ibid. p. 145.
5 Ruskin, J. – *Sesame and Lilies*. George Allen, London, 1893. p. 58.
6 Ibid. p. 59.
7 Clark, R. – *Victorian Mountaineers*. Batsford, London, 1953. p. 137.
8 Stephen, L. – *Playground of Europe*. Longman, London, 1871. p. 272.
9 AJ Vol. LXII, p. 39.
10 Bicknell, J. (ed.) – *Selected Letters of Leslie Stephen*. Macmillan, London, 1996. Vol. I, p. 87.
11 *The Times* 24 Aug. 1871.
12 AJ Vol. V, p. 238.
13 Smythe, op cit. p. 228.
14 Blackwood's Magazine No. DCLXXII Oct. 1871.
15 AJ Vol. V, p. 239.
16 Ibid. p. 240.
17 Engel, C. – *They Came to the Hills*. Allen and Unwin, London, 1952. p. 145.
18 Ruskin, J. – *Deucalion and other studies in Rocks and Stones*. (Library Edition Vol. XXVI). George Allen, London, 1909. pp. 103–4.
19 RI – T. Huxley to J. Tyndall 13 May 1874.
20 AJ Vol. V, p. 235.
21 Stephen L. – *Playground of Europe*. Longman, London, 1871. p. 304.
22 Ibid.
23 AJ Vol. V, p. 235.
24 Ibid. p. 240.
25 Stephen, op cit. pp. 150–151.
26 AJ Vol. V, p. 189.
27 Ibid.
28 Ibid. p. 198.
29 Bicknell, op cit. Vol. I, p. 252.
30 Clark, op cit. p. 187.
31 AJ Vol. XIII, p. 419.
32 Engel, op cit. p. 146.
33 Ibid.

34   Bonney, T. – The High Alps of Dauphiné. Longman, London, 1865. p. xv.

Chapter Twenty-Three

1   Clark, R. – *An Eccentric in the Alps*. Museum Press, London, 1959. p. 21.
2   Ibid. p. 20
3   Ibid. p. 18.
4   Ibid. p. 32.
5   Ibid. pp. 60–61
6   AJ Vol. IV, pp. 322–3.
7   Ibid.
8   Clark, op cit. p. 63.
9   Ibid. p. 64.
10   AJ Vol. V, p. 130.
11   Ibid.
12   Ibid.
13   Clark, op cit. p. 66.
14   Ibid. p. 67.
15   Ibid. p. 68.
16   AJ Vol. IX, p. 133.
17   AJ Vol. VII, p. 91.
18   Ibid.
19   AJ Vol VIII, p.179.
20   Ibid. pp. 195–6.
21   Clark, op cit. p. 98.
22   Ibid.
23   Ibid. pp. 101–2.
24   Ibid. p. 100.
25   Coolidge, W. – *A Run Through the Dolomites in 1876*. Ben Johnson, York, 1902. p. 3.
26   Ibid. p. 4.
27   Ibid. p. 13.
28   AJ Vol. VIII, p. 198.

Chapter Twenty-Four

1   AJ Vol. VIII, p. 177.
2   Engel, C. – *They Came to the Hills*. Allen & Unwin, London, 1952. p. 182.
3   Ibid. p. 189.
4   AJ Vol. IX, p. 121.
5   Ibid. p. 123.
6   Ibid. p. 125.
7   Ibid.
8   Ibid. p. 129.
9   Ibid. p. 130.
10   Ibid. p. 127.
11   Ibid. p. 131.
12   Engel, op cit. p. 193.
13   Clark, op cit. p. 131.
14   Ibid. p. 117.
15   Conway, M. – *Episodes In a Varied Life*. Country Life, London, 1932. p. 60.
16   Clark, op cit. p. 132.
17   Ibid. p. 74.

Chapter Twenty-Five

1 Mummery, A. – *My Climbs in the Alps and Caucasus*. Fisher Unwin, London, 1895. p. 68.
2 Engel, C. – *The Came to the Hills*. Allen & Unwin, London, 1952. p. 225.
3 Conway, W. – *Episodes in a Varied Life*. Country Life, London, 1932. p. 34.
4 Conway, W. – *The Alps from End to End*. Constable, Lkondon, 1895. p. 3.
5 Engel, C. – A History of Mountaineering in the Alps. Allen and Unwin, London, 1950. p. 177.
6 De Beer, G. – *Travellers in Switzerland*. Oxford University Press, London, 1949. p. 414.
7 Stephen, L. – *Playground of Europe*. Longman, London, 1871. p. 1.
8 Ibid.
9 Whymper, E. – *Scrambles Amongst the Alps*. Murray, London, 1871. p. 304.
10 De Beer, G. – *Travellers in Switzerland*. Oxford 11 Dormandy, T. – *The White Death*. Hambledon Press, London, 1999. p. 1.
12 Ibid. p. 155.
13 Seth-Smith, M. – *The Cresta Run*. Foulsham, London, 1976. p. 14.
14 AJ Vol. IV, p. 326.

Chapter Twenty-Six

1 Conway, M. – *Episodes in a Varied Life*. Country Life, London, 1932.
2 BL – Add. MS 63090 E. Whymper to father 17 March 1894.
3 Conway, M. op cit. p. 60.
4 Clark, R. – *An Eccentric in the Alps*. Museum Press, London, 1959. p. 135.
5 Ibid. p. 159.
6 Ibid. p. 161.
7 Ibid. p. 167.
8 Ibid.
9 AC – Whymper, E. – 'A Letter Addressed to the Members of the Alpine Club.' p. 4.
10 Clark, op cit. p. 170.
11 Ibid. p. 169.
12 Ibid. p. 172.
13 Ibid. p. 173.
14 Ibid.
15 Ibid.
16 MC – MS 593 W. Coolidge to Wilson 30 July 1900.
17 Ibid.
18 Ibid.
19 Ibid.
20 Clark, op cit. p. 174.
21 BL – Add. MS 63112 J. Davidson to E .Whymper 14 May 1900.
22 Clark, op cit. p. 175.
23 Ibid. p. 174.
24 Ibid. p. 175.
25 MC – MS 593 W. Coolidge to Wilson Feb. 11.
26 BL – Add. MS 63112 J. Davidson to E .Whymper 9 Jan. 1905.
27 BL – Add. MS 63112 E. Whymper to J. Davidson 24 Oct. 1905.
28 Ibid.
29 SPRI – MS 822/29 Whymper's Journal 1905.
30 Smythe, F. – *Edward Whymper*. Hodder and Stoughton, London, 1940. p. 298.
31 BL – Add. MS 63112 Memorandum from Robert Whymper.
32 BL – Add. MS 63112 E.Whymper to H. Montagnier 9 Dec. 1910.
33 BL – Add. MS 63112 E. Whymper to H. Montagnier 16 April 1911.

34   BL – Add. MS 63112 E. Whymper to A. Whymper 28 July 1911.
35   BL – Add. MS 63112 E. Whymper to H Montagnier 22 Nov. 1908.
36   Ibid.
37   BL – Add. MS 63112 E. Whymper to H. Montagnier 16 June 1911.
38   Clark, op cit. p. 193.
39   Smythe, F. – Edward Whymper. Hodder and Stoughton, London, 1940. p. 318.
40   Clark, op cit. pp. 196–7.
41   Ibid. p. 197.
42   MC – MS 593 W. Coolidge to H. Wilson 3 July 1919.
43   MC – MS 593 W. Coolidge to H. Wilson 31 Dec. 1916.
44   MC – MS 593 W. Coolidge to H. Wilson 25 Dec. 1918.
45   MC – MS 593 W. Coolidge to H. Wilson 11 June 1919.
46   Clark, op cit. p. 211.
47   Conway, M. – *Episodes in a Varied Life*. Country Life, London. 1932. p. 28.
48   Ibid. p. 29.
49   MC – MS 593 W. Coolidge to H. Wilson 6 Oct. 1918.

Chapter Twenty-Seven

1   Engel, C. – *A History of Mountaineering in the Alps*. Allen and Unwin, London, 1950. p. 212.
2   Ibid. p. 214.
3   Stephen, L. – *Playground of Europe*. Longman, London, 1871. p. 109.
4   Engel, op cit. p. 223.
5   Ibid. p. 224.
6   Stephen, op cit. p. 266.
7   AJ Vol. XLVIII p. 373.
8   AJ Vol. XLVI p. 375.
9   Ibid. p. 377.
10   Harrer, H. (trans. Merrick, H.) – *The White Spider*. Flamingo, London, 1995. p. 32.
11   AJ Vol. XLVII p. 379.
12   Ibid. p. 374.
13   Harrer, op cit. p. 41.
14   Ibid. pp. 43–44.
15   AJ Vol. XLVIII p. 369.
16   Harrer, op cit. p. 54.
17   Ibid. p. 55.
18   Ibid. p. 54.
19   AJ Vol. XLVIII, p. 365.
20   AJ Vol. IL, p. 283.
21   AJ Vol. L, p. 9.
22   Harrer, op cit. p. 99.
23   Ibid. p. 83.
24   Ibid. p. 123.
25   Ibid. p.124.
26   Ibid. p. 125.
27   Ibid. p. 126.
28   Engel, op cit. p. 228.
29   Harrer, op cit. p. 126.
30   Heckmair, A. (trans. Sutton, G.) – *My Life as a Mountaineer*. Victor Gollancz, London, 1975.
31   Harrer, op cit. p. 126.

INDEX